# PSYCHOANALYTIC THEORIES OF DEVELOPMENT

PHYLLIS TYSON, PH.D.

ROBERT L. TYSON, M.D.

# PSYCHOANALYTIC THEORIES

# OF DEVELOPMENT:

# AN INTEGRATION

FOREWORD BY ROBERT S. WALLERSTEIN, M.D.

*Yale University Press   New Haven & London*

Published with assistance from the foundation established in memory of
Amasa Stone Mather of the Class of 1907, Yale College.

Designed by Nancy Ovedovitz and set in New Baskerville type by
Keystone Typesetting, Inc. Printed in the United States of America by
Vail-Ballou Press, Binghamton, New York.

*Library of Congress Cataloging-in-Publication Data*
Tyson, Phyllis
Psychoanalytic theories of development : an integration / Phyllis Tyson,
Robert L. Tyson ; foreword by Robert S. Wallerstein.
p.   cm.
Includes bibliographical references.
ISBN 0-300-04578-6 (cloth)
0-300-05510-2 (pbk.)
1. Developmental psychology. 2. Psychoanalysis. I. Tyson, Robert L.
II. Title.
BF713.T97   1990
155—dc20
90-32688
CIP

A catalogue record for this book is available from the British Library.

The paper in this book meets the guidelines for permanence and
durability of the Committee on Production Guidelines for Book
Longevity of the Council on Library Resources.

10   9   8   7   6   5   4   3

*To the memory of*
*Arthur P. McCoard, Frank McCoard, Harry Kravitz, and*
*Bertha Tyson, who supported our development and would have*
*loved to see this book.*

# CONTENTS

## PART SIX / THE SUPEREGO

## PART SEVEN / GENDER

## PART EIGHT / THE EGO

# FOREWORD

It has become a truism that contemporary psychoanalysis is beset by an increasing diversity of theoretical perspectives. This is not what Sigmund Freud, the founding genius of psychoanalysis, intended or expected. In fact, Freud made strenuous efforts throughout his lifetime to define clearly the parameters of his new science of the mind and to hold it together as a unified enterprise against destructive or diluting pressures or seductions from without and also against fractious human divisiveness from within.

But we also know the story of Freud's failure in the realization of this intent. Intense and painful struggles led to the secessions of gifted adherents striving to imprint their own differing intellectual perspectives upon the body psychoanalytic. The creation of the famous committee of the seven ring holders who, through the strength of their collective intellectual conviction, loyalty, and achieved leadership positions, would try to guarantee the stability of Freud's central psychoanalytic doctrine, failed in its aim. For already in Freud's lifetime there arose the alternative Kleinian metapsychology with its focus shifted onto the centrality of the earliest life experiences within the matrix of the dyadic attachment between mother and child, and the dominance within that arena of the vicissitudes of the aggressive (or death) drives. Within this enlarged (as well as shifted) psychological focus onto the experiences of preoedipal life, the Kleinians felt enabled to deal therapeutically with patients suffering more severe pathology than did the closer followers of Freud's metapsychology, with its focus on the centrality of the oedipal phase and the resolution of oedipally based conflict to which only the psychoneurotic patients who could develop so-called transference neuroses were felt to be amenable.

The history since then is a familiar one. Next came the development of the British object relational perspective with its wholly new metapsychology of an ego dedicated not to drive discharge but to object seeking, as a new independent or middle group between the Freudian and the Kleinian. Then, in subsequent years, came the Bionian perspective as an extension from the Kleinian, and the Lacanian as a distinctively French and linguistically centered psychoanalysis. And in America—

until that point the one region in the world where Freud's vision of a unified psychoanalysis had persisted through the hegemony of the ego psychological metapsychology paradigm articulated in claimed direct descent from Freud's own late developing ego psychology—the rise of the challenge of Heinz Kohut and his self psychology focused around the centrality of the vicissitudes of narcissism. And there are still others (to a lesser extent new directions), such as Mahler's developmental perspective, Schafer's new idiom ("action language") for psychoanalysis, and so on.

It is characteristic of each of these contending theoretical perspectives within psychoanalysis, to which we each have our commitments and allegiances, that each claims to be more comprehensively applicable to the entire gamut of amenable patients, and to be more efficacious in understanding and in cure, than its rival perspectives. The psychoanalysis of Freud, originally a psychology of drive and expanded later into a psychology of the ego as well, was seen to be the first scientific psychotherapy that could elucidate the nature of psychoneurosis and bring about an etiological cure with all the psychoneurotic patients amenable to it. The Kleinians, who focused originally on work with children and then with adults more deeply disturbed than simply psychoneurotic, evolved a metapsychology and a derived therapeutic that was declared to be also a better (more thorough, deeper) treatment of the classically neurotic as well. Similarly, Kohut's self psychology arose out of a concern with the seemingly refractory treatment problems of those with narcissistic personality disorders. But the technical interventions as well as the theoretical explanatory constructs that were originally tailored to the understanding of the therapeutic needs of this specific segment of the psychopathological spectrum, the narcissistically disordered, were then also declared to be a better explanatory system and a better therapeutic for the classically psychoneurotic as well. The point here is simply that each contending theoretical perspective in psychoanalysis, however narrowly defined its original base of inquiry and intervention within the domain of psychoanalytic application, is soon broadened to become a proclaimed superior metapsychology and intervention system for all those whose mental and emotional distress bring them within the psychoanalytic professional orbit.

Given this overall state of affairs that characterizes our discipline, with its welter of rival metapsychologies, the question naturally arises of how we can best understand what still holds us together as common adherents of a *shared* psychoanalytic science and discipline. That is, what do our diverse theoretical perspectives still have in common so that they are all recognizably psychoanalysis in terms of fundamentally shared assumptions about the human mind and the way in which we understand its functioning, and—as perhaps the other side of the same coin—what differentiates us, all together, from all the other non-psychoanalytic theories of mental life?

My own response to these questions, which I have developed at length elsewhere, is that our common ground cannot be reached at this time within our general theories. I feel that our metapsychologies in their current stage of historical development, in the looseness of their articulation with the observable and the empirically testable clinical phenomena of our consulting rooms, are beyond the reach of scientific study and therefore still only scientific metaphors, albeit perhaps heuristically useful ones. I believe rather that our common meeting ground is to be found only in the observable and testable clinical phenomena and in the experience-near clinical theory of conflict and compromise, of anxiety and resistance and defense, and of the inter-play of transferences and countertransferences that all our metapsy-chologies do share, despite languages that sometimes obscure this clinical commonality. Beyond that common clinical ground, I see at this point only scientific disadvantage in pressing for an effort at premature conceptual amalgamation or integration of our diverse general psy-choanalytic theories of the structure and functioning (and malfunc-tioning) of the mind. The reference frames of these theories or meta-psychologies are, to me, simply not sufficiently comparable—that is, not sufficiently in the same realm of discourse. Nor are any of them sufficiently linked to observable and therefore testable phenomena. They have for their own inherent heuristic purposes diverged too much and too abstractly, each into its own metaphoric rhetoric, within which its own adherents think and work congenially but beyond the realm of side-by-side scientific study, contrast, and comparison.

How do all these considerations relate to this—to me, extraordi-narily successful—effort by Phyllis and Robert Tyson to propound a coherent and useful conceptual integration of the same diverse pano-ply of psychoanalytic metapsychologies at the level of their underlying theories of development? For each of our diverse theoretical perspec-tives within psychoanalysis (except perhaps the Lacanian) has indeed elaborated retrospectively (and in some cases, to some extent, also prospectively observationally) its own developmental theory based on its own conception of the kinds of life experiences (that is, meanings given to happenings) that shape the unfolding organization of the personality in accord with its own theoretical constructions about how the mind hangs together and how it can be influenced toward change. For example, in accord with Freud's original drive psychology, the developmental focus was on the vicissitudes of the libido over the steps of the psychosexual developmental ladder, with its culmination in the appropriate resolution of the inevitable conflicts and ambivalences of the triadic oedipal constellation. With the development and elaboration of the counterpart ego psychology of drive modulation and management, the study of the development of varieties of ego functions, along the various developmental lines proposed by Anna Freud and amplified and extended by investigators like Spitz and Mahler and others, has come onto center stage. Similarly, Kohut's self psychology, with its concern for the vicissitudes of narcissism as the central developmental dynamic, focused on the developmental line of a cohering self, increasingly unified, effective in its deployment of its ambitions, talents, and ideals, and resistant to regressive and fragmenting pressures. And object relations theorists have focused especially on the developmental vicissitudes of object relatedness as the growing child navigates first the dyadic and then the triadic, and then the multipersonal world of increasingly complex and differentiated object embeddedness. That is, each of our divergent theoretical perspectives within psychoanalysis has laid particular stress on the development of a particular specifically relevant developmental strand or strands within the overall developmental process.

This development has led to a bewildering variety of psychoanalytic developmental perspectives more or less relevant to particular psychoanalytic metapsychologies. In addition are the studies of the developmental psychologists—Piaget being an outstanding example—bringing their own observational data and derived theoretical constructs to bear on our overall understanding of how human development proceeds. The particular (and monumental) task that the Tysons have set themselves has been to trace out these various developmental lines, as they are linked to the separate psychoanalytic metapsychologies and also to observables, and, by adhering as closely as possible to those observable indicators of these differing unfoldings—of the psychosexual, the object relational, the cohering sense of self and identity, the affective, the cognitive, the superego, the gender, and the ego developmental—to show the interrelatedness of all these strands as distinguishable but not distinct aspects of overall development. Each of these strands must be properly understood and related to all the others in an effort to comprehensively understand psychoanalytically the overall process of development.

In this endeavor—and at the level of understanding the overall developmental process as an integrated amalgam of *all* these perspectives, each brought into relation with all the others via its own observable indicators and their experience-near clinical formulation—the Tysons have been the first to risk the effort and to my mind have been as successful as anyone (or two) can be within the confines of a single manageable volume. This is to say that they have thoughtfully and imaginatively encompassed a vast array of literature across many domains of psychoanalytic and child development scholarship. Yet, given the vastness of the work and writing across these domains, experts within almost each area of inquiry might wonder if the authors have at times been too sweeping in their overviews, and have in places glossed over or ignored the full complexity or tentativeness of the data or the inference that can be permissibly generated from them. In that sense these experts can at times rightfully charge that their own scholarly niche has been somewhat shortchanged and not done full justice.

But the overall accomplishment of this book is elsewhere than in the chimerical pursuit of total comprehensiveness in all its complexity and subtlety. The Tysons here show us that it is possible, by tracing the developmental beginnings of our diverse psychoanalytic theoretical perspectives to the particular kinds of early life experiences that can be coherently linked to each of these particular theories of the structure of the mind, to show how the observable developmental indicators that link to each of these divergent theoretical perspectives can be brought into a meaningfully integrated fabric of understanding. And that by itself is a considerable achievement. Beyond that the contents of this book may then point toward one road to the ultimate creation of a truly unified and scientific general theory of psychoanalysis that will transcend our current metaphor-based divergent theorizing, by building incrementally upward from diverse observational data, painstakingly brought together in their interrelatedness and gradually progressing up the developmental timetable toward a more empirically based theorizing in each of the selfsame dimensions of adult mental functioning (drives, object, self, affect, cognition, ego, superego, and so on) in their interrelatedness and necessarily then in their integration—dimensions that today each find their main relevance in one or another of our noncompatible general theories or (metaphoric) metapsychologies.

Some psychoanalytic theorists—Kernberg is a good example—have been attempting to create an integrated and overarching psychoanalytic theory by a more partial or limited effort at amalgamation, for instance, in his case, by trying to amalgamate the object relational perspective to the ego psychological structural paradigm. It may well be that the Tysons' developmental approach to this vital theoretical task for our discipline will turn out to be the more promising just because it is at a level of conceptualization that can be more readily constrained by the requirements of the observable phenomena and the rewards (in terms of scientific testability) of lower-level, experience-near theorizing. That things will work out this way scientifically cannot of course be guaranteed, but the possibility is there, and this book does point that way. In addition to the heuristic and educational benefits of the synthesizing effort that the Tysons have intended, this book can also be seen as an at least equally important beginning on a direction of work toward ultimate overall theory integration within psychoanalysis. In that sense it has opened an exciting scientific vista.

—Robert S. Wallerstein, M.D.

# ACKNOWLEDGMENTS

Our idea to write an integration of psychoanalytic developmental theory began while we were working and teaching in London at the Hampstead Child Therapy Clinic, now the Anna Freud Centre. Agi Bene, Maria Berger, Marion Burgner, Dorothy Burlingham, Rose Edgcumbe, Anna Freud, Ilse Hellman, Hansi Kennedy, Sara Rosenfeld, and Joseph Sandler were among the many fruitful influences from whom we benefited at that remarkable institution.

The perennial need for students to integrate what they are taught seems more difficult to achieve as the developmental information explosion progresses, as exemplified by the first few scientific congresses of the World Association of Infant Psychiatry and Allied Disciplines (WAIPAD), 1980–1983. We are indebted to our colleagues in that organization, especially Eleanor Galenson, Justin Call, and Robert Emde for encouraging and supporting our interests in the field. Discussions with Margaret Mahler and John McDevitt have also been important to us.

We have learned from our patients of all ages, from our students, and from our colleagues. As in citing the literature, we are limited to mentioning only a few from among the many who could be named. We are grateful for the encouragement of Beverly Kilman, especially in the early stages of the work. We are most appreciative of the efforts of Martin Silverman, Vann Spruiell, David Stier, Amy Tyson, and Joan Zilbach who read versions of the manuscript at different stages. Philip Spielman in particular must be acknowledged as the most perceptive, persistent, and unfailingly knowledgeable and supportive critic and counselor we could have hoped for. None of these colleagues can be held responsible for any of our errors or omissions. Dr. Albert Solnit not only provided warm support but proved to be an efficient catalyzer toward publication. Glenn Miller of the Chicago Psychoanalytic Institute Library has given valuable assistance with references.

The consistent, seasoned, well-informed, sparkling, and friendly editorial critique of Natalie Altman has never left us without an ideal toward which to strive, and she has helped us to render lucid many ideas and passages that were more opaque than we had imagined. More recently, Cecile Watters has edited the manuscript with an unfailingly sharp eye, and Liza Altman has provided an in-depth index that is a model of comprehensiveness. Gladys Topkis's enthusiasm and knowledge have been important in the transition of this book from a wish and dream into a reality. Finally, the endless willingness of Kim Snow and the loyal and durable patience of Loretta Kramer, Carolyn Severy, and Lorraine Douglas, through the word processing of many drafts, have more than earned our gratitude.

# INTRODUCTION

This book grew out of the needs of our students. In teaching psychoanalytic developmental theory to students of psychoanalysis and psychology, and to residents in child and adult psychiatric training, we found them—and sometimes ourselves—perplexed by an array of often contradictory and mutually exclusive theories and overwhelmed by the rapidly growing mass of unassimilated information about infant and child development. When we ourselves were learning about psychoanalysis, we turned to Otto Fenichel's comprehensive landmark book, published in 1945, *The Psychoanalytic Theory of Neurosis*, which integrated the various theories then extant, as a way of getting our bearings. Our aim here has been to produce a kind of parallel to that work—to present a synthesis of psychoanalytic developmental theory.

Another difficulty confronting our students was the lack of easy access to the information they needed. Collections of individual authors' work are available, as are anthologies on selected topics and monographs that present a particular view; but otherwise, fragments of the theory are scattered throughout a multitude of publications. Another of our aims, therefore, has been to bring under one roof both traditional and more recent psychoanalytic theories of personality development and information concerning contemporary research in that area. The latter, when seen in the context of what preceded it, takes on an added dimension, and the student can view it with better understanding.

We maintain throughout a central focus on the intrapsychic—that is, on what occurs in the mind as it evolves. Although much recent developmental research focuses on the interpersonal, our attention is directed toward the way in which perceived and felt interpersonal interactions affect the origin, nature, and function of intrapsychic structures.

In our attempts to integrate the theories of personality development, we begin with those of Freud's ideas that have stood the test of time. We do this to show how current theories have evolved from this base. When evidence suggests that Freud was in error, we present

I

that evidence. Our stance has been determined predominantly by ego psychology, especially the structural theory, and by what Wallerstein (1988) has called the post–ego psychological age, in which the theories of ego psychology are progressively more informed by ideas and concepts originating from other areas both within and outside the purview of psychoanalysis. Most of all we have been influenced by what we have found clinically worthwhile, comprehensible, and coherent in our teaching and our daily practice of analysis with children, adolescents, and adults.

To formulate this integrated perspective, an enormous number of details and wide varieties of theoretical assumptions, clinical findings, and experimental data have had to be examined. To arrive at a view of an integrated whole, we have used an organizing framework derived from combining the ideas of Piaget, Spitz, and Anna Freud with more contemporary ideas from general system theory as described by von Bertalanffy.

In so doing we have come to a perspective that development is a continuous and discontinuous process involving a large number of interacting, intertwining systems (or structures), each with its own developmental sequence that must be considered in relation to the development of the others. We describe a developmental sequence for each of the major, simultaneously evolving systems* that make up the human personality. In describing them, we maintain that no one developmental phase holds a central position in relation to the final outcome and that no one system is superordinate to the others.

We recognize that the developmental perspective evolved from early psychoanalytic appreciation of the importance of childhood experiences to the adult personality. From the beginning, reconstructions of a person's past were crucial to the psychoanalytic method of treatment, and this, the genetic point of view, was central to psychoanalytic formulations. As analysts came to recognize that genetic reconstructions gave a distorted view of development, they gave more attention to the developmental process.

The developmental perspective has had its own evolution, which parallels the history of psychoanalysis. Analysts, moving from a central

---

*Throughout this book we use the terms *system* and *structure* interchangeably. Although Freud's final model of the mind came to be known as the structural model, it nevertheless can be viewed in a systems framework as we describe in part I, a structure being a relatively stable and slowly evolving system.

focus on the progression of the instinctual drives and the Oedipus complex, have offered a variety of alternative theories to conceptualize human development. Some of these theories have been criticized because they give priority to one aspect of development at the expense of other aspects. An integrated framework reduces the dangers of simplistic reductionism or unwarranted inferences regarding the effects of early experiences on subsequent pathology. The study of psychopathology has contributed immensely to our understanding of normal development, but the debt is now being repaid in the other direction. We hope that our efforts will make the complexity of the developmental process more apparent as well as provide a framework within which various points of view can be accommodated. A detailed and precise knowledge of "normal" development then can form the basis for a progressively more informed and profound understanding of deviant and pathological events in and between people, bringing with it possibilities for earlier detection, prevention, and more effective intervention.

The book begins with the history of the developmental perspective in psychoanalytic theory, followed by an explication of the developmental process and a description of the framework we use. We then present and discuss the major foci of interest and study in psychoanalytic developmental psychology in the following areas: psychosexuality, object relations, affect, cognition, the superego, gender, and the ego.

We have chosen this way of presenting our material over the traditional chronological or psychosexual phase approach in order to emphasize the broad array of interacting factors that contribute to manifest behavior at any chronological age, and also to make clear the importance of each system to the developmental process. Our approach, therefore, emphasizes interrelatedness and process rather than the individual's age and moves away from the notion of psychosexual or libidinal phase specificity. Experience has taught us that this advantage outweighs the disadvantages of any overlaps or duplications. The interdependent nature of all these systems, however, gave us some difficulty in organizing the book. We do not mind confessing to having had some moments of indecision—whether superego development should precede or follow gender development, whether ego development should precede or follow both superego development and gender development, for instance. But our uncertainties only added to our conviction regarding the validity of viewing the human personality in terms of interrelated, interacting systems. Each system relies on all the others, so each chapter relies on concepts contained in other chapters. Thus, we have been unable to avoid some anticipation, repetition, and overlap.

Because of the number of concepts and number of developmental stages involved in the description and integration of the developmental process, as an aid to the reader we chart the various sequences in the areas of the personality we are discussing. This chart is to be found at the end of chapter 2. Admittedly, such a graphic schematization risks oversimplification; we intend it only as a visual aid for mastering the integration of a very large body of data.

Newcomers to psychoanalytic terminology frequently are confused by the different meanings they find for one term or another as they read or listen. Rather than interrupt or unnecessarily burden the text with descriptions, we composed a casual glossary that briefly defines certain terms according to the way we use them.

For the sake of simplicity, we have used the generic *he* throughout. The text makes clear that we do not thereby imply that male development is the model on which human development is based. The same interest in simplicity decided us to use the term *mother* generically to refer to any mothering or caregiving figure.

Our book is a mix of our own views and those of others. We have throughout cited from the literature most familiar to us. We early recognized the impossibility of being exhaustive in this respect, and we are fairly certain that some excellent works do not make their appearance in the following pages. If we have failed to give credit where credit was due, the omission has been inadvertent.

# PART ONE

## THE

## DEVELOPMENTAL

## PROCESS

# CHAPTER I

## THE HISTORY OF THE

## DEVELOPMENTAL PERSPECTIVE

## IN PSYCHOANALYSIS

Freud once declared that psycho-analysis could not be like a philosophical system and produce a complete, ready-made theoretical structure. Instead, it would have to "find its way step by step along the path towards understanding the intricacies of the mind" (1923a, pp. 35–36). As the theoretical scaffolding of psychoanalysis has gradually taken shape, a developmental perspective has emerged as a major cornerstone. We begin with a brief survey of the evolution of this perspective to provide a context for our integrative approach to current developmental theory. Indeed, we think that a historical approach is always useful. It offers a means of evaluating contemporary thought and minimizes the proverbial tendency to reinvent the wheel.

### THE DEVELOPMENT OF THE
### DEVELOPMENTAL PERSPECTIVE

We first turn to the genetic point of view, for that is where the developmental perspective originates. A genetic, or more accurately, psychogenetic view of the personality is based on an interest in and knowledge of the ways in which an individual's past has influenced his current functioning. This perspective has been part of psychoanalytic theory since Freud's clinical work led him to investigate psychic conflict. Early in his thinking he conjectured that certain kinds of childhood experience were antecedents to adult neurosis, and he thought that a symptom of emotional origin could not be eliminated until this origin and its development had been traced. Indeed, Freud distinguished psychoanalysis from a simple analysis of composite psycholog-ical phenomena by declaring that it "consists in tracing back one psy-chical structure to another which preceded it in time and out of which it developed" (1913, p. 183), and he devised treatment techniques designed to reconstruct and understand the nature of early experi-ences. The first attempts to understand infancy and early childhood, therefore, were based on reconstructions of those early periods derived from clinical experience with adult neurotic patients.

Freud recognized, however, that reconstructions inevitably contain distortions. Consequently he recommended that psychoanalytic inves-tigations be supplemented by direct observations of children (1905b, p. 201). The case report of Little Hans (1909b) was a landmark in this direction. Although it focuses on the treatment of an infantile neu-rosis, it contains valuable information about the boy's experiences and his responses to them *in statu nascendi,* thus providing a developmental perspective—a view of the way things happen in contrast to an account of the way things happened.

Freud also recognized that there are pitfalls in the use of develop-mental knowledge. Just as apparent remnants of the past in the adult should not be equated with the developing child, it should also be appreciated that it is the psychic past that is important to psychoana-lytic theory. This psychic past reflects more the influence of conflict and defense than a veridical account of historical reality. Clearly, the psychological significance of early experiences may not be visible in statu nascendi; it becomes apparent only later in life. Because of this, psychoanalytic theory could not have evolved from child observation alone. It is through the psychoanalytic treatment method and the study of unconscious mental processes that the developmental impact of earlier life experiences comes to be understood. Freud seems to have had this idea in mind when he pointed out in the 1920 preface to the fourth edition of the "Three Essays on the Theory of Sexuality" (1905b) that although manifestations of sexuality in childhood had been observed by others, the crucial significance of the child's libidinal life emerged only from the psychoanalytic study of the unconscious. He commented that "if mankind had been able to learn from a direct observation of children, these three essays could have remained un-written" (p. 133).

Freud offered the first psychoanalytic theory of development (1905b) by proposing sequential stages of sexual development. In this theory he was positing not only a theory of infantile sexual develop-ment but also a theory of the interaction between constitution (innate maturational sequences) and experience. As he and others subsequently broadened this theory of development to include more of the latter, it became known as the theory of "psychosexual development" (1923b).

Following Freud's lead, Abraham elaborated on the concepts of oral and anal phases, identifying a sadistic component in each (1916, 1924a, 1924b). Some aspects of his theories remain useful today. Ferenczi, who was interested in the development of the sense of reality, expanded the scope of developmental theory into what would become ego psychology (1913). Melanie Klein, emphasizing the development of fantasy life, hypothesized that the infant experiences vicissitudes of aggression, rage, projection, and identification in the earliest weeks and months (1928, 1933, 1948).

When Freud introduced the structural theory, sometimes referred to as the tripartite model, he proposed that the mind was composed of three hypothetical psychic structures—the id, ego, and superego—that provide a stable underlying organization to experience (1923a). Later he added the idea that both innate features and the environment played varying roles of importance in the formation of these structures (1926), leading analysts to better appreciate the range of factors influencing development. Anna Freud (1936), Hartmann (1939, 1952), and Spitz (1959) were among the first to study the development of these psychic structures. In addition, Hartmann (1939) and, later, Winnicott (1956) began to distinguish in greater detail between the impact on the developmental process of innate, constitutional forces and that of experience and the environment. The mother-child unit thus became an important focus of attention as analysts acknowledged the contribution of the mother (the environment) to psychic structure formation. A developmental sequence of object relations eventually emerged as a result, as Anna Freud (1942), M. Klein (1928, 1933, 1952a, 1952b), Spitz (1959), and Mahler (1963, 1972a, 1972b) delineated stages in the evolution of the mother-child relationship.

Whereas Freud's understanding of the dynamics of the interpersonal and intrapsychic world began mostly with the Oedipus complex of the four- or five-year-old child, events in the period we now regard as infancy—the first three years of life—came increasingly into focus. (In Freud's time, infancy referred to the period from birth through the oedipal era.) With the growing emphasis on the earliest years, the problems with the reconstructive approach became even more apparent, and investigators tried to find other methods of understanding early development. The first efforts were in child analysis. Anna Freud demonstrated that the analysis of children yielded knowledge that could be incorporated into the body of psychoanalytic theory. Reflecting on these early years, she later said, "Child analysis proved unique in one all-important respect: it was the only innovation which opened up the possibility of checking up on the correctness of reconstructions in adult analysis. Now, for the first time, with the direct application of psychoanalytic treatment to young children, what had been merely guessed at and inferred became a living, visible, and demonstrable reality" (1970b, p. 210). She added later that although reconstructive work with adults was largely responsible for the psychoanalytic view of pathology, "child analysts appear to hold the key to the description of the course taken by normal infantile development" (1976, p. 85).

In addition to treating children with neurotic disorders, Anna Freud was also interested in learning about the developmental process. In 1926 she and some close colleagues (Dorothy Burlingham and Eva Rosenfeld, with Peter Blos, Sr., and later Erik Erikson as teachers) set up a small school in Vienna for children between the ages of seven and thirteen. It was designed for children whose parents were in analysis or who perhaps were in analysis themselves. Accordingly, it provided an opportunity to observe the ways in which psychoanalytic understanding could influence the educational process and, in particular, stimulated early observations of the interactions between development and education.

Analysts came to study progressively younger age groups in the pursuit of understanding the origins of normal and pathological development. Because the earliest periods of life are largely dominated by sensorimotor activity rather than verbal thinking and communicating, analysts adopted an observational approach. One of the pioneers in this area, Melanie Klein, developed her theories initially from observations of her own children (Grosskurth, 1986; Hughes, 1989).* In an effort to make more objective and systematic observations, Anna Freud and Dorothy Burlingham set up in 1937 an experimental day-care nursery for a group of toddlers from Vienna's poorest families. It was designed to collect information about the second year of life and the early steps away from the mother-child biological unity. This center, called the Jackson Nursery, was soon closed by the Nazis. Shortly after their move to London in 1938, however, Freud and Burlingham estab-

---

*Subsequently it has been widely accepted that attempts to treat or interpret to one's own child are contrary to the child's best interest.

lished a wartime center for infants and children who had been orphaned or separated from their families. The Hampstead War Nurseries became not only a landmark of residential child care but a center for psychoanalytic child research based on meticulously recorded observations of the children's behavior (A. Freud, 1942).

As the observational approach gained credibility, its use was extended to the study of the origins of psychopathology. Shortly after World War II, Spitz (1945, 1946a, 1946b) undertook a series of observational studies of infants in institutions and foundling homes where, although the infants were cared for physically, they received little stimulation or affection through interaction with a constant caretaker. Spitz's reports on the effects of these deprivations added both information and theoretical understanding about early development and psychopathology; he also documented his findings on film, a rarity in 1947 but a procedure that we now take for granted in laboratory studies of infants and young children and in teaching.

From these pioneering efforts in developmental research, a burgeoning new field has emerged, one that represents the convergence of two broad currents of endeavor. One stream, originating from within the framework of psychoanalytic thought and from Anna Freud's and Dorothy Burlingham's work, gathers data either from the clinical setting of child analysis or from longitudinal observations of children in naturalistic or standardized settings. The emphasis in these studies is on the process of development—that is, the differentiation of psychic systems and structures, the increasing complexity of intrapsychic life, the emergence of thought and fantasy, and the origins of psychopathology as well as ways to prevent it. These studies have considerably enlarged our knowledge of the many small steps in normal psychic development.

The second current typically proceeds by means of carefully designed experiments. It is now multidisciplinary, but it originated in laboratory experiments of the type Spitz conducted and came to incorporate many of the research methods of academic psychology. These experiments are usually carried out in a laboratory setting over relatively brief periods of time with infants in a state of quiet alertness; rarely are they observed at times of acute hunger or distress. The studies often have a more limited objective than longitudinal research; they are intended to test a particular hypothesis. The broadening scope of experimental work and the large numbers and wide diversity of subjects studied over the past few decades have led to an enormous expansion in our understanding of infants and, more impressive, of newborns.

As an outcome of more than eighty years of psychoanalytic interest (see P. Tyson, 1989a, for a review), we can now articulate a number of important characteristics of the developmental process. These we discuss in the following chapter. In addition, certain problems in understanding and using the data are now evident. Clearly, the actual child cannot be reconstructed simply from adult material, and the adult cannot be constructed merely by extrapolating from infant and child observations.

Sometimes the genetic point of view is applied in an oversimplified and reductionistic way, neglecting the "change of function" (Hartmann, 1939, p. 25) or secondary autonomy (Hartmann, 1950) that evolves as development proceeds. These terms refer to the fact that a behavior originating at one point in development may serve an entirely different function later on or become independent of the circumstances that determined its origin. The reaction formations (adoption of an opposite attitude to defend against an instinctual wish) formed in relation to toilet training are examples. Cleanliness in the older child or adult does not necessarily imply a wish to soil. Failure to recognize these factors leads to what some have called the genetic fallacy (Hartmann, 1955, p. 221)—that is, the tendency to attribute to later behavior the presence of the elements responsible for its origin. As an example, a dependent relationship in adulthood would be understood simply as a repetition of the person's early relationship with his mother.

As a result of this kind of thinking, adult psychopathology is automatically understood to signify either the persistence or the regressive recurrence of only the earliest developmental experiences. Then the remnants of early emotive functioning are viewed as diagnostic evidence of a severely disturbed primitive character disorder, with narcissistic, borderline, or psychotic features. Consequently, the later contributions to development are neglected along with the important possibility that a particular psychopathological disturbance may have originated at a later time rather than in the earliest months of life.

We believe this is unwarranted. Although one may see what looks like a remnant or a persistence of an earlier mode of functioning in an adult, this does not mean that the adult is functioning in the same way a child does at the time that mode of functioning originates. It is well known that later stages of development are colored by previous stages but that each stage makes its own contribution to the total personality. A typical example is the ambivalent adult with a defensive tendency toward dividing (splitting) positive and negative feelings.* Frequently such a descriptive picture is mistakenly taken as evidence of regression to or development arrested at a phase before these feelings were integrated. Such an oversimplification is like saying that a rapid division of cancer cells signals the recurrence of infancy; though there are cells that do indeed divide rapidly during infancy, this is not the same thing as cancer. Like the relationships between growth and cancer, the links between early developmental phenomena and psychopathology are not that simple. Intervening events play a crucial part in the eventual outcome. In addition to secondary autonomy and the change of function already mentioned, the principle of multiple function (Waelder, 1930) plays a role, in that drive, ego, and superego codetermine all mental functioning, both normal and disturbed. Waelder was referring to the overdetermination of all behavior, and the same approach can be fruitfully applied to any form of disturbance (Brenner, 1959, 1979). So even if an analytic patient finds the therapist's reconstructions extraordinarily helpful in making sense out of the past, what we understand as "psychic reality" may never have happened, at least in the way we reconstruct it.

Perhaps a more familiar problem is adultmorphic bias; the observer attributes phenomena occurring in infants and young children to structures, functions, or mechanisms that do not yet exist—for example, interpreting the infant's tongue protrusion as early imitation when it has been demonstrated to be a reflex response to the stimulus of a visual facial confrontation, a response that gradually fades away within a few months of birth (S. W. Jacobson, 1979). True imitation is more complex (Meltzoff, 1982, 1988). Another example is Melanie Klein's assertion (1928, 1958) that a young infant's behavior at the breast indicates fantasy activity, whereas research evidence indicates that the requisite mental capacity for fantasy is not available until a later age.

*Splitting* is a term that can be used in two ways. It can refer to a primitive defense in which things are kept apart that have not yet been amalgamated—for example, pleasurable and unpleasurable mental representations of the mother. It can also refer to a regressive defense in which things are separated *after* they have been amalgamated. For example, a mental representation encompassing all aspects of the mother can be divided into one with all the mother's "good," or pleasurable attributes and another with all the "bad," or unpleasurable ones; or mixed feelings about one person or oneself can be divided into pleasurable and unpleasurable feelings, one set of which is then often displaced onto another person. Unfortunately it is seldom specified in which sense the term is being used.

In this regard child analysis has yet another opportunity to make a contribution to our overall knowledge of development. As Anna Freud pointed out, the psychoanalytic treatment of children has already established itself as a means with which to gain access to the inner world of the child and to corroborate or refute theories based on reconstruction in adult analysis (1970b). More recently child analysis has also been able to provide a cross-check on assumptions and theories made on the basis of observational research. Since these ideas are usually concerned with the preoedipal child before psychic life is reorganized around the Oedipus complex, they are usually unavailable for reconstruction later by the adult analyst. But as more very young children come to be analyzed early in or prior to significant oedipal engagement, the analytic data illuminate early aspects of the developmental process, highlighting those issues and conflicts that need to be resolved before oedipal progression can take place (for examples see P. Tyson, 1977, 1989; R. L. Tyson, in preparation).

A recent controversy regarding the developmental process concerns when, if ever, the process ends. Several have suggested that the stage theory used to describe child development can be extended to the adult. Erikson (1950) was among the first to suggest that development is a lifelong process, and he elaborated Freud's psychosexual theory to include three adult stages, which he characterized as the person's attaining a capacity for intimacy, for generativity, and for ego integrity. Benedek (1959) added that parenthood could be viewed as a developmental stage, and Bibring et al. (1961) proposed that pregnancy also be viewed as a developmental stage. Gould (1972), Jaques (1981), and Dewald (1981) have suggested other criteria to describe adult developmental stages.

Colarusso and Nemiroff (1981) maintain that development continues throughout life, but instead of being tied to maturational stages in later years in the same way that it is earlier, it is defined by certain dynamic adult developmental tasks. These occur roughly within the chronological periods of early, middle, and late adulthood. In a similar way, Pollock (1981) discusses life-course expectancies, emphasizing that adult developmental sequences encompass many variables. Emde (1985) also asserts that development continues in an active way throughout life and that structural change does not stop with adolescence. Neugarten (1979) similarly thinks that psychological remodeling continues throughout life, but that adult development cannot be characterized by delineating discrete stages.

Settlage et al. (1988) have declared that although the stage model is useful for describing development in childhood and adolescence, it does not provide sufficiently specific criteria for adult development. They propose an alternate conceptualization of the developmental process defined in such a way as to encompass all periods of life. They consider the stimulus for development to be a disturbance of the previously adequate self-regulatory and adaptive functioning. This disturbance, or "developmental challenge" (which can be caused by biological maturation, environmental demand, a traumatic experience or loss, or the perception of a better possible adaptation), creates disequilibrium, with varying degrees of mental and emotional stress. A motivating tension, which can lead to regression, to psychopathology, or to development, is thereby created. If the motivating tension leads to attempts at resolution via forward development, a conflict is generated; its resolution leads to self-regulatory or adaptive structure formation or reorganization. New functions may result, and the integration of these new structures or new functions is marked by a change in the self-representation—that is, in the individual's sense of identity.

We agree that changes occur throughout the life cycle and that certain major life events (such as marriage and parenthood or a traumatic experience of loss) serve as stimuli for psychic reorganization. But we maintain that a maturational pull (or push) is central to the developmental process. In our view, the psychological changes that come about in step with maturation are distinguished by psychic structure formation, differentiation, and integration. The maturational pull is not present in adult life in the same way that it is in childhood and adolescence, and so the structural changes that do occur after adolescence are mostly related to adaptation; reorganization of existing psychic structures is involved, but not the formation of new structures. However, we see the reconceptualization of the developmental process proposed by Settlage et al. (1988) as a promising integrative effort that proposes a link between the psychological changes of childhood and adolescence and those of adulthood rather than simply equating the two.

## THEORIES OF THE DEVELOPMENTAL PROCESS

In his "Three Essays on the Theory of Sexuality" (1905b), Freud proposed a developmental sequence for the libidinal drive that remained the cornerstone of developmental theory until the advent of ego psychology. Then it became increasingly apparent that many factors in addition to sexuality contribute to the developmental process. Although some writers have made sweeping claims for the central or superordinate position of single components of development (for example, Kohut for narcissism and the self, Melanie Klein for aggression), others have considered the broad array of elements and struggled to find conceptual tools to convey the process of organization and integration. Of this latter group, we have been most influenced by the work of Piaget, Spitz, and Anna Freud. Each devised a comprehensive theory of development that every subsequent theorist has had to take into account in one way or another.

## Jean Piaget

Although he was an academic psychologist working outside the field of psychoanalysis, Jean Piaget was interested in the process of development, and his ideas have influenced psychoanalytic thinking since Hartmann recognized their importance to ego psychology (1953, 1956). Piaget focused particularly on behavior from the standpoint of adaptation. He saw the child's adaptation to the environment as his coming to an equilibrium between assimilating new information within already available categories and accommodating to new information by forming new categories, thereby altering internal structures. He thought that new experiences create tension within the system (disequilibration). By means of repeated assimilation and accommodation, the system gradually changes its internal structure and reestablishes equilibrium, so that development takes place. The transition constitutes a restructuring of previous schemata into a totally new organization. Equilibration is therefore a self-regulating process in which tension is created and then eliminated, and in the process the individual moves to increasingly higher stages of mental organization (Piaget, 1936, 1946, 1958, 1967).

Piaget concluded that mental development occurs through a series of stages, each marked by its particular dominant characteristics and with laws and a logic of its own. He emphasized that the stages follow an ontogenetic sequence. Although the time frame determining entry into a stage is not fixed and varies from population to population and from individual to individual, the serial order remains constant and is universal. Furthermore, each new stage begins with the sudden acquisition of a new cognitive capacity, followed by its consolidation and integration, leading to preparation for the next acquisition. Accordingly, the passage from an earlier to a later stage represents a spurt forward, so to speak, which is followed by an integration—hence the notion that psychic growth is both continuous and discontinuous. It has become commonly accepted that the period of structural disequilibrium that marks the entry into a new cognitive stage is typically accompanied by a heightened emotional vulnerability.

### René Spitz

Like Piaget, René Spitz was interested less in the unfolding of specific personality constituents than in their progressive integration and organization. But unlike Piaget, he was deeply interested in the early origins of psychopathology and in the psyche as a whole. Building on an unpublished paper presented in 1936 to the Vienna Psychoanalytic Society, he formulated in 1959 *A Genetic Field Theory of Ego Formation*. This became the basis for much of the psychoanalytic understanding of the developmental process.

Drawing heavily on embryological theory, Spitz saw development as a progression from instability to stability within a "field," which we today think of as a system. Having observed that major shifts in psychological organization and adaptation occur in the course of development, he concluded that in these instances some functions have been brought into a new relation with one another and are linked in a coherent unit. In his description, which he restricted to the first two years of life (we think it has broader relevance), he emphasized that the shifts are accompanied by new behaviors and new affective expressions, such as the social smile, stranger distress, and the "no" gesture. Spitz postulated that the appearance of these new affective expressions can be used as an indication or signal that a new level in psychic structural organization has been reached. He therefore called these new affective expressions "psychic organizers," although he thought they are not truly organizing but rather reflect an underlying advance in psychic structure formation, representing the integration of earlier behaviors into a new organization. The organizers also herald dramatic changes in interpersonal interaction and are followed by developmental consolidation of the new organization (Spitz, 1959, elaborated by Emde, 1980a, 1980b, 1980c). Spitz emphasized that development is both cumulative and epigenetic; that is, each developmental stage is built upon the previous one whether the developmental path is normal or pathological, and successive stages contain important and lasting new psychic formations that do not exist in preceding stages.

### Anna Freud

The concept of the "developmental line" has been used throughout psychoanalytic developmental theory as a metaphor representing sequential progress and emphasizing continuity and the cumulative character of development. Freud himself proposed the first such line, the maturational sequence of the libidinal drive. With the aim of finding a context within which to evaluate a child's personality, Anna Freud (1962, 1963) suggested that a series of predictable, interlocking, overlapping, and unfolding lines characterize development and that congruence or incongruence among them indicate normality or pathology.

In her formulation of developmental lines, Anna Freud emphasized their interactions and interdependencies—that is, the relationships among maturational sequences, environmental experiences, and developmental steps—as, each in his own way, had Piaget and Spitz. But whereas Piaget focused on the acquisition of new cognitive skills and Spitz looked for new affective expressions as signals of further organization in underlying structures, Anna Freud concentrated on understanding the underlying psychic determinants of specific behaviors. For example, she saw the manner in which a child relates to the mother as reflecting the integrated functioning of the id, ego, and superego, incorporating adaptive, dynamic, and genetic factors. She spoke of a line "from dependency to emotional self-reliance to adult object relationships," or of lines culminating in body independence "from sucking to rational eating," "from wetting and soiling to bladder and bowel control," "from irresponsibility to responsibility in body management." These "historical realities" reflected steps in the formation of underlying psychic structures and could help her understand the child's progress toward a more independent adaptation. She could then address such frequently asked questions as "What is the right age for entry into nursery school?" (1965, p. 57).

Anna Freud cautioned against reifying the developmental lines metaphor or interpreting it too concretely, arguing that development constitutes both progressive *and* regressive movement. She thought, however, that the comparison of progress along the several developmental lines offered a context within which to evaluate a child's emotional maturity or immaturity, normality or pathology, apart from the symptom. She anticipated that others would propose a variety of developmental lines and that an assemblage of developmental lines could "convey a convincing picture of an individual child's personal achievements or . . . of his failures in personality development" (1965, p. 64).

## DISCUSSION

The theories of Piaget, Spitz, and Anna Freud bring us to a view that the personality forms from the interaction among maturational and environmental influences and personal experiences and that development is characterized by continuity and by discontinuity. Progression proceeds along an array of pathways, each having a typical pattern of sequential, overlapping stages—hence development is continuous. Yet each stage has a unique organization with certain dominant characteristics that cannot be predicted from the preceding stage—hence it is discontinuous. The emergence of these characteristics, not a person's age, is the criterion of developmental progression. This means that each child progresses at his own rate and that developmental progress is judged according to the child's own past patterns rather than a norm established on a large population.

Progression along the various pathways is not smooth. Rather, it is characterized by major shifts, so that forward movement is followed by periods of integration and consolidation before preparation for the next forward shift begins. Some investigators have focused attention on these developmental shifts, and it is interesting that they agree as to when the shifts occur. The major shifts seem to take place at the ages of two to three months, seven to nine months, fifteen to eighteen months, about three years, seven years, eleven to thirteen years, fifteen to sixteen years, and eighteen to twenty years. Each investigator, however, labels the steps or stages according to his own framework and terminology. For example, Freud described sequential reorganizations of drive development. Piaget used these developmental shifts as indicators of cognitive integration and described stages according to the dominant mode of thinking in each. Spitz used developmental shifts as indicators of progressive reorganizations in ego development. Mahler (1972a, 1972b) also focused on the development of psychic structures, but she did so in terms of the infant's interactional experiences leading to object relations development. Stern (1985) likewise emphasizes the infant's interactional experiences in a framework of successive stages of the subjective sense of self, but he does not relate these stages to the development of the ego and the id. Anna Freud employed all these structural units and used manifest behavioral clusters to indicate progressive integration among them.

Until now, theorists have made few attempts to integrate these various perspectives on development. Indeed, Greenberg and Mitchell (1983), in discussing drive theory and object relations theory, maintain that the different models that characterize psychoanalytic thought are not simply organizational devices; rather, they reflect different visions of reality and so cannot be meaningfully combined or integrated. We disagree. Although each theory approaches the personality from a different angle, we find that the structural model of the personality can be employed at several levels of abstraction (see Rothstein 1983, 1988, for elaboration) and that it is sufficiently elastic to accommodate an integration of many models. We are convinced that an integration of theories and models is essential for a comprehensive view of personality formation. We also believe that effective intervention in the treatment of a child, or in reconstructing the childhood of an adult, demands a comprehensive understanding of all the overlapping factors influencing the individual's development. Therefore, a theoretical integration seems highly desirable. This is our aim, and after a more detailed discussion of the characteristics of the developmental process, we will illustrate the ways in which the theories can be integrated by presenting a comprehensive psychoanalytic perspective on human development.

# CHAPTER 2

## THE THEORY OF THE

## DEVELOPMENTAL PROCESS

The evolution of Freud's theory and technique of psychoanalysis has been based on the genetic point of view that certain childhood experiences form the basis of the adult neuroses. Since this view proceeds with reconstructions from adult analysis, the "reconstructed child" telescopes many of the small steps and experiences through which the actual child has passed. The genetic view emphasizes drive development, internal conflict, traumatic experiences, and the infantile neurosis; that is, it emphasizes the understanding of the developmental impact of childhood experiences and seeks to find the origins of the particular difficulties that brought the person to psychoanalytic treatment.

In contrast, the developmental perspective includes not only an investigation of internal conflicts and the infantile neurosis but also takes into account the origin and development of the psychic structures that contribute to adaptation as well as those that enter into conflict or bear on its course. The developmental point of view, which looks for the actual child rather than the reconstructed child (A. Freud, 1970b), has been immensely enriched in recent years by knowledge gained from methods of data gathering not available to Freud when he proposed the first theory of development in 1905. These include child analysis; direct observation of children in preschool, nursery, day-care, or hospital settings; longitudinal studies; laboratory experimental investigations; and data from related fields such as child development, cognitive psychology, and central nervous system developmental research. The developmental perspective seeks to integrate this fund of knowledge into a view of the developing child (Settlage et al., 1977).

The relationship between the genetic and the developmental points of view is a complementary one, reflecting Freud's "complemental series" (1905b, 1916–1917). One might say they represent two ways of

21

looking at the same part of the elephant. The genetic point of view looks from the present to the past and is particularly concerned with psychopathology. Its context is psychoanalytic therapy, and it requires thinking about the past in order to explain the present, recognizing that all earlier aspects of psychic life are potentially active and can influence current functioning. The developmental perspective looks forward with a focus on the process of psychic structure formation; that is, it considers how psychic structures and functions come about from the combined influence of innate givens, maturational sequences, and individual experiences to contribute to the ever more complicated labyrinth of intrapsychic life.

If we examine the process of this psychic development with the knowledge and tools currently available, we see a process characterized by change and plasticity that involves an integration and organization of biological, behavioral, and psychological components (Sander, 1983). It evolves from simple to more complex forms of organization and function, and the resulting functions and structures constitute advances in self-regulatory and adaptive capacities (Settlage et al., 1988). To the biologically minded, psychic development can be compared to embryological development. We are born with a blueprint of potential psychic developmental courses determined in part by a maturational timetable. We are born also with a capacity to interact with others, with a variety of already active cognitive functions, and with certain bodily needs and peremptory urges, all of which influence our unique individual experiences and contribute to the range and variation of our developmental path. Interactions with others in combination with maturational influences, individual experiences, and inner needs, urges, wishes, and feelings lead to the formation of an underlying stable organization of psychic structures that characterize a unique personality.

To study this process, we first describe innate givens, experiential factors, and the resulting integration into organized psychic structures. We then discuss the process of development and delineate a conceptual framework within which to integrate the great range of features contributing to the process.

## THE INNATE

Since Hartmann (1939) asserted that certain cognitive, perceptual, and motor functions are innate and provide the infant a state of "preadaptiveness," researchers have made explicit the enormous range of innately determined functions that contribute to the infant's competence and profoundly influence his developmental outcome. In addition to cognitive functions, they have described many details of the infant's temperament (which includes activity levels, rhythmicity, adaptability, threshold levels, the intensity of his reactions, and his distractibility or his persistence and attention span [Chess and Thomas, 1986]), his innate intellectual potential (influenced by his sensorimotor, visual perceptual and visual motor skills, and his ability to receive, express, and process language), the ease or difficulty with which he achieves homeostasis, and various special hypersensitivities or difficulties in integration that affect his preadaptiveness to cope with his environment.

The infant's propensity for activity is a major finding of contemporary developmental research. Far from being a tabula rasa, opening and flowering by virtue of environmental input or genetically determined plan, the infant actively participates in and shapes his development, utilizing his own special array of constitutional factors. This view contrasts sharply with the early idea that the infant is a helpless and passive recipient of developmental forces. Rather, the infant actively engages in human interaction, regulates himself, is resilient to potential pathogenic influences, monitors experience according to what is pleasurable or unpleasurable, and adapts to his environment. To describe each of these briefly will set the stage for a more comprehensive discussion in the chapters that follow.

The infant comes into the world predisposed for participating in human interactions. Bowlby (1969, 1973, 1980), for example, has stressed the infant's predisposition for attachment. As more knowledge has accumulated about the infant's contributions to development, researchers have come to recognize the importance of the infant's abilities to initiate, maintain, and terminate interactions with others. Brazelton and his colleagues have convincingly demonstrated that the infant anticipates social interaction and that when his expectations are not met, he employs a variety of techniques with which he attempts to engage his mother (see Brazelton, 1973, 1982; Brazelton et al., 1975; Brazelton and Als, 1979; Tronick et al., 1978).*

*As we noted in the introduction, we use the term *mother* generically throughout this book to refer to any mothering figure. We recognize that at times fathers may function as the primary caregiver as may grandparents and many others, but we agree with Call (1984) in preferring the term *mother* over the term *caregiver* because it includes rather than excludes the mother's subjective experience with her infant.

Self-regulation is an innate capacity that is basic to all living systems. Developmental research demonstrates that the neonate arrives equipped with an organization of state-related, endogenously determined regulatory behaviors that maintain physiological homeostasis. With the innate capacity for learning and adaptation and for using neurophysiological and morphological functions to cope with the environment, the newborn moves steadily toward developing a psychological system that regulates behavior. Self-regulation thereafter is considered an important ego function (Spitz, 1957; Wolff, 1966; Sander, 1969, 1980; Spitz, Emde, and Metcalf, 1970). Psychoanalytic developmental research has demonstrated the ways in which psychogenetic factors, early environmental influences, or a combination of the two, contribute to the structuring of self-regulatory processes that function adaptively or fail to do so (Greenacre, 1952a; Spitz, 1959; Weil, 1978). Affects play a major part in this regulation. At first the mother responds to the infant's inborn affective facial expression, and her response facilitates the infant's physiological homeostasis; later the infant uses his mother's and eventually his own affects as a signal of safety or danger (Emde, 1980b; Call, 1984). This monitoring of affects is an example of the combination of innate and environmental influences that contributes significantly to self-regulation.

The human infant is also enormously resilient, with a strong tendency to return to the course of development after some deviation or deflection. This observation has forced clinicians to reevaluate the pathogenic effects of single traumatic episodes. They have even had to reconsider the idea that major environmental interferences such as maternal deprivation or chaotic environments always and inevitably have irreversible adverse effects (see A. Freud, 1955; Emde, 1981; Harmon, Wagonfeld, and Emde, 1982; Anthony and Cohler, 1987).

Another innate given is the capacity to distinguish between what is pleasurable and what is unpleasurable and to prefer the former. Memories of his experiences guide the infant's subsequent choices, as peremptory urges impel his behavior. Freud recognized that the experiences of pleasure and unpleasure had motivational impact and that the bodily sources of pleasure changed over the course of development. He took these factors into account when he formulated the stages of psychosexual development, the libido theory (postulating a pleasure-seeking psychic energy), and the dual-drive theory. Because new information about development has brought about progressive revisions and modifications in libido theory, we no longer view infants and children simply as energy-possessed, pleasure-seeking creatures, though we recognize that the wish for pleasure as well as sexual and aggressive urges clearly have a dynamic influence on the growing child's behavior.

Adaptation is a crucial function of the child's innate capacity for activity. Hartmann (1939) distinguished between the individual's state of adaptedness to the environment and the developmental process by which that state is brought about. The adaptational process has been described as being either *alloplastic* or *autoplastic* (Freud, 1924c; Ferenczi, 1930). Alloplastic adaptation (analogous to the Piagetian concept of accommodation) refers to the individual's capacity to elicit responses from the environment or to relate to the environment primarily according to internal needs, schemes, or wishes. These capacities are crucial in earliest infancy when the infant must be capable of eliciting a response from the environment to meet his survival needs. But for the older child or adult to continue to manipulate the environment as the sole or major means of meeting his inner needs may be indicative of pathology. Autoplastic adaptation (analogous to the Piagetian concept of assimilation), by contrast, is the ability to make inner or psychic modifications in response to perceptions of the environment. This requires reality testing and in most cases implies compromise or at least a delay of gratification.

## THE EXPERIENTIAL

Innate capacities provide the limits within which later developing psychic structures can operate, and physiological functioning provides a preadapted means of adapting to the environment. As Benjamin was careful to emphasize, "Not only can innate differences in drive organization, in ego functions, and in maturational rates determine different responses to objectively identical experiences; *but they can also help determine what experiences will be experienced, and how they will be perceived*" (1961b, p. 34). Psychological functioning, however, is not innate, and, so far as we can determine, it is not available at birth (Spitz, 1957). Rather, psychic structures coalesce gradually through a series of individual experiences in interaction with others. And so, in addition to the infant's innately determined developmental potential, we have come to appreciate individual experiences as having a crucial developmental impact.

The infant may have an innately determined predisposition for participating in human interactions, but from those interactions a plethora of individual experiences accrue. The infant has a profound effect on his mother, for example, and his innate capacity to engage her or his failure to do so influences the course of his development (see Fraiberg, 1968, 1974; Bell, 1974; Lewis and Rosenblum, 1974; Bell and Harper, 1977). Benedek (1959) has suggested that the mother's gratification in satisfying her infant's needs, as well as her frustration when she is unable to do so, affects her own emotional life and, reciprocally, that of the infant.

Spitz (1963) has also emphasized that mother-infant reciprocity influences both the mother and infant. He stressed the asymmetry of reciprocity, noting that what the mother contributes is different from what the baby contributes, yet "each of them is the complement of the other, and while the mother provides what the baby needs, in his turn . . . the baby provides what the mother needs" (Spitz and Cobliner, 1965, p. 96). Kris (1953) examined the mutual fit between the needs of the mother and those of the infant and how they vary over time. More recently Chess and Thomas (1986) have discussed the same idea and point out that the quality of fit between caregiver and infant is as significant a contributor to the infant's development as is the infant's endowment.

An important outcome of contemporary developmental research has been the understanding that the mother and infant form a developing interactional system in which each partner has different competencies continually affecting and reinforcing the behavior of the other. Early in development this interactional process becomes so complex that very often later aspects of pathology cannot be attributed to the behavior of either partner (in contradistinction to the irresistible tendency among some clinicians to blame later pathology on what are presumed to be the mother's failures, a simplistic application of the genetic view emphasizing only the ways the mother shapes the infant's behavior).

The infant's experiences of interactions with others form the basis of memory. The infant constructs a sense of his personal reality on the basis of this memory. Reality must therefore also be seen as the product of the infant's activity and individual experiences.

## PSYCHIC STRUCTURE FORMATION

In the course of development, the innate and experiential elements we have described combine to form a hypothetical underlying stable organization of psychic structures, a process sometimes referred to as "psychic organization" or "structuralization." Mother-infant reciprocal interactions provide the early context. Through affectively invested interactions with the environment, and memories of these, the infant builds mental representations of himself, the other, and their interaction. Through various processes of internalization (incorporation, introjection, and identification), psychic structures also emerge from these interactions.

Not only do psychic structures emerge in the context of mother-infant interaction, but the difference between the psychic functioning of the mother and that of the infant has a developmental impact. Their interaction provides a learning context wherein the psychological functioning of the infant is lifted to successively higher levels of organization and structuralization (Loewald, 1960; Settlage, 1980).

Interactions with the mother at times lead to conflict, which also plays an important role in psychic structure formation. Conflict is not associated only with pathology; it is ubiquitous and inevitable, a "part of the human condition" (Hartmann, 1939, p. 12). Challenge and frustration, polarity and paradox, coherence and uncertainty, all characterize the developmental process (Sander, 1983). We are continually challenged by dissonance and incompatibility (G. S. Klein, 1976b), and our attempts to resolve them spur psychic functioning. In other words, conflicts begin as external, between two persons, mother and infant. We are born with an inherent capacity to resolve these conflicts by environmental manipulation or internal compromise—alloplastic or autoplastic adaptation. Eventually these conflicts are internalized, and internal compromises, mediated by ego functioning, are made to resolve them. In this way, psychic structure continually develops and is modified. Nagera (1966) has usefully clarified this, as he distinguished among developmental conflict, developmental interference, internalized, or neurotic conflict, and infantile neurosis.

Developmental conflict, sometimes with accompanying symptoms, is normal, characteristic, predictable, and usually transitory. Every child experiences developmental conflicts to a greater or lesser degree at each developmental state when, for example, a mother makes specific, phase-appropriate demands (such as toilet training) that clash with the child's wishes.

Environmental influences are sometimes so grossly out of harmony with the child's needs that the resulting distress interferes with forward development. Such developmental interference may lead to a variety of pathological deviations, depending on the child's age and developmental level at which they occur. Early interferences tend to have a more profound impact that may or may not be reversible. Neglect, for example, in earliest infancy jeopardizes the infant's survival; in the second year neglect may delay language acquisition and interfere with the formation of the cognitive structures underlying abstract thinking (Weil, 1978). Surgical intervention is another potential developmental interference. When it is performed at the peak of the infantile genital phase, the child may interpret the surgery as punishment for oedipal wishes, which may exacerbate castration anxiety or penis envy. Performed earlier, before firm senses of body and self are established and mentally represented, surgery may so overwhelm the child as to undermine his sense of body integrity and his self-regulating functions (Greenacre, 1952a). Developmental interferences have a pervasive influence and may determine the outcome of subsequent developmental conflicts.

Ordinarily, what begins as conflict between external demands and inner wishes becomes conflict between inner demands and inner wishes. We then speak of *internalized,* or *neurotic conflicts.* The first steps in conflict internalization are evident as early as the second half of the second year (Mahler, 1975b). Then the toddler experiences conflicting wishes, as between the wish for his mother's love, which begins to have conditions, and the wish for unrestricted gratification; an optimal consequence is that internal modifications are made. For example, instead of the toddler's pursuing and enjoying anal pleasures, reaction formations interfere and he seeks cleanliness in identification with his mother's wishes.

Phase-specific oedipal conflicts are superimposed on these early internalized conflicts, and one possible result is that an *infantile neurosis* takes shape. (This takes place in the period we now view as early childhood, not infancy.) An infantile neurosis implies a functioning superego and refers to a certain structure and organization of the mind wherein particular wishes and impulses (usually drive-related wishes of the Oedipus complex, but other wishes can also be involved) come into conflict with internalized standards and moral directives of the emergent superego, and internal modifications and compromises (instead of attempts to manipulate the environment) are made in response to the conflict. The infantile neurosis can be crippling and interfere with development, yet the underlying conflicts are normal, and adaptive efforts toward their resolution facilitate independent psychological functioning.

Although most internal conflicts begin with interactions with the external world that are subsequently internalized, a special category refers to active, unresolved, and partially unresolvable conflicts between opposing trends in the personality. Ambivalence, the balance between femininity and masculinity (often referred to as bisexuality), and activity and passivity are examples of such inner conflicts.

## THE DEVELOPMENTAL PROCESS

The formation of intrapsychic structures from innate and experiential elements is characterized by forward spurts and backward slides. Thus, it is a discontinuous process. Forward spurts occur because of what Abrams (1977) refers to as developmental transformations. From time to time, various elements, capacities, or functions (cognitive functions, or the emergence of a new erogenous zone leading to further psychosexual development, for example) mature according to a biologically determined pattern and timetable. Such maturation leads to transformations within the system. These transformations are not normally dependent on or influenced by the environment, and each child must progress according to his individual pace.

Forward development also occurs because of developmental integrations. That is, various independently emerging components and functions come to be linked and to work in relation to one another, forming a new, coherently functioning organization. This new organization is more complex than any one of its contributing elements. The coupling or organizing of a variety of functions into a coherent system is the essence of ego structuralization. The nodal points at which various functions come to be linked, marking stages in ego formation, are characterized by notable advances in a child's self-regulatory and adaptive capacities and, therefore, by notable changes in behavior.

Each nodal point is characteristically followed by a period of regression and developmental consolidation. A forward move in one psychic system or another creates an imbalance among the psychic systems that disturbs the prior equilibrium. Earlier modes of functioning, earlier developmental issues, conflicts, defenses, and forms of adaptation, must now be reworked. (Piaget conceptualized a similar process for cognitive development, which he called décalage [1932].) Each successful reworking brings a higher level of functioning within each psychic system as well as a higher level of integration among the psychic systems as the mental apparatus matures. This is not to say the child "grows out of" his insufficiently resolved conflicts or persisting problems. Instead, he "grows around" them; they thereby distort the subsequent developmental course.

Kris introduced the concept of "regression in the service of the ego" (1952, p. 177), emphasizing that regression should be considered a part of normal development. A basic psychoanalytic assumption is that all forms of psychological phenomena, although superseded by later forms, remain potentially active; given sufficient stress, a functional (not temporal) regression may take place in the sense that more satisfying or less conflictual modes of functioning that arose earlier are again utilized. Repetition in psychic functioning is therefore common, as every aspect of experience, every developmental issue, remains intact, evolves and is potentially viable throughout life. As Jones commented, "The individual *recapitulates* and *expands* in the second decennium of life the development he passed through during the first five years. . . . these stages are passed through on different planes at the two periods of infancy and adolescence, but in very similar ways in the same individual" (1922, pp. 398–399). It is also characteristic of the evolving personality to experience "repetition in the inner world of what has taken place in interaction with the outer world" (Loewald, 1965, p. 90). Repetition as we refer to it here differs from the repetitive behavior Freud (1920) attributed to the "repetition-compulsion" that is a result of psychopathological forces. Repetition in the sense we are using it is part of the psychic processes of internalization and structuralization.

Abrams (1977) pointed out that the manner in which developmental progression contributes to the personality is highly variable. Not only do major organizational shifts that are due to transformations or integrations lend discontinuity to the process, but continuities can also be identified. The patterning of interpersonal relating (Emde, 1988a) or modes of ego functioning (S. Brody and Axelrad, 1970, 1978), for example, have been shown to retain some recognizable characteristics throughout development.

Considering the discontinuities and continuities of the developmental process, the difficulties in describing "normality" become increasingly apparent. A particular child develops at faster or slower rates in some areas than in others. Development in some areas relies more on maturation, in others, on environmental interaction and individual experience, and in still others, on the integration and synthesis of elements from previous stages. Because of this, Neubauer observed that "the attempt to unify the various divergent modes of the developmental processes exposes the inherent problem in the psychoanalytic theory of development. It is their complexity that makes it so difficult to find appropriate relationships between various ego functions and id-ego functions" (1984, p. 21). The complexity of the developmental process makes the varieties of normality and of psychopathology infinite.

## A PROPOSED VIEW

The previous discussion has made it clear that an extensive range of psychic functions contributes to the developmental process. The purpose of this book is to delineate an integrative framework within which to view that process, one that is responsive to the challenge of complexity and yet will allow for an examination of a large number of component parts. When Freud's (1923a) structural hypothesis is viewed in an evolutionary manner that takes account of contemporary developments in the field, we believe it can account for this developmental process and can accommodate the findings of modern developmental research. This is because the structural model can be approached at various levels of abstraction. One such level is the experiential—those everyday affectively laden experiences, fantasies, and memories of ourselves, alone and with others, which shape self- and object representations that collectively form the representational world (Sandler and Rosenblatt, 1962). Another level of abstraction is the nonexperiential—the hypothetical structures id, ego, and superego that create an underlying organizational structure for the personality and that, in turn, function to organize everyday experiences.*

Also, since a structure refers to a relatively stable, slowly evolving system, and since the structural hypothesis was proposed to allow us to consider the dynamic interaction among various psychic processes, the structural hypothesis fits in very well with contemporary emphasis on systems theory. Briefly, this theory was explicated by von Bertalanffy, who contrasted it with the then prevailing behavioristic or "robot psychology" view of human beings: "In contrast to physical forces like gravity and electricity, the phenomena of life are found only in individual entities called organisms." He explains that an "organism is a system, that is, a dynamic order of parts and processes standing in mutual interaction" (1968, p. 208). There are open and closed systems: the former are open to influence and modification from outside; the latter are not. The mind and its constituent parts (as well as our

---

*Strictly speaking, nonexperiential refers to all the hypothetical aspects of psychic functioning, such as defenses or other psychic mechanisms, as well as the psychic systems or structures. The nonexperiential elements of psychic functioning are an integral part of our theory but not a part of our experience. Sandler and Joffe (1969) note that "the nonexperiential realm is intrinsically unknowable, except insofar as it can become known through the creation or occurrence of a phenomenal event in the realm of subjective experience" (p. 82).

theories about it, we hope) is an open system, as we are always open to influence and modification from outside as well as inside forces.

General system theory has become increasingly influential with psychoanalytic theorists, and some analysts, beginning with Bowlby (1969, 1980), and including Peterfreund (1971), Rosenblatt and Thickstun (1977), Basch (1977), Sander (1983), Stechler and Halton (1987), and Boesky (1988), find it useful. We, too, find it helpful not as a replacement for the structural model but as a way of describing the structural model in greater functional detail. By viewing the mind as an open system, one with a dynamic order among its component parts, characterized by a continuous exchange with the environment and by increasing elaboration and differentiation, we believe we capture the spirit of Freud's thinking. Describing the structural hypothesis this way helps account for the many factors and levels of abstraction involved in the evolution of motivation, defense, and conflict resolution that make up the essence of human experience.

Seen from a system perspective, the process of development can be conceptualized as the evolution of a number of functions that come to be linked and associated with other functions forming a system. Many systems evolve in this way, and the developmental trajectory of each intertwines with that of the others. These various systems eventually coalesce to form the relatively stable organizing structural units of id, ego, and superego, which maintain a dynamic equilibrium with each other and with the external world.

The developmental process, accordingly, takes place through the differentiation, organization, transformation, and reorganization of a variety of networking, branching, and interrelated systems. In every system, the form taken at each stage is affected by the development of all the other systems in interaction with the environment. That is, the infant begins life with a number of innate potentials. As infant and mother come to form a stable interactional system, the organizing influence of that system gives psychological meaning to innate physiological functions. This becomes evident as the infant distinguishes between what is pleasurable and unpleasurable in association with affective feedback responses from the mother. These distinctions mark the earliest steps in the formation of the id as a motivational system (Loewald, 1978; P. Tyson, 1988).

Progress in object relations can be inferred as the infant-caregiver interactional system leads to the formation of stable, enduring patterns of relating. In addition, experiences of interaction facilitate the infant's gradual development of a sense of the mother and a sense of himself in interaction with her. Soon the infant begins regulating exchanges with the mother (Stern, 1974b; Beebe, 1986), behaviors that imply that the ego is beginning to take shape as an organized and organizing, self-regulating psychic structure, which moves beyond the endogenous, state-determined regulatory system available to the newborn.

Over time the infant's sense of the other and sense of himself become more enduring as mental representations of self and other begin to accrue; these, in turn, foster his increasing sense of individuality. In addition, various of the mother-infant interactions lend gender specificity to the emerging sense of self, and as the infant makes enduring identifications with one or the other parent, gender identity becomes established. Over time, through various processes of internalization and identification, the mother-infant interactional system fosters the child's gaining greater capacity for independent functioning, since identifications with the caregiving mother have helped him gain greater ego strength. At the same time, a growing sense of social connectedness encourages the internalization of rules and expectations, ideals and moral codes, as early stages in the functioning of a superego system become evident. Early superego functioning, together with greater independence in psychological functioning, ensures greater stability of interpersonal harmony and supports expansion and greater elaboration of object relations.

As psychic functions come to be associated and interdependent in this developmental process, a more integrated organization among the systems emerges. An appropriate analogy would be the child's learning to write. At first the letters have little association with one another, but eventually they become grouped to form the child's name and then other words. Ultimately words become grouped to form sentences, and sentences form stories.

In this description the word *process* should be emphasized, for no one point or pattern ever recurs, and no one system is ever a fixed and final attainment; new additions or modifications may be made throughout life. Furthermore, if we consider the infinite complexity of all the elements cascading together in the developmental process, a large measure of unpredictability is characteristic, and yet there is a predictability and stability to the overall pattern. Also, no one system is superordinate nor can any one system be considered in isolation from the others; no one system is causally related to, derived from, or explanatory of another. Rather, all are interdependent, but the rela-

# DEVELOPMENTAL STAGES OF MAJOR PSYCHIC SYSTEMS

| Psychosexual Phases | Object Relations | | | Conflict | Affects |
|---|---|---|---|---|---|
| | | Object | Self | | |
| Oral | Dyadic | Reciprocity Dialogue | Core self | | Social smile |
| | | Libidinal object | Body self | Developmental conflict (if severe developmental arrest) | Social referencing |
| Anal | | Practicing | Mentally represented self | | |
| | | Rapprochement | | | Affect/idea linked |
| | | Libidinal object constancy | Self-constancy | Internalized conflict | Signal function |
| Infantile genital | | Narcissistic | | | |
| | Triadic | Oedipal positive negative | Identity integrated | | |
| | | | | Infantile neurosis | |
| Latency early | | | | | |
| | | Family romance | Self-responsibility | | |
| late | | | | | |
| Preadolescence | | Regression | Shifts in body self | | |
| Adolescence early | | | | Conflict externalized | |
| | | | Body self-reconsolidation | | |
| middle | | Deidealization | | | |
| | | | Identity crisis | Conflict reinternalized | |
| late | | Disengagement | Stability of identity | | |

| Cognition | Superego | Gender | | Ego |
|---|---|---|---|---|
| | | *Girl* | *Boy* | |
| Sensorimotor (0–2 years) | | Sex assignment | Sex assignment | Social smile |
| | | | | Libidinal object |
| | | Body differentiation | Body differentiation | |
| | Introjects and ideals form | | | |
| Representational thinking | | Primary femininity | Primary masculinity | Communication |
| | Comply object | | | |
| Preoperational | | Female role identification | Disidentify mother | Internalized conflict |
| Primary and secondary processes fluid | Comply introject | | Fear castration (mother) | Signal function |
| | | Anatomical preoccupation | Anatomical preoccupation | |
| | Identify Ideals/ introjects | | Male role identification | |
| | | Change of libidinal object | Fear castration (father) | |
| | Guilt | Conflict in object choice | Conflict in object choice | Infantile neurosis |
| Concrete operations | | Practice gender role | Phallic narcissism | Pleasure in industry |
| Primary and secondary processes separated | Superego autonomous | | | |
| | | | Regression | |
| | | Menarche | | |
| | Regressive personification | | Castration anxiety | Reorganization: labile affects |
| Formal operations | | Reconsolidate femininity | Revise ego ideal | |
| Fluidity between primary and secondary processes | Modify ego ideal | Object choice conflict | | |
| | | Sexual preference set | Sexual preference set | Ego supremacy: mood stability |
| Primary and secondary processes separated | Self as authority | | | |

© Phyllis Tyson and Robert L. Tyson

tionships among them are not strictly proportional. It is the integration among the systems, however, that promotes adaptation at increasingly higher levels of psychological functioning.

With this framework, misconceptions of the concept of "stage" can be addressed. Each system has a series of stages—that is, a predictable pattern in the order of acquiring certain functions or in achieving various levels of integration among its functions. Each stage, therefore, represents a nodal point along the developmental continuum where a certain level of functional integrity can be identified. Pine (1985) criticizes analysts for seeing everything in a particular period as relevant to the dominant libidinal stage. If we conceptualize a number of simultaneously evolving systems, however, each with its own developmental trajectory with various stages, it becomes apparent that several stages coexist; then the stages in one system must be considered in relation to stages in the other systems, with no one system being superordinate.

In our conceptualization of development, we rely on the ideas of Spitz, Piaget, and Anna Freud. We adhere to the emphasis placed on epigenesis first by Erikson (1959) and maintained by Spitz and Piaget—that is, on sequential stages each with new, dominant characteristics—rather than on chronological age. We also find most relevant their stress on the discontinuity of the developmental process—forward movement followed by integration, consolidation, and preparation for the next forward shift.

We also find the concept of developmental lines a useful metaphor to convey the interwoven, overlapping, branching network of simultaneously evolving psychic systems that constitutes the developmental process. This metaphor offers a framework not only for understanding the process but also for examining its details more closely. The metaphor remains useful, however, only to the extent that a developmental line is understood to refer to the sequential changes in any one of many personality systems and represents a cyclical and spiraling pathway, one that is not linear in nature.

Our use of the concept of developmental lines differs from Anna Freud's reference to behavioral clusters representing the integration of id, ego, and superego elements. We formulate sequential developmental stages for the more hypothetical, nonexperiential psychic systems and structures such as the ego and superego. To do so requires extrapolations from clinical observations to theories about conscious and unconscious mental functioning. We also formulate developmental lines for object relations, a sense of self, and gender identity. These rely on the experiential, but our formulations involve extrapolations from the experiential to theories of psychic functioning.

Drucker has said, "The forging of a theory that accounts not only for both stability and continual change over the course of development but also for the possibility of varying kinds of interactions among organismic systems and functions is indeed a challenge" (1981, pp. 44–45). We hope to show that by utilizing a system approach to the structural model, employing the metaphor of developmental lines, and filling in details of the developmental stages of many evolving systems, we can go a long way toward meeting that challenge.

Of course, delineating the developmental trajectory of any one system or viewing one system in relation to the others is a descriptive exercise. It is not meant to be a metapsychological formulation but more like a map-making procedure utilizing developmental landmarks. Just as points on a map do not indicate the likelihood of traffic jams at intersections, so steps in a developmental trajectory do not always convey the potential conflicts at each developmental stage.

As an aid to the reader, we have schematically charted hypothesized steps in the various lines of development (see figure 1). We realize that such a graphic representation runs the risks of oversimplification and reification, and does not account for different levels of abstraction. Nevertheless, some may find it a useful tool in following the developmental progression in the simultaneously evolving, intertwining systems we discuss.

With this approach, we move away from the building-blocks, or "Lego" idea of development (R. L. Tyson, 1986) according to which each piece of developmental experience is assumed to be built solidly on top of the preceding piece; that is, simple links between early and later behavior are assumed. Ours is a more plastic model—made of a substance like Plasticine that never dries up—in which the shape and configuration of various cascading and intertwining strands change as evolution and development proceeds. In this way the shape at any one time is never predictable, although there is a predictability to the pattern. Finally, the configuration of the whole is never static, but is continually evolving.

# PART TWO

## PSYCHOSEXUALITY

# CHAPTER 3

## PSYCHOSEXUALITY:

## A THEORETICAL OVERVIEW

At a time when prevailing social, scientific, and psychological opinion held that childhood is free of any evidence of sexuality, Freud declared the opposite, thereby provoking a storm of shocked opposition. He nevertheless went on to propose the libido theory, which stresses the influence of sexuality on psychic life. His clinical experience—his self-analysis and his patients' fantasies, associations, and recollections from childhood—led him to conclude that sexual urges provide a motivation for psychic functioning. He supposed that some kind of force or psychic energy lies behind sexual behavior and suggested that this energy be called "libido." He thought that libido is crucial in personality development and that it leads to sexual strivings that begin at a much earlier age than had been previously believed. In addition, he became convinced that many disturbances of adult functioning are based on vicissitudes of early childhood sexual development. Because of the painfully conflictual nature of early sexual experiences and fantasies, they are largely no longer accessible to conscious recollection; they succumb to *infantile amnesia*. The chief task of the psychoanalyst, therefore, is to uncover and interpret to the patient these mostly sexual contents of his Unconscious.

For almost forty years, the concepts embodied in libido theory provided a developmental foundation for psychoanalytic thought and the technical procedures of psychoanalytic treatment. With the introduction of the structural hypothesis and the dual-drive theory, in which the aggressive drive was awarded equal status with the sexual drive, "instinctual drives" (a designation that has come to refer to both sexual and aggressive strivings) were located within the domain of the id, which largely although not completely encompassed the Unconscious system in the topographical model. As the work of Anna Freud (1936) and Heinz Hartmann (1939), with their emphasis on ego functioning, began to broaden the theoretical and technical foundations of psychoanalysis, the id and libido theory lost their positions as the sole measures of psychoanalytic understanding. Nevertheless, they remained essential to the therapeutic and theoretical endeavors of most analysts. Even in the face of recent cogent criticisms of libido theory, the framework of psychosexual development and the concept of instinctual drives retain their clinical usefulness.*

There are many excellent summaries of libido theory (for example, Sterba, 1942; Fenichel, 1945, pp. 33–113). In what follows our emphasis is chiefly on those aspects that have been affected by recent research and are closely interrelated with other developmental systems.

---

*In his early work Freud attempted to provide a biological basis for his formulations and to use terminology consistent with contemporary advances in other sciences. He was strongly influenced by his teacher Ernst Brücke, himself a student of Helmholtz, who believed, along with other nineteenth-century scientists, that the principles of contemporary physics would eventually provide explanations for all natural phenomena, including the psychological. Consequently, Freud used the terms of energy—its *conservation, displacement,* and *discharge*—as metaphors for psychological functioning. Psychic energy, or libido, was an attribute of emotions that had the capacity to impel the mind to activity; the chief function of the mental apparatus was to harness, deploy, and regulate this mental energy, or "excitation." George Klein (1976b) points out that essentially Freud's libido theory encompasses two theories. One emerged from clinical experience and the other, more abstract, involved a quasi-physiological model of energic forces seeking discharge. Klein argues that while the clinically based theory remains useful because it is susceptible to continued empirical testing and growth, the more abstract is less useful, for the models on which it is based are out of date, and it emerged more from a need for theoretical consistency with other disciplines than from data. Klein's ideas have been very influential as an increasing number of analysts question the theory of psychic energy. We too find ourselves inclined to abandon the concept of psychic energy in its concrete meaning referring to some actual physical form of psychic energy. But the idea of an instinctual drive as an idea, an affect, an impulse, a wish that has motivational impact—that is, it impels the mind to activity—remains clinically useful. Therefore, if at times we use terms such as *libidinal investment,* it should be understood that we refer to a loving attachment, not a hypothetical quantity of psychic energy.

## THE LIBIDO THEORY

Freud's "Three Essays on the Theory of Sexuality (1905b), to which he added substantially in 1915, contains all the major elements of libido theory and psychosexual development. In this work he used the term *sexual* to refer to sensual pleasures derived from any body area or organ, not only the genitals, and *libido* to refer to the hypothesized energy underlying sexual pleasure. Although it is commonly believed, erroneously, that Freud equated libido totally with sexuality (especially genital sexuality), he later clarified that libido should be thought of more broadly as love, or a "love-force," with sexuality just one manifestation of libido. He also emphasized that

> we do not separate . . . what in any case has a share in the name "love"—on the one hand, self-love, and, on the other, love for parents and children, friendship and love for humanity in general, and also devotion to concrete objects and to abstract ideas. . . . We are of the opinion, then, that language has carried out an entirely justifiable piece of unification in creating the word "love" with its numerous uses, and that we cannot do better than take it as the basis of our scientific discussions and expositions as well. (1921, pp. 90–91)

In emphasizing the broader meanings underlying Freud's concept of libido, we wish to make it clear that although throughout this book we will use the terms *libido, sexuality,* and *sexual drive* more or less interchangeably, this broader meaning is implied.

Freud maintained that the instinctual drive is always unconscious. Only the associated fantasies or peremptory impulses derived from it can reach awareness. He conceptualized the libidinal drive in terms of its source, aim, object, and pressure. The *source*, he thought, is a somatic, perhaps even hormonal one that gives rise to continuous stimulation. He maintained, however, that the drive itself is purely psychological, that it is "the psychical representative of an endosomatic, continuously flowing source of stimulation" (1905b, p. 168).*

Although Freud was uncertain about the source of an instinct, he nevertheless described certain body "erogenous" zones—the mouth,

*Freud was not always consistent about whether he viewed the instinct as something purely psychical—in which case, instinct and its psychic representative are identical—or as something nonpsychical that comes to awareness only through an associated idea or affect which then is, in effect, the psychic representative. The psychological concept became the basis of the psychoanalytic theory of motivation, however. See Strachey's discussion, *S.E.,* 14:111–113.

anus, and genitals—that, when stimulated, bring pleasure and gratification. Although all these zones are potentially active from birth,
Freud observed a maturational sequence according to which each zone
is more prominently in focus or is the source of greatest pleasure—that
is, it is "phase dominant"—at various times during early childhood.
Hence, his theory of psychosexual development with oral, anal, and
infantile genital (which came to be known as phallic) phases was based
on the maturational progression of the focus on the erogenous zones.

The *aim* of the instinctual drive is gratification. Freud maintained
(1915a) that although the ultimate aim remains unchangeable, there
may be different paths leading to that aim. Therefore gratification may
be sought through a variety of acts that stimulate body erogenous
zones, such as sucking, defecating, or genital masturbation. When
climactic orgasm is physiologically possible, the achievement of orgasm
is, according to the libido theory, the aim that comes to consolidate
within it all earlier gratifications. Freud characterized infantile sexuality as "polymorphous perverse" in that, as in adult perversions,
every kind of excitation in any erogenous zone is potentially available
as the maximal source of pleasure.

The person through whom, or in regard to whom, the drive is able
to achieve its aim has come to be known as the *object*. In earliest infancy
the infant is thought to respond to or attach to the gratifying functions
performed by the mother rather than to the mother as a "whole object." The mother or the caregiver is therefore sometimes referred to as
the *part object* or *selfobject*, depending on which theoretical framework is
being used.

Freud viewed the instinctual drives, because of their peremptory,
impulsive quality, as the prime motivators of the mind. All mental
activity was accordingly drive-related. The *pressure* of an instinctual
drive, then, referred to the amount of force, or the "measure of the
demand for work which it represents" (1915a, p. 122). In accord with
nineteenth-century scientific thinking, Freud attributed the varying
intensity of sexual impulses to varying amounts of metaphorical energy, or libido.

Whereas Freud viewed all motivation as derived from the instinctual
drives, recent theoretical work proposes broadening the origin and
range of possible motivation, thereby loosening or dissolving this obligatory conceptual link (see Lichtenberg, 1989, for a survey and discussion). Affects, object-related needs, or narcissistic needs are viewed as
having the same kind of motivational intensity as needs having a
somatic base and are thought to be deserving of equal status. Broaden-

ing the definition of motivation to include such factors does not, however, exclude the sexual drive.

An additional characteristic of the instinctual drives is their extraordinary "plasticity" or "mobility." Particular actions by means of which satisfaction is sought may be repressed, shifted, or altered, and satisfaction achieved in disguised forms if necessary. Zones also change during the course of development, as do the objects through whom gratification is sought, in fantasy or in reality. Once the final object choice is made, reached through resolution of the Oedipus complex and completion of the adolescent process, the individual typically achieves maximal libidinal gratification through genital sexual intercourse. Nevertheless, the pressure of drive needs at any developmental level may result in a shift or change in aims and objects in the search for gratification, with a corresponding change in fantasy life.

Sexual fantasies may be object-directed, but sexual gratification is frequently autoerotic. In infancy and childhood, sexuality is necessarily autoerotic, the child's own body being the only means through which gratification is available under normal circumstances. The child freely uses his own body and experiences sexual pleasure from all its areas.

Freud observed that particular characteristics and symptoms of a range of adult emotional disorders bore a resemblance to certain behaviors in childhood. He and his colleagues, especially Abraham and Ferenczi, elaborated the theory of libidinal development to better explain their observations. They concluded that though ordinarily the child's environment varies in its responsiveness to his needs, either excessive gratification or excessive frustration may disturb the otherwise peaceful process of development. As a consequence, quantities of libidinal and/or aggressive energy are "left behind" and are attached to particular mental representations of that period. These way stations along the developmental course are called silent "fixation points." They give no indication of their presence until the individual encounters some particular stress or difficulty that he cannot cope with by any of the usual mechanisms of defense. Then he resorts to regression whereby a change in behavior reveals a shift to some behavior characteristic of an earlier developmental level. If the fixation point is not "silent," the person is deemed to have been "arrested" at that stage, implying that further development did not take place.

This explanation was satisfactory given the knowledge available at the time; now, however, it seems a concrete and mechanistic attempt to explain the vicissitudes of emotional conflict and characteristic behavior patterns. Anna Freud later (1965) made it clear that progression and regression are observable, integral parts of normal development. Regression is no longer conceptually limited to drives alone; for example, it may be seen to occur also in ego and superego functioning. Furthermore regression should not be thought of as a temporal phenomenon in the sense of returning to; rather, it is a reversion to safer sources of pleasure or a utilization of earlier learned behavior patterns or modes of relating. Rather than being understood as a spot along a continuum where energy is deposited and to which the psyche must return to gather up its formerly abandoned energy, a fixation point is more helpfully viewed as a thought, a wish, or a behavior associated with pleasure or with pain that continues to be emotionally significant for the individual. One can see the continuing influence of the particular thought, behavior, or means of gratification especially at times of stress.

A common error in psychoanalytic theorizing is always to view the later appearance of earlier wishes, conflicts, or modes of functioning automatically as indications of significant disturbances in the earliest months of life. A classic critique of the problem by Sandler and Dare (1970) uses the concept of orality as an illustration. An infant in the first year of life may be regarded as being orally dependent, but dependency longings cannot always be considered as arising in the first year of life. As Sandler and Dare point out, such longings are likely to occur at any phase at times of stress, when the child wishes to have what he fantasizes was true earlier.

Erikson (1950) was the first to make the important distinction between *drive expression*, as in behavior specifically directed toward drive gratification, and *mode of functioning*. The latter refers to a characteristic manner of obtaining gratification or relating to objects. The person may find a means of gratification originally associated with a particular phase or erogenous zone a useful way of expressing wishes and conflicts at a subsequent time. It persists, but without its former ties to the zone and phase of origin; thus it achieves secondary autonomy (Hartmann, 1939). For example, an infant's biting during the oral phase may be a way of deriving pleasure, but at that time it is unlikely to be accompanied by wishful fantasies or hostile intentions directed toward another person, inasmuch as cognitive and self-object differentiation have not progressed this far (even if the recipient of the infant's bite is likely to think otherwise). The child, however, may use this oral mode later to express his object-directed hostility, and he may engage in a variety of destructive fantasies. But though the oral mode persists, this does not imply that forward development has not taken place—that is, the person is not "arrested" or "fixated" at the oral level of drive development—and there is no reason to think that other means of satisfaction are absent. It is now generally agreed that the intricacies of development are such that later psychopathology cannot be predicted or explained simply on the basis of so-called libidinal fixation points.

## DUAL-DRIVE THEORY

As more clinical information accumulated and more observations required theoretical accommodation, Freud (1920) expanded instinctual drive theory to include an aggressive or destructive counterpart. His clinical observations led him to the conclusion that feelings of anger and hostility result in conflict and unconscious guilt in the same way that sexual wishes do and that these negative feelings are similarly defended against. Indeed, he observed that many impulses contain both sexual and aggressive elements, and that various clinical phenomena, including sadism, masochism, and ambivalence, can be explained in terms of varying degrees of conflict between these elements or their fusion. Freud also thought that nondestructive forms of aggression provide motivation for activity and mastery just as the libido does. For these reasons he postulated that the libidinal and aggressive drives are fundamental.

Freud's conceptualizations of aggression were always problematic. Since he had proposed a biological basis for libido, he felt it necessary to provide one for aggression. But aggressive impulses were not related to specific body zones, so no source was obvious unless aggressive impulses could be viewed in close association with sexual ones. Indeed, in his first model of the mind Freud thought of aggression as a component of the sexual drive: "The history of civilization shows beyond any doubt that there is an intimate connection between cruelty and the sexual instinct" (1905b, p. 159). Although aggressive impulses are associated with the expression of libidinal urges, they frequently appear to be a reaction to external stimuli. This observation led Freud, at another time, to describe aggression as an ego attitude in the service of self-preservation (1915a, pp. 137–139).

Later (1920), in a philosophical mode completely divorced from clinical observation, he postulated the existence of a fundamental and lifelong conflict between a death instinct (Thanatos) and a life instinct (Eros). The aggressive drive, he believed, arises from an organically based death instinct; the principle by which he believed it to operate was that the organism strives to dispose of excitation and reach the ultimate state of Nirvana, or total absence of excitation. Even as libido was the energy of the "life force," "destrudo" was the energy of the death instinct. This revision was of monumental importance and has provided fuel for theoretical polemics for decades.

Today the followers of Melanie Klein are the chief proponents of the death instinct, unlike others who find it problematic and unnecessary (Parens, 1979). Nevertheless, a dual-drive theory of libidinal and aggressive drives persists and has almost universal clinical application. Sexuality and aggression are thought to be intimately bound up together with the developmental phases of infantile sexuality; both are seen as sources of conflict, and defenses are employed against the awareness or expression of each. Repression or inhibition of aggression may interfere with sexual gratification at any developmental level. In early childhood, problems in the expression of aggression may be apparent in feeding disturbances (the food may be, for example, unconsciously equated with mother, so that eating means devouring mother), fragility of emotional attachments, and inhibition of curiosity and intellectual achievements. At the other end of the spectrum, one may see exaggerated aggressive manifestations ranging from overemphasized assertiveness to unmanageable destructiveness. These may come about, according to the dual-drive theory, if for some reason the aggressive urges are not combined with or adequately "bound" with love—sexuality in its larger sense. This may happen because early deprivations, object loss, or child abuse interferes with the libidinal attachment (see A. Freud, 1949).

## THE STRUCTURAL MODEL AND PSYCHOSEXUALITY

The structural hypothesis (1923a) followed shortly after Freud introduced the dual-drive theory; there he grouped the instinctual drives under the heading "id." There are many unresolved problems regarding current psychoanalytic understanding of the id (see Arlow and Brenner, 1964; Schur, 1966; Hayman, 1969). While not attempting to resolve those issues, we think it is helpful to view the id less as a "seething cauldron" and more as a system of motivation encompassing processes that have a peremptory quality and that function to impel the mind to activity in search of gratification. Loewald makes a similar suggestion (1971, 1978) in his argument that the id is an organization related to reality and to objects. That is, instinctual drives are organized within object relations and also organize object relations and reality. He emphasizes that as a mental representative of organismic stimuli, an instinct is a mental force or stimulus that may simply be described as the most primitive element or unit of motivation (1971, p. 119). In this sense, the id and instincts contribute to the organization of the mind (the mental apparatus) and are organized by it.

In introducing the structural hypothesis, Freud (1923b) recognized that sexual development involves many more issues than he had previously thought, leading him to a significant revision. He realized that he not only needed to take account of shifts in erogenous zones and related wishes and fantasies; he had also to consider the child's developing relations to objects, his developing internalization of prohibitions against drive expression, and his intellectual efforts to come to terms with his sexual and aggressive impulses. Sexual or libidinal development, then, came to be *psychosexual* development, referring to the organization that evolves at successive developmental stages as all these factors coalesce.

Freud's concept of psychosexual development gradually modified the ways in which analysts viewed the stages of libidinal development. Whereas early expositions of the libido theory describe distinct stages (Sterba, 1942), infant and child observation has led to the awareness that all three erotogenic zones, oral, anal, and genital, are active to some degree from the first months of life, with peaks of relative ascendancy (Greenacre, 1952a). The dominance of one organization over another is in part maturationally determined, but long before any type of organization achieves dominance, one or another of its characteristic functions may have already appeared. Each stage also gradually blends into and becomes intertwined with the next, so while later developed pleasures may have become the central focus, earlier sources of pleasure persist or remain available.

Agreement that Freud's dual-drive theory has clinical merit is general, but it is not without its critics. They have especially attacked the "quasi-physiological" aspects of the theory that states that energic forces seek discharge (G. S. Klein, 1976b; Rosenblatt and Thickstun, 1977; Compton, 1981a, 1981b). Another vulnerable point has been the notion that the dual-drive theory is simultaneously applicable to normative and pathological events. Peterfreund (1978) and Milton Klein (1980) believe that a separate theory is required. The evolutionary nature of Freud's model has also been criticized on the ground that it suggests the supremacy of heterosexual genital sexuality and procreation and implies that all other forms of sexual pleasure are deviant, arrested, or otherwise abnormal (Schafer, 1974).

In the face of these criticisms, Freud's scheme of dual drives and of psychosexual development nevertheless remains of value to many analysts in their clinical work. This is true especially if the instinctual drive system, the id, according to the structural model, is viewed as one among several simultaneously emerging systems. Instinctual drive theory enhances clinical discrimination among various kinds of impulses and their sources, facilitates understanding of the meaning of urges, feelings, and defenses of varying intensity, and places the patient's conflicts and symptoms in a coherent developmental context. It thus augments the precision and effectiveness of the analyst's interventions.

Clearly, psychosexual developmental theory today is much more complex than the original version of libido theory; it has been revolutionized by increased knowledge of early childhood development and greater understanding of ego and superego development, gender identity, object relations, and other areas treated in later chapters of this book. In fact, it has become impossible to speak of drive development without reference to all developmental phases and to all these other areas. Consequently, in the following chapter we maintain the focus on drive progression for heuristic purposes, with the understanding that there are a number of related developmental issues to be covered in subsequent chapters. We use the term *drive*, or *instinctual drive*, to refer to a mental representative that has motivational impact; we do not imply energic forces seeking discharge.

# CHAPTER 4

## THE STAGES OF

## PSYCHOSEXUAL DEVELOPMENT

Hartmann (1939, 1950, p. 79) maintained that both ego and id evolve from a common matrix. He thought the newborn's behavior was such that it was difficult to say what would later be ascribed to ego functioning and what would be considered an instinctual drive, the domain of the id. Indeed, he was uncertain whether the newborn's behavior represented psychological functioning at all, and so he referred to earliest life as the undifferentiated phase.

We view the integration and structuralization of ego and id as interrelated; neither system is operative at birth in a psychological sense, and both evolve in the context of object relations. The biological underpinnings of instinctual drives are present at birth, but it is the environment's affective responses, evoked by the infant's neurophysiological, state-related reflex patterns, that gradually lend shape to pleasurable and unpleasurable, loving and hating, mental representations. They then combine to form instinctual drives and the id as a psychic structure.

Recent observations of infants seem to support the notion that drives differentiate gradually. It is generally agreed that more is going on in the earliest months than simply drive gratification. For example, a newborn will interrupt a feeding to look at a novel stimulus, and such a stimulus unassociated with drive gratification can prolong wakefulness. Stern indicates the limitations in drive theory as applied to observations of infants under one year of age. He suggests that motivation may be reconceptualized in terms of many discrete, interrelated motivational systems that eventually achieve higher or lower hierarchical standing (1985, p. 238). Lichtenberg, (1988, 1989) expresses a similar idea. Gaensbauer (1982) comments that though the dual instinct theory has proved to be of theoretical and clinical utility, it is a mistake to look for direct manifestations of instincts in the infancy period. Rather, the number and form of the instinctual drives during infancy become defined through mother-infant affective interaction (see also Loewald, 1971, 1978).

## THE ORAL PHASE

When the infant is between two and three months of age, one can observe a gradual distinction between his expressions of pleasure and unpleasure, with pleasurable experiences organized around sucking.* Freud recognized that the gratification of hunger and the pleasurable stimulation of the oral mucous membrane during sucking are distinctly separate and represent the satisfaction of different needs. Thumb sucking is often present in utero, and sucking in infancy is considered an innate reflex linked to the rooting reflex, but there is no way to ascertain whether this activity has any psychological meaning for the infant. Sucking and feeding experiences, however, provide the context of many of the earliest mother-infant interactions, and as memory traces of pleasurable sensations come to form, they are organized around such experiences. During pleasure sucking, the entire attention of the infant is concentrated on this rhythmic activity, and he frequently combines it with rubbing some part of his body—an earlobe or the genitals, for example.

Observations by Spitz (1945, 1946a, 1946b) demonstrate the dramatic and devastating effects on early development when the infant receives insufficient stimulation during the first year of life. The infants he studied were in a foundling home where their hunger needs were met, but they were left alone for long periods of time and sucking and other pleasures in the context of affective interaction with a caretaker were largely absent. They suffered profound developmental retardation in all spheres, part of a syndrome he termed *hospitalism*. In other reports (Spitz and Wolf, 1949; Spitz, 1962; confirmed by Provence and Lipton, 1962), Spitz described how early genital masturbation or play, which he observed to be present in all infants with a sufficiently good mother-infant relationship, tended to be replaced

---

*Expressions of pleasure and unpleasure are viewed by some primarily as affective reactions (Emde et al., 1976) and by others as early evidence of drive differentiation (Brenner, 1982). Perhaps the most we can say at present is that affects and drives are fundamentally related.

with other autoerotic activities when the relationship was a problematic one and tended to disappear altogether when the mother was absent, as in the foundling home. Clearly, the feeding situation is crucial, but the amount and kinds of stimulation available, as well as the affective climate of the caregiving environment, are as important to the normal developmental sequence as is food itself.

Dowling (1977) had an unusual opportunity to study the importance of oral experience in ego and drive development when he observed and graphically described seven infants born with congenital esophageal atresia. Because of this abnormality such infants are normally fed through a tube directly into the stomach, so feeding is unrelated to the infants' sucking activity or to satiation. Surgical repair to establish esophageal continuity and oral feeding in these infants was not undertaken until after the age of six months (and on occasion much later), so Dowling could study the influence of sucking and related innate oral reflexes apart from the gratification of hunger. He observed the emergence of a particular pattern of passivity and of motor, affective, and social retardation, which persisted long after the corrective surgery. He followed the developmental progress of these infants for up to twelve years. In some infants, Dowling was able to prevent these consequences by arranging for the mother to bottle-feed the infant normally while the usual gastric-tube feeding was in progress; the milk ingested by the infant's sucking drained out via a surgically fashioned fistula. Sucking was not only stimulated but associated with hunger satiation in these infants, and they developed normally. Dowling concluded that this demonstrated that integrated development requires, in addition to adequate mothering, an intricate sequential pattern of phase-appropriate sensory experiences beginning with sucking and the swallowing of food, and including cyclic patterns of hunger and satiation. This information also dramatically supports the idea that the drives are not structuralized at birth but coalesce from antecedents, given the availability of an average expectable environment. Not surprisingly, early distortions of developmental experience have a broad impact over many developmental lines as the child grows up.

In the second six months a new form of oral sensual satisfaction normally appears—that of chewing and biting. The pain and discomfort associated with the eruption of the first set of teeth are relieved by the infant's essentially non-object-related biting activities, but this masticatory use of the teeth also appears to provide instinctual gratification. As the infant begins to explore the world about him more actively, he uses his mouth as the principal organ of exploration. With pleasure he puts everything within reach into his mouth, and his attempts to chew every attainable object give ample evidence of the instinctual pleasure associated with the "oral zone."

During this same period, more finely differentiated aggressive-appearing behavior can also be seen, from which we may infer progressive differentiation of libidinal and aggressive drives. By age seven to nine months, stimulus-bound, short-lived, situation-specific, object-directed anger in response to restriction and frustration emerges (Spitz, 1953; Greenacre, 1960; Parens, 1979; McDevitt, 1983). One can also observe nonhostile forcefulness and assertiveness in pursuit of aims and interests. Hitting, biting, scratching, pulling, kicking activities are evident in the child's exploratory activities, often mixed with pleasure and affection and directed toward the object, such as pulling the mother's hair or playfully biting her.

Although Stechler and Halton (1987) view assertion and aggression as arising from distinctly separate systems, with assertion associated with structure-building functions and positive affects and aggression related to self-protection, we understand the situation differently. If assertion and aggression do originate separately, they become intertwined so quickly that their separate origins are not easily discernible. The balance or proportion that results depends on the environment's responses to the infant's activities.

Indeed, Abraham (1924a) called this second six months of life "oral sadistic," assuming that the biting activity is hostile and combines sexual and aggressive gratifications. He believed that sadistic character traits or tendencies in certain of his adult patients were direct carryovers from infantile forms of oral sexual gratification. Burgner and Kennedy (1980), however, point out that sadism implies an *intent* to hurt; it is unlikely that the infant of this age (six to fourteen months) can form such an intent because he lacks the capacity to form symbolic representations and to make mental distinctions between his own body and that of others. Nursing mothers, however, because of the pain inflicted on them often misunderstand the infant's pleasure in biting as an expression of sadistic hostility, and they respond with hostility. This is a typical adultomorphic misinterpretation of infant behavior, and it quickly leads to a contamination of the infant's originally nondestructive but object-related assertion. The infant comes to associate the biting, hair-pulling activity with the distress the mother's angry attack arouses in him, and so the activity takes on a hostile, destructive content, a consequence Greenacre described (1960).

## THE ANAL PHASE

Pleasurable sensations are probably associated with experiences in the anal area soon after birth—for example, during the mother's ministrations around diaper changes—and maturational influences lead to a prominent increase in anal erogeneity as the second year progresses. The toddler now can easily be observed enjoying pleasures associated with anal and urethral functioning such as withholding and expelling, as well as pleasures derived from touching, smelling, and looking. Withholding, in addition to expelling of feces and urine, may become a means of obtaining autoerotic pleasure as greater sphincter control is achieved coincident with myelinization of the nerve pathways, a maturational event that also enables the child to walk. As symbolic thinking emerges, urine and feces may become associated with object-related conflicts, particularly as mother's earliest demands are often in regard to toileting functions. These body products may also become endowed with fantasy content and so come to be viewed as a gift, a baby, a bomb, or even a penis, or as a means of manipulating mother. Progressive physical maturation brings greater control over excretory processes as well as over locomotion, providing sources of narcissistic pleasure.

In a study of seventy toddlers during the second year of life, Roiphe and Galenson identified a number of signs indicating the onset of the anal phase; their clear descriptions allow the clinician to spot important landmarks. These include (1) changes in bowel patterning, including diurnal variations, diarrhea, and/or constipation and stool retention; (2) behavioral changes during or directly preceding defecation, such as squatting, facial flushing, straining, grunting, pulling at the soiled diaper, abrupt interruption of other activities, the "inward gaze" of concentration on inner sensations, hiding in corners or separate rooms, and sitting on the toilet or "toidy" seat; (3) behavioral changes directly following defecation, including signaling for or resisting diaper change and playing with, smearing, or attempting to eat the stool; (4) affective concomitants of defecation, including excitement, pleasure, shame, or anxiety; and (5) anal-area "self-exploration" (1981, p. 60). Toddlers of this age also demonstrate great curiosity about the toileting activities of peers, siblings, and parents and enjoy a wide variety of anal-derivative play.

In an early comment on what later came to be thought of as part of aggressive drive development, Freud hypothesized that an urge toward mastery dominates the pregenital libidinal organization (1905b, p. 193). Now the toddler has a greater sense of his body and a greater ability to control its movements. Yet when efforts at mastery fail, object-directed anger often accompanies the frustration. Containing hostile aggression alongside positive loving feelings about the mother—that is, learning to tolerate a degree of ambivalence—becomes a crucial developmental issue of anal-phase development. The presence of many divergent developmental trends produces disequilibrium and disharmony, and the toddler's tendency to regression is a sign of the back-and-forth movement of the developmental processes. He is easily overstimulated and quickly overwhelmed, which frequently leads to his giving vent to rage and frustration. Even when he is under little stress, fretful clinging and whining behavior may appear along with other expressions of unhappiness, and chaotic affective states manifested in temper tantrums are not unusual.

The characteristic object-related hostile aggression emerging at this age led Freud to label it the sadistic-anal phase (1905b, note added 1915). Instances of directed aggression are abundant, particularly in the play of toddlers when they bite, kick, and scratch one another in attempts to acquire a wished-for toy, often in identification with the aggressor, that is, using hurtful behavior that they had once experienced (Parens, 1979; McDevitt, 1983). Although the toddler's cognitive capacities are now significantly advanced over the level when biting first became important, we nevertheless again question the designation of sadism. A clear intention for acquisition and mastery may be apparent, but it is unlikely that the toddler appreciates the hurtful consequences of his aggressive actions; it is therefore unlikely that a "sadistic" intent to hurt accompanies attempts at mastery. But as noted earlier in connection with the nursing mother, the other person's retaliatory response to being attacked eventually brings aggressive meaning to the behavior. Such an observation may have led Freud to comment, "It may be assumed that the impulse of cruelty arises from the instinct for mastery. . . . Cruelty in general comes easily to the childish nature, since the obstacle that brings the instinct for mastery to halt at another person's pain—namely a capacity for pity—is developed relatively late" (1905b, p. 193).

The intense anger and hostility the toddler is capable of in this phase provide a challenge to his immature ego. Surges of aggression and sexual excitation may combine and easily overwhelm his tenuous control, adding anxiety to his affective burdens. Insufficient protective intervention or an angry response from the object who is needed as an auxiliary ego may serve to exaggerate phase-specific ambivalence. Either or both parents may impose their own sadomasochistic conflicts in

forms of interaction that further compromise the child's ego functioning and result in later psychopathology.

It has long been noticed that a heightened curiosity and interest in
the genitals, an increase in genital self-stimulation, and an emerging
awareness of the genital distinctions between the sexes accompany
anal-phase manifestations (Ferenczi, 1924; Fenichel, 1945; Greenacre,
1952a; Kleeman, 1976; Roiphe and Galenson, 1981). Roiphe and
Galenson (1981) report that all seventy of the children in their study
developed a new quality of genital behavior during the second year.
Genital curiosity and concern appeared along with anal interests, and
the toddlers generally "discovered" or showed greater awareness of the
anatomical differences between the sexes. The child's reactions to this
discovery, dependent on a number of factors, may influence object
relations and the emerging feelings about the self in various ways.

## THE INFANTILE GENITAL PHASE

The final period of infantile sexuality is heralded by a concentration
of sexual interest and excitement in the genitals. Oral and anal interests and the component instincts—for example, looking (scopophilia),
exhibiting, and smelling—are now encompassed in the context of
genital masturbation, which becomes dominant. In contrast to the
genital interest and curiosity of the anal phase, Freud noted that at the
height of this phase, "interest in the genitals and in their activity acquires a dominating significance which falls little short of that reached
in maturity" (1923a, p. 142). He therefore originally called this the
*infantile genital organization.*

Freud's understanding of the infantile genital phase was limited to
the male, and so he termed this the phase of phallic primacy (p. 144).
He commented, "Unfortunately we can describe this state of things
only as it affects the male child; the corresponding processes in the
little girl are not known to us" (p. 142). He believed that both the boy's
and the girl's interest during this period was primarily directed toward
the phallus, and so he came to use the term *phallic phase* to refer to the
infantile genital organization of both sexes. This designation, however,
has its critics (for example, Parens et al., 1976).

Current psychoanalytic theory includes the formulation of separate
lines of psychosexual development and gender identity for males and
females; it also accommodates the interest shown by little girls in their
own genitals and those of the male, together with the boy's interest in
his complete genitals (Bell, 1961; Yasmajian, 1966, 1967), as well as

those of the female. As we now understand that children of both sexes become preoccupied with genital interests and anatomical features and differences from about the third year, Freud's original term, *infantile genital organization,* or a slight modification, *infantile genital phase,* may be more apt than *phallic phase* to describe this period. By adopting this term we distinguish early childhood genital concerns from the adult genital phase that emerges at puberty, and we also move away from a phallocentric model.

Girls become genitally oriented as they enter the infantile genital phase and experience an upsurge of erotic sensitivity. They localize the genital area and learn how to bring about sensual excitement and pleasurable erotic suffusion involving the clitoris and vagina as well as an inner genital rhythmic discharge (Kestenberg, 1968). This is then generalized to a pleasurable feeling throughout the body. Heightened genital sensations lead to a fascination with the body, both her own and others'. Fascinated with her mother's genitals and breasts, she idealizes mother and her body and wishes she had one like it. Varieties of breast envy and penis envy and anxieties about inferiority accrue as the girl is confronted by her immature sexual state.

With drive progression to the infantile genital phase, the boy's attention is also drawn to his genitals. Exhibitionism reaches its height, and the boy may feel simultaneously excited, pleased, anxious, and puzzled by the sometimes overwhelming nature of his penile erections and detumescence. Typically, the boy comes to idealize father and father's large penis and wants to acquire one like it for himself, a wish that often leads to castration anxiety based on a fear of retaliation.

Fears of castration may cause the boy to masturbate to determine if his penis is still intact, but the increased excitation reactivates the incestuous fantasies, and a cycle of compulsive masturbation may be established. Although some masturbation helps the boy to master his sexual excitation and provides some discharge and relief of tension, compulsive masturbation is maladaptive—it increases rather than decreases tension.

The infantile genital phase overlaps with two object-related phases, preoedipal, or narcissistic, and oedipal. The preoedipal phase is dominated by gender-identity tasks; the child's interest focuses on consolidating a sexually differentiated, narcissistically valued body image and establishing gender-role identifications.

The second phase is dominated by the sexual vicissitudes accompanying the object-related tasks of the Oedipus complex. Freud observed that with drive progression, children of this age soon begin to show evidence of developing an Oedipus complex (1905b, note added 1915). That is, they form strong attachments to their parents, begin to have sexual feelings toward both parents, and compete with each parent in turn for the affections of the other. They also begin to ask questions about anatomical differences and where babies come from, and they construct theories to explain their observations. These theories, Freud conjectured, were linked in the child's mind to sexual fantasies and were relevant to later neurotic illness. He recognized that children's frightening conscious and unconscious fantasies associated with sexual excitation stimulate conflicting attitudes toward their parents and are accompanied by intense feelings of love and hate. Clear examples of these wishes, fantasies, and conflicts have been demonstrated by analytic work with children. Many derivative forms and generalizations from these conflicts and the defenses employed against them have also been demonstrated in analytic work with adults, although sometimes less clearly.

Traditionally, the Oedipus complex is discussed in the context of psychosexual development. But the child's engagement in it implies not only drive maturation but also progress in object relations and gender identity. Furthermore, the internal compromises the child makes to cope with the conflicts engendered by the Oedipus complex (usually the formation of an infantile neurosis) imply progress in ego and superego development. The identifications made in the course of oedipal resolution also imply elaborations to the sense of self. Indeed, Rangell described the Oedipus complex as the climax of infantile instinctual life, the nucleus of the neuroses, and the "organizing umbrella of future life" (1972, p. 7). Freud referred to it as the juncture from which all later developments proceed (1905b, 1925b). That it is appropriate to discuss the Oedipus complex in all these areas of development exemplifies our view that development does not take place in isolation within any one system. A balanced approach to the developmental process takes all systems into account.

Because the child has sexual feelings toward each parent, the Oedipus complex is traditionally discussed in terms of positive and inverted, or negative forms (so called in analogy to a photographic print, not to imply a value judgment). In the positive Oedipus complex, the child focuses libidinal wishes on the parent of the opposite sex and perceives the same-sex parent as a feared rival. The child then comes to fear loss of love as well as retaliation from the idealized same-sex parent because of the fantasies, hopes, and wishes held toward the other parent.

Because of the child's idealizations and identifications made with the parent of the same sex in the course of establishing gender identity, libidinal wishes toward that parent are also in evidence throughout the infantile genital phase. In this inverted, or negative Oedipus complex, libidinal wishes are directed to the parent of the same sex, and the parent of the opposite sex is seen as the rival. Typically the child resolves the negative oedipal conflict by taking the parent of the same sex as the object of the ego ideal and by making identifications with the ideal as part of superego formation.

The child's rivalrous oedipal wishes arouse enormous conflict because of the intense love and hate, envy, and hostile competition, all amplified by identifications with and wishes for love from each parent. Accordingly, the child is pressed to find some resolution or to abandon his painful, conflicting wishes and feelings. The next two to three years are devoted to the elaboration, control, partial resolution, and relinquishment of the Oedipus complex.

Freud's theory of psychosexual development lacks the crucial concept of gender identity (Kleeman, 1976), a fundamental idea that brings together sexuality, object relations, ego and superego development, and the sense of self. Because a comprehensive understanding of oedipal dynamics involves all these psychic systems, a more complete discussion of these dynamics will be postponed until we discuss gender identity.

## LATENCY

Freud borrowed from Wilhelm Fliess the phrase "period of sexual latency" (1905b, p. 178, note 1) to refer to a time of diminished overt sexual manifestations from the sixth or seventh year of life until puberty. He thought that during this period sexual impulses are overcome by repression and that the reaction-formations of morality, shame, and disgust are built up as well as aesthetic ideals (1905b, p. 177, 1925a). He viewed this phase as resulting from a combination of biological processes, cultural and educational influences, and a reorganization of the ego's defensive structure partly influenced by superego development. Although Freud believed there was a diminution of sexual activity during this period, he pointed out that latency was in fact an educational ideal (1905b, p. 179). Development diverges from this ideal at many points and often to a considerable degree. Fragmentary manifestations of sexuality escape sublimation and break through, and many if not most children engage in some sexual activities throughout the latency period.

Our present understanding of the latency period derives from Freud's emphasis that it is a far from uniform state. The child undergoes many developmental changes during these years, and sexual latency is relative rather than absolute. To a certain extent the child has given up, resolved, or repressed the libidinal wishes of the oedipal phase because of ego and superego development. Now the child more consistently experiences parental expectations and prohibitions as demands lodged within the mind, and the painful affects of shame and guilt serve to restrict the pursuit for libidinal satisfaction and reinforce repression of oedipal incestuous wishes. Furthermore, the ego is stronger and more in control (rather than at the mercy) of drive activity, and sublimation of drive activity becomes possible at the same time that more adaptive means of gratification are found.

Nevertheless, masturbatory activity and masturbation fantasies are almost universal in normal children from middle to late latency into puberty (Fraiberg, 1972; Clower, 1976). Fraiberg has pointed out that a certain relief through masturbation may be very important for the child's psychic stability. When masturbation fantasies and activities are forcefully suppressed, ego restrictions result and the child may complain of boredom and become limited in his freedom to play and pursue other activities.

The fate of masturbation and instinctual urges during latency depends, first, on the extent to which the child can displace, disguise, or replace the oedipal incestuous wishes originally associated with the masturbatory activity. Second, an expanding environment helps dilute the genital urgency (Greenacre, 1948) by providing the child with pleasurable learning and social experiences that increase the opportunity to develop sublimations. These in turn give him sources of positive self-esteem, which help counterbalance masturbation guilt. Third, the child becomes better able to cope with guilt over sexual urges, fantasies, and masturbatory activities as his defensive organization becomes stronger and more elaborate with the growth of ego functions.

## GENITAL PRIMACY AND ADOLESCENCE

The relative equilibrium of the latency period is interrupted by the biological changes of puberty, during which genital sexual impulses become intensified and the erotogenic zones become further subordinated to the primacy of the genitals (Freud, 1905b, p. 207). There is now general agreement that distinctions should be made between prepuberty and puberty, and between preadolescence and adolescence. Prepuberty and puberty refer to the physiological, anatomical, and hormonal criteria of sexual maturation. Prepuberty begins with the emergence of secondary sexual characteristics including those not visually noticeable; puberty starts with menarche in girls and with the first ejaculation, or with the presence of live spermatozoa in the ejaculate, in boys (Galenson, 1964). Preadolescence and adolescence refer to the complex psychological and developmental facets of the age period spanning roughly the years from eleven or twelve to nineteen or twenty. These psychological and developmental issues include but are not limited to the psychological tasks involved in the adjustment to sexual maturity.

*Preadolescence*

Current opinion holds that the initial adaptation to the increase in hormone secretion is significantly different for boys and girls (for example, Erikson, 1956; Blos, 1962, 1970, 1979). The task of both sexes in preadolescence is to cope with the profound and rapid physical body changes by making appropriate adjustments to the body representation and dealing with the newly intensified sexual drive with its increase in genital sensitivity and reactivity. This is manifested in boys by the increased frequency of erections and in girls by breast development and vaginal as well as more generalized bodily sexual sensations, which can be confusing because their sexual nature may not be immediately recognized. Both girls and boys employ a range of phase-specific defenses (A. Freud, 1936, 1958) including first of all regression, stimulated by increased drive intensity brought about by the rise in hormone secretion, and then various defenses against the consequences of the regression.

Characteristically, regression in the preadolescent boy is to a rather broad pregenitality, manifested by a recrudescence of anal, urethral, and oral interests, preoccupations, and pleasures. The girl's regression is along different lines, seen chiefly in a shift in her attitudes reviving her relationship to the preoedipal mother. As Blos notes, however, "The boy's preadolescent regression is more massive than the girl's; it is action-oriented and concretistic. In the first onrush of pubescence, the boy turns away, with derision and contempt, from the opposite sex" (1970, p. 27). This dramatic turning away is attributed to the resurgence of castration anxiety that accompanies the increased intensity of sexual feelings, with fantasies of the feared phallic female uppermost.

The preadolescent girl struggles against the regressive pull to the preoedipal mother by defensively assertive heterosexuality, perhaps preceded or accompanied by an active "turn toward reality" and a heightened curiosity about sexuality in general. Regressive tendencies assert themselves peripherally and secretively (Deutsch, 1944; Blos, 1962, 1970).

### Adolescence

Pubertal maturation—the occurrence of menarche in the girl and the first emission in the boy—marks the end of preadolescence and the beginnings of adolescence. Drive progression is now toward genital primacy; pregenital indulgences occur chiefly in the context of regressive moves, and sexual pleasures progressively center on genital activities and functions.

The first menses and first emission are not equally recognized by contemporary society as markers of this developmental transition. Girls are usually better educated and prepared than are boys. Similarly, although there are many references in the psychoanalytic and developmental literature to the impact of menarche and its meaning to the young adolescent girl, references to the first ejaculation and its meaning to the adolescent boy are rare (for example, Fenichel, 1945, p. 111; R. A. Furman, 1975). Because boys have no control over spontaneous ejaculations but must experience them passively, they may interpret the sensations as primarily feminine in nature rather than as confirming their masculinity. Indeed, one man remembered experiencing his first spontaneous ejaculation during bathing, and he thought something terrible was wrong with him. Furman, on the basis of the analysis of a boy who was able to talk about his experience at the onset of ejaculation, suggests that boys may defend against awareness and verbalization of this experience because it can "be both so confusing and distressing as to preclude discussion until after full emissions actually begin, at which time there is little inclination to look back on the period that preceded them" (1975, p. 229). Our clinical experience with the analyses of adolescent boys and young men confirms that the first emission is a developmental marker as poignant for the boy as is menarche for the girl (see P. Tyson, in press, for a clinical example).

The biological changes have a profound influence on psychic development. Together with the accompanying surge of hormonally stimulated impulses, they arouse conflicts from earlier developmental levels, upsetting the balance between superego and ego, between drives and defenses achieved during latency, and contribute a new, intensified drive quality to psychic activity. The intensification of such sexual and aggressive drive pressures revives earlier preoedipal and oedipal incestuous wishes and related conflicts. These may now be particularly threatening because the adolescent has the necessary equipment for the completion of heterosexual intercourse.

Not only is there now potential for fulfillment, but with cognitive maturity the adolescent recognizes the full meaning of the infantile incestuous fantasy. As a result, he feels an increased need to repress the content of earlier wishes; at the same time, efforts to win freedom from earlier taboos against sexual gratification, essential to genital sexual adjustment, add to the current conflict. As the body is the source of sexual gratification, masturbatory impulses intensify. Masturbation in adolescence holds the potential of being an avenue for trial action for genital activity, a way in which the adolescent can take possession of his newly matured sexual body, and a means by which he can take responsibility for his sexual wishes (Laufer and Laufer, 1984).

Not surprisingly, conflicts surrounding masturbation become intense because the accompanying fantasies are derived from oedipal incestuous wishes. The adolescent must find avenues of instinctual discharge that will ensure the optimal degree of instinctual and emotional freedom needed in order to build adult sexual relationships. This involves making mature identifications with parents who are sexually active and who will grant the adolescent indulgence in sexual activities (Jacobson, 1961). A successful adult genital sexual organization requires that incestuous wishes continue to be repressed while these crucial identifications are made. These identifications may be extremely difficult to make, however, because a view of the parents as beyond sexuality is bound up with the incest taboo.

But the behavioral inconsistencies common among preadolescents and adolescents are due not only to the biological changes and more intense sexual feelings and impulses of this period. In addition there is remarkable and rapid physical, cognitive, and social growth. These combined pressures challenge the ego's defensive and integrating functions and lead to rapid and wide shifts in mood and to actions impelled by these moods. These swings are frequently in reaction to experiences with particular people and events; each adolescent responds according to his individual style, determined by earlier identifications, values, social learning, and the momentary state of ego strength, defenses, and superego restrictions.

The degree of anxiety of which the adolescent becomes aware is related to the strength of the drives in relation to ego and superego capacities and functions. Mood and behavioral changes and transient symptoms often reflect significant conflicts between and within the various psychic structures, as well as attempts at compromise formation. A major difficulty may arise if, as often happens, the biological, cognitive, and social changes occur before the ego and the superego are equipped to handle them. In girls, for example, early onset of secondary sexual characteristics like breast development and an early menarche deprive the girl of full latency consolidation, straining otherwise adequate capacities. When younger, the child could rely on the parents to provide auxiliary ego functions to control acting on sexual drive impulses. But in adolescence, with drive intensification and the physiological and anatomical development of genital potential, emotional closeness to the parents arouses incestuous conflicts and rekindles the unresolved strivings of the Oedipus complex. The parents cannot play the same role as before; they can no longer serve an auxiliary ego function for the adolescent.

The young person must find new objects for the satisfaction of both dependent and sexual needs ("object removal," Katan, 1951). This requires a long period of adjustment during which the adolescent not only separates from his parents as sexual objects and as objects of affection and dependency but also individuates from their idealized and authority-bearing representations; he ceases to rely on them as authority figures.

These many intertwining factors will be discussed throughout the rest of this book. Suffice it to say here that, in terms of psychosexual development, the main shift in adolescence is to the primacy of the genital zone. The principal tasks of adolescence are to come to terms with sexuality, including the sexually mature body, and to achieve a new balance among the drives, the ego, the superego, and objects of both the past and the present.

# PART THREE

## OBJECT RELATIONS

# CHAPTER 5

## AN OVERVIEW OF THEORIES

## OF OBJECT RELATIONS

The plethora of studies on object relations in the past few decades may give the impression that the concept is of more recent origin than is actually the case. The notion of the object was present in Freud's ideas from the beginning, when he described the object as the vehicle for instinctual gratification. He examined object relations primarily in connection with drive expression but made no attempt to describe a developmental progression of evolving object relations independent of the drives. In addition, his major formulations pertain to the Oedipus complex, and he admitted he had little understanding of the nature of preoedipal object relations (1931).

Definite progress has since been made in understanding the early development of object relations. To minimize any confusion caused by the current array of theories, we briefly review in this chapter the developmental contributions of those authors who have had a major impact on the field or who have offered a fairly systematized theory of object relations development. This review provides a background for the next two chapters in which we describe developmental pathways for object relations and for the subjective sense of self.*

### THE EVOLUTION OF OBJECT RELATIONS IN FREUD'S THINKING

Freud recognized that significant perceived and felt interactions with others affect the origin, nature, and functioning of intrapsychic

*Throughout this discussion it will be useful to keep in mind the distinction between interpersonal relations and object relations. The first has to do with the actual interactions between people. Object relations (or "internalized" object relations) refers to the intrapsychic dimensions of experiences with others—that is, to the mental representations of the self and of the other and of the role of each in their interactions.

structures. As early as 1895 he said that experiences of gratification or of frustration vis-à-vis the object provide the impetus for registering durable memories (1895b). Consonant with his interest in establishing drive theory, he focused on issues of gratification and frustration in his affect-trauma (drive-discharge) and topographical models in which the object is the vehicle through which drive gratification is sought and obtained. At the start of life the object is experienced in relation to libidinal satisfaction; instinctual drives are said to be pleasure-seeking and rapidly become object-seeking, or object-dependent, as memories of interactions accrue. In his "Project for a Scientific Psychology" he wrote, "The wishful state [of the hungry infant] results in a positive *attraction* towards the object wished-for, or, more precisely, towards its mnemic image [mental representation]" (1895b, p. 322). Freud retained the view of the object as secondary to the drive, stating later that the object "is what is most variable about an instinct and is not originally connected with it, but becomes assigned to it only in consequence of being peculiarly fitted to make satisfaction possible." Moreover, the object, he added, "is not necessarily something extraneous: it may equally well be a part of the subject's own body" (1915a, p. 122).

In the topographical model Freud stressed the pathological impact on development of traumatic experiences with the object, emphasizing how unconscious wishes and fantasies can transform otherwise indifferent experiences with an object into traumatic ones, leaving troublesome and noxious memories. But he shifted focus in relation to the concept of the object when he proposed the structural theory. Instead of emphasizing the importance of the relationship to the object being secondary to that of drive gratification, he stressed the individual's nontraumatic experience with objects and the ways in which these form an interface with drives, ego, and superego. Although his focus was more on functioning than on structure formation, he did observe that identifications with the object were central to ego and superego formation (Freud, 1923a, 1924c).

Freud made another important addition to object relations theory when he revised the theory of anxiety (1926). He noted that in early infancy the ego is easily overwhelmed by stimuli, but, he said, "when the infant has found out by experience that an external, perceptible object can put an end to the dangerous situation . . . the content of the danger it fears is displaced from the economic situation [the fear of being overwhelmed] on to the condition which determined that situation, viz., the loss of the object" (pp. 137–138). Because of the helplessness of the infant ego, the object has the task of regulating anxiety, and

Freud implied that later deficiencies in ego function are ultimately due to the influence of both the strength of instinctual impulses and the object's lack of success in regulating the infant's state (pp. 155–156). Freud proposed a sequence of object-related anxieties and associated fantasies, which he assumed correlated with the phases of psychosexual development (fears of object loss, loss of the object's love, castration, and superego punishment). Finally, he added that the helplessness and dependence of infancy establishes these "earliest situations of danger and creates the need to be loved which will accompany the child through the rest of its life" (p. 155). In this last statement, Freud clearly sees both object-related experiences and experiences of libidinal gratification as being equally important for psychic structure formation and optimal development, and suggests the two are linked through experiences of love or of fear and anxiety.

## MELANIE KLEIN

Melanie Klein was one of the earliest contributors to the theory of object relations. She derived many of her theories from observations of her own children and from the analysis of other children, many of whom she thought to be psychotic. From this work she demonstrated the importance of early preoedipal object relations to development and to the emergence of psychopathology, thereby challenging Freud's emphasis on the Oedipus complex. Her theory was largely based on Freud's affect-trauma and topographical models—that is, she adhered to and extended the theory of a death instinct and developed a unique and complex terminology. One of her basic tenets was that all conflict is based on the prototypical struggle between the life and death instincts (1948). This conflict is inborn and operative from birth. Indeed, birth itself is experienced as an overwhelming trauma that gives rise to persecutory anxiety in relation to the external world. The infant's first object, which exists in the mind of the infant as an object separate from the self from the start, according to Klein, is the mother's breast, which is felt to be hostile because of persecutory anxiety. Klein emphasized throughout her work the primacy of the drives, which are essentially equated with object relationships (Greenberg and Mitchell, 1983, p. 146).

Klein postulated that the ego, unconscious fantasy, and the capacity to form object relations, experience anxiety, and utilize defense mechanisms are all available at birth. Fantasy, as she viewed it, is the mental representative of an instinct, so that every instinctual impulse has a

71

corresponding fantasy; this means that instinctual impulses are experienced only through fantasy, and the function of fantasy is to serve instinctual impulses.

Since the infant looks at the mother from a new position or in a new way, Klein uses the word *position* to describe what non-Kleinian analysts call stages of development (1935). The first position, during the first three months of life, is known as the *paranoid-schizoid* position (1946, 1952a, 1952b), paranoid because of the infant's persistent fear of persecution from the external bad object, the breast, which is also internalized or introjected in an effort to destroy it. This now internal and external bad object derives from the death instinct. The schizoid idea comes from the propensity for splitting "good" and "bad." She introduced the term *projective identification* in the context of discussing how she imagined the infant at this point handles his hostile feelings toward himself and toward the mother (1946). In fantasy, hated and dangerous parts of the self are split off (in addition to the earlier splitting of objects) and projected into the mother in order to injure, control, and take possession of the object; the hatred against parts of the self is now directed against the mother. "This leads to a particular form of identification which establishes the prototype of an aggressive object-relation. I suggest for these processes the term 'projective identification'" (p. 8).

As Spillius describes it, "Klein defined the term . . . almost casually in a couple of paragraphs and, according to Hanna Segal, instantly regretted it" (1983, p. 321). It has become widely used with broadened meaning and often equated with projection (p. 322; Meissner, 1980; Sandler, 1987).

In addition to the death instinct, the life instinct or libido also attaches itself to the breast as the first external object. This good breast is also internalized through introjection in an effort to preserve it, so that the struggle between the life and death instincts is represented as a struggle between an ideal breast and a devouring breast. The two "form the core of the super-ego in its good and bad aspects" (1948, p. 118). The characteristic fear in the first three months is that the bad persecuting object will get inside the ego and destroy the ideal internal breast and annihilate the self. Related to this is the role of envy, which also exists from birth. Since the ideal breast is held to be the source of love and goodness, the ego strives to emulate it. If this seems impossible, the ego wishes to attack and ruin the good breast to rid itself of the source of envy. The infant attempts to split off the painful affect, and if this defense is successful, the gratitude introjected into the ideal breast will enrich and strengthen the ego (Klein, 1957).

If development is favorable, and in particular an identification is made with the ideal breast, the infant begins to tolerate his death instinct and resorts less to splitting and projection, with a lessening of paranoid feelings and furthering of ego integration. Good and bad aspects about objects come to be integrated, and the infant sees the mother as both the source and the recipient of good and bad feelings. The infant, now about three months old, moves to the *depressive* position (Klein, 1935, 1940, 1946, 1952a, 1952b). Now his deepest anxiety is the fear that he has damaged or destroyed the object of his love, and he seeks to introject the mother orally—that is, to internalize her—so as to protect her from his destructiveness. Oral omnipotence, however, leads to a fear that the good internal and external object will be devoured and destroyed anyhow, so that even attempts to preserve the object are experienced as destructive. In fantasy the dead, devoured mother lies in pieces inside the infant. Feelings of loss and hopelessness, hence depressive, characterize this phase. Yet this depression furthers development by mobilizing superego development and the Oedipus complex. Under the influence of persecutory and depressive anxieties, both boy and girl turn from the mother and her breast at the height of the *oral-sadistic* phase (at about eight or nine months) to the father's penis as a new object of oral desire (Klein, 1928). Oedipal wishes at first focus on fantasies of depriving the mother of penis, body contents, and babies. These eventually come under the influence of the important reparative trends of the depressive position as the superego consolidates, so that, in fantasy, these are restored to the mother (Klein, 1940).

This abbreviated summary of Klein's ideas does not do them justice, but it does illustrate some major differences between Kleinian theory and our views. Kleinian theory is primarily topographical rather than based on Freud's later structural theory, so her concepts do not relate to ego functioning as we understand it. The Kleinian ego, for example, is more like the self, with none of the self-regulating functions proposed by Freud in the structural model. Fantasy to her is the concrete expression of a drive, not a compromise between impulse and defense derived from ego functioning, in the course of which reality is taken into account. Her contention that the capacity for fantasy is available from birth is not supported by evidence from cognitive psychology or the neurosciences. Anxiety is an ever-threatening traumatic influence that overwhelms the ego; it does not serve a signal function as Freud suggested in the structural theory of anxiety (1926). Although Klein described a wide array of defenses, a preponderance of "good" experience over "bad" is more important for maintaining internal harmony than is the use of successful defense mechanisms as conceptualized in the structural theory.

In the Kleinian view, the fundamental conflict from birth is between two innate drives rather than between evolving psychic structures, and it is not moderated by ego functioning. Accordingly, interpreting unconscious sexual and aggressive impulses vis-à-vis objects is central to Kleinian technique. Furthermore, in her view, since the conflict is between two innately determined drives, it is hardly affected by subsequent development except in form; thus environmental influences and individual experiences have little developmental impact, a view of development significantly different from the one we propose. As Sutherland expressed it, "she seems to most analysts to minimize the role of the external object almost to that of confirming the fantasies [allegedly] produced from within by the activity of the instincts. She thus appears at times to create a kind of biological solipsism rather than a conceptual framework for the evolution, from the earliest stages, of structures based on experience with objects" (1980, p. 831). Finally, although Klein's theory is usually called an object relations theory, to her the importance of the object is secondary to that of the drives; there is little in her theory to account for the effects of the real qualities of the object or for the role of dialogue and reciprocity with the object in the infant's development.

These comments should make it clear that there are few similarities between the Kleinian and the contemporary Freudian psychoanalytic views based on the structural theory, even though they use apparently similar language. (For summaries and critiques of Kleinian theory, see Waelder, 1936; Glover, 1945; Bibring, 1947; Joffe, 1969; Kernberg, 1969; Yorke, 1971; Segal, 1979; Greenberg and Mitchell, 1983; Hayman, 1989.)

On the other hand, Scharfman (1988) points out that Klein's efforts did direct psychoanalytic attention to the preoedipal child and, in particular, to preoedipal object relations. Concepts about object representations that are formed from projections and introjections have become part of the psychoanalytic lexicon. More classically Freudian analysts may differ from Klein in their understanding of these concepts, but it was Klein who first used some of the concepts that are now central to what has become known as object relations theory.

## ANNA FREUD

Anna Freud was particularly critical of Klein's ideas and of her treatment approach, especially with children. Their few attempts at dialogue and debate seem to have aroused intense emotions in the two rather than bringing about rapprochement.

Anna Freud's observations of infants and small children in the Hampstead War Nurseries, where they were separated from their parents for long periods, formed the basis for her view of object relations development (1942). She described the infant as being governed by need sensations in the first few months of life, the mother's role being primarily that of need satisfier. She noted, however, that babies separated from their mothers even at this early stage show signs of upset, some attributable to the disturbance of routine and some to the change from the particular intimacy with the mother (p. 180).

In the second six months of life, the relationship to the mother continued beyond moments of physical need. Much later, Anna Freud described this as the stage of object constancy—that is, the mother is the constant libidinal object, and the child's libidinal investment in her continues regardless of the degree of his gratification (1965).

She thought that in the second year of life the mother-infant attachment acquires the strength and variety of adult human love as the attachment comes to its full development and all the child's instinctual wishes are centered on the mother (1942, pp. 181–182). She observed that this "happy relationship" is followed and mitigated by the feeling of ambivalence and then of rivalry; with the emergence of these conflicting feelings, the child "enters into the whole complicated entanglement of feelings which characterizes the emotional life of human beings" (p. 182).

In the next stage, during the years three to five, inevitable oedipal disappointments and the parents' withdrawal of love as they increasingly try to "civilize" the child make him quick to anger. The child's momentarily violent death wishes toward the parents appear to be confirmed by separation, arousing enormous guilt and intense pain. In the Hampstead War Nurseries, Anna Freud observed that this pain interfered with the child's enjoyment of the parents on those occasions when visits were possible. Indeed, she realized that the intensity of grief following separation indicated possibly serious consequences for later adjustment, and she formulated possible consequences of separation to accompany each developmental phase.

Many of Anna Freud's observations were astute and remarkably similar to contemporary developmental research. But unfortunately her formulations were buried in the first *Annual Report of the War Nursery* and did not receive much attention. In addition, she did little to elaborate or confirm her early observations, and the developmental line of object relations she formulated later (1965) did not draw on, refer to, or do justice to the wealth and sensitivity of her early observations.

## JOHN BOWLBY

John Bowlby began his work in Anna Freud's wartime nurseries and was also influenced by Klein's ideas and especially by ethological research. His emphasis on infant attachment has had a fruitful impact on infant developmental research, and his approach has contributed to the current view of developmental systems. (For critiques, see Hanly, 1978; Brody, 1981.) Bowlby's theory has found favor especially among developmental psychologists who have studied attachment behavior (see Ainsworth, 1962, 1964; Ainsworth et al., 1978) and have, more recently, applied his ideas to studies of infant competence and intellectual development (see Papousek and Papousek, 1984). He has contributed significantly to the theory of the mother-infant relationship (1958, 1960a, 1960b, 1969, 1973, 1980).

Bowlby is critical of psychoanalytic theory for what he sees as its stress on the infant's primary need for food and only secondary need for attachment to the mother. He believes that the main issue for the infant is the need for an unbroken attachment to the mother. He proposes that the propensity for attachment is a biologically based inborn instinctual response system and is at least as important, if not more important, a motivator of infant behavior as oral drive gratification. Bowlby's basic assumption is that human infants begin life with at least five highly structuralized response systems—sucking, crying, smiling, clinging, and following or orienting; some of these are active at birth, and some mature later. The response systems activate maternal response behavior, which provides feedback to the infant systems, activating certain behaviors that mediate attachment. When the infant's instinctual response systems are activated and the mother figure is unavailable, separation anxiety, protest behavior, and grief and mourning occur.

Although most analysts have concurred with Bowlby's observations of the infant's propensity for attachment, there has been considerable criticism focusing on his challenge to the dual-drive theory, his conceptualization of the tie to the mother, and his claim that the infant's grief and mourning response is comparable to that of an adult. Schur (1960; see also A. Freud, 1960) argued that the primary biological instinctual response systems should not be compared with the psychoanalytic concept of libidinal drive, since an instinctual drive was understood to refer to *psychological* experiences and mental representations (although Freud was not always consistent in this usage [see Strachey, *S.E.*, 14:111–113]). Spitz (1960) added that whereas innate response patterns may trigger the first psychological processes and thus underlie both libidinal drives and object relations, biological and mechanical response patterns alone are not sufficient. Rather it is through the process of development, which includes ego development and learning through environmental responses, that innate reactions gradually assume psychological meaning. Spitz also questioned Bowlby's ideas about the infant's experience of grief, since a certain degree of perceptual and emotional maturation and self-object differentiation is required to maintain object relations, which are necessary in order to experience loss and grief.

The debate continues to the present. Bowlby has elaborated his work consistent with information-processing theory. He views attachment behavior as mediated through organized behavioral systems activated by certain signals of internal or external origin; the activation ceases on receipt of other signals. He asserts that there is no way to explain attachment behavior in terms of a buildup of psychic energy, which is then discharged (1981). He presents his hypothesis as an alternative to the concept of libido and does not think it can be integrated into psychoanalytic theory as it now stands, a statement suggesting that Bowlby sees psychoanalysis as frozen in a drive-discharge model.

## THE BRITISH SCHOOL

While ego psychologists were elaborating their theories, a parallel development in Great Britain began with innovative ideas about object relations—for example, that object relations, and therefore an ego and some sort of self-concept, exist from birth. The "British School" (to be distinguished from the "English School," a term that refers to Melanie Klein and her followers) developed its own tradition and concepts of self. Members of this school eventually formed a large part of the Independent Group of the British Psycho-Analytical Society, alongside the Kleinians and the "B" Group of Freudian analysts (now called the

Contemporary Freudians). Prominent contributors of the Independent Group were Balint, Fairbairn, Guntrip, and Winnicott (Sutherland, 1980; Kohon, 1986).

Fairbairn (1954, 1963) and Guntrip (1961, 1969, 1975, 1978) were among the most theoretically consistent of the British School of analysts. They did most of their clinical work with a group of adult patients who were very difficult to treat, described diagnostically as schizoid. Their emphasis on the importance of early object relations led them, in contradistinction to the Kleinians and the Freudians, to see drives as unimportant in psychic structure formation. They believed that instinctual activity was simply an example of the activity of structures, including that of the self. Balint (1959, 1968) emphasized the importance of the preoedipal dyadic relationship, asserting that subsequent characteristics and psychopathology derived from disruptions of that early mother-child relationship.

Probably the most familiar in this group is Winnicott who was a pediatrician, an adult and child analyst, and a prolific writer. He was not a systematic theory builder, but he made a number of clinically pertinent commentaries that have been extraordinarily helpful to analysts in understanding early aspects of the developmental process. For example, his well-known aphorism (1952) "There is no such thing as a baby"—meaning that any theoretical formulations about an infant must include formulations about the mother, as he thought the dyadic relationship was more important than the contributions of either partner—emphasized that considerations of infant attachment must be balanced by considerations of the "good enough" mother's emotional investment in her child. His concept of the "true self" and "false self" (1960) reflected his conviction that the infant is intensely object-related from birth and that the ordinary devoted good enough mother must inevitably fail the infant. The result is the infant's compliance with the mother's wishes and presumed sacrifice of true-self potential. Winnicott thought that optimal development of self-esteem depended on the mother's capacity for affective "mirroring" (1967); when a mother is depressed or otherwise unable to reflect her delight and pleasure in her infant back to him, his development may be influenced in a variety of pathological ways.

Winnicott (1953) also introduced the idea of transitional phenomena in a study of how the infant uses the mother to facilitate independent functioning. He saw that a favorite blanket, for example, helps soothe an infant because it is associated with pleasurable interactions with the mother. The transitional object, he assumed, is a symbol that helps bridge the "me and not-me" world as the infant becomes aware of separation. A largely uncritical literature (except for Brody, 1980) devoted to transitional phenomena has evolved from this idea, extending far beyond the realm of infancy and figuring especially prominently in the area of creativity (for example, Grolnick and Barkin, 1978).

Winnicott's ideas have found particular favor in American psychoanalysis. His emphasis on the dynamics of mother-infant interactions has led to a greater awareness of the functioning of the analyst within the analytic situation. Modell, for example (1969, 1975, 1984), suggests a shift in emphasis in psychoanalytic understanding from a one-person perspective to that of a two-person system, which puts a greater focus on the analyst's role and participation in the analytic process. Modell has also taken Winnicott's ideas and those of others of the British School into account in explaining the relationships between experiences in infancy and later emotional illness. Kohut (1971, 1977) and his colleagues have also made extensive use of Winnicott's ideas, particularly his mirroring concept, and they describe dynamics of early mother-infant interactions that are thought to lead to empathic failures and adult psychopathology.

## RENÉ SPITZ

René Spitz was a pioneer in infant observational research carried out to increase our understanding of early object relations and the way in which interactions with others affect the origin and functioning of psychic structures.

Shortly after World War II Spitz, as we mentioned in the last chapter, undertook a series of observational studies of infants in institutions and foundling homes where they were physically cared for, but received little stimulation or affection from a constant caretaker. Spitz's movies (1947) of emotionally starved, developmentally delayed babies staring vacantly at the camera dramatically illustrated the destructive effect of maternal deprivation on infants. In addition to documenting disturbed object relations, he demonstrated deficits in drive, ego, cognitive, and motor development, and showed that, in extreme cases, maternal deprivation leads to infant death (1946a, 1946b, 1962; Spitz and Wolf, 1949).

Spitz expanded his ideas with laboratory experiments (1952, 1957, 1963, 1965; Spitz and Cobliner, 1965), focusing on the role of affect and dialogue. He introduced the concept of mother-infant reciprocity

(1962) in the context of Harlow's well-known work with infant monkeys reared with inanimate surrogate mothers—wire frames with feeding bottles inside, some covered in terry cloth (1960a, 1960b). Spitz recognized that affective reciprocity between mother and infant stimulates and allows the infant to explore the environment, facilitating expanding motor activity, cognitive processes and thought, integration, and mastery. He believed that mother-infant reciprocity is a complex and meaningful nonverbal process that influences both mother and infant and includes a two-way affective dialogue going beyond the infant's attachment to the mother and the mother's bond to the infant.

Spitz also paid special attention to the early stages of unfolding object relations and to the ingredients necessary to establish the libidinal object, accomplished when the infant makes it clear that mother is preferred above all other objects. He formulated three stages in the development of the libidinal object: (1) the preobjectal or objectless stage, which precedes a psychological relationship; (2) the stage of the precursor of the object, which begins with the social smile at two to three months and indicates the beginnings of a psychological relationship; and (3) the stage of the libidinal object proper. He was especially interested in the implications for healthy ego development of these successive achievements.

## THE WORK OF EGO PSYCHOLOGISTS

Freud's introduction of the structural theory aroused interest in the role of the object in psychic structure formation, leading to an increasing focus on the direct study of infants and young children. It is of some historical interest that these contributors of three and four decades ago had to rely on knowledge of the Hampstead reports and of Spitz's then current work, in addition to reconstructions from analytic work with children and adults, for no other analytically framed systematic child observational data were as yet available. Nevertheless, concepts such as Hartmann's "average expectable environment" (1939) and Winnicott's "good enough mother" (1949, 1960) reflected the interest in early development and the recognition of the importance of the mother for optimal development.

Hartmann was particularly interested in the way in which the ego develops (1939, 1953, 1956). He disagreed with Freud's assertion (1923a) that the ego is a part of the id modified by the influence of the external world and that conflict with the mother is central to ego development. He argued that certain ego functions are available at

birth, that they do not emerge from conflict but have "primary autonomy," and that they are part of a "conflict-free sphere." He also suggested that all psychic structures are undifferentiated at first, pointing
out that no ego is observable in the sense of the ego as it operates later
and that the state of the id is also unknown. It is therefore impossible to
disentangle functions that will later serve the ego from those that come
to be attributed to the id.

Hartmann, in accordance with the metapsychological currents of the
times, was also interested in clarifying the concept of ego (1950, 1952).
Freud's term *das Ich* (which Strachey translated as "ego") contained two
meanings in the original German—an experiential self (that is, an
experiencing sense of oneself as a separate person with a continuity of
identity) and, especially after he posited the structural theory, a hypothetical psychic structure. Hartmann made conceptual distinctions between the ego as a substructure of personality or a system defined by its
functions (1950, p. 114), the self as "one's own person"—that is, the
whole person (p. 127)—and the self-representation as part of the ego
system where it exists as a counterpart to the object representation
(p. 127). His attempts to clarify the term *ego* led to a redefinition of the
concept of narcissism. Instead of a libidinal investment of the ego (as
meaning self at the time Freud introduced the concept, but easily
confused with the ego of structural theory), Hartmann suggested that,
according to structural theory, narcissism should be viewed as a libidinal investment of the self, or more correctly, of the self-representation.

According to Brenner, Hartmann made these distinctions rather
offhandedly at a meeting of the New York Psychoanalytic Society, and
although distinguishing self and ego was not Hartmann's main point,
the discussion following his presentation apparently had great impact.
Brenner recalls that "Edith Jacobson, who was in the audience, was
very taken with what Hartmann had said and they had a lively discussion. . . . the idea of using the term, 'self,' clearly appealed to her . . .
and from that time on it became a familiar psychoanalytic term" (1987,
p. 551).

Jacobson was enthusiastic about Hartmann's distinctions between
the ego as a psychic structure, the self as a whole person, and self- and
object representations. She found these concepts especially useful in
understanding processes of internalization during early psychic development and the formation of particular kinds of pathology thought
to have early origins. She constructed a developmental framework for
the emergence of the experiential sense of self, proposing that early
representations of self and of object cluster around pleasurable and

unpleasurable experiences, so that representations of a "good" and a "bad" self and object emerge before those of integrated representations. Unfortunately, she was not precise in her terminology and used the terms *sense of self, sense of identity, self-awareness,* and *self feeling* interchangeably (1964, pp. 24–32), for there was little interest yet in making these further distinctions.

With the introduction of thinking about the sense of self, the topic of the child's emerging sense of identity and its disturbances came to the fore. Erikson (1946, 1956) suggested that identity formation is a life-long ongoing process, one that is a part of psychosocial as distinguished from psychosexual development, intimately involved with the surrounding culture and the individual's ultimate role in society. To him, a sense of identity includes an awareness both of "continuity to the ego's synthesizing methods" (1956, p. 23) and of elements in common with one's cultural group.

Greenacre offered a more precise formulation, stressing that a sense of identity emerges in relation to and in comparison with another (1953a, 1958). As she defined it, self-awareness depends on the formation of separate mental representations of self and of object and comes with the ability to compare these representations. A "stable core" of identity accompanies this sense of self-awareness. She distinguished this from the simple comparison of perceptual images that is possible from early infancy by virtue of cognitive functioning. Greenacre noted that despite the early "stable core" of identity, the sense of identity always remains susceptible to influence by changes in the individual's relationships to his environment.

The concepts of self- and object representations as applied to the theory of identity and narcissism led others to elucidate affective aspects of the self, self-esteem regulation, the role of the superego, and the way these relate to narcissistic disturbances (see, for example, Reich, 1953, 1960). Sandler (1960b) suggested that an early step in the formation of self- and object representations is the active perception of the object; this perception serves as a protection from being overwhelmed by unorganized stimuli and is therefore accompanied by a definite feeling of safety, which the ego attempts to preserve. Once formed, self- and object representations form what Sandler and Rosenblatt (1962) refer to as a "representational world," which Rothstein (1981, 1988) suggests can be viewed as a substructure of the ego that takes an active role in mental life.

Hartmann, Jacobson, and Sandler all viewed the development and maintenance of self- and object representations as among the most basic functions of the ego and superego. Evolving concepts of these representations, however, have gradually become the basis for a variety of theories primarily concerned with self- or object relations, theories that have become separate from rather than integrated with structural concepts (see J. G. Jacobson, 1983a, 1983b, for a review and discussion).

Further conceptual ambiguities and diversity of opinions about the formation of psychic structure followed and continue to exist. The ego-self distinction and the suggestion of a conflict-free sphere have led some theorists to limit their thinking about structure formation to the Oedipus complex and the infantile neurosis. Kohut (1977) and his followers (see Tolpin, 1978; Stechler and Kaplan, 1980), for example, argue that considerations of conflict and the structures of the tripartite model are more relevant to the later years of early childhood—that is, to the resolution of the conflicts of the Oedipus complex (it is as if the superego begins only then, and so only then can one talk of the id, ego, and superego as internalized structures). This view is extended to the formulation of pathological syndromes in which an infantile neurosis does not seem to play a role, contributing to a general impression that psychopathology reflecting primarily preoedipal elements is best conceptualized within an object relations framework. On this basis, an artificial dichotomy is made between psychopathology that results from deficit and psychopathology that results from conflict. Theories based on object relations or on self psychology then lead to sometimes unwarranted conclusions about the etiological role of environmental deficiency, relegating considerations of conflict, neurosis, and the usefulness of the structural model to neurotic symptoms of supposedly later etiology.

These theories appear to be based on two misconceptions: one, that Hartmann's distinction between self as a whole person and ego as structure means that the two are mutually exclusive, and two, that Freud gave up the experiential implications of the term *das Ich* with the structural model. The richness of Freud's original concept was thus lost with the English translation and Hartmann's and Jacobson's distinctions. Although initially clarifying, these distinctions and classifications made by Hartmann and Jacobson have resulted in significant theoretical confusion and ambiguity. For example, a number of analysts now limit the term *ego* to its abstract systemic meaning, view it as a relic of outdated mechanistic structural metapsychology, and refer primarily to the experiential part of the concept, utilizing notions about the vicissitudes of self- and object representations.

It appears, however, to be impossible to think about psychoanalytic psychology for very long without referring to a nonexperiential, conceptual, internal world of psychic structures. Consequently, one finds the originally experiential concept of the self being described as a structure, with the various functions of the discarded ego ascribed to it. In this way, as Spruiell (1981) points out, the self has taken on the multiple ambiguous meanings that were the province of *das Ich*. This is true of Kohut's concept of the "superordinate self," of Stern's (1985) idea that the sense of self is the organizer of development, and of Sander's (1962, 1964, 1983) and Emde's (1983, 1988a) references to the organizing and self-regulatory processes of the self. Indeed, their descriptions sound strikingly similar to Freud's (1923a, 1926) and Hartmann's (1950) discussions of the organizing, regulating functions of the ego. Reflecting on Hartmann's dedication to the clarification of psychoanalytic concepts, Brenner mused that this current ferment in American psychoanalysis "was introduced by, of all people, Heinz Hartmann" (1987, p. 551).

A consequence of the separation of structural concepts and object relations theories is the appearance of two kinds of theories of motivation. The first sees motivation as primarily associated with the seeking of drive gratification, the object being secondary to instinctual pleasure. The second takes as primary the wish to repeat early pleasurable interactional experiences with objects. It holds that either an inborn propensity for attachment (Bowlby, 1958, 1969) or a wish to maintain safety (Sandler, 1960b, 1985) has motivational importance equal to drive gratification. Unfortunately, the two theories have become polarized by being kept separate. The first tends to underestimate the importance or even the existence of motivations other than drive needs, whereas the second tends to stress object relations and ego functions while undervaluing drive needs.

Hartmann was interested in the process of development and how relations with others led to stable, independently functioning psychic structures. He criticized oversimplified views of a "bad" or "good" mother that took into account only one aspect of the developmental process. He pointed out that sometimes later ego development compensates for "poor" early object relations and, conversely, that so-called good object relations may become a developmental handicap if the child doesn't utilize them to strengthen his ego but remains dependent on the object (1952, p. 163). Hartmann believed that the child's resiliency and the experience of later developmental stages account for the ultimate outcome and suggested that ego development and object relations are correlated in various ways—for example, by the extent to which object constancy is achieved. He said, "There is a long way from the object that exists only as long as it is need-satisfying, to that form of satisfactory object relations that includes object constancy" (p. 163). He thought Piaget's (1937) concept of "objectivation" of the object (when an integrated, cognitive mental representation is maintained, by about eighteen or twenty months [see Fraiberg, 1969]) was relevant, but that more was involved in a psychoanalytic concept of object constancy.

Following Hartmann, others have employed various notions of object constancy, but the lack of consistency makes the concept confusing. Some theorists emphasize the infant's attachment to the mother, an attachment that remains intact in spite of life-threatening pathological situations such as child abuse (Solnit and Neubauer, 1986), but this attachment does not facilitate independent psychological functioning. Others focus more on the functioning of the intrapsychic representation of the mother. These distinctions become important when we try to understand and treat neglected and abused children, or to understand adults with particularly noxious memories of early experiences but whose psychological functioning nevertheless appears to be largely intact. To illustrate the range of different meanings using similar terminology, consider the formulations of Spitz, Anna Freud, and Mahler.

Spitz and Cobliner (1965) refer to the *constancy of the libidinal object* when they describe the way in which, by eight months, the mother is established as the consistently preferred object of the infant's libidinal drive. Once the mother becomes the libidinal object, substitutions of caregiver are no longer easily accomplished.

Anna Freud's concept of *object constancy* is similar in stress and in timing to Spitz's idea of the constant libidinal object in that she stresses libidinal investment. She said, "What we mean by object constancy is the child's capacity to keep up object cathexis irrespective of frustration or satisfaction. At the time before object constancy the child withdraws cathexis from the unsatisfactory or unsatisfying object. . . . The turning towards the object takes place again when the wish or need arises. After object constancy has been established the person representing the object keeps this place for the child whether he satisfies or frustrates" (1968, p. 506).

Whereas both Anna Freud and Spitz emphasize aspects of the approximately eight-month-old infant's attachment to the mother, Mahler concentrates on an intrapsychic dimension—the mental representation of the mother and the manner in which it functions. She uses the term *libidinal object constancy,* writing that this is achieved when the intrapsychic representation of the mother functions as the mother had previously functioned, to provide "sustenance, comfort, and love" (1968, p. 222). In Mahler's view, a first step in the process requires a firm attachment to the mother as the constant libidinal object (as proposed by Spitz and Anna Freud). The second step is the integration of a stable mental representation. This includes not only cognitive integration but some resolution of anal-phase ambivalence, so that the positive and negative affects can be integrated into a single representation (McDevitt, 1975, 1979). With an integrated, durable inner representation to which he can cling when frustrated or angry, the child is able to derive progressively more comfort from the internal image. Mahler maintains that libidinal object constancy is never fully achieved; it is a lifelong ongoing process. Yet we recognize that once some measure of it has been attained, interpersonal relationships can progress to more advanced forms; now the individual may achieve both mutuality and independence. Failure to attain this developmental goal gives an infantile, dependent, narcissistic quality to the individual's interpersonal relationships. Mahler's use of the object-constancy concept confirms Hartmann's idea that we can judge an object relation to be "satisfactory" only if we also consider what it means in terms of ego development (1952, p. 163).

## HEINZ KOHUT

Kohut (1971, 1977) says that just as physiological survival depends on a specific physical environment that includes oxygen, food, and a minimum temperature, psychological survival depends on particular components in the psychological environment, including responsive, empathic selfobjects.* "It is in the matrix of a particular selfobject environment that, via a specific process of psychological structure formation called *transmuting internalization,* the *nuclear self* of the child will crystallize" (Kohut and Wolf, 1978, p. 416). Kohut's self psychology maintains that a cohesive superordinate self, the optimal outcome of the developmental process, results from beneficial interactions between the child and his selfobjects and is made up of three major constituents: basic strivings for power and success, basic idealized goals,

*Kohut's self psychology has evolved a new set of terms. *Selfobject* is defined as a person in the environment who performs particular functions for the self, functions that have the effect of evoking the experience of selfhood—that is, of a cohesive self structure (Wolf, 1988, p. 547).

and basic talents and skills (p. 414). This structure is built on empathic responses from the mirroring selfobject that facilitate the unfolding of the infant's grandiosity, exhibitionism, and feelings of perfection, and that also enable him to build an idealized parental imago with whom he wishes to merge. Through minor, nontraumatic empathic failures of the mirroring and idealized selfobject, a self and its functions gradually replace the selfobject and her functions.

But traumatic failures of the selfobject, such as grossly insufficient empathy when the mother or selfobject falls short in her mirroring function, will result in a variety of defects of the self. An empathic failure to mirror, for example, will disrupt the infant's contentment with his archaic self and lead him to introject a faulty parental image and develop a fragmented self. His injured narcissism arouses narcissistic rage and leads him to fantasies of his grandiosity, so that normal infantile narcissism, rather than diminishing gradually, now increases as a result of this failure of the selfobject. Kohut maintains that not until the defect in the self is healed can structural conflict typical of the oedipal phase arise.

Many cogent critical reviews of Kohut's theory are available (see Loewald, 1973; Slap, 1977; Slap and Levine, 1978; Schwartz, 1978; Calef and Weinshel, 1979; Stein, 1979; Friedman, 1980; Wallerstein, 1981; Blum, 1982; Rangell, 1982). We limit our own comments to the pathogenetic role Kohut gives to the parents, his view of the drives, his view of the developmental process, and his method of theory construction.

We think that Kohut gives inordinate prominence to the pathogenic role of the parents, implying that their pathogenic personality and the pathogenic features of the environment are what account for pathology of the self. This view is reminiscent of Freud's early affect-trauma model, in which adult psychopathology was thought to be the result of childhood seductions. Freud soon realized that sexual and aggressive impulses arising within the child's mind also contribute to conflict. But in Kohut's thinking, "Drive experiences occur as disintegration products when the self is unsupported" (1977, p. 171), as if the child is a helpless, passive recipient of forces from outside. Such a view of development is certainly contrary to a developmental process wherein innate potentials and the *activity of the infant* share with environmental experiences the responsibility for the final outcome.

Furthermore, according to Kohut's theory, progression to oedipal wishes and conflicts is precluded by self pathology. This is to say that developmental pathology in one developmental system causes arrested development in other systems, an idea not substantiated by clinical experience. Problems in narcissism, in self-esteem, or in ego functioning may lend a particular form to preoedipal strivings and to the Oedipus complex, as well as a particular form to their resolution, but they do not stop the process of development. Finally, as we mentioned earlier, there are problems with retrospective developmental theories constructed on generalizations from conjectures about infantile sources of adult psychopathology (see Brody, 1982).

Nevertheless, we are indebted to Kohut for reemphasizing the need for empathy, as a way of knowing about the other, within the mother-child relationship and in the analytic relationship. Also, his emphasis on "experience-near" concepts (ideas that are close to the clinical situation rather than burdened with elusive metapsychological formulations) reminds us of the importance of maintaining clinical relevance in our theories.

## OTTO KERNBERG

Kernberg's focus is on integrating psychoanalytic theories. Over the years he has adapted a number of the ideas and assumptions about psychic development proposed by Klein, the British School, Mahler, and others, combining them with Jacobson's (1964) theories into what he calls an ego psychology–object relations theory with broad applications to nosology, assessment, diagnosis, and treatment technique (1975, 1976, 1980a, 1984, 1987). The manifold difficulties and contradictions in this enterprise have been well cataloged and criticized (for example, Heimann, 1966; Calef and Weinshel, 1979; Milton Klein and Tribich, 1981; Brody, 1982; Greenberg and Mitchell, 1983).

Briefly, Kernberg proposes a theory of development in which affects are the infant's primary motivational system; these become organized into the libidinal and aggressive drives, always vis-à-vis interactions with a human object that is more than a vehicle for drive gratification. The id, ego, and superego derive from self- and object representations that have become internalized under the influence of various affective states. These states influence or determine the characteristics of what has been internalized—for example, whether the superego is harsh or the ego is sufficient for the tasks confronting it.

In our view, his postulates regarding early development reflect a retrospective adultomorphic bias; they are based on reconstructions made during the treatment of severely disturbed adults and do not sufficiently account for the wide range of possible developmental experiences and outcomes. For example, there is little to explain the impact on the child's development of the nature of real experiences as contrasted with the force of introjects and fantasies; there is also little to clarify the differing effects of a mother's responses to the growing child's needs or the different developmental consequences of similarly noxious experiences in different children. Kernberg, however, has elucidated developmental aspects of the adolescent process of falling in love, and he has made valiant and interesting efforts to integrate and systematize central aspects of developmental theory from several authoritative sources (1974a, 1974b, 1977, 1980b). In so doing he has eliminated many ambiguities to provide a useful structure for the clinician to use in working with a spectrum of severely disturbed adult patients.

## HANS LOEWALD

Strictly speaking, Loewald is not an object relations theorist, but he stresses the importance of drives and the central synthesizing role of the ego in an object relations context (1951, 1960, 1971). He emphasizes that drives and objects do not exist in isolation from each other. Drives organize object relations and thus reality, and at the same time object relations and reality organize drives. Loewald rejects the idea of drives resulting from the impingement of biological stimuli on the psychic apparatus and instead sees drives as being created by the psychic apparatus (1971, 1978). That is, he considers a basic function of the mental apparatus to be to generate mental representations, the most primitive of which are representations of pleasure and unpleasure. Thus, drives, ego, and objects are created by the mind in the context of the original unity of the mother-infant interaction. "Understood as psychic phenomena or representatives, instincts come into being in the early organizing mother-infant interactions. They form the most primitive level of human mentation and motivation" (1978, p. 495). The id as a psychic structure, therefore, originates from the interactions of the infantile organism and its human environment.

Loewald does not formulate a cohesive theory, nor is that his intention. Instead he reinterprets and redefines psychoanalytic concepts on the basis of new data and new understanding. Although he rejects certain of Freud's basic tenets—for example, biology is the basis for psychology—he also preserves and paves the way for a return to other Freudian concepts and to classical theory (Fogel, 1989). He is guided by his goal "to correlate our understanding of the significance of object relations for the formation and development of the psychic apparatus with the dynamics of the therapeutic process" (1960, p. 221).

Although Loewald makes analogies between the therapeutic process and mother-infant interaction, he does not make naive reconstructions to infancy. Rather, he considers the ways in which patterns of interaction are recapitulated in the transference, the ways in which disorganization and reorganization leading to integration at higher levels are characteristic for the developmental process and the therapeutic process, and the ways in which the metaphor of a higher and lower organization is characteristic to both. That is, just as the higher organization of the mother's psychic structure lifts the infant's psychological functioning to successively higher levels of organization and structuralization, the "tension" between the psychic functioning of the analyst and that of the patient creates the potential for the patient's psychic reorganization as the analysis proceeds.

Finally, Loewald considers the complexity of the individual, anticipating in many ways the current emphasis on system theory. In his earlier work he rejected a narrow focus on the Oedipus complex and stressed that preoedipal influences also need consideration; his more recent papers (1979, 1985) reaffirm the centrality of the Oedipus complex for analytic work.

We find Loewald's ideas particularly helpful because of the balance in his approach. His consideration of complexity, his recognition of the contribution of all stages of development, and his emphasis on the operational synthesis between drives, objects, reality, and the synthesizing function of the ego are all ideas we use and build upon throughout this book.

## MARGARET MAHLER

Mahler and her colleagues studied normal babies and normal mothers longitudinally in a naturalistic playroom setting, observing the emergence of object relations over the first three years of life. Like Spitz, Mahler was particularly interested in the way in which intrapsychic structures are built up from the normal mother-infant relationship. She came to this study from a background of working with deeply disturbed infants and young children, so in studying normal children she endeavored to discover what contributes to the emergence of intrapsychic structures that eventually enable the child to function independently of the object and what contributes to pathology of those structures (Mahler and Gosliner, 1955).

Influenced by the work of Hartmann and Jacobson, Mahler assumed that the mental representations of self and object that come to form are basic to ego and superego formation and functioning. She assumed that although the very young infant is able to make perceptual distinctions among various aspects of the outer world, only gradually is he able to form an integrated mental representation of the mother, and only gradually can he forge a unique, stable, and mentally represented sense of himself as distinct from his primary love object. Mahler hypothesized that these mental representations of the object and of the self are gradually built up from progressive steps in the development of relationships with objects, and so she set herself the task of trying to determine the nature of those progressive steps.

The data from this research enabled Mahler and her colleagues to conceptualize developmental progression in terms of what she called the *separation-individuation* process. This process, which became basic to Mahler's theory of object relations development (1963, 1972a, 1972b), has two distinct but intertwining aspects. *Separation* refers to the process whereby the infant gradually forms an intrapsychic self-representation distinct and separate from the representation of his mother (Mahler, 1952; Mahler et al., 1975); this does not imply a physical, spatial distancing from the parent or a dissolution of the interpersonal relationship but rather the development of an intrapsychic sense of being able to function independently of the mother. *Individuation* refers to the infant's attempts to form a unique individual identity, to assume his own individual characteristics (Mahler et al., 1975, p. 4). Optimally separation and individuation proceed together, but they may proceed divergently with a lag or precocity in one or the other.

Mahler described the separation-individuation process as beginning at four to five months of age and as comprised of four predictable, observable, and overlapping subphases: *differentiation, practicing, rapprochement,* and *on the way to object constancy.* In addition, Mahler distinguished two phases prior to the onset of the separation-individuation process, one in the first four weeks (the *normal autistic phase*) and one from the second to the fourth or fifth month (the *normal symbiotic phase*).

In her descriptions of the separation-individuation process, Mahler described the evolution of infantile feelings of omnipotence and the accompanying sense of grandiosity that underlies normal self-esteem development as well as certain later pathology. In particular, she emphasized the expansion of psychic systems that accompanies the evolution of interpersonal relations, pointing to the important role of conflict, at first interpersonal and eventually intrapsychic. She described those aspects in the mother-infant relationship that eventually contribute to libidinal object constancy in which the comforting functions originally provided by the mother become intrapsychically available. She thought that establishing libidinal object constancy facilitates independent ego functioning. Mahler (1971) also described implications for pathological ego functioning when there is a disturbance in the mother-infant relationship.

A persistent problem in psychoanalytic theory making has been to find concepts and language adequate to convey meaning about processes that cannot be quantified or objectified, but only inferred. The frequent use of metaphors to express these concepts often has the unfortunate consequence of the metaphors being taken literally. When new knowledge accrues, the old metaphors become less useful, and the concepts as well as the metaphors may come to be regarded as invalid. Consider Freud's concept of psychic energy, for example. The idea of physical energies seeking discharge is no longer apt, yet clinically we continue to observe variations in the intensity of emotion or in the intensities of impulses and strivings for gratification. Mahler's terminology is another example, especially the phrases she used to describe the earliest months of life. There is no question that pathologically based and retrospective metaphors such as "autism," "symbiosis," "stimulus barrier," "delusional common boundaries," and "hallucinatory somatopsychic omnipotent fusion" present problems (see Peterfreund, 1978; Milton Klein, 1980). Nevertheless, many of Mahler's observations and formulations about the infant's behavior during these early months are perceptive and remain relevant even if the labels themselves no longer hold.

The validity of Mahler's work has been criticized. Brody (1982) faulted her research methods, saw a degree of subjective bias in her findings, and thought she had a tendency to state hypotheses as conclusions. Mahler's notion that the infant begins life in an autistic state, cut off from the world by a stimulus barrier like a chicken embryo in an eggshell (a metaphor taken from Freud, 1911)—not engaged by or related to social stimuli—has rightly been questioned (see Peterfreund, 1978; Lichtenberg, 1981, 1987; Stern, 1985). Mahler herself attempted to redress this issue by suggesting that "awakening" (Stern, 1985) or "semi-autistic" (Harley and Weil, 1979) would be better phrases. Stern (1985) also questions the validity of Mahler's idea that self and object are undifferentiated at birth, noting that the data of infant research provide ample evidence that the infant perceives inside and outside, self and other, from birth. This criticism reveals a basic misunderstanding between many infant researchers and psychoanalysts. Psychoanalysts are concerned with the building up of intrapsychic structures. Physiological preadaptedness is available at birth, but there is no evidence to suggest that psychological structures capable of forming and maintaining intrapsychic mental representations of self and other are available at birth.

Stern also criticizes the basic premise of Mahler's theory of separation-individuation. He understands Mahler's describing the child's growing independence and autonomy as implying the dissolution of interpersonal object ties (p. 243). We think Mahler is actually describing an *intrapsychic* process whereby the child can eventually function on his own and not be helplessly dependent on the mother, but meanwhile retains the interpersonal tie to the mother. With increased stability of inner structures the child can move to progressively higher levels of object relating, maintaining and deepening interpersonal ties.

In spite of some valid criticisms, we believe that Mahler made a fundamental contribution to the psychoanalytic understanding of the evolution of object relations. Of particular importance is her making explicit that the appropriate emotional availability of the caregiver and the affective interchange between mother and infant are vitally important features in promoting the formation of psychic structures that eventually facilitate independent emotional functioning. Mahler's attention to the details of the affective mother-infant interchange has promoted considerable research related both to the mother-infant relationship and to the father-infant relationship (for the latter, see Abelin, 1971, 1975; Cath et al., 1982; Pruett, 1983, 1985). The results have added to our knowledge of normal development as well as to our appreciation of the emergence and prevention of pathology. In addition, her pioneering in naturalistic longitudinal child development observation, one of the few such projects undertaken by a psychoanalyst, has provided a model for and an impetus to subsequent infancy research. Even if increasing knowledge of the details of infant development should lead to some modification or change in emphasis of her theory, particularly her conceptualization of the earliest phases, her observations remain valid. By conceptualizing the process of separation-individuation, Mahler offered an integrated theory for preoedipal object relations that complements theories about the Oedipus complex and makes it possible for a developmental track of object relations to be constructed that can parallel and be integrated with drive theory and theories of evolving psychic structure.

## DANIEL STERN

Stern is one among many contemporary infant researchers who are studying object relations in the first three years of life. But unlike those who study selected aspects, Stern has formulated an integrated theory for the earliest stages in object relations development. In contrast to ideas derived from Freud's structural theory and the notion that intrapsychic structures emerge from interpersonal interactions, his focus is on the infant's inner subjective experience and its interpersonal context. This focus on the sense of self, present to some extent from birth, is "not encumbered with or confused with issues of development of the ego or id" (1985, p. 19), for Stern maintains that the self is the primary organizing principle. Stern brings to his studies a wealth of data from his own and others' carefully and often ingeniously constructed laboratory experiments with infants and their mothers.

Drawing on inferences about the infant's subjective life from his observational data, Stern suggests that as new behaviors and capacities emerge they are organized and transformed into organizing subjective perspectives about the sense of the self and the sense of the other. Stern is particularly concerned with the interpersonal context of these emerging senses, and so, to emphasize the importance of this connectedness, he suggests that each emergent sense of self defines a new form or domain (sphere of influence or activity) of social relatedness— that is, a "sense of self with other" grows along with a sense of self and sense of the other.

Although each sense of self and each domain of social relatedness emerges during a sensitive developmental period, Stern emphasizes that they should not be thought of as phases; rather they are forms of self-experience and forms of social interaction that, having emerged, remain intact as organizing principles through life.

Stern proposes four senses of the self: a sense of emergent self (birth to two months); a sense of a core self (two to six months); a sense of a subjective self (beginning seven to nine months); and a sense of a verbal self (beginning around fifteen to eighteen months). Alongside the emergent sense of self is a domain of emergent relatedness; alongside the core self is a domain of core relatedness; a domain of intersubjective relatedness parallels the sense of a subjective self, and a domain of verbal relatedness parallels a sense of a verbal self.

In many ways, Stern's work is influenced by and builds on the work of Spitz, Bowlby, Anna Freud, and Mahler. He builds on their views of the developmental process—the successive phases begin at similar nodal points of developmental transition—and he pays great attention to the infant's interactions with his mother. Yet Stern sets himself apart. He treats existing psychoanalytic developmental theories as redundant and in need of being entirely rebuilt, and he uses a series of his own newly invented, at times confusing, metaphors. He thereby substitutes one set of jargon for another.

At times Stern's criticisms of psychoanalytic developmental theories are valid, but as Solnit notes, he uses these criticisms artificially to heat up the debate between developmental psychology and psychoanalysis (1987b). His lack of a historical perspective, moreover, results in his failing to consider the many significant ways in which psychoanalytic developmental theory has been modified and changed since 1900 in response to criticisms similar to his own. Therefore, his rendition of psychoanalytic theory sounds particularly narrow. Furthermore, in our view, his emphasis on subjectivity and the interpersonal at the expense of the intrapsychic takes insufficient account of the contribution of inner forces to the developmental process, especially the process of internalization.

On the other hand, Stern's laboratory studies with infants and their mothers have made significant contributions to our knowledge of the details of early development. His sensitivity to mother-infant interactions and the self-regulatory capacities of the infant in these interactions has increased our understanding of the emerging sense of self and of ego development.

## SUMMARY

The evolution of theories of object relations begins with the history of psychoanalysis itself. It has been a long and difficult pathway, beginning with Freud's earliest notions, expressed in "Project for a Scientific Psychology" (1895b). The relationships among object relations, drives, affects, psychic structure formation, and the sense of self, and the relationship between the intrapsychic processes associated with object relations and interpersonal relations have all been controversial issues.

In this chapter we have presented the ideas of a variety of contemporary object relations schools. Those theories that have evolved from observations of infants and children provide the foundation for our discussion in the next chapter of the developmental evolution of object relations, followed by a discussion of the development of the sense of the self.

# CHAPTER 6

## OBJECT RELATIONS DEVELOPMENT

In describing a developmental framework for the evolving stages in object relations, we focus especially on the way significant perceived and felt interactions with others affect the origin, nature, and functioning of intrapsychic structures. We have found the ideas of Spitz and Mahler particularly helpful for the earliest stages because they base their formulations on direct observational data rather than reconstructions and because their focus is consistently on the intrapsychic.

Finding an apt and acceptable term for the period immediately after birth has always posed difficulties. Hartmann (1939), as we noted in chapter 4, labeled it the *undifferentiated phase* (Hartmann, Kris, and Loewenstein, 1946), meaning that neither the ego nor the id was structuralized and that mental representations of the object and of the self were not yet formed. The term, however, has often been misinterpreted by students and analysts alike to imply that the infant is not capable of some *perceptual* distinctions between self and object.

Spitz preferred to call this first stage *objectless,* or the stage of the *preobject,* to stress that there cannot yet be a psychological object because psychological functioning has not yet been established (1957). Mahler et al. labeled this the phase of *normal autism,* explaining that in comparison to later stages, the neonate is minimally invested in external stimuli (1975). Anna Freud similarly stressed the infant's lack of psychological functioning and total dependence on the mother by referring to the "biological unity between the mother-infant couple" (1965). The problem with these labels is that they imply little interaction between mother and infant so that she is viewed as easily interchangeable; we know from infancy research, however, that this is not the case even within the first week after birth (Burns et al., 1972). The evidence is that the infant is preadapted to participating with the mother in establishing a coordinated reciprocal pattern of sensorimotor interaction within which an affective feedback system is quickly established. Because of this, we believe the term *primary reciprocity* most aptly describes the first phase in the development of object relations.

Mahler's term *normal symbiotic phase,* although derived from observations of pathological development, was meant to convey the formation of a secure, intimate attachment. Spitz, too, was interested in attachment, but he stressed the importance of dialogue in order for attachment to take place (1963, 1964, 1965; Spitz and Cobliner, 1965). Given that the idea of dialogue places greater emphasis on the infant's activity and self-regulatory capacities, we think *beginnings of dialogue* best describes the second phase of object relations, highlighting the reciprocal affective climate necessary for attachment.

In what follows, we trace the evolution of object relations from these earliest beginnings through the preoedipal phases, using Mahler's framework for the separation-individuation process. We next describe the vicissitudes of object relations development in the infantile genital phase and the Oedipus complex, and then discuss later evolution during latency and finally during adolescence. Our emphasis will be more on the earlier years of life where the bulk of recent research has focused, and where perhaps the most dramatic change in object relating and hence the most significant steps in psychic structure formation occur.

## PRIMARY RECIPROCITY: A PHYSIOLOGICAL PRELUDE TO OBJECT RELATIONS

Most researchers agree that we are born prepared to participate in reciprocal interaction. Sander (1975) conceptualizes this reciprocity as part of the infant's biologically derived, preadapted behavior for engaging in the *process* of adaptation. For some time after birth the infant's behavior is predominantly affected by endogenously determined regulatory processes (Sander, 1962, 1964); the principal task for mother and infant is to regulate and stabilize sleep-wake, day-night, and hunger-satiation cycles and, in so doing, maintain homeostatic equilibrium (Anders, 1982). This, too, is part of the mother-infant reciprocity. Indeed, as Call (1984) stresses, reciprocity at birth employs several physiological systems in both mother and infant, including the visual, auditory, and kinesthetic systems, and even states of psychophysiological arousal. Call found that the infant's sucking rhythms interact with the psychophysiology of the letdown reflex in the breast-feeding mother. The coordination among interacting systems, Call maintains, is demonstrated by the newborn's anticipatory approach behavior at feeding.

Anders and Zeanah (1984) conclude that the sophisticated biological endowment of the infant enables it actively to seek and respond to appropriate sensorial and affective feedback. Optimally, an affective feedback system is soon established in which parent and infant mesh various behaviors in mutual interchanges, such as in looking and arousal, voice and movement, and voice and directed facial looking (Sander, 1975; Als et al., 1979; Brazelton and Als, 1979; Meltzoff, 1985). In this way a private, exclusive form of communication is developed between mother and infant, which provides a foundation for competent psychological functioning.

## BEGINNINGS OF DIALOGUE

Around two months of age a noticeable shift occurs in the infant's behavior. He begins to demonstrate an active anticipation of reciprocal exchanges, an active seeking for social interaction, and an emerging capacity for self-regulation. Mahler stressed that the important psychological achievement for the infant, beginning with the second month until four to five months, is the establishment of the mother as the cardinal love object and the formation of a firm attachment to her. The nonspecific smiling response, which soon becomes specific to the mother (Spitz and Wolf, 1946), is an important indicator of this attachment and serves to organize and consolidate it. From this point on the infant's activities, affects, and perceptions all appear to increasingly focus on the interpersonal interaction with the mother as the two engage in active dialogue.

Spitz's observations convinced him that the most important aspect of the mother-infant relationship is the affective climate (1965; Spitz and Cobliner, 1965). He believed that an affectively motivated, continuous, mutually stimulating dialogue of action and response provides the milieu from which object relations and intrapsychic structures emerge. He described the dialogue as beginning in, but soon extending beyond, the nursing situation. Call suggests that these feeding experiences be viewed as the organizers of the most salient of early interactions with the mother (1964); Loewald thinks that these interactions offer a setting for the early structuring of pleasure and unpleasure (1971, 1978). As Wolff pointed out, however, much more than need satisfaction quickly comes into play in the mother-infant dialogue (1959, 1966).

Many authors have pointed out that this early dialogue, in which the infant's wide-eyed gaze is met by the mother's adoring look, provides the roots of competence and reality-based self-esteem. A range of positive feelings from contentment to joy become associated with competent interactions when the infant is able to elicit appropriate responses from the mother and when the mother-infant dyad is able to repair inevitable breaches in the empathic tie (Tronick and Gianino, 1986).

Call describes details of the dialogue in terms of nonverbal facial expression, bodily action, vocalization, response, and playful interactions and games, which provide the basis for the development of a private, exclusive form of communication with the mother (1980, 1984). The primary purpose of this early communication system is mutual holding, maintenance, and enrichment of the duality, and it becomes, according to Call, the organizing principle for later forms of communication, including affects, gestures, and the acquisition of speech.

The infant takes more and more control over games and interactions, and by three or four months he is frequently their initiator, terminator, and regulator. In a series of studies, Sander (1962, 1964, 1983), and Stern (1974b) and his colleagues (Beebe and Stern, 1977; Beebe 1986) document that although the mother continues to have the major organizing and regulating responsibility, by the time the infant is three or four months old, mother-infant games take on a patterning that facilitates self-regulation within the exchange. The patterns of these reciprocal interactions are remarkably tenacious. Continuities in relationship patterning have been demonstrated from early interactional patterns established in infancy, through the toddler and preschool ages, into later life, and even across generations (Emde, 1988a, 1988b).

The early regulation of self and other established through reciprocal exchanges also makes an important contribution to the development of self-regulatory ego functioning. Follow-up studies have found that patterns of self-regulation established in early infancy are persistent through adolescence (Brody, 1982). When the mother provides excessive, insufficient, or unpredictable stimulation or is persistently not in harmony with the infant's attempts to elicit a response, or with the infant's rhythms, the infant's competent self-regulatory functioning may be undermined; furthermore, these early noxious influences may be apparent later in the ways the individual copes with anxiety, as described, for example, by Greenacre (1941) and Weil (1978).

Sandler and Sandler (1978) suggest that, in addition to what we have mentioned, mother-infant interactions provide the context for the earliest formations of self- and object representations. As representations of self and other slowly form in the infant's mind, they include representations of these subjective, interactive experiences, or "role relationships." Stern (1985) calls the preverbal representations of these experiences "RIGs," or "Representations of Interactions that have been Generalized." He conjectures that RIGs form the basis of memory and are the basic unit for the representation of the self. This idea may have merit, for it is known that although memories of preverbal events may not be subject to later recall, action patterns and procedural memories appear to persist and contribute to expanding areas of the infant's competence (Papousek and Papousek, 1979, 1984; Lichtenberg, 1987). Relationship patterns are an example. Developmental research has demonstrated that early experiences cannot be used to predict later functioning, but the demonstrable durability of relationship patterns over time substantiates an assumption explicit in the psychoanalytic concept of transference (Freud, 1905b). We assume that these patterns are tenacious because they are a part of self- and object representations from their earliest formation.

## SEPARATION-INDIVIDUATION

### Differentiation and the Libidinal Object

Beginning sometimes as early as four months, and certainly by five or six months, the infant begins to show interest and curiosity about the world beyond the mother-infant dialogue. As soon as he is motorically able, the infant makes his first tentative moves at breaking away from the close physical proximity of the mother. Consistent with her metaphor of a "symbiotic orbit," Mahler thought it seemed appropriate to name this new outward look "hatching."*

Mahler's hatching coincides with Piaget's Stage 3 of sensorimotor intelligence, when the infant discovers that his actions influence external objects and his interest shifts from the action to the effect of the

---

*Mahler attributed the marked shift in the infant's functioning at this time to central nervous system maturation of the perceptual-conscious system. She assumed that before this time, a "stimulus barrier" protected the infant from being bombarded with overwhelming external stimuli. Insofar as recent research has documented the remarkable ability of the neonate to recognize and differentiate stimuli of several sensory modalities, the idea of a stimulus barrier is no longer tenable or necessary (Esman, 1983). It seems that many maturational and experiential factors underlie this shift, not the least of which may be development in ego functioning facilitating the infant's integration of stimuli into new behavioral patterns (Lester, 1983).

action (1952). Intentionality in the infant's behavior becomes apparent for the first time, and he begins to distinguish between ends and means.

Although the infant shows interest and curiosity and explores the world around him, his pleasure and sense of security and well-being depend on his being able to elicit an appropriate response from his mother. Mahler recognized that as the infant explores away from the mother, he stays in close proximity to her and continues to need her as "home base." Now the infant establishes a visual pattern of "checking back to mother," who emotionally "refuels," sometimes through physical contact but often merely with visual or auditory cues. The infant's curiosity and wonderment are thus in the context of "basic trust" and confidence in the relationship, as evidence accrues that the mother is now the *libidinal object* (Spitz, 1959). The affective investment in the mother appears to be sustained in spite of frustration or gratification (A. Freud, 1968).

This basic trust is particularly apparent in the infant's reactions to strangers. When confronted with a strange person or situation, he typically reacts with some degree of distress. Yet, if the attachment to the mother is secure, the infant will eventually show more curiosity than distress toward the stranger (Mahler and McDevitt, 1968; Bowlby, 1969; Rheingold, 1969; Brody and Axelrad, 1970; Ainsworth et al., 1978). In what is often a subtle and momentary interaction, the infant looks to mother for an affective clue of safety or danger. In response to her reassuring smile, he gleefully explores. Should she frown in distress and anxiety, he breaks into tears, withdraws from the strange situation, and returns to mother's side. Emde (1983) documents the ways in which this "social referencing" system acts as an auxiliary ego function and guides the infant in future action—in deciding whether to explore or to withdraw and return to the safety of the mother.

As he is forming a sense of self and other from the reciprocal exchanges with the mother, the infant also forms a sense of the relationship, which Stern (1985) calls a sense of "intersubjectivity" and Emde (1988a, 1988b) understands as the beginning of a sense of "we." Now the infant seeks to share experiences about events and things. As feeling states become increasingly imbued with love and hate and a variety of other positive and negative affects, the infant gradually learns that these affects are potentially shareable with someone else.

Winnicott's concept of the transitional object is relevant to the infant's developing object relations (1953, 1959). The favorite blanket or soft toy usually has some association to early pleasurable experiences shared with the mother and the infant's attachment to it often becomes most intense at times of separation from the mother such as bedtime or moments of distress. This suggests that it functions to maintain some illusion of the mother's presence or at least of her soothing, safe-keeping functions during times of separation. In the usual course of events it disappears at about the time libidinal object constancy is established, confirming Spitz's observation that "the transitional object is indeed transitional in the sense that it partakes of both worlds, the archaic world of the conditioned reflex on the one hand, the ego-regulated world of object relations, of the psyche, on the other" (1965, p. 179). With the establishment of libidinal object constancy the inter-nalized image of the mother, hence the ego, takes over the soothing, regulating functions of the transitional object.

### The Practicing Phase

The mastery of upright locomotion propels the infant into what Mahler characterized as the practicing phase. Displays of emotional elation and exuberance are typical of this time as the young toddler finds himself exhilarated by his own capacities and enamored with the world and his daily discoveries. The relationship between mother and toddler includes a progressively widening variety and interchange of feelings and behaviors as the toddler, now with the ability to move away from and back to mother, explores an ever widening world and be-comes accustomed to the experience of physical separation and its psychological consequences.

Toward the end of the practicing phase, between fifteen and eigh-teen months, the toddler appears more reliably able to maintain and regard an image of the mother separate from himself and his immedi-ate actions, suggesting greater stability in evolving self- and object representations. Mahler and McDevitt (1968) used the toddler's be-havior during short separations from mother as evidence for this con-clusion. In the mother's absence the toddler shows what Mahler and McDevitt called "low keyedness" (1968), a diminished interest in the surroundings, increased sensitivity to minor mishaps, and what can best be described as an air of preoccupation. Mahler infers from this behavior that the toddler can now for a time retain, evoke, and begin to use an intrapsychic representation of the mother, which, in her ab-sence, is sufficient to sustain some degree of well-being; he no longer requires her constant presence (McDevitt, 1975). Burlingham and Freud (1944) noted, however, that separation from the mother for any extended length of time may disrupt the relationship in harmful ways, and this may have lasting effects. On her return, the toddler may look at her face with stony indifference, as if she were a complete stranger, suggesting not that the internal representation has disappeared but that his inner relationship to her has been altered.

Individuation proceeds rapidly during the second year, and Mahler describes how, after the exhilaration of the practicing phase, the child negotiates the final process of "psychological birth" (Mahler et al., 1975). New behaviors emerge: the toddler brings material objects to mother and wants her to engage in common exploration and discovery; interest in persons other than mother, such as father, siblings, and other children, becomes more apparent; attempts to imitate the mother or father also appear. These behaviors suggest that a consolidated and relatively stable representation of the self and of the other has accrued. Piaget (1952) found that the toddler can now manipulate reality by thought, not just action, which also supports the conclusion of an integrated mental representation of self and other.

*Rapprochement*

Sometime around sixteen to eighteen months, the rapprochement phase,* characterized by dilemma, paradox, and wide affective swings between love and hate, appears. In comparison to the elated practicing toddler who easily wanders away from mother, the rapprochement toddler may be distressed even when mother is available. Mood swings and temper tantrums accompany alternating rejecting and clinging behavior. Mahler has inferred that progress in cognitive development makes the toddler acutely aware not only of emergent skills but of his smallness and psychological separateness, which brings feelings of loneliness and helplessness. Cognitive advances facilitate language expression and symbolic play. Now the toddler can think about things, and fantasy life becomes possible. With this, it becomes apparent that the toddler forms wishes of how things ought to be as well as a clearer idea of how they are.

So the toddler realizes that his wishes and his mother's do not always coincide; he cannot always coerce her to gratify him. He is not the omnipotent majesty (we imagine) he imagined himself to be! The change from the euphoria of the practicing subphase to depressive

*The term, from the French, refers to "an establishing, or especially restoring, of harmony and friendly relations" (*Webster's 1980 New World Dictionary*, 2nd college ed., p. 1177).

moods, distress, temper tantrums, and a constant concern about the mother's whereabouts during rapprochement is dramatic.

The characteristic acquisitiveness, envy, indecision, ambivalence, and negativism of the anal phase emerge, and the toddler is confronted with the dilemma of intensely ambivalent feelings and incompatible aims. He wants to be independent, to function on his own. Now is the time of expanding opportunities to develop and to exercise skills and controls. Optimally the toddler gains growing confidence and pleasure in his increasing competence in regulating tension states, feeding, dressing, protecting himself, and establishing bowel and bladder control, as long as his mother allows him to own his own body and is herself sufficiently competent in channeling her child's assertive impulses and in "absorbing aggression" (Furman, 1985). For now the toddler wants things his way, and he assertively attempts to arrange life to suit himself. Yet he also loves and wants to feel loved and comforted by his mother, and his sense of well-being is dependent on this love. But all sense of loving and being loved may disappear at times when hate and anger take over. The sense of being alone and unloved arouses tremendous anxiety and further mood instability. This heightened ambivalence, with accompanying temper tantrums and regressive behavior, can be understood as the external manifestation of an emergent intrapsychic conflict between the toddler's wish for individuation, independence, assertiveness, and control and his wish to please mother and to keep her love. And so, as Sander has pointed out, the toddler oscillates between stubbornly asserting himself against the wishes of his mother and, in the next moment, enjoying the familiar pleasure of "fitting together" (1983, p. 343).

The rapprochement subphase typically leaves its imprint on character style in some way or another, for we all maintain some need for separateness, for closeness, for autonomy, and for dependency (Kramer and Akhtar, 1988). The individual's later management of these dilemmas as well as the manner in which the ego functions in the face of anxiety will reflect the way in which rapprochement conflict is resolved. When, as McDevitt (1975) describes, hostile feelings outweigh affectionate ones, the maternal representation may become so distorted by the projection of violent and angry feelings during times of crisis that the child is not able to feel positively about his mother or about himself. The mother is then not able to function as an auxiliary ego and foster successful conflict resolution.

If, however, the toddler, instead of being overwhelmed, can accept and tolerate an upsurge of rage against his frustrating mother, recognizing that she is the same person he loves at other times, he can then integrate "good" and "bad" self- and object images into stable representations. Seeing mother as "mostly good," the toddler more often wishes to please, temporarily giving up drive gratification for the more rewarding love of the mother. Internalization and identification proceed smoothly, enhancing the independence of ego functioning.

### The Beginnings of Libidinal Object Constancy

To the extent that the child forms an integrated maternal representation that can function to provide comfort and support in mother's absence, enabling the child to be less dependent on and therefore to function more separately from the mother, we can speak of the child having attained some measure of libidinal object constancy. To attain this measure of inner security, the toddler must resolve conflicts between his wishes and his mother's prohibitions and manage to tolerate ambivalence. Then his loving and angry feelings about her come to be more solidly encompassed by a single representation of her (McDevitt, 1975). He can better temper and tolerate his disappointment and rage, since his frustrating experiences with mother are counteracted by memories of her gratifying, loving, and comforting behavior.

If this representation can hold together even when the child is angry or frustrated, it begins to take on a new function. That is, the positive quality of the images evoked from the mental representation of the mother takes on a comforting function, and the child in identification with his comforting mother is better able to comfort himself (Furer, 1967). Ego functioning progresses because the child, instead of being overwhelmed by the intensity of his affects, is now better able to regulate himself whether or not mother is immediately available. This is because a part of his integrated representation of her includes expectations of her behavior—such as her regulating and comforting responses to his distress. With these internally available, the child is not so dependent upon her physical presence to stabilize his functioning (Pine, 1971). Mahler locates the beginnings of this accomplishment in the third year, but emphasizes that it extends beyond that age; it is relatively open-ended and may never be fully achieved.

It is in this area that Kohut's idea of selfobjects—that we rely throughout life on others to provide comfort and love and thus maintain inner feelings of well-being—finds a place. We do not think Mahler intended to imply that achieving libidinal object constancy meant that one could comfortably live in autonomous isolation from others.

Rather, our relations with important others endure and mature. Indeed, Pine (1974) points out that people vary all through life in their capacity to take comfort from the internal memory or image of the love object as opposed to the need for contact with a real object for comfort and pleasure. Pine adds, however, that since it *is* internal, the representation can be shaped to represent both wish and reality. In that way, the internal object can potentially be better than the real object, and so it can function as an important internal regulator of longing and rage, as well as of self-esteem.

The developmental significance of libidinal object constancy is not only that the child can integrate the loving and affectionate with the angry and hostile views of the mother; it is also that the child is reassured that their basically loving relationship will continue in spite of brief separations or temporary feelings of anger and resentment. In other words, the child can sustain a constant relationship with the mother in spite of the vicissitudes of frustration and gratification that occur with development (Burgner and Edgcumbe, 1972). Now the child shifts from almost exclusively self-centered, demanding, clinging behavior to being able to engage in more mature, ego-determined relationships characterized by affection, trust, and some (though limited by cognitive immaturity) regard for the interests and feelings of others.

The development of libidinal object constancy is usually accompanied by the attainment of a degree of libidinal self constancy—that is, by the capacity to sustain a unified self-representation encompassing all the different, affectively toned ideas about one's self. This step is reinforced and stabilized by increasing ego capacities for impulse control and self-reflection, which allow the child a greater degree of self-control and pleasurable feelings of mastery. This step usually also elicits pride and reinforcement from the mother, enhancing the child's feeling of being lovable.

## EARLY ROLE OF THE FATHER

Although our discussion so far has concentrated on the mother-child relationship, we do not mean to imply that the father and other family members do not play an important role. Several investigators describe the various ways that the father contributes to the process of self-object differentiation in the first year of life (Loewald, 1951; Mahler and Gosliner, 1955; Abelin, 1971, 1975). Pederson and Robson (1969) found that the infant makes early perceptual distinctions between the parents, and a discernible attachment to the father is evident by at least eight months of age. Burlingham (1973) and Yogman (1982) observed definite differences in the ways in which fathers and mothers play with their infants, as well as in their handling of boys and girls. Fathers in general tend to play more actively and more physically with their infants. Kramer and Akhtar (1988) emphasize the positive benefit this has for the practicing toddler; within limits, the stimulating effect of physical prowess enhances the toddler's greater awareness of body parts and body self. Herzog (1980, 1982) suggests that another important role for the father is to help the infant develop the capacity to modulate aggression. Absence or loss of the father during the first eighteen months of life can contribute to behavioral and affective disturbances that may not be recognized until later.

The father also plays a major role in helping the toddler resolve the conflicts of the rapprochement phase. As a less "contaminated" object, the father may be able to mediate between the mother and toddler, provide extra "refueling" at times of distress, and serve as an additional object for identification. Indeed, early signs of identification with the attitudes of the father are apparent by about eighteen months (Mahler et al., 1975). As development proceeds the child makes selective identifications with both mother and father.

It is only relatively recently that direct observational father-child studies have been undertaken (for example, Gunsberg, 1982) and that the impact of the absent father has been studied (for example, Neubauer, 1960; Herzog and Sudia, 1973; Herzog, 1980; Wallerstein and Kelly, 1980; Burgner, 1985; Wallerstein and Blakeslee, 1989). Pruett (1984, 1985, 1987) focused on intact families with a primary nurturing father and a working mother; he found that in stressful circumstances the children tended to turn first to their fathers, indicating that the "cardinal object representation" (Mahler, 1961, p. 334) in these families was the father rather than the mother. Even though the primary caretaker was male, there seemed to be no gender-identity or gender-role difficulties in the children studied. Signs of oedipal involvement appeared to be typical in those children developmentally far enough along to manifest them, and development disturbances or psychopathology were mild or absent. Lamb (1981, 1984) has reported on social changes in family patterns and the many opportunities these provide for shifts in the traditional contacts children have with their parents during their upbringing; we are just beginning to learn about the intrapsychic consequences.

## TRIADIC OBJECT RELATIONS

Up to this point we have been describing dyadic object relations. Now that researchers have paid more attention to the father's early relationship with the infant, we have come to understand more clearly that the infant is able to relate in different ways to a variety of persons simultaneously. Once the small child reaches the infantile genital phase and is preoccupied with genital impulses, however, object relations become more complex.

During the early part of the infantile genital phase, object relations remain dyadic, and the child's focus in object-related interactions is on narcissistic, gender-related issues. The child idealizes his same-sex parent and seeks an intimate, affectionate attachment to this parent; this attachment ideally facilitates the child's forming those identifications that enhance a sense of masculinity or femininity. Now the child seeks an exclusive relationship with each parent; that is, he seeks to be the center of attention so that he can receive praise and admiration for his emergent masculine or feminine characteristics. And so he jostles and competes with one or another parent or family member to gain this position and admiration.

Progress in gender identity includes establishing gender-role identity according to which the child usually wishes for a different role in relation to the parent of the opposite sex; together with the pressure from infantile genital phase drives, this step ordinarily leads to a shift in object relatedness. From dyadic relatedness the child shifts to triadic object relations as he becomes engaged in the Oedipus complex. (The dynamics of the oedipal phase are more fully described in part VII.) With regard to object relations, three aspects of the oedipal phase should be noted: the triangular nature of object relations, the impact on psychic structuralization, and the influence on narcissistic balance.

The achievement of triadic object relations of the Oedipus complex implies a change in the nature of the child's fantasy; from simply wishing an exclusive relationship with one or the other parent in efforts to be the center of attention, the child's fantasy is to replace and to play the role of one parent with the other. The child's loyalty conflicts, libidinal wishes, and fears of punishment change in character as fantasy life becomes more absorbed with Oedipal wishes. Earlier conflicts between competition and identification, and between libidinal wishes and prohibitions, become stronger, adding to the child's distress. Fears of castration, body damage, and loss of parental love are intensified in reaction to the child's wishful fantasies, and he struggles to work out solutions to these many conflicts in his life.

Some examples might be helpful. One five-year-old girl was preoccupied with competition with her mother. She dramatized her conflicts through play with Barbie dolls in which she staged beauty contests between Barbie and Skipper, the adolescent doll. Ken, Barbie's mate, was usually given the role of the judge. Skipper was empathically concerned about hurting Barbie's feelings, yet she wanted to win the contest because the prize was a date with Ken. She proudly announced that she was a "daddy's girl," and said she wished she could have large breasts like the Barbie doll or her mother. Although she felt herself to be her father's princess, mother remained Queen, leading her to feel inadequate and envious, jealous of her mother. Then when her mother bought her the stylish clothes she longed for, her guilty feelings disrupted her self-confidence, her pleasure in her femininity, and her pleasure in the shared activity with her mother.

A five-and-a-half-year-old boy played at setting up a house with Popeye and Olive. Popeye was strong and liked Olive, but robbers wanted to marry Olive, too. Popeye caught them trying to steal Olive and put them in jail where they got their heads chopped off. On another day he pretended that Superman and Wonderwoman got married, and they had Superboy; Superboy grew up and married Superwoman, and Spidy was their son. "No! No girls," he suddenly demanded, defending himself from mounting excitement and oedipal conflict, "because I can see Superwoman's boobies! The fathers want to be with their sons." His play then switched to the escapades of Superman and Superboy.

As these examples illustrate, the concept of triadic object relations refers to the description of the conflictual vicissitudes of oedipal rivalrous relationships. Involvement in the Oedipus complex—characterized as it is by love and genital excitement for one parent arousing hate, death wishes, fears of retribution, and competition with the other parent, and yet love and admiration for the rival—indicates the establishment of full triadic object relations. It also marks the highest possible level of both libidinal organization and available object relations for the young child (see, for example, Lebovici, 1982). The triangular nature of oedipal object relatedness and of oedipal object-related conflicts furthers psychic structuralization and complicates the child's narcissistic balance.

Although preoedipal developmental conflicts can potentially become neurotic conflicts as parental prohibitions and directives are internalized, the rivalry inherent in oedipal relationships creates the potential for the infantile neurosis, during the course of which the child identifies with parental directives and moral standards, and superego development progresses accordingly. Not only are representations of the parents' observing, judging, punishing, and rewarding functions, distorted though they may be by the child's projections, now increasingly to be found within the child's mind, but identifications with these make oedipal rivalrous wishes increasingly conflictual. The pain produced by the infantile neurosis therefore provides the momentum for resolving oedipal conflicts. Consolation as well as fortification of ego functioning is, however, found in idealizations and identifications with various aspects of the parent of the same sex. The greater strength of ego functioning that results from superego consolidation then facilitates oedipal resolution, which requires relinquishing the push for immediate gratification of sexual aims and for replacing and playing the role of one parent with the other. With oedipal resolution the child becomes increasingly able to guide, protect, correct, and punish himself. His parents' ideals and standards, or the versions he has internalized, are now his own.

The narcissistic vulnerabilities of the child in the oedipal phase are considerable, although the declarations and manifestations of oedipal love may not always be visible to the adult observer. The optimal balance between narcissistic mortification and developmentally appropriate narcissistic gratification falls somewhere between complete oedipal rebuff and complete oedipal victory. Even the most loving parent must disappoint the child because the child's wishes far exceed the possibilities of reality. Sooner or later, in order to preserve self-esteem, the child must come to terms with the reality of his relationship to his parents and his sexual immaturity.

Those children who enter the oedipal phase with feelings of competence and positive self-regard derived from affective interactions with their parents are not devastated by oedipal disappointment. Their capacity to defend against and relinquish incestuous wishes helps them to begin to delay, defer, and accept the notion that displaced oedipal wishes can be gratified in the future. Furthermore, the child's advancing identifications with the idealized parent of the same sex provide an increasing source of self-esteem.

Thus, to the extent the child's capacities and the environment allow, narcissistic equilibrium can be maintained by the child's finding substitutes for the parents and sublimations of his drives. This process is aided by a growing number of internal prohibitions, a greater capacity for internal regulation by an increasingly wide repertoire of available defenses, and by the concomitant repression of oedipal sexuality. Growing intellectual capacities also allow the child to find gratification in sublimations, so they can enjoy and take pride in their cognitive as well as their physical activities. Their widening social relations provide additional avenues for pleasurable relationships as well as greater scope for displacement and substitute gratifications. Therefore, although painful, oedipal failure normally will not be traumatic but will further the developmental process, as maturational factors propel the child toward latency.

## OBJECT RELATIONS IN LATENCY

By giving up conscious efforts to achieve an incestual relationship with one or the other parent, the child brings about a change in their relationship. Now relations with each parent can be affectionate, even if continuously affected from the child's side by the nature of repressed wishes and conflicts, the nature of parental representations made during earlier stages of object relations development, and a newly powerful superego. Indeed, the child becomes noticeably more independent from his parents as latency progresses, especially with regard to matters of right and wrong because the superego is increasingly experienced as an internal presence. These intrapsychic forces become crucial and permanent unconscious ingredients of his object relations, deeply affecting his behavior and his relations with others.

"Family romance" fantasies (Freud, 1908) are typical of early latency. These fantasies originate in disappointments in oedipal love and also serve as a defense against incest fantasies; they thus facilitate the child's efforts to distance himself intrapsychically from his parents. Feeling slighted by his parents, who at times, he perceives, prefer each other to him, the child compensates in fantasy for his narcissistic injury and disappointment. Accordingly, he imagines himself to be an adopted child or stepchild and believes that he is of noble or supernatural birth and merely placed in this family until bigger and better opportunities come along. Family romance fantasies betray oedipal disappointment and disillusionment as the child sees that his parents are not, as he thought, perfect and omnipotent. This phase-appropriate disillusionment in the child's major objects, a continuing task of development (Winnicott, 1953), is counterbalanced in the child's fantasy by the relative grandiosity of his fantasied "true" parents. Similar functions and origins have been attributed to fantasies of having a twin (Burlingham, 1952), to imaginary animal or human companions (Nagera, 1969; Myers, 1976, 1979), and to an interest in the superheroes of comics and television (Widzer, 1977). Many of these fantasies become further elaborated as latency progresses.

The older latency child also steadily turns away from preoccupation with fantasy and toward objects in the real world. A significant aspect of this shift is manifested in social relations, which become much more important during latency. "The world of his play interest engulfs the child with new hopes, new disappointments, and gratifications," says Peller, who points out that in these circumstances the child begins to make identifications with peers or equals in addition to his parents and teachers (1954, p. 191).

Same-sex peer groups provide opportunities for consolidating gender identity, for displacing oedipal object–related conflicts, and for distancing from the oedipal objects. Buxbaum, seeking an intrapsychic explanation for the two marked periods of group formation in childhood—at the onset of latency and in adolescence—concluded that "whereas the young child finds in the group support for his new-found physical independence from mother, the adolescent finds reassurance for his moral independence from home" (1945, p. 363). Buxbaum points out that the child entering latency has a readiness to form new relationships especially because he needs to find new sources of libidinal gratification. Group activities (as well as school [Peller, 1956]) do this in displaced or sublimated ways. In addition, the group can often tolerate relaxing of superego standards; Golding dramatically portrayed group acceptance of otherwise forbidden activities, such as the overt expression of sadistic impulses, in his novel *Lord of the Flies* (1955). A socially acceptable form of latency group formation is team games, often with elaborate attention paid to who plays in which leagues.

## OBJECT RELATIONS IN ADOLESCENCE

Blos (1967) has described the principal object relations tasks of adolescence as a process of "second individuation," which includes two intertwining processes—separating from and giving up the parents as primary love objects, and finding substitutes outside the family. (Katan [1951] calls this disengagement and "object removal.") "Giving up" also requires the adolescent to relinquish the parents (of the past and of the present) as authority figures. Although these two processes are clearly intertwined, for purposes of clarity we discuss the first here and postpone a full discussion of the second until we deal with superego development.

A crucial aspect of the second individuation process is the deidealization of parental object representations formed in earlier childhood, perhaps ten or more years before. At that time, the child's thought processes were egocentric and he viewed the parents as wonderful and ideal because of the central position they held in his life. Even as he clings to the ideal image of these all-loving, all-fulfilling ideal infantile object representations, the adolescent harshly criticizes his parents, whom he now tends to see as inadequate, disappointing, and unfair. The resulting interpersonal strife causes the adolescent to feel a loss of internal support and a sense of emptiness, accompanied by a sense of painful alienation and object hunger.

The adolescent turns to his peers because of his need for relationships to gratify drive derivatives, to relieve his sense of emptiness, and to support his self-esteem as he pushes forward in his developmental task toward psychic independence. The peer group supplies nonjudgmental support as the adolescent attempts to resolve inner conflicts related to early infantile object ties. The nuances of peer and group relationships have a "practicing" quality, for the intimate relationships established at this time do not require a permanent commitment; the adolescent is therefore free to experiment with others and with his own self in new situations with an increasing sense of independence. This independence retains an "as if" quality until the adolescent can come to terms with the idealizations of his parents. Also, the relationship to the peer group may be altered when feelings of romantic love bring together a couple who maintain their relationship by displacing part of their aggression onto the group (Kernberg, 1980b, p. 33).

In a kind of second rapprochement, the adolescent tries to resolve early infantile ties. In serving progressive aims, the regressive revival of infantile object relations may arouse an intensity of ambivalence reminiscent of the original rapprochement phase. Blos (1967) points out that the revived ambivalence characteristically creates in the adolescent a mass of labile contradictions in affect, impulse, thought, and behavior. Fluctuations between the extremes of love and hate, activity and passivity, masculinity and femininity, fascination and disinterest, and regressive longings for dependence as well as independent strivings are hence all age-appropriate. One can therefore understand the characteristic negativism of adolescence not only as an expression of hostility but as a necessary means for the individual to protect the ego from "passive surrender" (A. Freud, 1958), enabling him to take a necessary step forward in his individuation process.

At age fifteen, Gene worried his parents because of his apparent interest in drugs, his defiance of their authority, and his increasingly poor academic performance in spite of his high intelligence. When they made an appointment with a psychiatrist for an evaluation, he ran away from home and couldn't be found for several days. Gene's father finally found him sleeping in a tree in the backyard. To his parents' surprise, he allowed them to escort him to the renegotiated appointment time. He brought himself to subsequent sessions, and as the analytic work unfolded, he made clear that he wanted to be the one to decide when to come and for what reasons. He had not told his parents of his increasingly distressing nightmares and anxiety attacks for which he wanted help, but which he also felt he should be able to handle by himself.

The adolescent also experiences himself as not perfect, which leads him to reevaluate his own ideal self-image. Often a painful intrapsychic struggle ensues between competition with the idealized image of the parent and the not-so-perfect self-image during the course of deidealization. One seventeen-year-old described writing an essay for a class assignment. "Words came easily in the beginning, but then dad [a college professor] got in there; he can write so well! Then I got angrier and angrier; I hate him! The essay was terrible—I couldn't finish!" Of this process, Blos writes, "Indeed I feel inclined to say that the process of deidealization of object and self represents the most distressful and tormenting single aspect of growing up" (1979, p. 486).

To the extent that the adolescent is able to differentiate the omnipotent, idealized object representations of his infancy from the parents of his current life, he will be able to establish "friendly," respectful relationships with his parents and still feel himself to be independent of them. Early identifications with parents, which formed the basis of the superego, then lose some of their significance and sway, and the adolescent is freer to identify with selected aspects of his parents and in so doing, modify the ideal self-image to something more realistic. These identifications, however, are associated more with the ego than with the superego. Indeed, Freud commented, "At the time at which the Oedipus complex gives place to the super-ego they [the parents] are something quite magnificent; but later they lose much of this. Identifications then come about with these later parents as well, and indeed they regularly make important contributions to the formation of character; but in that case they only affect the ego, they no longer influence the super-ego, which has been determined by the earliest parental imagos" (1933, p. 64).

We think the importance of the second individuation process of adolescence is frequently underestimated. An adult's complaint that his parents were inadequate and unempathic when he was a child often reflects his failure to deidealize infantile objects and thereby complete adolescent individuation. Once this process is completed, normally or through the help of psychotherapeutic intervention, the person often comes to view the parents as quite "good enough" or at least to have some compassion for their shortcomings.

The process of individuating or disengaging from infantile objects may last well into late adolescence and early adulthood. If it is successful, this internal process gradually lessens the painful ambivalence of the preoedipal and oedipal object ties, and a progressively more mature, mutually satisfying relationship with the parents emerges. At the same time, the individual establishes new and more satisfying and stable extrafamilial love relationships, and as his capacity for mature love and intimacy develops, he can share deeply felt emotions with friends and lovers. Optimally, love relationships ultimately provide a context within which the person can experience independence and mutuality as well as profound sexual pleasure (Erikson, 1959; Kernberg, 1974a, 1974b, 1977, 1980b, 1980c; Person, 1988). Although other factors play a part, the ending of adolescence depends to a significant degree on the extent to which the individual's object relations conflicts, incompatibilities, and attachments can be reconciled and integrated with the demands of reality in what Blos terms "adolescent closure" (1976).

## SUMMARY

The course of object relations development is rewarding and enriching, although at times painful. The earliest phases in this process are still shrouded from view, for in spite of extensive research efforts we can still only guess what is going on in the mind of the infant. Taking the findings of developmental research into account, however, we have designated the first phase as "primary reciprocity" and the second as "the beginnings of dialogue." We then described the subphases of separation-individuation, the dynamics leading up to and including oedipal triadic object relations, and the implications for ego and super-ego development. In a discussion of object relations vicissitudes during latency and adolescence, we described the obligatory alterations, modifications, and revisions in object relations that are an expected and necessary part of adolescent development.

# CHAPTER 7

## THE DEVELOPMENT OF A

## SENSE OF SELF

As we discussed earlier, reciprocal exchanges with others beginning at birth lead to the formation and modification of intrapsychic structures. A subjective sense of self also emerges from and in relation to such interactions. This chapter is concerned with the sequential steps in the evolution of this subjective sense of self.

### HISTORICAL BACKGROUND

Concepts of the sense of self, the self-representation, and self as structure, and how these relate to the structures of the tripartite (id, ego, superego) model of the mind, have been subjects of increasing psychoanalytic interest and debate. Kohut (1971, 1977) conceptualizes development in terms of a self structure, and he maintains that this self encompasses and is supraordinate to the structures of the tripartite model. Stern (1985) similarly contends that the study of the development of the various subjective senses of self should be a central psychoanalytic focus separate from the study of the ego. He considers the sense of self the primary organizing developmental principle.

In contrast, some authors argue that a separate theory for the development of the self is unwarranted, as the emergence of a sense of self is part of the separation-individuation process and is adequately conceptualized in the theory of object relations (for example, Loewald, 1973; Mahler and McDevitt, 1980; McDevitt and Mahler, 1980). Others add that both an experiential subjective sense of self and a nonexperiential organizing psychic structure are contained in the concept ego, and that an increasingly integrated sense of self evolves with ego development (Spruiell, 1981; P. Tyson, 1988).

Historically, this debate arose from efforts to understand the phenomena of narcissism in terms of structural theory (Hartmann, 1950); a major impetus was the need to treat patients suffering from what is currently described as severe narcissistic disturbances and problems of borderline personality organization. Freud's (1914) seminal statement on narcissism had left him deeply dissatisfied ("I do not like it particularly, but it is the best I can do at the moment" [Abraham and Freud, 1965, p. 167]; "I have a strong feeling of its serious inadequacy" [pp. 170–171]). His dissatisfaction seems to have been based on the fact that there were two levels of abstraction in his use of the term; one was an underlying metapsychological concern with the energic investment of the self, and the other referred to an array of psychological phenomena and behaviors. Pulver points out that the power of the psychoanalytic concept of narcissism was that it related a range of specific phenomena—sexual perversion as the primary source of sexual satisfaction, a stage of development, a type of object choice (that is, based on some aspect or wished-for aspect of the self), a way of relating to the environment, and aspects of self-esteem—to something more general, that is, the love of one's self. In other words, "the sensual love of one's self existed as an underlying motivation in certain behavior which was not overtly sensual" (1970, p. 321).

In the topographical theory of the time (as we discussed in chapter 5), Freud's term *das Ich,* translated as "ego," referred to the whole person in the sense of the experiential subjective sense of self rather than exclusively to a psychic system as it came to imply later. A link between the emphasis on narcissism and current psychoanalytic interest in the self was made by Hartmann's distinction between ego and self in his attempts to understand narcissistic pathology according to the structural model (1950). He clarified that Freud's referring to a narcissistic investment of the ego should be understood as an investment of the (experiential) self, not an investment of the (nonexperiential) ego as a system. This distinction led to a shift in focus from the ego of structural theory to the sense and eventually the structure of the self.

Despite semantic and conceptual difficulties, questions about the nature of the experiential sense of self remain vital. Various concepts of the self have been offered throughout the history of psychoanalytic thought. They played a central role in the theories of what has been called "the alternate schools" of psychoanalysis, including Adler, Jung, Horney, and Sullivan. The definitions of self employed by these various theoreticians have in common "the subjective, creative, experiencing aspects of the psyche" (Ticho, 1982). These subjective, experiencing aspects have attracted a great deal of recent research interest as attention has turned to observational studies of infants.

## ESSENTIAL ELEMENTS OF A SENSE OF SELF

Several schemes are available to conceptualize the emergence of the sense of self, each of which approaches the issue in a distinctive way. Lichtenberg, for example, says the development of a sense of self takes place in four periods. First, before self-differentiation, "islands of experience" form, and in a second era, more ordered groupings of self-images coalesce. Third, these bodily self-images (images of the self in relation to distinctly separate objects) and grandiose self-images gradually become integrated into a cohesive self, which in the fourth, and final phase of the development of self brings order and focus to mental life and is reflected in ego functioning (1975). Stern outlines four successively emerging "senses of self," each with an associated "domain" of interpersonal relatedness (1985). Mahler and McDevitt trace the emergence of a sense of identity and of self-constancy in relation to experiences in the mother-infant dyad and the separation-individuation process (1980; McDevitt and Mahler, 1980). Kohut focuses on the way in which selfobjects, through transmuting internalizations, crystallize into a nuclear self structure (1971, 1977). Kernberg also views the self as a structure; he describes in some detail five stages of the development of self structure involving steps in the integration of "good" and "bad" self- and object representations (1976).

We believe that the infant's formation of an integrated or coherent sense of self with a continuity over development is a long process that relies on and reflects synthesizing and integrating ego functions. Our focus, therefore, is on the experiential, subjective sense of self, not on the self as a structure. Accordingly, our account of the development of the sense of self is organized in terms of the gradual integration of various kinds of unconscious, preconscious, and conscious self-experiences and related self-representations. For heuristic purposes, we categorize these experiences in terms of bodily experiences, self-and-other experiences, and a spectrum of affective experiences.

*Bodily experiences* are at first associated with biological needs and state regulation. Activities such as sucking and sensations linked to them and to hunger, satiation, arousal, attentiveness, and sleep-wakefulness cycles form the most basic layer of self-experience. As the range of the infant's mental impressions about his body gradually expands, he begins to develop a primitive sense of his body's boundaries and a greater facility in manipulating it (eye-hand-mouth coordination, turning over, paddling away, and so on). Freud thought the emerging differentiation of body boundaries through a synthesis of various body experiences was the result of early ego functioning and indicated one of the early stages in the sense of self; hence he referred to a body ego.* Body image and concern about it remain central aspects of self-experience throughout life. Experiences of illness, medical or surgical intervention, body growth and change—all arouse a range of conscious and unconscious fantasies and anxieties about body issues that may play a central role in pathology. In addition, self-esteem is often partly dependent on whether or not the perceived body image conforms to a wished-for body image: "a person's own body, and above all its surface, is a place from which both external and internal perceptions may spring" (1923a, p. 25).

*Experiences of the self in relation to and as gradually differentiated from the object* also contribute to the subjective sense of self. From his early work on, Spitz emphasized that every infant can exist only in context with and in reciprocal relationship to a mother or caregiver. Winnicott's aphorism "there is no such thing as a baby" (1952) expresses this sentiment. Over thirty years ago Mahler began pioneer studies to determine the ways in which the infant's reciprocal interactions with the mother contribute to the emerging sense of self. This work has resulted in the concepts of "hatching" (Mahler and Gosliner, 1955), the "mutual cueing" dialogue and the infant's need for "refueling" (Mahler et al., 1975), "social referencing" and the sense of "we" (Emde, 1983), and intersubjective relatedness, or "a deliberately sought sharing of experiences about events and things" (Stern, 1985, p. 128). All these concepts attest to the importance of the affective ambience of mother-infant reciprocity for the infant's emerging sense of self. Current research has detailed the infant's elaborate preadaptations for participating in human interactions. Bodily experiences, therefore, soon come to be closely bound up with the activities of the caregiver— mother or other. It is through actual experiences of physical contact during the mother-child reciprocal interaction that the infant quickly learns that pleasure and safety are experienced in interaction with the mother. Through these experiences, body boundaries—that is, their mental representations—gradually become firmly established as the

*Perhaps a better translation would be "body-self," for Freud was clearly referring to a part of the self aspect of *das Ich,* not to the ego as a psychic structure.

infant builds a representation of himself, representations of his objects, and representations of himself in interaction with his objects. The patterns of interaction established during reciprocal exchanges contribute to a sense of continuity throughout development, as these patterns are reactivated in interpersonal contexts throughout life.

*Affectively meaningful experiences,* first pleasure and unpleasure and then discrete emotions that are gradually differentiated, add further dimension to the sense of self. Affective expressions are at the heart of interactional experiences and are central to body experiences. They guide caregiving—for example, the infant's cry signaling the mother that he needs attention. Through pleasurable and unpleasurable experiences the infant learns about his body and eventually learns to control the comings and goings of pleasant and unpleasant sensations. A range of such positive emotions as joy or interest slowly emerges from interpersonal interactions. These help create incentives for social interaction, exploration, and learning, and add to an emerging representation of an ideal state of affective well-being (Joffe and Sandler, 1967). This wished-for state initially depends on the presence of the object who is viewed as ideal. Wishes to maintain this ideal relationship gradually lead the child to internalize or to construct meaningful inner rules and standards as he becomes increasingly concerned about what is and is not approved of.

Eventually the affective ideal state comes to be dependent upon an internal ideal (the ego ideal, part of the superego). Then maintaining self-esteem depends upon superego functioning, because the level of self-esteem reflects the extent to which the self measures up to the ideal.

The importance of the affective aspects of self-experience has been emphasized by Spruiell (1975) and by Emde (1983, 1984) who describes a biologically based "affective core" or "affective self." This affective core provides continuity to experiences of ourselves over the course of development in spite of the many ways we change. It also enhances interpersonal interactions, for it "ensures that we are able to understand others who are human" (Emde, 1983, p. 180).

## THE DEVELOPMENT OF A SENSE OF SELF

### Earliest Beginnings

The question of the means by which the infant's sense of self and its mental representation become distinguished from his perception of the surrounding world has long preoccupied psychoanalysts. Hand-mouth coordination (Hoffer, 1949, 1950a, 1950b), visual perception (Spitz, 1957; Greenacre, 1960), changing states of internal tension (Freud, 1930), and social interaction (Mahler et al., 1975; Emde, 1983; Stern, 1985) have been variously held accountable. It is now abundantly clear that the infant possesses a remarkable degree of preadaptive potential for direct interaction with his mother, interaction that includes a perceptual, motor-affective dialogue. Even from birth, the infant's response to his mother is distinctive and shows attentiveness or stimulus seeking as well as a capacity for stimulus avoidance.

It should be kept in mind, however, that in the first few weeks most mother-infant interactions are linked to issues of physiological regulation (Sander 1962, 1964) or homeostasis (Greenspan, 1981), during which time there is a gradual shift in the infant from endogenous to exogenous functioning (Emde and Robinson, 1979). As part of this shift, greater psychological functioning becomes evident with the appearance of the social smile. Greater individual differences soon become apparent, differences that, in association with different responses by individual mothers, lend an increased affective coloring to various mother-infant interactions. The interaction between the infant's equipment and early experience leads, after a few weeks, to the emergence of what Weil calls a "basic core" of fundamental trends in the mother-infant dialogue (1976). This basic core places each infant within a wide range of developmental possibilities, ranging from harmony to imbalance. It is also within this basic core that the instinctual drives become orchestrated with emerging object relations.

*Beginnings of a Dialogue and Building a Core Sense of Self*

Early in life the infant's bodily experiences, self-other experiences, and affective experiences are mostly in the context of the mother-infant dialogue. By two or three months, the range of interactions with the mother extends beyond feeding experiences. Affectively meaningful mother-infant playful exchanges, which include not only visual but also tactile and kinesthetic bodily experiences, provide the context in which the infant begins to build some basic sense of himself and some sense of the other as distinct, continuous, and separate. We can thus infer that from the basic core of the mother-infant interaction, the infant builds what Stern (1985) refers to as a "core self" and a "core other," or what Emde (1983) calls the "affective core," emphasizing the affective aspects of the interaction.

Increasingly the infant participates in the interaction with the mother as a full partner and plays an important role in regulating the level of excitation. Stern (1974b, 1985) describes how the infant, using gaze aversion, cuts out stimulation that has risen above the optimal range, and with gaze and facial behavior, seeks out stimulation when excitation is minimal. Call (1980) emphasizes that ordinarily a wide variety of intermodal reciprocal activities involving the visual, sensorimotor, auditory, and kinesthetic modes of interaction is seen as infant and mother communicate.

A striking example of the infant's interaction potential—or perhaps *need* would be more accurate—is provided by the "visual violation" experiments of Tronick et al. (1978) that offer an unusual interface with the origins of normality and psychopathology. Two video cameras with a split-image display follow the movements of both mother and baby who face each other. The mother is asked to look above the infant's head instead of into his eyes and to keep her face and body as immobile as possible while doing so (so as to violate the normal expectation of interaction). The results are dramatic. First the infant tries to recapture the mother's gaze visually by looking around corners, moving his eyes from side to side, moving his head back and forward, in clear attempts to reestablish visual interaction. Before long the infant becomes distressed and reaches out for contact with the mother using his arms, legs, and body, as well as leaning forward with his head. Finally the infant gives up, his posture collapses, and he withdraws. This is soon followed by renewed attempts to contact the nonreciprocating, blank-faced, distant mother. Following the experiment the mother reengages herself with her infant, and very shortly they are able to regain their communication.

Winnicott describes the vital "mirroring" role played by the mother in the early stages of emotional development. He asks, "What does the baby see when he or she looks at the mother's face?" "Ordinarily," he suggests, "what the baby sees is himself or herself" (1967, p. 112). This is Winnicott's way of saying that the mother's pride and joy in her baby will be reflected in her face and that the infant's experiencing of this reflection forms the basis of his feelings of well-being and safety. This crucial contribution of the caretaker has been stressed by Kohut (1971, 1977), who emphasizes that the infant's survival requires a specific psychological environment—the presence of responsive, empathic selfobjects who are proud of the child and, by reflecting this pride back, confirm his innate sense of vigor and vitality.

Tronick's experiments vividly demonstrate how the infant depends on and needs appropriate reciprocity. The infant's response to the mother's brief failure to mirror allows inferences to be drawn about the effects on an infant's development of a mother's depression or her inability to interact with her baby (Tronick et al., 1977, 1978). It is a mistake, however, to assume that all later pathology is a reflection of a real failure of the mother during this period, as Winnicott and Kohut suggest. Indeed, Tronick's experiments also show the infant's resilience within the experimental setting. We certainly cannot ignore the sensitive dependence of the child's development on early circumstances, but such work as Tronick's helps us to avoid the tendency to blame mothers without considering the full range of factors involved in the developmental process.

### A Body Self or Primitive Self-Feeling

By about seven to nine months of age the infant's behavior suggests that the range of impressions about the body is expanding. The baby appears to recognize his feet and can easily find his thumb. From the original physiological sensations from which fragmentary images of body parts in states of need or excitation arise, the infant appears to put together, via more stress-free experiences, a crude yet more durable and coherent body schema. Although there is disagreement as to the ways in which the infant experiences self and other in the first few months of life (for example, Stern, 1985, p. 101; Lichtenberg, 1987), by the second half of the first year what Mahler and McDevitt (1968) call a primitive "self-feeling" with a primarily pleasurable feeling tone seems to be available.

The affective quality of the mother-infant interaction makes an important contribution to this pleasurable feeling tone. When the mother, in mutual cueing or social referencing interchanges, reflects back to the practicing infant a sense of safety, as well as her delight in his exploratory activities, this provides a foundation on which the infant can build a sense of self-confidence and self-love. Not only is the quality of their interaction reflected later in the reciprocal quality of interpersonal interactions, but A.-M. Sandler suggests that the seeds of object constancy and self-constancy are sown during this time through the mutual cueing dialogue. Experiences of repeated scanning of the constant libidinal object who interacts with the infant, even at a distance, to provide him with a sense of security and feeling of mastery lead eventually to a sense of object constancy. "However, with self-object differentiation, . . . another constant object, an object with an equally enduring identity, also emerges for the child. This is the child's own self" (1977, p. 199).

## *A Sense of Self as Objective and Mentally Represented*

By about fifteen to eighteen months several developmental advances are evident to justify the conclusion that toddlers can by now conceive of and refer to themselves as objective entities separate from their own immediate actions and the actions of others and that a mentally represented sense of self has emerged. Behavioral evidence for this assumption is provided by the toddler's realization that it is his own reflection he sees in the mirror (Amsterdam, 1972; Schulman and Kaplowitz, 1977; Lewis and Brooks-Gunn, 1979; Emde, 1983). Also, as the capacity for symbolic play and the use of language emerges, self-descriptive expressions appear.

Toddlers now not only can conceive of themselves as objective entities but can also evoke representations of objects or events that are not present, and they can think about these representations. This objective sense of self with an emergent capacity for self-awareness and self-reflection brings what Greenacre referred to as a "stable core of identity" (1953a, 1958). This sense of identity, or "core identity," should be distinguished from Stern's "core self" that he says emerges with the ability to make simple perceptual comparisons of self and other. The capacity for self-awareness and self-reflection heralds broadening horizons interpersonally and intrapsychically. Upright locomotion, anal-phase psychosexual development, and differentiation of the self as male or female with "core gender identity" (Stoller, 1968a) add breadth and depth to the self-representation. Emerging verbal skills and a capacity to reflect upon the intentions and will of the object as separate and different from the toddler's own desires arouse conflict, at first developmental and potentially intrapsychic. In addition, memory and fantasy combine, and for the first time the toddler can entertain and maintain a wish of how reality ought to be (Stern, 1985). Interpersonal interaction now includes past memories, present realities, and increasingly, some ideas of a future. These several currents combine to inaugurate the rapprochement subphase of separation-individuation (Mahler et al., 1975), a phase crucial to the emerging sense of self.

Just as the toddler becomes increasingly aware of his wishes for independence for autonomy, as well as his wish for pleasurable ongoing interpersonal interactions, he also becomes aware of his mother's increasing demands for compliance. This means relinquishing a degree of instinctual gratification as well as a degree of grandiosity in exchange for cooperation. Angry at enforced restrictions, the toddler becomes aware of his vulnerability and his dependence on his mother's continued love and support. Feelings of rage arouse the toddler's fears of the loss of mother's love, and intensely ambivalent feelings challenge his capacities to integrate the range of pleasurable, or "good," and unpleasurable, or "bad," images of the self. The toddler's ultimate ability to meet the challenge to some extent depends on the parents' ability to empathically yet effectively enforce prohibitions, restrictions, and minimal standards. By watching the mother's or father's affective expressions, the toddler determines what is and what is not approved behavior. His cooperation ensures that the sense of togetherness will be maintained as he comes to internalize the rules of the relationship as part of early superego formation; his lack of cooperation guarantees interpersonal turmoil and lonely isolation.

### Libidinal Self-Constancy

With increasing success at controlling bodily urges and complying with parental standards, the child learns more appropriate ways of expressing independence and autonomy without sacrificing interpersonal ties. He also begins to develop a self-representation within which the different affectively toned images of the self are integrated. Consequently, he can maintain self-love, and his overall feeling about himself remains basically positive in spite of occasional outbursts of anger or frustration, which may bring self-criticism and unpleasurable reflections about himself as superego functioning becomes evident. In this way, self-esteem can be maintained and a libidinal self-constancy is established parallel to libidinal object constancy.

Self-constancy does not imply a consistent and rarely changing view of one's self as this overview might suggest. Rather, it is a total gestalt that optimally has a basically positive organizational background within which there is a wide array of specific conscious and unconscious self-images, any one of which may push forward as the organizing focus at any given time (Eisnitz, 1980). "Libidinal refueling" from the constant object is needed on occasion in order to maintain an integrated, essentially positive sense of self (R. L. Tyson, 1983). Such refueling is also ultimately derived in part from the loving superego, as one lives up to internalized ideals and standards.

With the establishment of libidinal self and object constancy, a durable, stable, and mostly positively regarded sense of one's self as differentiated from and separate from others has been established. This sense of self is experienced as an active agent capable of giving impetus and direction to the child's expanding psychic functioning.

### An Integrated Identity and Self-Responsibility

The sense of self takes on wider dimensions during the infantile genital phase. Genital sexuality with its sense of urgency brings an entirely new sense of the body into awareness; mastery of infantile sexual urges, acquired gradually over the course of early childhood, involves taking ownership of and responsibility for the body. It is in relation to the new urgency of genital sexuality that core gender identity becomes solidly consolidated, as sexuality and a sense of separate and unique identity come to be combined. The child now forms durable identifications with the parent of the same sex, and the sexually differentiated and narcissistically valued body image that ideally results serves as a positive source of self-esteem. Gender identity adds to the child's core of identity a sense not only of "who" he is but of "what" he is (Beres, 1981). This provides a basis for engagement in the Oedipus complex.

The many systems of development we discuss throughout this book converge with the formation of the Oedipus complex. The synthesizing functioning of the ego in integrating the multitude of resulting interacting conscious and unconscious thoughts, wishes, fantasies, conflicts, anxieties, defenses, and resolutions, together with the identifications made with both parents during the course of elaborating and trying to resolve the Oedipus complex, lead to an integrated sense of identity not present earlier.

Loewald believes that the Oedipus complex, with all the complications the concept carries, is a watershed in individuation: "The Oedipus complex, with its basis in instinctual life, stands as a symbol in psychoanalytic psychology of the first delineation of man's love . . . a symbol of the clear awakening of his life as an individual. It takes form through his passionate involvement, in love and hate, with his first libidinal objects, and through the limitations placed on this involvement which throw him back on himself" (1985, p. 442). Loewald calls this process "soul making."

The extremes of love and hate and the loyalty conflicts of the Oedipus complex mark a crossroads in psychic development. One possible outcome is for the child to continue in a hopeless narcissistic quest for perfection (Rothstein, 1980), striving to confirm his omnipotence. Then, attempting to manipulate the environment, he insists on his entitlement. When his wishes (oedipal or preoedipal) are not granted, he maintains the angry sense of being cheated, insisting his parents are unfair and "mean." Another outcome is for the child to struggle to identify with the values and morals of the parent. In this case the superego becomes established as an inner voice of authority, and although conflict and turmoil may persist, it is internal, giving the child the potential for a new sense of autonomy and independent functioning. With internalization of oedipal conflict, resolution or relinquishment of oedipal goals, and superego consolidation, the superego plays an increasing role in the sense of self and of identity. That is, because of its functioning in self-evaluation, judgment, and reward or punishment, a sense of self-responsibility begins to appear.

The expanding social life during latency makes additional contributions to the sense of self. In particular the sense of self-responsibility becomes even firmer as the superego becomes more fully internalized and autonomous. Now the child optimally begins to admit, at least at times, to being at fault. Vicissitudes in self-esteem are also a poignant aspect of latency, as elation or sadness and loneliness ensue when the child is included or excluded by a favorite friend or group.

### Adolescence and Identity Stability

Biological changes, shifting moods, different familial and social relations, and new responsibilities during adolescence further elaborate the sense of self. These elements sometimes bring with them a potential for what Erikson calls an "identity crisis" (1956). But the successful completion of the adolescent process, which we describe further in several chapters of this book, involves experiences in relation to bodily changes, affective experiences, and experiences in social relatedness. They all enable the adolescent to come to a fully integrated sense of self, with a stable sense of identity.

## SUMMARY

We have described the formation of the sense of self, indicating that we view this evolution as involving body experiences, experiences in relation to objects, and affectively meaningful experiences. There are many changes in the body and in body image throughout development. There are also many vicissitudes in object relations, as we discussed in the previous chapter. Affective experiences in relation to the body, to objects, and to the sense of self and self-esteem also shift and change throughout development. There is, however, an impressive continuity of the sense of self through it all.

# PART FOUR

## AFFECT

# CHAPTER 8

## A PSYCHOANALYTIC

## PERSPECTIVE ON

## AFFECT THEORY

Affects are central to our psychic lives and to our interpersonal worlds, and so questions about the nature and functioning of affects in psychic life have been part of psychoanalytic theory from the beginning. For Freud, anxiety seemed to be the most pressing of affects because it was the most prominent of his patients' difficulties. He was, of course, aware that other affects existed, to which, he said, his ideas could be applied equally well (1895b, 1896). In his early thinking he equated affects with psychic energy as the source of motivation (1894). Later he thought of affects as manifestations of the unconscious drives (1915b, p. 152). Still later he thought that they could come to serve as protective signals, acting in tandem with defenses, and that therefore they were ego functions (1926a). More recently affects have been described as conflict-free ego functions (Emde, 1980a, 1980b) and as prime movers, the motivational system that underlies drive structuralization (Loewald, 1978; Kernberg, 1982).

Theories about affects are confused and confusing since each writer tries to define the relevant concepts and phenomena (some more explicit than others), and each set of definitions is different. In addition, the terms *affects, emotions,* and *feelings* are often used interchangeably, which further blurs the concept of affects.

We define *affects* as mental structures having motivational, somatic, expressive, communicative, and emotional or feeling components, as well as an associated idea or cognitive component (see Compton, 1980; Knapp, 1987). We prefer to reserve *feelings* or *emotions* for the experiential or behavioral aspect of affects—that is, for one portion of what we see as a composite structure.

Knapp's exemplary reviews of affect theory in psychology, neuropsychology, and psychoanalysis are benchmarks in orientation to and clarification of these issues (1981, 1987). Summarizing characteristic features of affective experiences and behaviors, he notes that affects are experienced with vividness and immediacy and are felt to have an imperious or urgent quality. They are also experienced in a quantitative range from faint traces to massive and intense reactions; more than one may appear at a time; they tend to persist and to be linked with accompanying bodily or visceral processes; and they seem to have relatively stereotyped expressive patterns. That affects have such a striking array of characteristics raises fundamental neurophysiological and psychosomatic issues.

## HISTORY AND DIRECTIONS OF AFFECT RESEARCH

As Tomkins (1981) points out, the long history of the study of emotions begins with Aristotle and subsequent philosophers theorizing for over two thousand years about the nature of primary emotions and "passions." Next came the biologists, with Darwin's (1872) classic statement of the evolutionary significance of the expression of the emotions, establishing that human beings and their closest zoological relatives use the same configurations of specialized muscular movements for the facial expression of basic emotions. Biologists, particularly ethologists, have continued this research. Psychologists have also developed an extensive literature on the topic. The turn-of-the-century James-Lange theory of emotions might be considered a foundation for the contemporary theories of academic psychology. According to this theory, emotional experience results from the conscious perception of various bodily changes, so that these changes are the cause of the emotion, not the outcome and not one of its concomitants (Eysenck et al., 1972, p. 572).

Darwin's ideas of the evolutionary significance of expressive manifestations of emotion became the basis for what is by now a large body of research studying the *expression* of affect. The theories and studies of Tomkins (1962, 1963), who revived Darwin's thesis, have come to have wide appeal; Tomkins was the first to devise a reliable method of identifying and classifying affect on the basis of facial expression. He identified nine discrete categories: interest-excitement, enjoyment-joy, surprise-startle, distress-anguish, fear-terror, anger-rage, shame-humiliation, contempt, and disgust. Tomkins (1970, 1978) insisted that affect is primarily facial and skin behavior, and that biologically based inherited programs anchored in the central nervous system control facial muscle responses as well as autonomic visceral and motoric responses. These programs are triggered by different rates of neural firing (1981). Tomkins inspired others, particularly Carroll Izard (1971, 1972) and Paul Ekman (1984; Ekman and Friesen, 1975), to conduct empirical studies of the universality of facial manifestations of discrete categories of emotion. Cross-cultural research with large numbers of subjects has demonstrated that specific facial expressions are correlated for the expression of happiness, surprise, distress, fear, anger, sadness, and disgust across cultures and even between species. There is some evidence for similar correlations in infancy (Demos, 1982).

For the psychoanalyst, however, an individual's expression of a particular emotion does not tell the observer what that particular emotion means to that person. Expressive behavior is often assumed to have a communicative intent, but it is frequently overlooked that feelings influence perception and thought; therefore the emotion and the associated idea aroused in the observer may lead him to attribute to the other a meaning that was not intended, a situation that often enough leads to misunderstanding.

Recent research in the neurosciences, reviewed by Schwartz (1987), indicates that affects and their action sequelae have distinct neurophysiological bases. It can be said that affects require anatomically identifiable neural circuits; that the perceptible, felt accompaniments of affects are linked to neurophysiological activation of parts of the brain, including the hypothalamus, limbic system, midbrain, and pons; and that associated facial, postural, vocal, visceral, and action patterns are affect-linked and subcortically integrated patterns of motor response. Schwartz, attempting to make bridges between the neurosciences and psychoanalysis, suggests that these patterns come to have psychological meaning to the individual through various learning processes.

The cognitive assessment perspective of affects also has been an active area of research. Lazarus, Kanner, and Folkman, for example, assert that emotion is "a product of cognitive activity" which leads both to action impulses and to patterned somatic responses (1980, p. 212). Mandler maintains that emotional expression is the result of a cognitive assessment of the world and internal states (1980, p. 229). The problem we see with most cognitive studies of affect, however, is that they do not consider unconscious affect. In an effort to accommodate the presence and importance of unconscious mentation, Rosenblatt (1985) takes a system-theory approach and views affect as the subjective experience of feedback-appraisal processes operating as part of numerous motivational systems.

Linguistic investigators have scrutinized the ways in which affects shape and are shaped and conveyed by words. Shapiro (1979) helpfully describes how affects are encoded in speech and decoded by the listener; the "emotional music" of speech, or its absence, has been the focus of other work (Deese, 1973; Sifneos, 1974; Edelson, 1975). Schafer suggests that the clinician concentrate on the active intent behind passive metaphors. This leads him to the position that affects are essentially adverbial, for example, someone is speaking angrily (1976, p. 169); that emotions cannot be experienced (p. 301); and that emotions in preverbal infants exist simply on the basis of their actions and facial expressions (pp. 354–356). (This is reminiscent of Tomkins's views discussed above.)

The scaffolding for a psychoanalytic theory of affect is provided by investigations of emotional expression and of the associated neuroendocrine, peripheral, and central nervous system processes, and by studies dealing with the cognitive, behavioral, and linguistic dimensions of affects. Again, Knapp (1987) has reviewed these complementary approaches. The scaffolding, however, does not tell us about the intrapsychic dimension of affect that lies behind the moving facial muscles and the firing neurons. In our view, the intrapsychic meaning and experience of affect do not exist as a consequence of the facial muscles or the firing neurons; they are another dimension, and that psychoanalytic dimension is our focus.

As a background, we first examine Freud's contribution to the understanding of affect. Although his writings on affect were primarily concerned with anxiety, we believe that his latest (1926) ideas on the subject can be generalized to other affects. Given Freud's background and interests, it is not surprising that philosophical, psychological, and biological currents would find expression in his work. After discussing Freud's ideas, we consider the relationships between affect and drives, affects and objects, and affects and the ego.

## FREUD'S THEORY OF AFFECTS

In Freud's earliest theory of affect, an event in the external world stirs up an affective response in the person that for various reasons—

such as a connection to a related incompatible idea—cannot be expressed. He then tries to suppress or forget it; but in so doing, he does not get rid of (or "discharge") the motivationally powerful "quota of affect" (or "sum of excitation") that was attached to the affect and related ideas, and various symptoms result. Treatment based on this theory consists of recovering in consciousness the event or related, fended-off idea with its associated feeling, bringing about a discharge or catharsis of the feeling and a disappearance of the symptoms. Psychotherapy, or the "talking cure," provides an alternative to the action impelled by the feeling (1894, 1895a, 1895b).

In this "hydraulic model," the greater the repression, the more intense or powerful the affect. Because the external event is regarded as the inciting agent, inducing a psychically traumatic situation that overwhelms the person with unmanageable excitation (or feeling), this theory has come to be known as the "affect-trauma" model (Rapaport, 1953; Sandler, Dare, and Holder, 1972).

In topographical theory, developed over a period of twenty-five years, Freud still linked affect, energy, and motivation, though in a more complex way. He defined the instinctual drive as a mental representative of a biological force, so the instigating event arises internally rather than being of external origin. The drive provides a constantly present motivational force (1915a, pp. 118–119); its accumulating energy causes unpleasurable feelings, particularly anxiety, whereas a variety of emotions, chiefly pleasurable, results from processes of discharge (1915c, p. 178). Freud added that emotions are associated with ideas or thoughts, so that by recognizing our feelings, we can "know" what is going on in the depths of our minds and can identify the needs striving for gratification (1915c, p. 177).

That feelings and ideas are linked remains central to the psychoanalytic theory of affects (Brenner, 1974). They are frequently separated for study, and although such separation is probably an unavoidable artifact of the way the concepts are defined, certain problems derive from it. For example, affects are identified almost exclusively by the nature of the conscious feelings we experience, and the role of unconscious fantasy is underestimated in that experience (Arlow, 1977).

The topographical theory was helpful in understanding many clinical situations, but as Freud's experience grew he found it more and more difficult to conceptualize affects—particularly in regard to the feelings of anxiety and guilt—as based on a buildup of drive energy. These difficulties contributed to his formulating a new structural theory of the mind in which the major divisions were based on mental functioning rather than conscious or unconscious states of awareness (1923a).

Following this, Freud (1926) gave up the quest to find the source of affects and considered instead their influence on psychic functioning. He devised a theory with two important aspects relevant to affects. First, he proposed that affects (although he discussed mostly anxiety, he suggested that the theory was generalizable to other affects) can have a traumatic influence on ego functioning. In something of a holdover from the affect-trauma theory, he proposed that excessive excitation, whether from real environmental situations (such as a sexual seduction or physical abuse) or from instinctual sources, arouses anxiety of such an intensity that the ego's organizing, synthesizing, and defensive functions are overwhelmed, rendering it helpless. Freud thought that such traumatic situations are particularly characteristic of, though not limited to, infancy and early childhood when the relatively immature and weak ego is easily overwhelmed.

Second, Freud proposed that affects can facilitate adaptation by signaling danger. Since anxiety is the original reaction to helplessness, it can be reproduced later as a reaction to the perception of a potentially dangerous situation: "Anxiety is therefore on the one hand an expectation of a trauma, and on the other a repetition of it in a mitigated form" (1926, p. 166). He noted, however, that "the ego, which experienced the trauma passively, now repeats it actively in a weakened version, in the hope of being able itself to direct its course" (p. 167). And so, when the person perceives some inner danger (intrapsychic conflict between drive and prohibition) or outer threat, the feeling of anxiety appears, linked to the idea, image, or fantasy of the threatening situation. By utilizing the perception of the affect to evoke defenses appropriate to the danger situation, helplessness can be avoided and the feeling intensity can be kept to a minimum; then it does not become disorganizing to ego functioning. In this way affects can be viewed as having an organizing, adaptive, and motivating influence, part of an ego response to avoid repeating the trauma by anticipating danger. "The individual," he wrote, "will have made an important advance in his capacity for self-preservation if he can foresee and expect a traumatic situation of this kind which entails helplessness, instead of simply waiting for it to happen" (p. 166).

Freud conjectured that ego maturation brought with it improved abilities to anticipate what Rangell termed the "helpless, overwhelmed, traumatic state" (1968, p. 391) by means of progressively better utilization of affects as signals. Danger is here viewed as being either external, resulting in "physical helplessness if the danger is real," or internal, as from conflict, resulting in "psychical helplessness if it is instinctual" (Freud, 1926, p. 166). Consequently, we can say that after achieving the degree of maturation and development that permits the signal function to operate, drives are not proximal motivators, but affects are.

Freud added an important link between the two forms of anxiety: "When the infant has found out by experience that an external, perceptible object can put an end to the dangerous situation . . . the content of the danger it fears is displaced from the economic situation [painful helplessness] on to the condition which determined that situation, viz., the loss of object" (1926, pp. 137–138). Now the anxiety experienced in reaction to the danger is experienced when a situation likely to bring a repeat of the danger is expected. He thought that each stage in psychosexual development contains potential dangers, and so he proposed a sequence of situations with related fantasies and anxieties that correlated with psychosexual development—fear of loss of the object and of the object's love, fear of castration, and fear of superego punishment (guilt).*

Freud's signal theory of affect made clear that from very early in life, the infant's unpleasurable distress and pleasurable sensations quickly become object-related as well as associated with drive frustration or gratification. In addition to its significance for object relations theory, the signal theory soon led to greater recognition of the importance of early infantile experience for later healthy personality functioning.

## CURRENT PSYCHOANALYTIC UNDERSTANDING OF AFFECT

Freud's final model did not resolve all problems with the theory of affect, and the ambiguities are reflected in the subsequent psychoanalytic theorizing on the subject. Confusion remained about whether affects are best seen as drive-discharge phenomena, as Freud's earlier theory suggests, or as ego functions, as in the signal theory. Nor was it clear whether affects other than anxiety could serve the signal function. Over the years theorists have devoted much attention to these two

---

*Nowadays we recognize that at least the first three of these danger situations can be anticipated shortly after the toddler has the capacity for fantasy formation and that they characteristically arise in association with the developmental conflicts of the second year as well as later. The correlation with psychosexual stages is therefore no longer especially helpful.

questions. For example, even though Jones (1929) assumed that the signal theory applied to a variety of feelings and wrote about fear, guilt, and hate, and Fenichel (1941) described how rage, anxiety, excitement, disgust, and shame all come to be "tamed" and used as signals by maturing ego functioning, it was not until the 1950s, with the work of Rapaport (1953) and Jacobson (1953), that the signal theory was accepted as relevant to other feelings. Jacobson even thought the signal function might apply to positive feelings such as elation, although Schur (1969) believed there are conceptual difficulties with the concept of signal pleasure.

Freud (1926) does make it clear that affects and drives are related. He also is definite that affects are related to ego functioning, and that affects must be viewed in conjunction with object relations as well. Contemporary psychoanalytic theories deal with affects mostly in relation to one or more of these subjects.

## Affects and Drives

Freud maintained throughout his writing that affects and drives are closely linked in a variety of ways. For example, in his last formulation of the subject (1926), affects and drives are related in both aspects of the theory. In the signal theory, affect signals danger. The internal danger is a conflict between a sexual or aggressive impulse seeking gratification and an ego or superego prohibition. In the trauma aspect of the theory, overwhelming stimuli early in life can originate either from external sources or from sexual and aggressive impulses, but in either case they can arouse an intensity of feeling that disrupts ego functioning. Similarly, in panic attacks at any time of life, ego controls may fail and the feelings become overwhelming (see Fenichel, 1945).

This discharge version of affect, in which the internal source of affects derives solely from drive activity, has been sharply criticized, particularly by those who believe that the concept of psychic energy is untenable (see Rosenblatt and Thickstun, 1977; Rosenblatt, 1985). An early criticism came from Jacobson (1953), who observed that ego functioning as well as direct instinctual gratifications such as eating and sexual intercourse are often accompanied by the expression of intense feelings. She made the important point that while orgastic experiences include various levels of tension, the feeling corresponds neither to the tension nor to its discharge but rather to the change in tension. This is consistent with Freud's position that pleasure and unpleasure do not relate to variations in quantity or intensity but to something qualitative, perhaps a rhythm or temporal sequence of changes (1924b, p. 160).

Jacobson thus emphasized that a drive-discharge theory of affect generation is insufficient. Her comments, however, appear limited to conscious feelings and raise further questions about connections between drive theory and the pleasure-pain principle (Rapaport, 1953). We believe her ideas make it clear that a comprehensive psychoanalytic theory of affects must account for the full spectrum of affects, for the circumstances in which they appear, and for the mechanisms by which they are brought about (see Rosenblatt, 1985, for a similar view).

Disagreement remains over whether indications of pleasure and unpleasure should be viewed as the earliest evidence of drive activity as Freud assumed (for example, 1905a, 1923a; see Brenner, 1982) or as early affective expressions (see Emde et al., 1976). There is no question that drive and affects are related, and the probability is that increasing knowledge of very early development will reveal important connections between them. For example, Weil (1978) has pointed out that excessive frustration of oral stimulation or substantial delays in satisfaction of hunger undermine primitive ego synthesizing processes, lead to early and exaggerated expressions of aggression, and set the stage for anxiety readiness, with anxiety and rage primitively intertwined. Thus extremes of the intensity of drive-related, very early experience can significantly influence the emergence of particular affects and their control.

Viewing affects and drives as interrelated also makes it possible to consider sources of early motivation other than drives. Several writers suggest that a variety of motivational systems are apparent very early in infancy and that these become hierarchically organized as development proceeds (for example, Gaensbauer, 1982; Stern, 1985; Lichtenberg, 1989). Indeed, as we mentioned in discussing psychosexual development, it has been suggested that the affective ambience of mother-infant interactions contributes to the structuralization of the drives and the id as a psychic system. Loewald (1971, 1978), for example, thinks the infant's amorphous urges and reflex activities become coordinated and organized into drives, and acquire aim and direction in so doing because they become associated with environmental responses that reduce tension and engender pleasure. The form taken by the libidinal drive thus represents the result of a "creative" process emerging from biological preadaptations and mother-infant affective reciprocity (see also Kernberg, 1976; Gaensbauer, 1982; P. Tyson, 1988).

Schwartz (1987), as we mentioned earlier, has sought to integrate the neurosciences, learning theory, and psychoanalysis. In his opinion, learning processes combine with affects so that later, as the infant matures, he learns to distinguish oral, eliminative, and genital sources of sensory stimuli and learns to manipulate his body to bring about pleasurable and eliminate unpleasurable sensations. Memories of sensations associated with zonal maturation and stimuli contribute to the behavior on which Freud (1905b) based his psychosexual theory of libidinal development.

Other writers emphasize that the aggressive drive, like the libidinal drive, derives its form from biologically predetermined, stereotyped affectomotor responses to danger in interaction with a mother's angry, frustrating, depriving, sadistic, or abusive behavior (see Greenacre, 1960; Galenson, 1986; Stechler and Halton, 1987). Accepting this view, we conclude that the structuralization of both sexual and aggressive drives can be understood as products of the interaction of innate underpinnings, early affective experience and expression, and environmental response. Furthermore, the affective tone of environmental responses to infant expressions of pleasure or distress and unpleasure makes an ongoing contribution to the organization of libidinal as well as aggressive drives.

The infant's sucking behavior provides an example. Oral mucous membrane stimulation by thumb sucking is often present in utero. Sucking itself is an innate reflex, but we have no evidence that sucking has psychological meaning for the neonate. Sucking and feeding experiences, however, provide the context for many of the earliest interactions in which mother-infant reciprocity is established. As it acquires psychological meaning, sucking is therefore associated with pleasurable oral stimulation, hunger satiation, and pleasurable experiences with the mother. The biological underpinnings, the object, and the affective components can be viewed as contributing to the process by which pleasurable sucking becomes structuralized as a component of the oral drive.

The combination of these factors was established by the researches of Spitz (1945, 1946a, 1946b) and Dowling (1977), which we described in chapter 4. Spitz's babies were fed and given every opportunity to suck, but they were deprived of mother-infant reciprocity; Dowling's babies had the advantage of some of the affective ambience of mother-infant reciprocity, but they were deprived of the oral stimulation and gratification of sucking. Both populations showed profound deficiencies in drive expression and ego functioning. Only when the pleasurable affective climate associated with mother-infant reciprocity and gratification of sensory stimuli were combined soon enough did the babies survive and thrive in all realms of psychological and physical development.

These observations emphasize that, though the biological underpinnings of the instinctual drives and the id as a psychic structure are present at birth, the id, like the ego, is not yet differentiated (Hartmann, Kris, and Lowenstein, 1946). The evidence suggests, in contradiction of Freud's early theory, that instinctual drives become differentiated and acquire psychological meaning through the mother-infant affective dialogue. It is the affective interaction that plays the crucial role in the differentiation, integration, and consolidation of those phenomena that eventually come to be classified as manifestations of a libidinal or aggressive drive.

### Affects and the Ego

Since Freud's idea that affects could serve ego functions, a major emphasis in psychoanalytic thinking and, more recently, in developmental research has been given to the delineation and elaboration of the role of affects in the development and functioning of the ego. Spitz, for example, observed that the coupling of various functions within the ego system as it becomes increasingly organized and capable of organizing behavior was accompanied by a new affective expression. This expression then introduced dramatic changes in interpersonal interaction and led to new adaptive behaviors, following which there seemed to be a developmental consolidation of the new organization. He thought these affects—the social smile, distress at eight months, and negativism—could be used as indicators of progressive levels of ego development.

The role of affects leading to psychic trauma and the undermining of ego development has also been intensively studied (Spitz, 1945, 1946a, 1946b, 1950, 1964; A. Freud, 1951, 1967; Greenacre, 1952b, 1967; Rangell, 1968; Weil, 1978; Ritvo, 1981). These authors describe various noxious results that arise from traumatic situations, traumatic situations being "any conditions which seem definitely unfavorable, noxious, or drastically injurious to the development of the young child" (Greenacre, 1976, p. 128). More recently, Shengold (1989) has responded to the growing cry to understand more about the traumatic effects of child abuse and deprivation. He notes that deliberate, repetitive, and chronic tortuous overstimulation, alternating with emotional deprivation, at a time when a child is totally dependent on the adult environment, elicits a terrifying combination of helplessness and rage. To survive, the child must suppress these feelings and deaden his emotions. One woman described her adaptation: the people in her dreams had no faces! The effect of the overwhelming trauma, Shengold declares, is "soul murder."

Anna Freud wrote that since the tolerance for the influx of upsetting environmental stimuli and for sensations of unpleasure through frustration, deprivation, or terrifying overstimulation increases with maturation and ego development, the individual is most vulnerable in infancy and early childhood (1967; see also Rangell, 1968). Should the mother-infant relationship be fraught with disturbance, the infant is subjected to the effect of long-lasting situations that, in contrast to "shock trauma," result in what Kris called "strain trauma" (1965, p. 324). Another variety of disturbance results from repetitive, diverse failures of the mother over time to protect or shield the infant or young child. Khan referred to these as "cumulative trauma" (1963). Both strain trauma and cumulative trauma may undermine the structuralization of ego-synthesizing functions.

Freud's concept of signal affect represented a different aspect of ego development and led to a major step in understanding the problem of adaptation. The relatively low intensity of anxiety that functions to signal danger, internal or external, means that instead of being overwhelmed by feelings, we are better able actively to control and regulate our circumstances and our response.

The signal function requires a cognitive appraisal—we must be able to identify and acknowledge the affect before it reaches overwhelming proportions. We must also identify, consciously or unconsciously, the underlying conflict and danger. Memory and fantasy then make anticipation possible (Noy, 1982). For example, a child may anticipate in conscious or unconscious fantasy the consequences of satisfying various conflicting wishes that are seeking gratification; the consequences may include helplessness, object loss, loss of love, guilt, castration, or other catastrophic events. The child then has the choice of allowing gratification of one or another wish, blocking its expression entirely, modifying its form by various defenses or compromise formations, or otherwise adapting behavior according to the assessment of danger. The choice he makes depends on his capacity to tolerate frustration and delay gratification. If he has sufficient capacity, the child responds with defense and compromise, forestalling an increase in the intensity of emotion and restricting it to manageable proportions. Therefore, a degree of ego maturity and strength is implied by the child's ability to use a small sampling of his own affects as signals for behavioral modification, thereby limiting the feelings to a minimal intensity.

Consider two examples. Susie, age four, plays mother and baby; the baby is bad, so the mother kills her. The next day Susie is less able to displace in fantasy her hate and death wishes toward her mother. The impulses are projected, experienced in relation to the analyst as a transference figure, and the anxiety associated with the conflict overwhelms her capacity for control. She runs into the analyst's room, terror written across her face, shouting "Don't you touch me, you mean, horrible, naughty little girl!" Becoming provocative, she picks up a pair of scissors, tries to attack her analyst, and then breaks into screaming sobs and crawls under a chair when the scissors are taken away. She sobs helplessly for several minutes until finally she is able to accept the offer of a quiet story.

Johnny, also age four, is playing that his family and the analyst's family are together on a boat trip. The analyst is supposed to announce dinner, but she makes a mistake and announces it incorrectly. Johnny becomes furious and throws the doll representing her overboard to be eaten by a whale. Johnny suddenly feels the urge to urinate and on his return cannot remember what he had been playing.

Susie, who had little capacity to identify her feelings, felt helpless and so required outside help to regulate them. Johnny was able to perceive both his mounting anger and his fantasied retaliation, leading to a momentary experience of anxiety. He used the perception of this anxiety together with fantasy (anticipation of the loss of his beloved therapist, or loss of her love, or castration, and the painful sadness and guilt he would feel) and instituted a defense (flight and repression). By responding in this way he limited his experience of the feeling so that he was not overwhelmed and did not feel helpless. Rather than overwhelming the functioning of his ego, Johnny's momentary affective experience served to facilitate ego functioning by organizing his response.

Although the way we describe it, Johnny's signal function appears to be partly conscious, more often the function is unconscious. Arlow (1977) comments that as affects come to be associated with conflict, any of the related components—the somatic, the emotional, the expressive, or the associated idea or fantasy—may be repressed, totally or partially. Johnny experienced anxiety about the possible consequences for only a fleeting moment. With development, the signal function becomes more or less automatic. Indeed, one of the frequent consequences of analytic therapy is that we become more aware of our feelings and of the associated unconscious fantasies.

The capacity to use the signal function is not a given; it does not automatically accompany affect. It is an important developmental achievement. Once it becomes available, usually beginning sometime in the third year, it serves adaptation since the signal use of affects prevents the child from becoming overwhelmed by states of helplessness. With ego development comes greater differentiation of affects, of expression of feelings, and greater recognition of affects and hence greater self-regulation and control over the disorganizing effects of affects. Pathological states in which feelings are repeatedly experienced as overwhelming indicate a faulty signal function and suggest pathological ego functioning (for examples, see Ritvo, 1981). Greenacre (1941) suggested that one source of such pathological ego functioning was related to affective experiences in early life. She proposed that severe traumas, overstimulation, lengthy exposure to frustration, and unrelieved organismic distress all function to undermine the emerging ego. As a consequence, affects overwhelm and disorganize rather than foster the ego's synthesizing and regulating functions. Neurophysiological patterning may be affected, producing a special sensitivity to physiological anxiety responses—a "predisposition to anxiety." She thought such a predisposition, when combined with constitutional predilections, might increase the severity of neurotic disorders (see also James, 1960; Weil, 1978).

### Affects and Object Relations

Our contemporary appreciation of the interrelatedness of affects and object relations originated with Spitz's concept of mother-infant reciprocity (1962, 1963). He wanted to emphasize the importance of a basic two-way, nonverbal, meaningful communication process, an affective *dialogue* between mother and infant that influenced both of them and provided the basis for the establishment of object relations. As we described in our discussion of object relations, Spitz first introduced this concept in a discussion of Harlow's work with infant monkeys raised with inanimate surrogate mothers, pointing out that the absence of an affective, reciprocal dialogue between the infant and surrogate mother had a broadly destructive influence on the baby monkeys' development.

As we mentioned earlier, mother-infant reciprocity is the foundation for the development of the sense of self and of object relations.

Failure to establish and maintain mother-infant reciprocity results in affective disturbances and interferes with development in a variety of psychic systems, as shown by Anna Freud (1941, 1942, 1949), Spitz (1946a, 1946b), Harlow (1960a, 1960b), Harlow and Zimmerman, 1959), Bowlby (1960b, 1961, 1969), and many other later researchers.

Specific studies of the role affect plays in mother-infant reciprocity have been revealing. For example, mothers seem "pretuned" to respond to what they perceive as the infant's expression of emotion. At the start of extrauterine life, endogenously determined, state-regulated, reflex behavioral patterns such as quiescence or fussiness account for most of the observable behavior of the neonate. Beginning with these primitive patterns, the infant progresses to more and more explicit facial expressions, sounds, and bodily actions. These expressions help consolidate the mother's healthy narcissistic and empathic identifications with her infant by means of which she makes inferences about the infant's inner state. His behavior therefore facilitates the establishment of the reciprocal affective feedback system between him and the environment, an achievement that ensures survival (Basch, 1976; Call, 1984).

Infants also come "tuned" or attuned to read the mother's emotions, and their behavior indicates that they expect to find emotional expression on the mother's face. As early as three months of age the infant becomes upset, withdraws, and then tries to reengage the mother if she has been coached to become "still-faced" in the middle of an exchange, as we described earlier (Tronick et al., 1978). By the second half of the first year, the infant appears to make use of perceptions of the mother's emotional expressions as he "checks back" to "refuel" (Mahler et al., 1975) and to use the mother's facial expression as a clue as to whether or not he should proceed in a strange situation, an affective exchange called "social referencing" (Sorce et al., 1981; Emde and Sorce, 1983).

Stern has introduced the term *affect attunement* to describe his way of seeing mother-infant reciprocity. Affect attunement refers to the mother's capacity to behave in a way that matches the infant's pace, intensity, and inner emotional state without imitating the exact behavioral expressions (1984, p. 7). Mismatching, or misattunement, results in observable disruptions in the infant's state or play. The importance for favorable development, Stern believes, is that the infant's experience of attunement enables him to realize "that internal feeling states are forms of human experience that are shareable with other humans" (1985, p. 151), and because attunement operates by means of nonverbal metaphor, it represents a necessary step in the use of symbols and language. Stern has thus taken Spitz's concept of mother-infant dialogue, studied it closely, and filled in many previously unrecorded details of this interaction.

## SUMMARY

Interest in affects is not limited to psychoanalysis, and we have briefly referred to the variety of disciplines engaged in their study. The many theories that have emerged over the past hundred years attest to the interest in the subject, and highly controversial issues related to affect theory remain. We have pointed out that the psychoanalytic view maintains that intrapsychic meaning and the experience of affect do not exist as a consequence of the movement of facial muscles or the firing of neurons. Affects, because of their relationship to the drives, ego functioning, and objects, come to have specific meaning to each individual over the course of development.

We now turn to the development of the functioning of affects, particularly the evolution of the signal function of affects.

# CHAPTER 9

## THE DEVELOPMENTAL

## EVOLUTION OF AFFECT

The cry of the newborn signals need states to the mother and elicits affective responses from her. The nature of her responses is determined by what she thinks and feels about her baby's cry (Call, 1984). The reverse situation—the infant's perception of the mother's responses in the context of his need states—will only gradually come to have subjective meaning for him. His own emotions, communicated to the mother in his cry or other facial expressions, will also only gradually come to have subjective meaning.

The capacity to use the signal function of affects does not exist at birth. Systematic studies of infant development in the first few weeks of life (for example, Spitz, 1950; Brody and Axelrad, 1970) demonstrate no evidence of the kind of ego functioning required for the signal function—that is, the ability to integrate perception, memory, recall, and response (Freud, 1926). Although the infant clearly possesses from birth a significant amount of perceptual and other central nervous system activity, integration of these factors emerges only gradually (Sander et al., 1979).

Emde (1984) studied maternal perceptions of infant affect expression and described a cross-sectional study of 611 mothers of infants ranging in age from birth to eighteen months. A majority of the mothers reported observing interest, enjoyment, distress, surprise, anger, and fear in their infants by three months of age. A major difficulty in the study of affects in infancy, for both the casual and the systematic observer, has been the irrepressible tendency to attribute to the infant an inner emotional state based on his facial expression. The judgment is frequently biased by the response aroused in the observer. Also, the infant's emotional state is frequently judged to be what the observer imagines he would feel in similar situations or would indicate with similar facial expressions or behavior. Basch pointed out that Darwin made this adultomorphic error when he failed to recognize that facial configurations are expressive *reactions* and that the underlying meaning of particular reactions has to be established independently (1976, p. 719).

Facial expressions of affect reflect an inborn capacity to communicate, but they represent only one of a number of aspects of affects that take part in increasingly varied environmental experiences as development proceeds. As a consequence the person's entire affect structure, including associated ideas and subjective feelings, becomes increasingly distinctive, even though a facial expression he displays may be judged identical to that displayed by another. Certain psychopathological states demonstrate that the link between facial expression, emotions, and affect is not an obligatory one. In this as in other lines of development, there are innumerable small steps and intersecting pathways that contribute to the total affective experience.

There is a related tendency to attribute to the infant an *intent*—for example, the intent to communicate. Clearly, an infant's cry has expressive and communicative value; it is well recognized that the expression of affects influences and guides the caregiver (for example, Wolff, 1959; Rycroft, 1968; Bowlby, 1969). The varied integrated cognitive skills necessary for intentional communication are not present at birth and develop only gradually. Prior to the time when the infant can initiate intended communication, we view the inveterate human tendency to attribute, project, or externalize emotions to others as a necessary component of "good-enough mothering" (Winnicott, 1967) or of the optimal "affective climate" (Spitz, 1947) and the "average expectable environment" (Hartmann, 1939).

## SMILING

The captivating smile of a small infant has a legendary power to induce the belief in the observer that the infant's emotions match his own. J. M. Barrie capitalized on this in *Peter Pan:* "When the first baby laughed for the first time, the laugh broke into a thousand pieces and they all went skipping about and that was the beginning of fairies." It is no surprise, then, that the infant's social smile is taken to mean that he feels pleasure, just as his cry is translated into the affects of pain, anger, or rage. Indeed, the social smile was the first organizer designated by Spitz (1959) to indicate growth in ego organization. Smiling, however, is a good example of the emergence and differentiation of facial expressions that are available at or soon after birth but only later become associated with pleasurable feelings and an intent to communicate.

Emde and Harmon (1972) have described two "systems" of smiling. The *endogenous* system, available at birth, operates solely on the basis of particular physiological factors. It appears in states of sleep or drowsiness, whether after feeding or not, and has been found to be associated with the rapid eye movement (REM) sleep state. Indeed, infants with significant congenital brain defects can produce as much endogenous smiling as normal infants (Harmon and Emde, 1971; Oster, 1978). Endogenous smiling has been observed to decrease between the second and third months postpartum.

*Exogenous* smiling, or the social smile, is produced in response to external stimuli. These smiles occur at a later age, beginning irregularly about the end of the first month; they use the previously established motor pattern, so they may be observed while the endogenous smiling system is still in operation. The timing of the appearance of exogenous smiling is genetically predetermined, as Freedman (1965) demonstrated by finding that monozygotic twins are significantly more concordant in this respect than are dizygotic twins. The landmark studies of Spitz and Wolf (1946) established that although the infant's exogenous smiling can be evoked by a range of stimuli, it was most regularly produced by confronting the infant with a particular gestalt of human facial elements; these consist of nose, two eyes, and forehead, and some motion, such as nodding, presented *en face*. The infant's smile disappeared if this configuration was presented in profile or if one of its elements was missing. It was found that the face need not be human; the same response could regularly be elicited by properly prepared masks or even balloons. Indiscriminate exogenous smiling quickly becomes well established, but later, once the infant has formed a firm attachment to the mother, her face becomes the most potent elicitor. Indiscriminate smiling diminishes after this, with some variation in the rate of decrease apparently depending on the nature of the child-rearing environment.

The example of the emergence of smiling demonstrates that although the equipment is available, and the newborn smiles whether awake, drowsy, or asleep, this cannot be taken as indicating the infant's wish to communicate pleasure, or even of the experience of pleasure, nor as evidence of interchange with another person, all of which the smile comes to mean at a later time. It also shows that the second form of smiling to appear begins as a stereotyped, nondiscriminatory emotive display made in response to a specific visual stimulus. It can be said, therefore, that psychological meaning becomes associated with a smile only after the smiling facial expression itself has appeared and has gone through some evolution in connection to the source of the stimuli that elicit it and to the ego's capacity to make perceptual discriminations. The display itself is no sure indication of what the infant feels.

## PSYCHOLOGICAL MEANING AND MEMORY

The question remains, when does the initial stereotyped, nondiscriminatory display become associated with psychological meaning? As already mentioned, the infant's early expressive displays such as those of pleasure and unpleasure contain biologically meaningful messages vital for adaptation and survival (Emde, Gaensbauer, and Harmon, 1976; Emde, 1980a, 1980b), but only gradually do they come to be linked in the *infant's* mind with gratification or frustration of the needs of hunger and comfort. Soon, though, these expressions also become linked with the need for the stimuli of human interaction as memory traces are laid down and as the infant increasingly comes to associate gratification of his needs with the presence of a familiar caregiver. An additional question is, what is required, and at what age, for the infant to make these links among need gratification, the presence of the recognized mothering person, and feelings of pleasure? It is the conjunction of these three elements that gives an affect psychological meaning for the infant, following which affect evolution and differentiation would be expected to occur.

Simple observation suggests that what is required to make these links is memory. Because the infant reliably smiles on recognizing the human face at about three months, one might conclude that this is when the infant makes the link between the experience of pleasure and seeing the mother. But whereas the three- to four-month-old infant can distinguish between the mother and unfamiliar people in a variety of ways, using visual and other perceptual modes of recognition such as smell (Montagner, 1983), the observations of Spitz and Wolf (1946) show that the visual configurational stimulus is nonspecific and need not be a human being. Therefore, more than facial-recognition memory is required for an affect to have psychological meaning. It is probable that such meaning begins in the context of the infant's capacity to distinguish mother from other on the basis of recognition of a number of maternal features (McDevitt, 1975), which increase as evocative memory becomes available. It has been found that differential looking at the mother's face emerges at about seven weeks, beginning in the region of her eyes (Haith et al., 1977), so that over the weeks and months the infant is repeatedly exposed to all the many details, variable and invariable, that go into the gradual construction of the maternal representation.

Many observers agree that the infant has a well-established specific attachment to the mother by the fourth or fifth month; by seven or eight months he gives unmistakable indications of missing and wanting the mother in her absence; she is no longer so easily "interchangeable" (McDevitt, 1975). Such responses suggest the beginnings of recall or evocative memory, a developmental achievement that Piaget (1936) thought occurred only later, at about eighteen months, when representational thought is established and language use is well under way. More recent experimental investigations have explored non-language-based memory systems in early infancy (see Stern, 1985, for a review). Nachman and Stern (1984) provide some evidence for the early presence of an affect memory system and suggest that affective experiences enhance recall as early as seven months, the period also suggested by McDevitt's report. Memory operating in this way would play an integral role in building affect components into mental representations, lending confirmation to Spitz's declaration that psychic functions evolve "on the foundations provided by affective exchange," which acts "as trail breaker for development" (Spitz and Cobliner, 1965, p. 140).

## STRANGER DISTRESS

Distress reactions to strangers have been observed and reported on by many writers (reviewed by Emde, 1980c).* Spitz (1959) designated their appearance as "the second organizer" of the psyche and thought they indicate the establishment of the libidinal object in the child's mind. He concluded that the infant's aversive response to a stranger and his turning to the mother confirm that the infant can discriminate between familiar and unfamiliar and that he prefers his mother. Spitz and Cobliner, (1965) also inferred that the perception of the stranger's face implies fear of loss of the mother. It is now known that the infant can discriminate between the mother's face and that of a stranger well

---

*Spitz called the observable reaction *anxiety*, but Katan (1972) suggests that *distress* is the more accurate term. *Anxiety* implies an associated idea such as a feared consequence as well as an underlying conflict, both of which require representational thinking, which emerges only later.

before seven to nine months; furthermore, reactions to separation are much less predictable or consistent than stranger distress and, if apparent, do not peak until later in the second year (Emde et al., 1976). Spitz's explanations of eight-month distress based on cognitive discrepancies or separation reactions are therefore insufficient and inaccurate.

Spitz's observation that the emergent distress indicates a significant developmental shift nevertheless remains viable. Studies have shown that discrete emotional expressions appear in a definite developmental sequence and that they are dependent on the maturation of the central nervous system. Certain cognitive capacities also appear to be related. Expressions of pleasure and unpleasure appear clearly by two to three months, but the expressions of fear, surprise, and anger become prominent only after seven to nine months, at about the time means-ends connections also begin to be made (Emde, 1980b; Emde et al., 1976). Accordingly, the appearance of stranger distress indicates the linking of means-ends correlations, anticipation of unpleasure, an emergent emotive (fearful) response, and avoidant behavior. The intensity of the infant's distress has also been likened to the quality of the mother-infant attachment, the more secure relationships being associated with distress of lesser intensity (Mahler and McDevitt, 1968; Bowlby, 1969; Rheingold, 1969; Ainsworth et al., 1978).

Now the mother's responses take on new usefulness and meaning for the infant. Although his own affects do not yet function as signals for him, "social referencing" becomes apparent. Beginning in the latter part of the first year (and continuing throughout life), the infant seeks out emotional information from mother (or a significant other) when confronted with unfamiliar situations, not just unfamiliar people. He then uses his mother's affective expression as an indication of her appraisal of safety or danger in the circumstances. Sorce et al. (1981) and Emde and Sorce (1983) describe an experimental setup in which this use of the mother's affective expression can be replicated and observed. After confrontation with a strange situation, the baby looks back and forth from the strange situation to mother; if the mother's response indicates, by a reassuring, happy smile, that the situation is safe, the baby explores. If her face reflects danger by a fearful expression, the baby typically breaks into tears and returns to her. The researchers concluded that the mother's affective signal guides the baby's subsequent behavior.

The experiments of social referencing demonstrate that the mother's emotional availability is crucial to the infant's ego development in two ways. First, her reassuring or warning affective responses become an integral part of the infant's appraisal system as she functions as an auxiliary ego, and, second, her affective interventions protect the infant's vulnerable ego from the traumatic effects of overwhelming panic. These observations lend support to Spitz's idea that the emergent distress is related to the mother's having become the infant's libidinal object, in whom he has established a sense of basic trust. She is now a reliable source of continuing safety. Instead of experiencing disorganizing panic in the strange situation, the infant, by using the mother's reassuring smile, is encouraged to explore. The mechanisms involved in stranger distress and social referencing therefore become foundations for the child's later use of his own affects as signals.

## AFFECTS AS MULTIFACETED PSYCHOLOGICAL EXPERIENCES

As mentioned earlier, we think of affects as mental structures having motivational, somatic, emotional, expressive, and communicative components, as well as an associated idea or cognitive component. As the infant develops, he gradually displays more differentiated affective behavioral patterns and more discrete emotional expressions; through these he elicits the appropriate environmental caretaking responses. His affective expressions do not yet, however, equip him for a reality-oriented adaptation to the world independent of his mother. As the toddler begins to be able to represent ideas and memories mentally and to construct wishes and fantasies (which requires the capacity to form connected ideas), he gradually comes to associate affective behavioral responses and their physiological counterparts with these ideas and fantasies. Now his own behavior and that of others begin to take on new meaning for him. It is this connection of affective behavioral response patterns with memories and ideas (conscious or unconscious) that takes the affect beyond an emotive display to become a psychological experience. Once a feeling is linked with an idea, it can be verbalized eventually. It is then more easily recognized, regulated, defended against, and controlled by the ego; mental activity is thereby disengaged from the obligatory or peremptory demands of the feeling.

The developmental distinction between an emotive display and affects as multifaceted psychological experiences makes it possible to distinguish separation anxiety or fear of loss of the object, the first anxiety in Freud's (1926) hypothesized developmental sequence, from stranger distress. This distinction was blurred by Spitz but suggested by Benjamin (1961a, 1963). Stranger distress is predictable; it is based on the emergence of fear and on making means-ends correlations. But as far as we can tell, stranger distress does not imply linking of the emotion with an idea or fantasy. Separation distress has a different and less consistent course of development than stranger distress. Reactions to separation have been reported as early as the fourth month (see Burlingham and Freud, 1942; Gaensbauer, 1982), but distress in anticipation of separation peaks in the second year (Tennes and Lampl, 1964).

In order for fear to be attached to an anticipated object loss, the child must have some capacity for mental representation, both of the object and of the self separate from the object, and a capacity to fantasize the consequences of being without the object. As the sense of self separate from the object begins to emerge, moments of feelings of helplessness appear. The toddler feels that the object's presence is needed to maintain his safety, and he anticipates helplessness with the perceived threat of loss of the object. Much later, fear of object loss also may become associated with neurotic conflict, in which case we can assume that many fantasies about the object and anticipated consequences for the self without the object have coalesced.

## THE SIGNAL FUNCTION

When development progresses sufficiently that feelings are linked with ideas and affects can come to serve a signal function, the child can better control and regulate his own affects instead of being overpowered by their peremptory and disorganizing effects. Researchers have paid relatively little attention to the developmental evolution of this function as compared to pathological states marked by its absence (see the clinical examples discussed by Hartmann, 1953; Ritvo, 1981; Kernberg, 1984).

We believe that the use of the signal function comes about through successful internalization of and identification with the mother's organizing and regulatory functions. It therefore can be seen to emerge alongside and in relation to libidinal object constancy (P. Tyson, 1988).

The use of affects as signals implies an ego capable of perceiving an affect, identifying the danger, and adjusting behavior accordingly with the help of defense and compromise. The question then becomes what it is that facilitates or provides for the development of the capacity to so perceive, identify, and employ defense and compromise. Freud pondered this question and commented, "Dangers are the common lot of humanity; they are the same for everyone. What we need and cannot lay our finger on is some factor which will explain why some people are able to subject the affect of anxiety, in spite of its peculiar quality, to the normal workings of the mind, or which decides who is doomed to come to grief over that task" (1926, p. 150).

Tolpin suggests that the capacity to use small amounts of anxiety and other affects as inner signals of conflict and danger begins with the mother's response to the infant's affective behaviors (1971; see also Ritvo, 1981). Structuralization and effective operation of the signaling function, however, are guaranteed only by the mother's timely and consistent response to the infant's expressed feelings and related behavior with actions that reduce his distress and provide a sense of comfort and safety, thereby supporting synthesizing and self-regulatory ego functions. The mother's initial success in such efforts may be apparent when the infant, by about eight months, begins to utilize the mother's affective signals as indications of safety or danger in social referencing exchanges.

The developmental conflicts of the anal-rapprochement phase typically arouse intense affective states, and greater demands are made upon the mother to balance her toddler's experiences of frustration and satisfaction. More and more the toddler begins to imagine the object-related fears Freud mentioned—fear of loss of the object, fear of loss of the object's love, and fear of punishment by the object. These fantasies have in common the anticipation of danger, together with a representation of the mother. In the toddler's mind, his safety appears to be dependent on the external, perceptible presence of his mother. And so he looks to her to prevent the overwhelming helplessness caused by exaggerated feeling states.

If the mother is not overwhelmed by the toddler's demands or distress, she can respond to his display of feelings with a balance between some tolerance of drive gratification and appropriate expectations of compliance. Such a regulating balance reduces distress, encourages the building of frustration tolerance and self-coping mechanisms, reassures the toddler of the enduring nature of the mother's libidinal availability, fosters internalization, and contributes to the development of an increasing capacity for affective control. Without timely intervention and the mother's empathic, regulating responses, still needed as an auxiliary ego, anxiety may disrupt ego functioning and create a state of helplessness and a sense of loss of the libidinal connection with the object, as exemplified in the toddler's temper tantrums (Yorke and Wiseberg, 1976). Such overwhelming helplessness is, we believe, a manifestation of traumatic anxiety as Freud originally conceptualized it.

Katan (1961) calls attention to the important affect-regulating function language serves. If words can be put to affective experiences, something that starts with the parent's labeling feelings, the child can begin to recognize, regard, and gain greater understanding of his feelings. Responses other than action are then more possible; action can be delayed, intentional communications can be established, and ego mastery and self-control accompanied by a sense of pride are facilitated. If a child does not learn to verbalize affects adequately, a discrepancy may develop between the strength and intricacy of affective states and the capacity for their expression. Without sufficient words, the child must rely on action or some other form of expression, such as somatization; in these circumstances there is minimal capacity to delay acting on impulse, which then undermines ego mastery, fosters conflict with the environment, and promotes rather than forestalls experiences in which the child is repeatedly rendered helpless and overwhelmed by affects.

If the mother is successful in her role as an auxiliary ego, the child will be able to identify with her attitudes toward libidinal and aggressive drives and also with her recognition, labeling, and appropriate regulating responses to the child's affective states. In other words, if he is to overcome his helplessness in the absence of the mother, the child needs the *constant internal presence* of the mother, together with the *internally available regulating and safety-keeping functions* of the mother. Successful internalization ensures that the child has significant resources for independent affect management. Once the object representation and its loving, comforting functions are stable internal resources, which Mahler proposed comes with libidinal object constancy (Mahler et al., 1975), then the object's function of responding to affective signals by the use of regulating and organizing activities becomes the child's ego function. Consequently, the child is able to recognize his own affective states and to utilize them as signals and respond with his own organizing, regulating, and protecting activities. It is in this way that the capacity to utilize the signal function effectively depends upon successful internalization and usually emerges along with the attainment of some measure of libidinal object constancy.

To return to Freud's (1926) question, we suggest that who is *not* doomed to come to grief over the management of anxiety is determined by the important self-regulatory capacity gained with internalization and the attainment of libidinal object constancy. The signal function strengthens the ego in dealing with the ever more pressing conflicts of development, especially those of the Oedipus complex.

The ability to respond in a timely fashion to the growing demands of conflict and thereby to keep painful affects within manageable limits largely depends on whether or not affects can function consistently as signals to organize ego functioning.

## FURTHER DEVELOPMENTS

The capacity to utilize the signal function may determine the way in which oedipal conflicts, the vicissitudes of their resolution, and the tasks of latency and adolescence are managed. The relative quiescence of the drives and expanding of cognitive skills in latency are facilitated by affects functioning as signals. Expanding cognitive skills also facilitate greater self-awareness, including awareness of affective experiences, which tends to further strengthen the signal function.

During adolescence, affects tend to be labile, and a variety of phase-specific defenses are needed to cope with widely shifting moods. Although mood swings are not limited to adolescence, they are particularly characteristic of that phase. The connection between affects and moods is an area of some ambiguity. Moods are relatively enduring, complex affective states that, Weinshel (1970) notes, are "slippery" to define, but he suggests that they are related to memories of early events. When certain provocative experiences arouse early memories they also arouse anticipations, and the early ego state is mobilized in the form of a mood. Arlow (1977) adds that although the provocative experience may be perceived unconsciously, the mood is evoked when this experience is sufficiently close to the underlying unconscious fantasy associated with the relevant early memory.

Mood swings are particularly related to the adolescent reorganization of the ego and the superego. We believe they can, like affects in general, serve a signal function, just as they can be pervasive and serve to disorganize ego functioning. Whether they overwhelm or serve as signals depends on the strength of the ego, a topic we discuss in some detail in the context of adolescent ego development.

## SUMMARY

Interest in affects is not limited to psychoanalysis, and in the last chapter we briefly referred to the variety of disciplines engaged in their study. Here we have concentrated on the intrapsychic dimension of affects and on the developmental acquisition of the signal function. We have noted that while the capacity for emotional expression is embodied in inborn behavior patterns, the psychological meaning that comes to be associated with these expressions is acquired only gradually. Before this time they are instrumental in engaging the caretaker so that an affective reciprocity between mother and infant can be established in an interactive dialogue. After a period in early infancy when intense emotional experiences can disorganize ego functioning, internalization and identification with mother's organizing and regulating response to the infant's emotional displays enables the child to use his own affects as signals of impending danger. Affects then come to function as signals that facilitate organizing and regulating functions of the ego. Although our discussion may have given the impression that the ingredients for establishing the signal function are well-known established facts, this is by no means the case. Many questions remain unanswered and much further study must be done. But from these two chapters we hope it has become evident that the contemporary concept of affect is an intricate and controversial one, as is the role of affect in psychic development.

# PART FIVE

## COGNITION

# CHAPTER 10

## A PSYCHOANALYTIC

## PERSPECTIVE ON

## COGNITIVE DEVELOPMENT

Ideas and fantasies, conscious or unconscious, are what give meaning, richness, quality, and nuance to our inner world. Linking ideas to impulses allows us to know about our instinctual drives and facilitates delayed action. The associated ideas and fantasies are what make our affective experiences psychologically meaningful and provide clues to our emotional state. Since ways of thinking also have a developmental evolution, a person's cognitive functioning, including his capacity to communicate, also tells us something about his past, his development, the conflicts in his life, and the ways he adapts to them. Knowledge of cognitive development, therefore, is advantageous for the psychoanalyst or anyone interested in the development of the human mind.

Understanding the evolution and structure of conscious and unconscious mentation is helpful in several ways. The links between ideas and feelings and the capacity to communicate are so basic to psychic life that an appreciation of cognitive development is necessary for an adequate understanding of ego formation. For example, the way in which a traumatic event influences a young child is affected not only by the nature of unconscious conflict and fantasy but by how the child perceives the event.

After a recent earthquake, a girl of two years ten months was heard to answer the phone by saying, "Hello! We just had an earthquake. I didn't do it, mommy didn't do it, daddy didn't do it, and my sister didn't do it. It just did itself!" (R. L. Tyson, 1989). We conjecture that the child's unconscious conflicts led her to feel responsible and so to repeat her reassuring words to others.

If therapeutic intervention is necessary either in childhood or later in adulthood, it is more likely to be effective if the therapist is mindful of distortions that may result from the immaturity of the child's cognitive skills. Also, developmentally early modes of thinking can persist and influence the adult just as do the contents of past memories, fantasies, wishes, and experiences with objects. Such persistence may influence the adult's perception of current reality and response to new information, and if the analyst recognizes early ways of thinking, his technical interventions will be better informed.

*Cognition* is a broad term that refers to any process through which we become aware of or obtain knowledge. It includes perceiving, recognizing, imagining, symbolizing, judging, memorizing, learning, thinking, and reasoning. Any or all of these processes may take place outside of awareness and may be profoundly influenced by our affective state.

Psychoanalysis recognizes two interrelated but distinctly different kinds of thinking—primary and secondary process.* Primary process thought is characterized by concretism, condensation, displacement, visual imagery, and symbolism; it is largely unconscious and the instrument for the expression of the inner subjective world. Primary process thinking is manifest through conscious and unconscious fantasy, fantasy play, day and night dreams, magical thinking, slips of the tongue, jokes, and artistic and creative activity.

Thinking governed by the secondary process can be conscious or unconscious. It is characterized by rationality, order, and logic. It relies heavily on verbal symbolism and functions chiefly in adaptation to reality.

With a few notable exceptions—for example, Hartmann (1939), Kris (1952), and Rapaport (1951, 1960)—psychoanalytic investigation has been mostly concerned with the primary process, whereas academic psychologists have focused chiefly on the development of secondary process thinking. Piaget recognized the two modes of mentation, but he found primary process thinking difficult to study and so, for empirical reasons, concentrated on the secondary process (see Anthony, 1957), forging a comprehensive theory about the growth of logical thought. Because psychoanalysts have been more interested in

*In designating one form of thinking as primary and one as secondary, Freud's goal was to indicate chronological priority. Since he thought one form of mentation was available to the mind at birth, he labeled that the *primary process;* the *secondary process* referred to later thinking associated with speech (Freud, 1900, p. 603).

understanding the meaning of the content of primary process symbolization than in its development, psychoanalytic theory does not have a comprehensive and well-studied view of the development of the primary process to correlate with the theory of secondary process development, and many questions remain.

Freud formulated his major ideas on the subject in 1895 and 1900 and made remarkably few changes after 1911, other than to relegate the primary process to the id and the secondary process to the ego, when he introduced the structural model (1923a). Since Freud, psychoanalytic investigations of cognition have been sparse and mostly confined to attempts to integrate Piaget's work with psychoanalytic theory, with varying degrees of success (see Anthony, 1957; Wolff, 1960; Décarie, 1965; Peterfreund, 1971; Silverman, 1971; Basch, 1977; Greenspan, 1979). Because Piagetian and other cognitive theories are not particularly concerned with unconscious mentation, Freud's ideas about the primary and secondary processes remain the basis of current psychoanalytic thinking about cognition.

## THE PRIMARY AND SECONDARY PROCESSES

One of Freud's earliest and most important discoveries was that unconscious mentation and logical, conscious thoughts are governed by different rules. Jones commented that "Freud's revolutionary contribution to psychology was not so much his demonstrating the existence of an unconscious, and perhaps not even his exploration of its content, as his proposition that there are two fundamentally different kinds of mental processes, which he termed primary and secondary respectively" (1953, p. 397).

Freud proposed that the primary process is the language of the Unconscious and that it functions according to the pleasure principle (1895a, 1900, 1911). His ideas were consistent with his drive-discharge model and the theory that the mental apparatus aims to maintain homeostasis. He described the primary process as facilitating drive gratification by distorting and disguising conflictual drive derivatives. Drive energy can then be discharged and pleasure obtained, because although drive impulses reach consciousness, they do so only in disguised forms. Freud maintained that the primary process is present in the mind from birth, and that with experience and development, the secondary process unfolds to inhibit and overlay the primary one. Because of the late appearance of the secondary process, "the core of our being, consisting of unconscious wishful impulses, remains inaccessible [and] these unconscious wishes exercise a compelling force upon all later mental trends" (1900, p. 603). Freud characterized the primary process as irrational, impulsive, and primitive—irrational because the connections among unconscious ideas do not seem logical; impulsive because since it is drive-related, it has a peremptory quality; and primitive because he thought it is available at birth and does not develop further.

Freud explained that at first, whatever the infant thinks of or wishes for is simply visualized, or as he put it, "presented in a hallucinatory manner," in accordance with the pleasure principle (1911, p. 219). His disappointment in not receiving the expected gratification leads the infant to form a concept of the real world and to seek ways to alter it. Motor discharge (action) is unlimited under the dominance of the pleasure principle; with the setting up of the reality principle, restraints on action are acquired by means of thought, and thinking as "trial action" delays gratification.

Freud emphasized that the crucial distinction between primary and secondary process thinking is the connection of visual images with words. "Thinking in pictures is, therefore, only a very incomplete form of becoming conscious" (1923a, p. 21). By linking a visual image to the word corresponding to it, a person achieves a higher psychical organization that makes "it possible for the primary process to be succeeded by the secondary process" (1915c, p. 202). He took clinical evidence of primary process functioning to indicate regression to more primitive states and said that the work of analysis is to supply the word links to primary process ideas (1923a). In that way they become understandable.

When Freud introduced the structural theory, he assigned the primary process to the id and the secondary process to the ego. In this context, it is the setting up of the reality principle and the connecting of unconscious ideas and visual perceptions with words that lead to the development of the ego. He commented, "It is easy to see that the ego is that part of the id which has been modified by the direct influence of the external world. . . . Moreover, the ego seeks to bring the influence of the external world to bear upon the id and its tendencies, and endeavours to substitute the reality principle for the pleasure principle which reigns unrestrictedly in the id" (1923a, p. 25).

## DISCUSSION

Freud's theory of thinking contains certain notable problems. The first is that a theory of energies and their displacement is linked with a theory of mentation. The second is the tendency to consider the primary and secondary processes as being separate and easily distinguishable, as if a mental activity reflects either one or the other rather than a combination of both. Third, the primary process tends to be seen as subjective, chaotic, and pathological, and the secondary process, as objective, orderly, and reality-oriented. Another problem is the linking of the primary process with visual-perceptual and sensory impressions and the equation of verbal symbolism with the secondary process. A fifth difficulty is the idea that the primary process is available at birth, but that it is soon taken over by the developing secondary process. This idea implies that the primary process itself does not develop, and consequently any indication of its presence suggests regression to more primitive mental states.

### An Energy Theory or a Cognitive Theory?

In Freud's formulation, the primary process refers both to what is responsible for distorting logical, rational thought in the search for gratification and to a form of mentation. Of course, both primary and secondary process thinking are often involved in the many ways in which gratification is sought. But to inextricably link one form of thinking to drive gratification confuses cognition with motivation. We believe psychoanalytic understanding is better served by keeping cognition and motivation separate; they are intertwined just as are other mental systems, but they are nevertheless separate systems.

Furthermore, if the secondary process is characterized by delay of gratification or discharge and by logical, rational thought, a child's impulsivity as well as his apparently illogical way of thinking would reflect the influence of the primary process. This way of categorizing mentation does not allow for any early developmental stages in logical thinking. But a developmental view permits us to understand secondary process thinking in terms of the individual's taking progressive steps toward maturity.

The two components, a mode of energy discharge or containment and a mode of thinking, both inherent in the theory of primary and secondary processes, contributed to Freud's uncertainty about the primary process and the nature of the unconscious (Reeves, 1965, p. 157). Was the primary process to be viewed as serving the inner subjective world, the Unconscious, the "core of our being," or was it to "be succeeded by the secondary process" (Freud, 1915c, p. 202), or could it be both?

Arlow and Brenner (1964) discuss the primary and secondary processes in terms of the structural theory. They suggest that since Freud spoke of the two in relation to mobility of drive cathexes, the thinking aspect of the theory should be dropped inasmuch as the concept of the primary process is broader than thinking. We agree with Arlow and Brenner that drive gratification should be considered apart from cognition. In our opinion, however, because drive gratification is only one of the many uses to which any combination of the primary and secondary processes may be put, we can achieve a greater clarification if we sever the link between primary process functioning and drive energy and retain the thinking aspect of the theory. Conscious and unconscious fantasying, for example, which combines the primary and secondary processes, reflects not only drive derivatives and the inner world of subjective reality but also elements of affective expression, defense activity, adaptation to the outer world, and moral judgment and punishment.

A five-year-old provides an example. She feels angry and cheated that the cookie her father gave her was smaller than the one he gave her sister; she is certain it was smaller because after she gobbled hers quickly, her sister still had over half a cookie. She then has a fantasy that her father has died, and she is the only one to go to the funeral.

This girl's age-appropriate immaturity along the developmental pathway of logical thinking led her to assume a size difference in the cookies because of the difference in speed of consumption; this is an illogical conclusion for an adult but a common one for a child of her age. Her conclusion that she was cheated had psychic truth nevertheless because it symbolized the nonfulfillment of her oedipal wish for her father's exclusive attention.

The child's fantasy reflected the primary process because it used magical thinking, symbolization, and visual imagery, and because it condensed the connections between the patient's anger and her death wish toward her father, her oedipal wish, and retribution for it. According to energy theory, however, the fantasy should be categorized as involving the secondary process because impulsiveness was delayed— her anger was expressed in thought, and she did not strike out at her sister or her father to discharge her anger.

By viewing cognition and motivation as separate systems, we can see that both the primary and the secondary processes were combined in the girl's fantasy. Reality testing and adaptation were served at the same time as were id wishes, affective expressions, defense activity, superego directives, and ego-synthesizing functions.

### Intermingling of the Primary and Secondary Processes

Although the primary process may appear to be employed chiefly in connection with the inner subjective world of "psychic reality" and the secondary process in connection with external "objective reality," they are intermingled in the course of maintaining harmony between the two realities. Indeed, cognitive processes can be looked at as operating along a spectrum with the primary process and the secondary process occupying opposite ends. Most mental functioning, then, would represent a balance between the two (Noy, 1979), which reflects id, ego, and superego functioning (Arlow, 1969).

One of the difficulties in distinguishing between the primary and secondary processes is that symbolism or symbolic thinking underlies both. Symbolic thinking occurs when one thing is used to stand for another, such as a visual image or mental representation used to stand for a person or thing—what Freud called thinking in pictures. When a word is used in this way, it is employed both in language and in representational thinking. Symbolism in representation, in thought, and in language is found in both the primary and the secondary processes. When symbolism is used in the expression of psychic conflict, however, the connection between the symbol and that which is symbolized is most often unconscious, especially in primary process functioning. The capacity to symbolize with the use of words and language is important for ego development and for the emergence of reality-oriented thinking.

Ferenczi (1912) and Jones (1916) usefully distinguished between symbolic equivalence and symbolic representation. The symbol and that which is symbolized can be experienced as identical—thus, symbolic equation; or the symbol can substitute for the original idea—thus, symbolic representation. Segal (1978) describes one patient who refuses to play the violin because he will not masturbate in public, whereas another will play the violin because, although the violin may unconsciously represent the penis for him, he still knows the difference. Edgcumbe (1984) suggests that the shift from symbolic equation to symbolic representation is important developmentally and relies on the capacity to perceive differences as well as similarities. We think the failure to make or sustain this transition has a great deal to do with pathological processes and is as yet insufficiently explored. (For further discussion of symbolism, see Rycroft, 1956, Renik, 1972, and Blum, 1978. On the distinction between symbol as a vehicle of thought and symbol as a means of communication or external referencing, see Mandler, 1988.)

Piaget (1937, 1946) also thought the capacity to symbolize (which he called the semiotic function) is crucial to development. He asserted, however, that once the capacity emerges, it has two separate developmental lines—a private ongoing system of symbols that hold an idiosyncratic meaning for the individual, and another based on language and an agreed-upon socially shared group of symbols. Language and logical thought, he presumed, eventually assume preeminence among the symbolic functions, serving thinking and adaptation directly and indirectly from early childhood on.

### Further Challenges to the Basic Theory

Rapaport (1951, 1960), one of the few psychoanalysts to study thought processes, challenged the basic premise of the primary process as primitive, chaotic, and pathological, and the secondary process as organized, logical, and reality-oriented. He pointed out that the organized, synthesizing, and socially relevant aspects of the primary process are evidenced in shared myths and animistic thought. Kris (1952) distinguished symbolic, personalized, subjective, and pictorial components of secondary process functioning, especially in creativity. Arlow (1969) wrote that the experience of reality, previously viewed as the province of the secondary process alone, depends on the interaction of perception and unconscious fantasy, that unconscious thought influences conscious ordered thinking, and that unconscious fantasy itself is constructed according to a logical scheme (a point also made by Holt, 1967).

Rapaport (1960, p. 843) and Arlow (1969) agree that all thought includes both the primary and the secondary processes and that optimal mental functioning relies on an equilibrium between the two. Clearly, as Arlow and Brenner (1964) point out, primary process functioning is not necessarily pathological or maladaptive, and indeed, Noy (1969) suggests that the absence of any evidence of the primary process may denote psychopathology.

The equation of the primary process with visual-perceptual and sensory impressions and the secondary process with verbal symbolism is also problematical. This assumption, which began with Freud's (1900) emphasis on dreams to delineate the primary and secondary processes, confuses mode of expression with psychic organization and function. Once language develops, it quickly becomes a vehicle for the secondary process and rational, logical thinking, and it constitutes a major resource for reflection, organization, and mastery, as well as communication. But one can also find a high degree of structure, organization, and logic in, for example, visual art forms, dance, and music, none of which relies on verbal symbolism. Furthermore, human interaction is mediated throughout life by nonverbal symbolic modes of communication (Langer, 1942), and verbal symbolism is a common mode of expression of primary process functioning, seen in parapraxes, jokes, and verbal condensations.

The idea that the primary process is primitive is also a subject of some controversy. Both Freud and Piaget perceived thinking in infancy to be different from that in later life, and both proposed that, with the onset of speech, a different form of thinking appears, which supersedes the earlier one. But they differed in that Piaget thought that mental representation, symbolization, and fantasy activity only begins with speech, whereas Freud believed that symbolization and fantasying takes place at or soon after birth as a function of the primary process. In this way he thought of the mental functions of the primary process as primitive, saying that they "are not altered by the passage of time; they have no reference to time at all" (1915c, p. 187). This led Noy to comment that Freud's view "means that the primary process is to be regarded as something that springs from nowhere, and develops toward nowhere, a strange group of functions for which there is nothing similar to be found among all other biological functions!" (1979, p. 174).

Longitudinal studies of child development amply demonstrate that behavioral and mental phenomena, regardless of their phase of origin, do not remain in their original forms but shift and change over time. As we already mentioned, early forms of logical thinking, though they may sound irrational to the adult, are nevertheless early forms of secondary process thinking that must evolve over time. So it may be with the primary process. Although the basic processes (condensation, magical thinking, and so on) may remain the same, the forms of expression over developmental time—whether seen in dreams, rituals, the art forms, or fantasy—reflect development in an underlying cognitive system just as the changes in logical thinking reflect that development. In other words, the primary and secondary processes can be seen as the lenses through which we can view the development of the underlying cognitive system. Indeed, Piaget (1946) seems to have thought similarly, for he discussed ways in which he thought children's dreams as well as their logical thinking at different ages reflect their level of cognitive development. Fast (1985) extends Piagetian concepts in an effort to reconceptualize primary process thinking. She suggests that the static, primitive, nondeveloping aspects of the primary process are those that have been excluded from cognitive reorganization as a consequence of the need for defense. In this regard, Noy (1969, 1979) contends that cognitive development as a whole, as well as that of its separate functions, requires that both the primary and the secondary processes reach optimal levels of development.

This brings into question the idea that the primary process is timeless. Clearly, we think not. What is timeless, however, are the unresolved conflicts, the libidinal wishes, the content of related fantasies, the poignant memories of traumatic or of unusually happy events, and so on. These persist in a timeless fashion in the unconscious. They may, however, acquire a different or additional meaning over time and be dealt with differently along the course of development. That is, at different developmental stages, earlier wishes and conflicts are reorganized according to the conflicts and also according to the different cognitive skills of the later developmental phase.

Contemporary developmental research suggests that what Freud described as primary process functioning is not available at birth. The cognitive abilities required for visual imaging and fantasizing as he described it do not begin to evolve until sometime between twelve and eighteen months of age. Although little research has been done in this area, we assume that the processes of condensation, displacement, and the like also do not emerge until about that time or even later. This implies that the primary and secondary processes begin to emerge at about the same time, each having roots in early infancy. Rapaport (1960) made such a suggestion, saying that both the primary and the secondary processes derive from an undifferentiated matrix, and that each has separate, intrinsic maturational factors. We agree, but though Holt (1967) suggests this common matrix is the sensorimotor modes of infancy, recent evidence suggests it is more likely that each emerges in early modes of perceptual analysis and recall that lead to the formation of a representational and symbolic system, which we discuss in the next chapter.

## CONCLUSION

Many conceptual difficulties in the psychoanalytic theory of cognition remain unresolved. We have reviewed Freud's theory and discussed difficulties with it. We nevertheless maintain that his concept of the primary and secondary processes, each having different organizational modes—one serving the unconscious inner world of subjective reality and one serving external reality—is extraordinarily valuable and has considerable developmental and clinical relevance.

We propose that the primary and secondary processes provide the lenses through which successive developmental stages in the cognitive system can be viewed. Nevertheless, problems remain, such as a time-table for the emergence of functions like condensation and displacement, which are utilized extensively by the primary process. In the next chapter we examine the steps in cognitive development.

# CHAPTER 11

## THE STAGES OF

## COGNITIVE DEVELOPMENT

The primary and secondary processes provide lenses through which to view the maturation of an underlying cognitive system. The two processes operate according to two organizational modes—the primary process is characterized by association, concretism, condensation, displacement, and magical thinking, and the secondary process, by rational thinking and logic. Although the two overlap, the primary process serves primarily the unconscious, subjective, inner world of psychic reality, and the secondary process is reality-oriented. Psychoanalytic studies have been mostly concerned with primary process manifestations over the course of development, whereas Piaget's work provided a developmental framework for the secondary process. In this chapter we rely on both processes in our description of the salient features of a psychoanalytic view of cognitive development.

### THE SENSORIMOTOR PHASE

The infant is born equipped with a variety of finely tuned, well-integrated systems of programmed reflexes and is capable of basic sensations (Prechtl, 1982). Some of these innate building blocks of cognitive growth disappear in a few months, whereas others persist and undergo developmental changes as they become incorporated into action schemes that operate in relation to objects and events. Those that undergo change, Piaget concluded (Flavell, 1977), provide the basis for the earliest, or *sensorimotor,* mental functioning that dominates the first two years and then persists throughout life. According to the theory of sensorimotor intelligence, the infant lacks the symbolic function and so does not have the capacity to evoke mental representations of persons or objects in their absence, nor does he have the capacity to manipulate mental images to form fantasies. Instead, his thinking during this period (divided into six substages) is related to his actions— that is, he acts in relation to objects that are perceptually present, and he shows a wholly practical, perceiving-and-doing, action-bound kind of intellectual functioning (Flavell, 1977).

For the analyst, the point at which some early representation of self and other forms is central to a theory of cognition. This is because the beginnings of primary and secondary process functioning as well as the beginnings of internalization and psychic structure formation rely especially on representation and symbolism.

Contemporary research points to the origins of both the thought processes in the stylized, playful, preimitative dialogues between mother and infant. These come to be established by two to three months of age following upon the "social smile." Spitz (1965), Call and Marschak (1966), Call (1980), and Stern (1974a, 1974b) describe these interchanges in detail. Parents typically respond to a baby's smile with vocalization, among other things; Call (1980) maintains that the vocal reciprocity established through these playful interactions provides the prelinguistic foundation for language acquisition (see also Bruner, 1974, 1977; Levinson and Call, 1987). Since secondary process logical thinking is based largely on language and the abstractions and concepts that become available through its use, the social smile can be viewed as an "organizer" not only of object relations and ego functioning but also of vocalization and mentation.

Parent-infant interactions also constitute the milieu for the formation of the first concepts about the self and the object. Spitz and Cobliner (1965) observed that infants in their fourth month will stare at the door after mother leaves. This suggests the infant has some ability to contemplate mother in her absence, an impression supported by developmental research. Bower (1974), for example, reports evidence that young infants establish cognitive object (or "thing") permanence by four to six months. He argues that infants may not search for objects hidden under a cloth, as called for in Piaget's experiments, only because they do not have the motor skills necessary to grasp and lift. Mandler (1988) maintains that, in any event, reaching for an object, that is, having a percept of it, is fundamentally different from having a concept of it. In studies designed to illuminate the beginnings of representational thinking, she demonstrates recall in infants of six months and sometimes in infants as young as four months. She writes that infants are born with the capacity for perceptual analysis—the ability to compare one perception with another; by making such comparisons, the infant begins to create concepts about objects, separately and independently from sensorimotor schemes.* These concepts form the basis of representations and symbols, which form a system of knowledge in an easily accessible format. Mandler thinks that only by evoking information from this system is recall or conscious thought possible. Therefore, recall in infants provides evidence that concepts about objects have begun to form. This does not imply that integrated representations of self and object are available at six months, but it suggests the process begins much earlier than Piaget had thought.

When means-ends connections appear, at about seven or eight months, the infant begins to use a particular visual perception as a sign that a particular event will follow. When events don't follow the expected sequence, distress accompanies the cognitive dissonance the infant is assumed to experience; this factor may contribute to the stranger reactions of the eight-month-old. That the infant anticipates an event following a visual perception indicates some form of accessible memory. That he looks to the mother and appears to use her facial expression as a source of information implies some inner concept of mother and memories of experiences of safety with her. These various observations lend support to the conclusion that certainly by the end of the first year the infant has available some elementary mental representations of his mother and himself.

Call emphasizes that it is not only the mother's face but the mother's voice that is important to the formation of mental representations. The voice, he says, is "like the smiling face, a dynamically moving, changing, and rhythmically-organized aspect of the infant's social interaction with the other" (1980, p. 278). The capacity for receptive language (comprehending spoken language even if not yet speaking) evolves from the vocal reciprocity established in the second or third month. Receptive language becomes more elaborate in the second six months and leads to the emergence of phonemes—units of significant sounds. Then, specific phonemes come to be integrated with feeling states, and the infant deciphers and responds to the meaning of his mother's facial-vocal configurations. This means that the social referencing we have described is based not on the mother's affective facial expression

*This differs from Stern's (1985) idea that it is the sensorimotor action patterns of early mother-infant interactions that form the basis of early concepts about the self and other. Clearly this is an area in need of further research.

alone but also on the infant's awareness of the mother's voice, gesture, and posture. "Smiling becomes organized in relation to vocalization," Call says, "and vocalization becomes organized in relation to a dynamically alive smile" (pp. 278–279). The voice and face, he concludes, become a locus for organizing affects and cognition.

In the next step the infant begins to use words as signals from others as well as other contextual information to anticipate and respond to his environment. Spitz pointed out that by the tenth to the twelfth month the infant has learned and begun to respond to the word and gesture "no" (1957, p. 13). This response, along with the infant's increasing ability to search for and locate named objects (Werner and Kaplan, 1963; Mandler, 1983), indicates the growth of receptive vocabulary, which also suggests further progress in representational thinking.

Play is the work of childhood. Play becomes a way of expressing wishful fantasies, a controlled means of mastering anxiety (Waelder, 1932), and a distinctive instrument for cognitive growth, useful for exploration and reality testing. Play thus underlies the growth of the primary and secondary processes (Plaut, 1979; Galenson, 1984; Moran, 1987; Solnit, 1987a). Whereas one can observe playful interactions between mother and child as early as two to three months, play in its own right emerges between eight and twelve months. This is the time when purposeful trial-and-error investigation, experimentation, and exploration characterize the infant's behavior. Novelty is actively sought as the toddler attempts to understand the world about him. Utilizing his ability to coordinate means and ends, the toddler finds new ways to approach problem situations and demonstrates further awareness of cause and effect. Mahler's designation of this period as the "practicing phase" recognizes the pleasurable, repetitive nature of the infant's play (Mahler et al., 1975).

Up to this point we have been considering the earliest evidence of mental representation and language formation—that is, the earliest evidence for forms of thinking that underlie both primary and secondary process functioning. In the second half of the first year, however, we also begin to see behavior that indicates a beginning differentiation of the primary and secondary processes. The first of these, we conjecture, is the creation and use of a transitional object (Winnicott, 1953, 1959). This may constitute the infant's first personally created symbol. It usually begins at the time of the developmental shift at eight months, when recognition memory is established, evocative memory is emerging (Busch, 1974; Metcalf and Spitz, 1978, p. 102), the mother becomes the libidinal object, and the infant begins to make means-ends connections and to react with distress at strangers or strange situations. Winnicott suggested that at times of mother-infant separation the transitional object functions for the baby to bridge the world of the mother and of the infant, that is, as a symbol of the mother. Inasmuch as the transitional object serves to maintain the subjective feeling of safety at a time when the infant anticipates disruption of safety, its use can be viewed as early evidence of symbolic representation. Since the infant is unaware of the connection between the symbol and that which is symbolized, we designate it as an early form of primary process organization.

"Magical phenomenalism" (Piaget, 1936), which Wolff (1960) and Holt (1967) suggest may form the basis of primary process magical thinking, appears between eight and twelve months. Piaget observed the infant's reaction to making a movement which was followed by an interesting new result independent of the infant's action. As the infant repeated the sequence over and over again, Piaget concluded that he believed his action was magic. As early as 1913, Ferenczi referred to this phenomenon as "magic gestures"; parents make gestures in response to the baby's gestures and facial expressions. Since the baby is unaware of his own expressions and has no intention of conveying meaning with them, the parents' responses appear as if "by magic." The magical results of the infant's gestures may incite him to further discovery, but they may also be a component of primary process magical thinking.

## SYMBOLIZATION AND THE BEGINNINGS OF AN INNER AND OUTER REALITY

Sometime between fifteen and eighteen months the toddler gives clear evidence of representational thinking by beginning to use personal pronouns to refer to himself and to others. With this, we can be sure that the toddler has an integrated representation of the object that allows him to evoke a remembered image of it in its absence. The toddler also has a greater sense of the object as separate from himself. In addition, communicative speech is definitely in use by now. One of the first words is "no" in imitation of the mother (Spitz, 1957). Spitz postulates that the "no" gesture is the first abstract symbol indicating the child's ability to exercise some judgment, to "think about things." The semantic "no" signals the emergence of useful, expressive, communicative language, the hallmark of the capacity to symbolize.

A host of behaviors follows, reflecting the increasing use of symbolism. The toddler uses his growing vocabulary to make his desires known, and he invents new means to solve problems. This suggests early reality-oriented thinking, or the secondary process. Between eighteen and twenty-one months the child's expressive vocabulary expands from about twenty to two hundred words, and he begins combining words to make simple sentences that are syntactically correct. The acquisition of novel, ordered, two-word expressions and questions is a developmental landmark as significant as the child's first words, and one that Blum (1978) suggests indicates a new level of organization and synthesis in psychic structure formation. These achievements enable the toddler to express his desires and needs verbally; he can now comprehend and ask simple questions.

In addition, the use of words helps the toddler begin to perceive his own inner state, his own affects, differences between his wished-for state and his actual state, and differences between his wishes and his mother's. Such discrepancies engender conflict between toddler and mother. But now, given his ability to manipulate symbols mentally, fantasied consequences (such as loss of love, loss of the object, bodily damage) emerge as does anxiety. Such fantasies increase the likelihood of internalization of conflict and identification with mother as a means of conflict resolution, an important step in psychic structure formation (see part VIII, "The Ego").

Evidence of fantasied wishes as well as fantasized consequences following conflict leads us to assume that the toddler is constructing, along with an outer world of reality, an inner psychic world, some of it conscious, some unconscious. For this he uses words and symbols to express wishes and fantasies, and he begins to use symbolic play to create personal symbols, choosing objects in the environment to represent other objects; he imitates the behavior of others not immediately present and he reenacts past events.

A notable example of early symbolic play is Freud's eighteen-month-old grandson's game of controlled disappearance and return of a toy, during which he gave vent to a long-drawn-out "o-o-o-o" (which Freud thought represented the German word for "gone") (1920, p. 14). Freud interpreted the boy's game as his attempt at active mastery over a passively experienced, unpleasant separation from his mother. Both linguistic symbolism and mental imagery appeared to be employed in the symbolization that seemed to become a substitute not only for the absent mother but also for the associated affect.

As symbolic thinking becomes richer, there is evidence of further differentiation between primary and secondary process functioning not only from the child's play but also from manifestations of unconscious processes. Now he can report having dreams (Metcalf and Spitz, 1978, p. 101). One of the earliest reports is of nineteen-month-old Anna Freud's dream of wild strawberries (Freud, 1900, p. 130).

We conclude that once symbolism becomes available—evidenced in deferred imitation, symbolic play, and language—it is employed in the service of both the primary and the secondary processes, the separate functioning of which becomes more apparent as development progresses. Language eventually appears preeminent among the symbolic functions associated with consciousness, reality testing, and adaptation; it is also a necessary tool for perception and understanding of the inner world of psychic reality as the child is increasingly able to use language to think about and reflect on his feelings, wishes, and conflicts.

Symbolic thinking brings the child to what Piaget described as the preoperational stage. The child can now use thinking as "trial action" as Freud described it; he can visualize operations mentally without having to go through the physical movements.

The preoperational child's images of reality are relatively static and concrete, and his thoughts close to overt action. He is not yet able to generalize from the particular or vice versa (induction or deduction) but proceeds from one particular to another and fluctuates between generality and individuality. For the preoperational child everything has a reason, an identifiable cause. Rather than constructing logical relationships, he makes associative connections, and so he establishes theories about the world and about his relationships with others in which fantasy and reality are not clearly distinguished. His thoughts are not particularly socialized but essentially egocentric.* Although he can show empathic concern for others, on the whole he is unable to take another's point of view. He thinks others think as he does. Events and experiences in the outer world are understood in terms of the inner world. The child has no useful concept of abstract notions such as space or time apart from personal experiences. Time is therefore meaningful only to the extent that it determines meals, play, sleep sequences, and the like.

Because nothing is fortuitous for the preoperational child, his ego-

---

*Cognitive egocentrism should not be confused with any of the psychoanalytic concepts of narcissism, however. The latter refer to the child's love of himself, some degree of which is necessary for healthy development, whereas the former simply limits his awareness of his position in relation to others (A.-M. Sandler, 1975).

centric thinking usually leads him to assume that the reason for any particular event is related to his own experiences and to his inner world of conscious and unconscious wishes and fantasies. Therefore he frequently confuses motive and cause, reality and fantasy. Sex differences are explained by the belief that something must have happened, a conclusion that leads to diverse anxieties and insecurities, the contents of which will vary according to age, gender, and experience. Death, divorce, and illness may represent to the child the fulfillment of a wish, thus reinforcing his egocentric and omnipotent view of himself; if he feels responsible and guilty about the wish and its consequences, as is often the case, a variety of fantasized harmful consequences may follow (E. Furman, 1974; R. L. Tyson, 1983).

Once language emerges, it quickly becomes a tool for thinking, organization, reflection, and mastery in secondary process functioning, as well as for the elaboration of an inner symbolic world in primary process functioning. Language fosters secondary process organization as it facilitates causal thinking, categorization, and abstraction. The use of language also furthers self-awareness and, ultimately, introspection, and it affects object relations as the child develops the capacity for sending, receiving, and understanding verbal messages—as he learns to communicate.

Communications fall roughly into two categories, those that are primarily informative in nature and those that have a controlling intent (Flavell, 1977). As the child's communicative skills improve, he becomes increasingly able to receive and transmit information and to convey his own thoughts and feelings to others, an important way of getting corrective feedback about his growing fund of information and ideas.

The young child also develops the ability to communicate to himself. He begins to think about his experiences, ideas, feelings, fantasies, and dreams. Putting thoughts and feelings into words aids in the control of drives and the modulation of affect and helps the child distinguish between the inner world and external reality (Katan, 1961). This ability to communicate to oneself is a requisite for evolving psychic structure formation and internalizing conflict.

Other communications have controlling goals. Their objective is to guide, shape, direct, or otherwise influence the recipient's behavior. The infant very early learns to understand controlling directives from mother. As the young child develops competence in verbalizing his needs and wishes, he is better able to communicate his own wish for control over what happens to him and control of others. Eventually language skills contribute to self-control, as thinking in words becomes a tool for trial action. Such self-control is reflected in Freud's remark, "The man who first flung a word of abuse at his enemy instead of a spear was the founder of civilization" (1893, p. 36).

Verbalization of sensory perceptions comes earlier and more easily than verbalization of feelings. Yet, as Katan (1961) pointed out, verbalization of the child's emotions, first by the parents and later by the child himself, increases his ability to distinguish between wishes and fantasies, on the one hand, and reality, on the other. In addition, integrating processes and reality testing are facilitated and lead to increased control over affects and drives because verbalization of feelings makes it less necessary to enact them. Weil notes, "It is easier to wait when words can promise future satisfaction" (1978, p. 479). Eventually the child carries out his self-management by inner speech or verbal thought (Luria, 1961, p. 61).

The enormous contribution of language to the mastery of emotions can be seen by the study of children with language delays. In the absence of the organizing framework that verbalization provides, these children remain more tied to sensorimotor action patterns, and their emotions tend to be largely enacted, leading to a variety of behavior problems.

Consider the example of a four-year-old boy who was just beginning to combine words into simple sentences. Aside from his severe language delay, his cognitive functioning and I.Q. seemed normal on testing. But his emotional development was severely compromised by the enormous frustration engendered by his inability to communicate his thoughts and feelings. Accordingly, his feelings had to be deduced from his progressively unruly behavior, and his play revolved largely around crashes with toy cars. That is, without the use of words, his emotional functioning seemed to be entirely action-bound.

In early childhood, the use of language, thinking, and playing are closely connected; the child uses words in self-directed ways, often talking aloud as part of his play, elaborating inner speech and thinking to himself more than communicating with others (see Vigotsky, 1934; Roiphe and Galenson, 1981). The use of play together with language and thinking helps the child integrate the various lines of development, as seen, for example, in Roiphe and Galenson's illustrations of how zonal arousal and object-related wishes are reflected in play patterns. In addition, play provides an opportunity to practice logical thinking and verbal expression as language becomes a resource of reflection, organization, and mastery. As the child becomes more ex-

pert in the use of language, he expands both his inner world of imagination and his understanding of the world of reality. Elaborations in
the use of primary and secondary modes of thinking become more
apparent.

This is particularly true as the child approaches the Oedipus complex, with the greater complexity and conflictual nature of the inner
world. The connections between the symbol and that which is symbolized become increasingly unconscious through repression and other
defenses; as a consequence, a larger number of symbols is utilized, for
example, to represent the wishes and anxieties of the Oedipus complex
and its antecedents. These symbols and themes have been immor-
talized in literature and mythology, as in stories of eating and being
eaten, fighting and conquering or being conquered, and romantic tales
of heroines and heroes representing the age-appropriate vicissitudes
of libidinal and aggressive strivings.

We have made inferences about the early structuring of an inner
world of psychic reality and an external reality sense, with the primary
process serving the former, and the secondary process the latter. We,
however, agree with Noy (1979) that these processes cannot be clearly
differentiated until the child develops a sense of reality sufficient to
classify objects according to their relationships to external reality and
to subjective experience. Inner needs and the wishes of subjective
experience, initially organized according to the primary process, can
then undergo "secondary revision" as attempts are made to verbalize
dreams or articulate emotional experiences. The child's concepts about
and experience of external reality similarly undergo revision as they
become organized according to their relevance to his subjective experience.

Even though some sense of reality begins early, it remains immature
and tied closely to personal experiences, and the rules of logic are more
related to inner than to external reality until the advent of latency.
Accordingly, the boundary between the primary and secondary processes remains fairly fluid throughout early childhood. This shifts
dramatically as the child enters latency.

## LATENCY

The spontaneous five-year-old, who easily verbalizes thoughts and
feelings and has free access to an inner world full of fantasies and
wishes, becomes transformed around the age of seven (plus or minus a
year). Now the child makes strenuous efforts to repress instinctual life

and maintain logical, rational thinking. Carefully constructed, stylized drawings and socially shared games with rules and objective goals become the order of the day, as the child tries to adhere to the much-emphasized social norms of the group. A firm boundary demarcates the primary and secondary processes, and the world of fantasy is confined to a private life.

Piaget's term, the stage of concrete operations, refers to the emergence of new cognitive skills that support an orientation to logic and reality. The child begins to think operationally—he can think about actions without having to go through the motions. He can think about opposite and complementary activities and can coordinate successive changes in time and space; his thinking is no longer dominated by the configuration he perceives at a given moment. Thus, in Piaget's terminology, mental operations become reversible and conservation is acquired. The child is also able to consider situations from a more objective, balanced, less egocentric point of view—Piaget calls this decentering.

The ability to decenter enables the child to think beyond a single aspect of a situation and to take account of two or more variables at once. Not only does the child's self-reflection expand, but he can consider another person's feelings, so that a true potential for empathy emerges. Although moments of empathy are apparent earlier, these are mostly related to the child's own interests and experience. A prelatency child will be sorry her mother has a cold, but chiefly because it interferes with her activity schedule. Because a latency child has the capacity to imagine how she would feel in her mother's situation and can understand that her mother has a reality separate from herself, she can empathize with her mother apart from whether or not her own wishes are affected.

Decentering and a self-reflective capacity are important for psychic structure formation, especially superego development. Increasingly aware of a socially shared system of moral rules and capable of reflecting on his actions, the child optimally begins to reevaluate his grandiose insistence on having his own way. He begins to understand that social acceptance depends on his modifying his actions to fit in with the needs and concerns of others. Self-reflection fosters greater self-control and makes it more possible to adhere to a socially shared system of moral rules. The replacement of outer control by inner control bestows greater autonomy on the child at the same time as it results in a greater propensity for neurotic conflict. Inhibition and control of drives and the postponement of action become more apparent.

As associative and magical thought yield to more objective and reality-oriented ways of thinking, the boundary between the primary and secondary processes becomes more firm. New cognitive skills add stability, so that instead of instinctual urges interfering with logical thinking and reality testing, drive components become unconscious and are kept in greater isolation.

Shapiro and Perry (1976) maintain that the separation of primary and secondary process thinking typical of latency is due to maturational factors. They have surveyed various fields of research all of which demonstrate a convergence at about age seven in the areas of brain differentiation, behavior, and maturation. From this they conclude that certain confluences in development—the resolution of the Oedipus complex, the structuralization of the mental apparatus into its three functional agencies, new levels of cognitive organization, and the replacement of outer control by inner control and organization—are not fortuitous but part of the design of the human organism. It is this design that permits higher-level mental organization, the hallmark of latency.

Shapiro and Perry further suggest that the new cognitive skills and higher organizational level of mental functioning fosters new approaches to old problems. Because of this, preoedipal and oedipal wishes and fantasies, dominated as they are by the animistic, associative, magical thinking characteristic of the primary process, become more and more foreign as they are split off from the more ordered logical type of thinking. Memory traces organized according to the associational form of thinking then become less available to consciousness. When ideas organized according to the primary process are raised to consciousness, they appear more and more archaic and less easily understood.

Nevertheless, primary process functioning remains alive and well and plays an important role in maintaining psychic equilibrium. Instinctual drives are also very much present, and without sufficient outlets for drive gratification, defensive activity increases. The child may show crippling ego restrictions and inhibitions, or symptoms may appear. Although the child's subjective fantasy life is now less often shared and is perhaps even less accessible to consciousness, drive derivatives are easily apparent especially in the child's solitary play, in fantasies, and in dreams. The family romance, or the variation thereof apparent in superhero stories as we described earlier, is often the subject of latency fantasy. Monsters frequently appear in fantasies, dreams, or nightmares as symbolic superego figures coming to punish, but the often uncontrollable aspect of the monster itself reflects an aspect of the impulses being defended against.

Drive derivatives are also apparent in other activities such as group play, where, especially in early latency, several children may elaborate a shared fantasy. Creative stories, perhaps originally in elaboration of a school assignment, or art projects, wherein some latency children begin to use devices such as caricature, also provide outlets for expression of drive derivatives. In addition, the more familiar modes of primary process functioning, such as jokes, slips of the tongue, and dreams, become more common as the wishes and fantasies of the oedipal years are relegated to the inner unconscious world.

Because of drive pressure and the ever-present threat of regression, certain age-specific modes of expression that integrate drive needs and defense requirements now appear. Although some of these may also carry over and become important later in life, they typically begin in and are characteristic of latency. Organized team sports, for example, provide outlets for competitive and aggressive strivings. Girls especially enjoy jumping rope or other repetitive rhythmic activities. Not only does this provide psychomotor outlets for drive pressures, but the accompanying rhymes provide a sublimated means of instinctual expression (Kaplan, 1965; Goldings, 1974).

In addition to physical activities, creative interests such as drawing, painting, and writing provide avenues for primary process thoughts with secondary process elaboration. Particularly imaginative and gifted children also sometimes create imaginary companions or fantasy twins, as we mentioned earlier, in part III. These fantasized companions may be the recipients of displaced unacceptable impulses as the child deals consciously with conflicts that would otherwise cause anxiety. The imaginary companion can share sadness, jealousy, anger, guilt, shame—all those feelings that the child fears would lead to punishment, criticism, or isolation if shared with a real friend or parent (see Freud, 1909b; Nagera, 1969; Myers, 1976, 1979).

In addition to creations of their own, latency children are avid consumers of the creativity of others. The capacity for reflective thought is indispensable to the success of children's stories, for it enables the child to clearly differentiate fantasy from reality. Were the child to confuse primary process–dominated imagination with secondary process–dominated logic, the stories would be frightening and overstimulating rather than pleasurable and enjoyable. Nevertheless, a discrepancy remains between the latency child's capacity to handle intellectual problems in an increasingly logical way and his distortion of reality whenever unconscious conflict is aroused. Unconscious conflict can disrupt the child's capacity to perceive, remember, think, and judge with "realistic objectivity" (Abend, 1982). A child may be able to recognize that a weight or volume remains the same no matter what the shape of the container in a school science experiment, yet remain vulnerable to feeling cheated when mother's piece of cake looks bigger. Therefore, reality testing remains quite variable. The child may be forced unconsciously to use the affective expressions of others as cues to whether or not a repressed impulse has found expression in derivative form. On occasion one even sees a kind of hypervigilance to this end in a child under pressure from intense inner conflicts. Because of this, in spite of increasing capacities for decentered objective reality testing, the latency child remains vulnerable to interpreting external events egocentrically.

## ADOLESCENCE AND OPERATIONAL SYNTHESIS

The rigid separation of external and internal reality characteristic of latency is replaced in adolescence by a more open interplay. The capacity for reasoning and for logical and abstract thinking reaches maturity. This combines with the fluidity of the psychic apparatus typical of adolescence (as described by Jacobson, 1961; Blos, 1968; and Rosner, 1972) during which preoedipal and oedipal conflicts are revived, provoked by the instinctual upheaval of biological maturation. The result is that thought processes in adolescence acquire a unique creativity frequently manifested in bursts of innovation and artistic expression not seen before or after. Noy (1978, 1979) suggests that such creativity, rather than being a regression in the service of the ego (Kris, 1952), is better understood as an "operational synthesis" between primary and secondary thought, whereby secondary process thought expands to include part of the primary process.

By middle or late adolescence, the capacity for what Piaget described as formal operational thinking becomes available.* The adoles-

*Piaget assumed that the individual reaches equilibrium in formal operations by about the age of fourteen or fifteen, by virtue of both the maturation of the central nervous system, which determines the ceiling of cognitive development, and the social environment's providing a stimulus and a milieu in which the maximum capacity can be realized (Inhelder and Piaget, 1958). Piaget assumed that central nervous system maturation and adult social roles dovetail at puberty. Although his assumption about the nervous system was not based on hard data, more recent research suggests that changes in brain organization

cent becomes capable of reasoning on hypotheses alone and he can mentally test his own thoughts. He constructs general laws, builds assumptions and theories, and mentally manipulates ideas, a process Piaget termed hypothetical-deductive reasoning. Cognition comes to be based more on form than on content, and on abstractions of things rather than on the things themselves. What is *actual* is replaced in importance by what is *possible* (Anthony, 1982) as the adolescent is able to formulate abstract, philosophical, ideal hypotheses and theories about the universe, the world, and society, as well as about his own present and future reality. Thinking becomes more systematic, and the adolescent becomes more able to reflect critically both on his thinking and on the products of his thoughts. In this way, a new descriptive and argumentative language makes its appearance, and beliefs can be subjected to methodical criticism (Anthony, 1982, p. 320).

Formal operational thought also influences the primary process, seen in more sophisticated forms of symbolization. Langer (1957) points out that symbols are vehicles for the conceptions of objects, not simply proxies for them. The form of the primary process as apparent in fantasy or creative activity, for example, evolves similarly and reflects abstractions and attention to form in addition to content. Although the thematic roots of a work of art or of a fantasy may derive from early childhood instinctual wishes, the form in which it is expressed by the

---

do occur in adolescence as measured by EEG changes, and that by age seventeen the EEG begins to assume the normal young adult form (Metcalf, 1979). P. Wolff (1981) noted that we know little about the finer details of structural change in the human brain after infancy. The dependence of brain function on myelinogenesis remains a debated point (McKhann, Coyle, and Benjamins, 1973).

Studies, however, demonstrate that major interhemispheric and intrahemispheric association pathways do not complete their growth until late in adolescence (Yakovlev and Lecours, 1967; Rakic and Yakovlev, 1968; Lecours, 1975). If maturation continues until late adolescence and into young adulthood, we should not expect equilibrium to be reached by the age of fourteen or fifteen.

Piaget's second determinant of cognitive maturity, the assumption of an adult social role, is also questionable at age fourteen. This may be true at certain levels of our society or in nonindustrialized societies, but one questions its validity in Western middle-class culture, where a psychosocial "moratorium" is more the rule (Erikson, 1968). Although puberty marks the beginning of psychological adolescence, psychological and social maturity may not be reached until sometime in the early to middle twenties.

adolescent or adult is highly evolved from that used by the young child. Indeed, the quest for "the perfection of form" (Langer, 1957, p. 208) with an awareness of harmony, balance, symmetry, and the reconciliation of opposites central to artistic creativity does not usually occur until the cognitive skills of adolescence are available.

In addition to the creative fluidity of adolescent thinking, the operational synthesis between the primary and secondary processes is also apparent in the characteristic, age-appropriate regression to and reinvestment of earlier wishes and conflicts alongside adult aspirations. As a consequence, the adolescent's thoughts may combine a search for a philosophy of life with narcissistic and personal issues, reflecting a kind of cognitive egocentrism. The adolescent conveys the belief that others *should* see the world and the problems of the world as he does, and he struggles to manipulate the environment accordingly. One sixteen-year-old girl dissolved into tears, shouting angrily, "I'm entitled to my own point of view," when she failed to convince her parents that her view was the "right" one.

Adolescent thinking also has an omnipotent quality, filled with dreams of revolution or social reform, which may interfere with an objective view of the position of others. When the adolescent comes again to decenter and consider multiple perspectives, a kind of confusion appears that is reflected in the characteristic ruminative quality of adolescent thought (Anthony, 1982). Then the adolescent is prone to oscillate between thinking and feeling, thinking about his thoughts and thinking about his feelings, a process illustrated by Anthony in the following quotation which he took from the writings of the sixteen-year-old Dostoevsky:

> To know more, one must feel less, and vice versa. . . . what do you mean precisely by the word know? Nature, the soul, love, and God, one recognizes through the heart, and not through the reason. Were we spirits we could dwell in that region of ideas over which our souls hover, seeking the solution. But we are earth-borne beings, and can only guess at the Idea—not grasp it by all sides at once. The guide for our intelligences through the temporary illusion into the innermost center of the soul is called Reason. Now Reason is a material capacity, while the soul or spirit lives on the thoughts which are whispered by the heart. Thought is born in the soul. Reason is a tool, a machine, which is driven by the spiritual fire. When human reason (which would demand a chapter for itself) penetrates into the domain of knowledge, it works independently of the feeling, and consequently of the heart. But when our aim is the understanding of love or of nature, we march towards the very citadel of the

heart. . . . what a lot of crazy systems have been born of late in the cleverest and most ardent brains! To get a right result from this motley troop, one would have to subject them all to a mathematical formula. And yet they are the "laws" of our contemporary philosophy! . . . I pity our poor father! He has such a remarkable character. [He] is wholly a stranger in the world. He has lived in it now for fifty years, and yet he has the same opinions of mankind that he had thirty years ago. What sublime innocence!

Periodic withdrawal into fantasy is yet another characteristic of adolescence. Although such withdrawal may signify in some adolescents a pathological turning away from reality, in others it can also lead eventually to better reality testing, as needs and goals come to be integrated with possible ways of realizing them (Hartmann, 1939). Fantasies also provide access to one's internal reality; earlier wishes and conflicts can now be reconsidered with the more mature psychic apparatus of the adolescent and his greater capacity for reflective and logical thinking. Insight into intrapsychic life often results, facilitating mastery of both internal and external worlds. When intrapsychic processes are perceived as dangerous and knowledge of them threatens psychic equilibrium, however, rigid defenses may be utilized to the extent that reality testing is interfered with.

As the adolescent process nears completion and character structure approaches maturity, educational and social pressures reinforce a separation of the primary and secondary processes. The primary process is increasingly confined to day and night dreams, fantasies, artistic creation, and symptom formation; it becomes more exclusively the "language" of the unconscious, and manifest communication and behavior become dominated by the logical thought of the secondary process system. Except where psychic reality interferes with objective reality testing, thinking becomes rational and logical.

Adaptive cognitive functioning and reflective thought, however, continue to depend on the optimal fit between the primary and secondary processes. While adhering to different rules and utilizing different modes of expression, primary and secondary process thinking must work in harmony in order for the individual to maintain the best possible emotional, social, and intellectual adjustment.

## SUMMARY

We have described a developmental sequence for cognition. We think that the primary and secondary processes are lenses through which to view the maturation of cognition. Both emerge from the stylized, playful, preimitative dialogues between mother and infant. The transitional object and magical phenomenalism are, we propose, early signs of the beginnings of the primary process. Speech is the hallmark of the capacity to symbolize. Once the child can symbolize, thinking as trial action becomes possible, and an inner world of psychic reality comes to be distinguished from the world of external reality. We can now hypothesize the beginnings of an unconscious, as dreams come to be reported. Although language development fosters reflection and mastery characteristic of secondary process thinking, the prelatency years are characterized by animistic, associative, magical thinking, and the primary and secondary processes merge and blend.

In latency, however, a sharp division is maintained between them, as the inner world of affects, drives, wishes, and conflicts and the private symbolism expressing them is kept apart from and becomes increasingly foreign to the world of objective reality. The capacity for formal operational thought becomes available in adolescence, and an operational synthesis is established between primary and secondary process thinking. With the waning of adolescence, once again separation between the primary and secondary processes is the norm, as the primary process becomes the "language" of the unconscious, and thinking becomes rational and logical.

# PART SIX

---

## THE SUPEREGO

---

# CHAPTER 12

## THE SUPEREGO: A

## THEORETICAL OVERVIEW

The superego is the psychic system that sets up and maintains moral standards and wished-for goals and ideals. When functioning optimally, it supports intrapsychic and interpersonal harmony and facilitates social adaptation. Although at times the "voice of conscience" seems nearly palpable, the superego, like the ego and the id, is not a concrete entity but a hypothetical concept, despite the shorthand convenience offered by the tendency to anthropomorphize.

There is abundant theoretical controversy about the superego, its development and functioning. Many of the current debates about the concept stem from some of the ambiguities or misconceptions inherent in Freud's writings on the subject. Nevertheless, since our present ideas are based on the foundation laid by Freud, we begin in this chapter with a brief survey of his work. We follow this by addressing some of the ambiguities and difficulties we find with the superego concept and then describe our basic premise about its constituents and functions. The next chapter takes up superego development. Since we believe that superego functioning and development are similar in both males and females, we treat the theory as a whole in these two chapters. Chapter 14 is devoted to an examination of gender differences in the superego, placing in context the wide variety of explanations that have been offered about superego development in the female.

### THE DEVELOPMENT OF FREUD'S SUPEREGO CONCEPT

Freud first made explicit his ideas on what later became known as the superego in his paper "On Narcissism" (1914).* Seeing that repres-

*Strachey (1961) traced the several antecedents of the concept, and Furer (1972) provides an extensive examination of Freud's thinking about the superego.

sion of instinctual impulses follows conflict with cultural or ethical ideals, he assumed that a person sets up an ideal standard in his mind against which to measure himself; then self-love or self-respect becomes dependent on a favorable comparison between oneself and that standard. Freud assumed that experiences with parents are largely responsible for the formation of ideals, that these ideals are later reinforced by further training and education, and that failure to maintain them leads to a sense of guilt or inferiority. He wrote, in summary (p. 100), that self-esteem is dependent not only on the residue of infantile narcissism and on receiving love from an object but also on maintaining ideal standards.

A few years later, continuing the idea of an internal critical agency "which even in normal times takes up a critical attitude towards the ego" (1921, p. 109), Freud delineated its functions more precisely. These include "self-observation, the moral conscience, the censorship of dreams, and the chief influence in repression" (p. 110). He added that all previous interactions with others may be repeated internally by means of this new agency (p. 130).

In 1923 Freud introduced the term *superego*. Although he was never consistent in his use of terms and often used the terms *ego ideal* and *superego* interchangeably, he introduced the superego as one of the structures in the tripartite model of the mind. In this essay he noted that the sense of guilt has dual sources. One results from internalizations and identifications with the parents formed on the basis of the child's real experiences of their criticisms. The other derives from the fact that oedipal mastery requires permanent vigilance of the superego against powerful id impulses and libidinal vicissitudes. A consequence of this vigilance is that though "the ego is essentially the representative of the external world, of reality, the super-ego stands in contrast to it as the representative of the internal world, of the id" (1923a, p. 36), and thus it embodies the expression of these impulses directed inward. Indeed, "the super-ego . . . can be super-moral" and then become immensely cruel (1923a, p. 54).

Freud based his superego theory on male development, and referring to the need to repress oedipal wishes, he supposed that hatred for the father arises when the boy perceives him as the obstacle to realizing these wishes. To preserve the father's love, the boy identifies with him, and it is from this identification that the superego derives the forbidding, punishing character of the father. By thus becoming the representative of the boy's relation to his father, the superego directs to the self all the unexpressed hostility the boy felt and might feel toward his father, so that the boy treats himself the way he imagines the father would treat him. Freud goes on to point out a paradox: "It is remarkable that the more a man checks his aggressiveness towards the exterior the more severe—that is aggressive—he becomes in his ego ideal" (1923a, p. 54). In other words, even though the hostility is not expressed overtly, it nevertheless leads to harsher superego demands and to a more intense sense of guilt.

In another essay written the same year, "The Infantile Genital Organization" (1923b), Freud acknowledged his lack of understanding of the early years of female development. This lacuna is especially apparent in his theory of superego formation and functioning in the female, which he began to develop in the 1923 essay and continued in 1925, "Some Psychical Consequences of the Anatomical Distinction between the Sexes" (1925b). Freud thought that inasmuch as it is the girl's acceptance of her castrated state that permits her oedipal progression, she has less motivation than a boy for superego internalization. Also, he believed the superego is derived primarily from identifications with the father; as the girl is usually more identified with her mother than with her father, he concluded that her superego must be weaker.

Freud next discussed his ideas about internal criticism in relation to the emergence of fears of punishment and the signal function of anxiety. He suggested that following oedipal resolution, the child no longer fears punishment from the external world as much as he fears the wrath of his own superego. "Putting it more generally, what the ego regards as the danger and responds to with an anxiety-signal is that the super-ego should be angry with it or punish it or cease to love it" (1926, pp. 139–140).

Starting in 1926, Freud elaborated certain aspects of the superego concept and explored its application to other fields. He noted, for example, that there is little to distinguish ego and superego functioning except as a result of psychic conflict, when their differences are manifested (1926, p. 97). He also examined the important role of the superego in the perpetuation of culture (1927) and in relation to the demands of society (1930).

Returning to the problem of superego severity, Freud (1933) clarified that the superego can be relentlessly severe, leading to guilt and a sense of inferiority even if the parents have not been threatening but kind and nonpunishing. In a final summary of his ideas, he added, "Its excessive severity does not follow a real model but corresponds to the strength of the defense used against the temptation of the Oedipus complex" (1940, p. 206). Freud expressed the belief that "the details of the relation between the ego and the super-ego become completely intelligible when they are traced *back to the child's attitude to its parents*" (1940, p. 146, emphasis added).

## CONCEPTUAL DIFFICULTIES IN FREUD'S THEORY

Confusion about the superego has arisen partly because Freud introduced the concept before his structural hypothesis, employing the term *ego ideal* (1914, p. 94). He spoke of the ego ideal as referring both to an internalized ideal image or standard for the self and to an agency that monitors the ego in relation to such an ideal image. In 1923 he added the term *superego*, but then proceeded to use the terms interchangeably. Because of the two concepts (an agency and a standard) and the two terms, disagreement has arisen as to whether the ego ideal should be considered a part of or separate from the superego (see, for example, Piers and Singer, 1953; Reich, 1954; Lampl-de Groot, 1962; Blos, 1974). As we see it, the ego ideal refers to a collection of specific mental representations that carry model, exemplar, or wished-for standards or ways of being. We view this ego ideal not as a separate agency but as a group of representations within the superego.

A common difficulty lies in fully comprehending superego severity. Although Freud makes it clear that its severity corresponds not to the wrath of the parents but to the strength of the defense used against instinctual temptations, he nevertheless implies in the next sentence that parental influence has a role, as it is the standards of the parents that are taken in by the superego (1940, p. 146). The implication of parental influence has led to a common misunderstanding that the superego represents *only the parents' attitude to the child*. It is as if the superego were merely a passive mirror of the actual circumstances in childhood. Kohut, for example, sees the critical and punishing features of the superego as residues of real experiences with parental authority, and superego approval as a direct replacement of parental approval and solely dependent on the original parents' capacity to be loving and approving (Kohut and Seitz, 1963, pp. 366–367).

We maintain that although parental influence makes a significant contribution to superego development, so does the child. Not only do instinctual drives and the defenses against their expression have a developmental impact on superego formation, but this influence may be magnified by the child's immature cognitive functioning that tends to distort events in the real world as they are happening and as they are remembered.

The timing of superego formation is another area of theoretical controversy. Freud proposed that the superego results from crucial identifications made with the father during efforts to avoid feared castration and to resolve oedipal conflicts (1923a, pp. 28–39). It is therefore formed upon oedipal resolution, which is why he described the superego as the "heir of the Oedipus complex" (p. 36).

Melanie Klein (1928) took exception to this late timing, although she viewed the motive as similar—to avoid bodily damage. She suggested that the superego forms during the oral-sadistic phase of the second half of the first year and that it is based on the introjection of frightening and punishing parental figures. These introjects result from the projection onto the parents of the infant's oral-sadistic impulses.

We are of the opinion that the views of both Freud and Klein are erroneous. We think the superego, like all other psychic systems, has a developmental line, with early roots in the first years of life. Freud's idea that the superego forms with oedipal resolution does not take into account early stages and conveys the impression that the superego appears suddenly. In regard to Klein's ideas, we know from developmental research that the complex functions she attributed to the infant, in order to be able to form the superego in the eighth or ninth month, do not exist at this time.

In the past few decades, analysts have reexamined both Freud's and Klein's positions and have suggested other formulations. Hartmann and Loewenstein (1962), taking an opposite position from Klein, maintained that superego structuralization can be assumed only when superego autonomy is achieved—that is, when the superego functions to maintain standards of conscience without external support. This placed superego formation sometime in latency. We think this is an extreme view. For one thing, the kind of superego autonomy Hartmann and Loewenstein describe is more of an ideal, and we know from child analytic work that the superego functions to punish long before it functions effectively to restrict temptation without significant external support. Indeed, superego autonomy may remain a relative term throughout life, with compromises of integrity (Rangell, 1974, 1980) a frequent hazard for many individuals.

Other more plausible suggestions have been made regarding superego development. Greenacre (1952a) suggested that superego development occurs in four stages: primitive roots in the first two years, the habit-training years of being good or bad, the struggle of oedipal renunciation at about age five, and the latency years, when the attainments of the oedipal struggle are reinforced by social influences and the individual's conscience fuses with social conscience. Jacobson (1964) and Mahler (1975a), we think quite rightly, drew attention to the role of preoedipal object relations and associated conflict in superego formation. More recently, Emde (1988a, 1988b) has described developmental research efforts focusing on what he calls "moral emotions," which evolve from mother-child interactions and function independently of the mother as early as age two or three.

These ideas reflect shifts away from Freud's primary emphasis on feared consequences and oedipal resolution for superego development. Now theorists are taking into account both the child's motivation to retain interpersonal and eventually intrapsychic harmony and his preoedipal as well as his oedipal conflicts. Perhaps because of loyalty to Freud's theory, however, many analysts have referred to preoedipal internalization of authority as a "superego precursor"; although this emphasizes the difference between early steps and the later integrated structure, it also perpetuates the neglect of early influences. In addition, it perpetuates the impression held by some that the structures of the tripartite model do not form until the appearance of the Oedipus complex and so the model is not useful when considering pathology of earlier origins. We hold the position that the superego has a long course of development beginning in infancy, and rather than refer to "precursors," we refer to early stages in the developmental trajectory.

A particularly thorny problem has been Freud's male bias in maintaining that the girl's superego is weak and unstable because she lacks castration anxiety and identifications with her father. This view has aroused much controversy, beginning with a number of Freud's contemporaries, including Jones, Horney, and Klein who disagreed with him. They insisted that the women they saw clinically suffered the pangs of guilt, shame, and low self-esteem at least as often as men. In the years since, various explanations have been offered in rebuttal of what is sometimes referred to as Freud's phallocentric view of this aspect of development. The idea that women have weaker, less stable superegos than men has generally been refuted in favor of differentiating between the structure of the superego and the content of the internalized ideals and standards. (In chapter 14 we examine the similarities and differences in superego functioning in men and women.)

## SUPEREGO CONSTITUENTS

Freud's clinical work led him to propose that an ideal standard becomes set up in the mind against which the person measures himself, an idea that has been widely accepted. We now consider the nature of that standard more fully.*

From Freud's comments, it seems that imperatives, moral standards, and ideal wished-for goals become the fabric of the superego. These accrue from the child's experiences of being observed, encouraged, challenged, judged, praised, rewarded, criticized, and punished by parents, teachers, peers, and other important people. Inasmuch as these elements come from a variety of sources and arise at various times during development, there may be little consistency among them. A fully developed, well-functioning superego in an adult is therefore better viewed as a homogenized and harmonized organization of divergent trends. Any categorization of the superego constituents will necessarily be somewhat arbitrary; but in order to more readily trace the origins and developmental courses of the various parts of the system, after a suggestion of Sandler (1960a, 1981) we distinguish introjects—by which we mean internalized directives, admonitions, or prohibitions—from ideals, or the wished-for standards or goals. In actuality, of course, they function together.

*Introjects*

As mental representations of objects and of the self are formed, certain ones stand apart from the others; indeed they may never be fully integrated. These are the representations that embody imperatives—parental rules and prohibitions, their dos and don'ts, shoulds and should nots. They also demand a particular role in relation to parental or other authority figures, and they eventually function as if they had parental authority and power. They then "carry on the functions which have hitherto been performed by the people in the external world" (Freud, 1940, p. 205). In this way, the superego continues to reflect the interactions between child and parent, as the "super-ego continues to play the part of an external world for the ego, although it has become a portion of the internal world" (p. 206). Emde (1988a) reports recent developmental research confirming Freud's notion. In a sample of three-year-olds, researchers found evidence that internal-

---

*We find it useful to discuss the superego in terms of its functions and constituents in order to facilitate understanding the origins and developmental courses of its various aspects. We recognize, however, that the idea of constituents may tend to concretize thinking about the system, thus unfortunately implying to some that it is a container with contents. Although we recognize the tendency to anthropomorphize the id, ego, and superego, it is inaccurate to view any system as a container with contents.

ized rules, without the physical presence of the parent, carry with them a sense of the "other" and a sense of the relationship.

### Ideals

The child forms various ideals on the basis of his experiences of joyful interaction with mother or father, during which he feels praised, encouraged, rewarded, and loved, together with the wish to retain and repeat these interactions. One can group together these mental representations that carry exemplar or wished-for standards or ways of being by using Freud's original term, *ego ideal.*

Freud and others have described many ideals, conscious and unconscious. They emerge as development proceeds, and at times some ideals conflict with others. To differentiate among them, Sandler and his colleagues (1963) suggest viewing the ego ideal as a composite of ideal object representations, ideal child representations, and ideal self-representations. We find this suggestion helpful, particularly in tracing the development of the many constituents of the superego system.

*Ideal object representations* form from the child's earliest impressions of the parents, whom he views as perfect and omnipotent. Ideal object representations become embellished over the course of early childhood and incorporate the child's wishful fantasies as well as joyful interactional experiences. These early images of omnipotence, magnificence, and perfection are remarkably enduring, and they become standards against which the subject may measure himself, future objects, or later impressions of his parents—for example, in adolescence.

*Ideal child representations* embody approved-of standards, morals, goals, and ideals that parents hold out to the child, and so to some extent they incorporate the introjects. Yet these ideals also represent the parents' fantasy about their ideal child, and very early the child gleans a notion of the "child my mother would like me to be." These ideals vary according to gender, culture, and social subgroup, and they are the vehicles through which gender- and culture-specific ideals are transmitted. This set of ideals largely emanates from the parents' superegos and contributes to what we call the conscience,* which, as

*Piaget (1932), Kohlberg (1963), and other psychologists refer to a child's development of a sense of morality. They are referring not to the functioning of an inner psychic agency that results from parent-child interactions but to the child's evolving cognitive capacities to deal with and accept abstract concepts of morality. These moral codes provide the content of what is held to be ideal, but they should not be confused with the structure or functioning of the superego.

Freud (1930) noted, serves to protect civilization. If the parents' standards are defective, or their behavior differs markedly from the directives they give the child, then the child's superego may contain similar defects (Johnson and Szurek, 1952) or show inconsistencies in functioning.

The *ideal self-representation* is a personal and unique view of the "self I would like to be" (Sandler et al., 1963). Many ideals coexisting unconsciously and consciously make up the ideal self-representation, which results in its being a more sophisticated mental construction than the earliest introjects and ideals.

The ideal self derives in part from aspects of ideal object representations—that is, representations of loved, feared, or admired persons. A second source is the "good," "desirable," or "ideal" child as conveyed by the parents. States of self previously experienced in reality or in fantasy provide a third source of ideal self-representations. These include memories, possibly idealized retrospectively, as well as fantasies of total reciprocal harmony, absence of frustration, or complete instinctual gratification during early infancy, or the fantasy of magical omnipotence and grandiosity typical of the anal phase. A person may retain throughout life some kernel of a wish to experience again those feeling states associated with harmonious reciprocity and omnipotence, that grand infant he once imagined himself to be. Jacobson notes that "the superego is the one area of the ego where the child's omnipotent fantasies find a safe refuge and, in a modified form, can be maintained forever to the profit of the ego" (1954, p. 105). The ideal self-representation thus becomes, as Freud pointed out, "heir to the original narcissism in which the childish ego enjoyed self-sufficiency" (1921, p. 110).

A fourth source for ideal self-representations is a current realistic assessment of oneself, of one's potentialities and limitations. This view of the self may be difficult to achieve because the various ideals embodied in the ego ideal often conflict. The differing ideals presenting themselves simultaneously may at best result in superego variability and flexibility. Less optimally, the conflict leads to superego unpredictability, inconsistency, distortion, and what Rangell has called "compromise of integrity" (1963, 1974, 1980). Reich (1960) pointed out that to continue to hope for impossible infantile wishes reveals a basic inability to face inner and outer reality. The capacity to take reality into account in building and modifying an ideal self-representation is a sine qua non for adaptation and emotional well-being throughout life.

## SUPEREGO FUNCTIONS

The superego functions to maintain intrapsychic and interpersonal harmony and to facilitate social adaptation. To accomplish this task, according to Freud, the superego "observes the ego, gives it orders, judges it and threatens it with punishments, exactly like the parents whose place it has taken" (1940, p. 205). From these and other comments, it seems clear that Freud conceptualized the essential superego functions to be self-observation and the instigation of defense as well as self-judgment leading to self-approval and self-reward or to self-reproach, criticism, and self-punishment (1914, p. 95; 1917, p. 247; 1921, pp. 109, 110; 1923a, pp. 36, 37; 1933, p. 65).

A handicap in distinguishing superego functions is that they are not directly observable, but must be inferred from thoughts, ideas, moods, fantasies, attitudes, emotions, and feelings (Beres, 1958). Furthermore, superego functions are not easily differentiated from ego functions. Indeed, the conscious and unconscious monitoring of one's own actions and thoughts is more correctly considered an ego function that can be in the service of superego aims. This *self-observation* operates to prevent or modify behavior that deviates from the standards of the superego (Freud, 1914, p. 95; 1921, p. 105; 1940, p. 205). Once affects come to serve a signal function, memories of past experiences contribute to the perception of situations that are likely to lead to a breach of superego standards, so that guilty feelings act as a signal to *instigate defenses.* Freud pointed out that the modus operandi of the superego is in accordance with parental observations and criticism; an important step in development is accomplished when parental prohibitions remain effective in the parents' absence (1914, p. 96; 1940, p. 205). It should also be kept in mind that superego functioning may interfere with self-observation, leading to deceptions about the self and the outside world (Hartmann and Loewenstein, 1962, p. 58).

The superego also serves the function of *self-judgment,* comparing the individual's behavior with that of the ideal and assessing the degree of conformity or transgression. If a significant discrepancy is observed between the actual self-representation and the internal standard or ideal, then aggressively driven self-criticism, reproach, and punishment follow, usually in the form of painful affects such as shame, guilt, anxiety, depression, or feelings of inferiority, all of which lead to a loss of self-esteem (Jacobson, 1946). Because superego punishment can be as peremptory and irrational as any id impulse, Freud (1933) concluded that an aim of therapeutic analysis (as well as of later developmental stages, especially adolescence) is to reduce superego influence on ego functioning.

On the other hand, self-judgment can lead to self-approval. Then identifications made with a parent's rewarding, praising, and taking pride in the child can function in place of the parent, so that the child rewards himself. Feelings of pride, self-respect, elation, and elevated self-esteem follow adherence to internal standards.

Freud underlined the importance of superego functioning for narcissistic equilibrium: "But the major part of the sense of inferiority derives from the ego's relation to its super-ego; like the sense of guilt it is an expression of the tension between them. . . . it is hard to separate the sense of inferiority and the sense of guilt" (1933, pp. 65–66). Also, he said, "The torments caused by the reproaches of conscience correspond precisely to a child's fear of loss of love, a fear the place of which has been taken by the moral agency. On the other hand, if the ego has successfully resisted a temptation to do something which would be objectionable to the super-ego, it feels raised in its self-esteem and strengthened in its pride" (1940, p. 206).

More often than not, analytic writers emphasize sadistic superego components and pay less attention to its benevolent aspects—loving, protecting, and caring. Nunberg was among the first to discuss the concept of the benign superego, suggesting that its origins lay in the preoedipal mother-child relationship (1932, p. 145). Kramer elaborated on the idea of the internalization of the preoedipal loving mother; he suggested that when this directing and supporting aspect of the superego fails to develop, the ego is left helpless in dealing with the id, which leads to a variety of pathological outcomes (1958). Schafer similarly points to a "loving and beloved" aspect of the superego. It represents the loved and loving, protecting, comforting, and guiding oedipal and preoedipal parents who, "even in their punishing activities, provide needed expressions of parental care, contact, and love" (1960, p. 186).

As part of the successful establishment of libidinal object constancy, the child internalizes and identifies with these loving, guiding, caretaking functions along with the punishing functions of his parents; identification with the "object-as-comforter" (Furer, 1967) enables the child ultimately to love, protect, comfort, guide, and feel proud of himself.*

*There is some disagreement about whether these comforting functions are located in the ego or the superego. Earlier we have implied they are ego functions, whereas Furer discusses them in relation to the superego. Perhaps we can say that this is another example of the way in which the two systems overlap, with ego functions serving superego aims.

The successful consolidation of the superego therefore provides a powerful potential source of well-being; it enables the child to become progressively less dependent on external sources for "narcissistic supplies," and it provides a way to avoid disappointment and frustration by encouraging the child to live up to internalized standards and ideals.

One characteristic of the superego is that it never becomes homogenized; therefore various ideals form and persist within the ego ideal. The individual's ability to maintain self-esteem may, accordingly, be an indication of the harmony or imbalance and conflict within the system—intrasystemic conflict (Hartmann, 1950). Persistently low self-esteem suggests the possibility of conflict among ideals. As one patient described it, his mother was afraid he would become a man and hence supported his artistic and intellectual endeavors; his father was afraid he would become a gelding and encouraged rough, aggressive activities. The patient complained that he couldn't win; when pursuing intellectual activities, which he enjoyed, he felt low self-esteem because he thought he wasn't really a man. Harmonizing ideals within the ego ideal is another developmental task particularly important to adolescence.

We now turn to the development of this psychic system. In the next chapter we trace superego development from the earliest formation of dos and don'ts to the structuralization of a system that functions not only to create painful affects of shame, guilt, and low self-esteem but to ensure compliance to moral standards without external auxiliary support.

# CHAPTER 13

## THE DEVELOPMENT OF

## THE SUPEREGO

The developmental history of the superego is a long one. Ideals and introjects begin to form very early in life and continue to be influential alongside components that are added later; preoedipal, oedipal, and postoedipal experiences all make significant contributions to superego functioning. Therefore, the superego undergoes transformations throughout development and sometimes throughout life.

### EARLIEST BEGINNINGS

We see the superego as deriving from the child's wish to retain the love of his parents and maintain interpersonal harmony and his understanding that this requires a negotiation between his own and his parents' wishes. To have this motivation, the child clearly must have had adequate experiences in pleasurable interactions with his parents, beginning in early infancy. Subtle conscious and unconscious exchanges of messages occur during these interactions, contributing to early reciprocity that forms the anlage for introject formation (see Stern, 1977; Brazelton and Als, 1979; Sandler, 1981; Emde, 1988a, 1988b). The differentiation of self from nonself and the formation of stable self- and object representations may be considered among the requisite early developmental steps for superego formation. Several analysts suggest that the infant's earliest experiences of gratification and frustration with the mother play an important role in stimulating perception and promoting differentiation (Jacobson, 1954; Spitz, 1958; Sandler, 1960a; Kernberg, 1976). Auditory, visual, and kinesthetic modes of perception all make contributions to the superego-to-be. The experience of "things heard" (Freud, 1923a, p. 52), the parents' restrictions and prohibitions as "physical primordia" to a prohibitive superego (Spitz, 1958, p. 399), the soothing experience of being rocked, and the recognition of the mother's facial expressions in her mirroring role (Spitz, 1958; Peto, 1967; Winnicott, 1967; Riess, 1978) all leave an affective imprint on self- and object representations that is later reflected in the qualities of introjects and ideals.

## FORMATION OF INTROJECTS AND IDEALS

By about seven months the infant begins to look for the mother's affective expressions to help him regulate his behavioral response at moments of uncertainty (Emde, 1980b). Research suggests that the capacity to understand prohibitions and commands follows shortly and may be present by about nine months (Spitz, 1957). Thereafter, the infant's experiencing maternal prohibitions at times of uncertainty contributes to introject formation.

The developmental advances that accompany upright locomotion also have an effect on superego formation. Soon after walking, the toddler becomes willful, negation emerges in speech, and parental preoccupations focus on teaching discipline in addition to nourishing (Maccoby and Martin, 1983). The toddler's experience with the disciplining parent becomes internalized; as a part of this process he can be observed to refer to the parent's emotional expression either before or after a prohibited act.

Early introject formation is based not on an integrated representation of the whole mother but on pleasurable or unpleasurable experiences related to pleasure-giving or forbidding-punishing images of the mother (Brody and Mahoney, 1964). In fact, introjects differ considerably from simple replications of the external object; in addition to the infant's perceptions of the external object, distorted as they are by cognitive immaturity, the introjects embody projections that exaggerate and distort the parents' prohibiting and threatening aspects (Jones, 1947, pp. 148–149). The qualities of the early mother-child relationship, the child's reactions to restriction and frustration, and his capacity to tolerate frustration combine to determine the qualities of the introjects. When there is increased tension, distress, anxiety, or frustration, or when the infant's tolerance of frustration is low, his perception of the parent becomes increasingly distorted, lending harsh and cruel aspects to the coalescing introject. Kernberg (1976) points out that when loving aspects of the superego do not develop, it retains a primitive, aggressive, and easily projected quality derived from intense oral-aggressive fixations.

The formation of ideals parallels introject formation. Early wishful images of an ideal state of the self are based on real or fantasied early experiences of safety, pleasure, and affective oneness within the mother-child dyad. This ideal state forms the bedrock of the ideal self-representations, to which the infant's sense of grandiosity and omnipotence in the practicing phase adds an active pleasurable component. Since parents at this time are usually viewed as omnipotent and perfect, these views provide the basis of ideal object representations. The ego ideal thus harbors the preoedipal child's grandiose wishes as well as his beliefs in parental omnipotence (Jacobson, 1964).

## COMPLIANCE WITH THE OBJECT

Developmental accomplishments in drive maturation, rapprochement ambivalence, and expansion of cognitive skills relevant to the second year of life, described earlier, interact with, influence, and are influenced by developments in superego structuralization.

Sander describes the salient issue of the toddler's second year: he "determines the mother's availability to facilitate his goal-directed intentions and to meet his specific needs," whereas the issue for the mother is to harmonize "her nurturance with her limits" (1983, p. 342). A basically loving, comforting, and regulating reciprocity between mother and child facilitates the child's acceptance of parental standards and rules. If rapprochement turbulence is severe, it may disrupt this pleasurable reciprocity to the extent that it interferes with the child's view of the parents as ideal; the toddler then has difficulties accepting mother's limits and superego development is impaired.

Typical developmental conflicts of the anal-rapprochement phase, in which the toddler's wish to express his will freely is countered by mother's demands for impulse restriction, creates the potential for intrapsychic conflict. When the toddler begins to recognize a difference between his mother's wishes and the inner world of his own impulses and desires, he becomes frustrated and angry; but because of earlier experiences of social referencing, he is also aware of the regulating comfort mother's love brings, even though mother's love now has some conditions. The toddler perceives at a remarkably early age that his mother also has an idea of her "ideal" child, perhaps because of his tendency to check mother's emotional signals either before or after a prohibited act as if seeking confirmation about it being right or wrong (see Emde, 1988a). He therefore struggles with incompatible wishes for free expression of his own will and wishes to be mother's ideal child and find reciprocal harmony. Ambivalence reaches new heights. But as pleasure in his omnipotence begins to wane, winning the approval of the idealized parent(s) becomes a major early source of self-esteem (an anlage for the later need for superego approval).

Ferenczi (1925) saw that toileting issues provide the context for some of the most salient early developmental conflicts and that compliance in the control of excretory functions indicates beginning internalization. He gave the name "sphincter morality" to compliance with parental demands. Unfortunately, the term has acquired a pejorative connotation because it refers to compliance with the demands of an idealized external object, regardless of inner standards, in order to gain love, recognition, or power.

Clearly, compliance does not guarantee eventual identification with the standards of the object. If a mother's standards are too high, or if she is highly critical and disapproving, or if a child's libidinal or aggressive impulses are particularly difficult for him to control, the toddler may experience few opportunities for success and reward, always feeling in danger of losing mother's love and comfort. To guard against such a loss, the toddler may overvalue and idealize parental standards and develop early and excessive reaction formations (Jacobson, 1964, pp. 96–100). This leads to the formation of perfectionistic and critical introjects, and the toddler strives to be always "good" as feelings of shame and disgust are turned on the self whenever drive derivatives find expression. Compliance with the wishes of the object is then used to defend against drive expression, particularly against object-directed hostile aggression. If extreme, such passive surrender may lead to dependency instead of autonomy, a loss of spontaneity may result, and compliance may become a pervasive character trait.* Ritvo and Solnit (1960) discuss some of the necessary ingredients for identification as contrasted to passive compliance.

Compliance to mother's demands, however, not only leads to modification of the toddler's behavior but also facilitates an internalization

*The formation of perfectionistic, critical introjects not only can lead to excessive compliance but can interfere with interpersonal relations. Introject demands became incorporated into ideal object representations, and when real people do not meet the idealized expectations, they are critically devalued. Consequently, the person tends to be continually disappointed in others as well as in himself; but because he remains excessively dependent on others for narcissistic supplies, he tends to move from one object to another, a problem first described by Freud (1914, p. 101).

of those demands and the formation of more cohesive introjects. Therefore, the child's compliance to mother's demands indicates the beginnings of internalized conflict. This is a central achievement of the anal-rapprochement phase, marking a significant step in superego development by the beginnings of internal controls, for the introjects come to be experienced (unconsciously) as an internal voice of authority.

From the developmental point of view, the toddler's experience of frustration now originates from three sources: the object's failure to fulfill his wishes, the toddler's abstinence in efforts to comply with his mother's wishes, and his efforts to comply with the increasing demands of introjects. The process of introject formation is often evident when the toddler, in a kind of early role-playing, punishes himself for misdeeds. He may say "No, no" to himself in identification with the aggressor, that is, in identification with his mother's saying "No" to him (A. Freud, 1936), slap his own hand, or show identification with the prohibiting parent in his gestures, facial expressions, inflections, actions, and attitudes (Spitz, 1957). The toddler at this stage, however, has not yet made the demands of the introject his own; he has not yet identified with the introject. He continues to need external reinforcement to bolster emerging internal standards.

Several observers have recognized the importance of the mother's empathy and consistency to the child's superego development, especially during this phase (Ritvo and Solnit, 1960; Winnicott, 1962b; Furer, 1967). Excessive gratification, inconsistency, or failure to set limits may be detrimental. Without the help and structure provided by the more mature adult, the toddler is deprived of opportunities to build his frustration tolerance slowly by the gradual titration of frustrating experiences. His establishment of inner controls is likewise delayed, and instead, unrealistic expectations of gratification from overidealized parental representations persist, interfering later with the possibilities of mature object relations.

Optimally, the mother empathically adapts her requests to the toddler's capacities rather than arbitrarily setting impossible standards or simply acquiescing to the toddler's demands. The toddler can then experience his conformity as pride shared with mother and does not have to feel his successful restriction of his wishes and impulses as frustration and humiliation or as a loss of omnipotence and control. He experiences such a mother as a stable, comforting, and loving authority figure; the toddler, by identification with her nonpunitive control, gains confidence in his self-control while building frustration tolerance. These ideal conditions contribute to the formation of an ego that, in interaction with the superego, will be nurturing and protective (Schafer, 1960).

In this regard, the emphasis currently given to empathy often overlooks how the subtleties of parent-child interaction affect the child's psychic structuralization. What is taken to be empathy may in fact be the mother's vicariously living out her own prohibited wishes through her child's unfettered behavior. Olden (1953) suggests that a mother's apparent empathy may be based on her own narcissistic needs more than the child's needs. In this case she may be inconsistent in her demands and apply inappropriate and inconsistent punishments. A mother who responds on this basis may, as Brody (1982) suggests, foster narcissistic demands in the infant and moral masochism in herself. The latter appears when, for example, the mother fears that making demands may unleash her own aggression and so she gives in at the first sign of her child's resistance. Inconsistencies in expectations and punishment delay internalization of conflict; instead of making inner compromises in an effort to comply with the object (and later the introject), the child maintains his fantasy of his own omnipotence and directs his efforts toward manipulating the object in the hope of having all desires met. The harsh and punishing qualities of the parent, exaggerated because of the child's anger that is projected, are then internalized and become part of the introject. Such an unfriendly inner world erodes the child's sense of safety, and sadomasochistic character traits often result, with the child showing a clinging hostile dependence on the object.

One four-year-old patient provides an example. Her favorite fantasy game is Cinderella, and she pretends her idealized fairy godmother gives her everything she wants. In reality, she screams with rage when *all* her wishes are not gratified and has a temper tantrum on noticing that her mother has two pillows and she has only one. She says she hates her mother, easily provokes her mother's angry attack, then feels that no one likes her, and fears that her mother will one day abandon her for another child. Her mother says she tries to be consistent, but she cannot tolerate being "mean"; setting and maintaining limits make her feel "mean."

The child's idealization of the parents is a normal part of superego development and essential to his learning to cope with his impulses. Winning the love of the idealized object gradually becomes as important as or more important than drive gratification. Indeed, Nunberg suggested that the child's earliest acceptance of parental restrictions is based upon his love for his parents. It is the love of his parents and his difficulty in tolerating painful ambivalence that foster the wish to comply and eventually to identify with their demands and expectations (1932, p. 145; see also Holder, 1982).

If the toddler lacks such an idealized view, parental love does not compensate him for relinquished gratification. Insufficient or prematurely lost parental idealization may compromise the child's sense of support in mastering instinctual impulses and deprive him of an important source of the sense of self-worth and accomplishment (Hartmann and Loewenstein, 1962, p. 61). He then feels little conflict between drive- and object-related wishes, and so has little motivation to comply with the object's wishes. Under such circumstances the child's conformity to mother's wishes, instead of leading to a sense of pride, may lead to a fear of loss of power and control, and passive surrender. His efforts to retain or regain the earlier, now idealized blissful state may lead to the pathological persistence of (or a later defensive regression to) early forms of self-aggrandizement. Such aggrandizement may later result in narcissistic object choices (Reich, 1960) and interfere with the individual's maintenance of self-esteem in that he remains vulnerable to a depressive response; when his "grand" view of himself is not sufficiently maintained he will feel injured, inferior, and enraged.

## INTERNALIZED CONFLICT AND COMPLIANCE WITH THE INTROJECT

Advances in cognitive skills between the ages of two and three years provide richer content and detail to the young child's thinking and fantasy life. This brings a potential for further superego structuralization. Now when the child is angry and does not conform to his mother's wishes or to her view of the "ideal child," he may anxiously imagine various consequences—loss of love, loss of the object, or punishment. To avoid these and the accompanying anxiety, the child begins to comply with the internalized dos and don'ts even when mother is absent, and the influence of the introjects expands. Only when the child is obedient to the mother's wishes in her absence can we infer the attainment of compliance with the introject.

Emde reports research that suggests children by the age of three have developed some capacity to comply with the introject. In an experimental situation, a young child is at play with a tester in a room full of toys. The mother comes in with two new toys, instructs the child not to touch them while she is gone, and leaves. The child then plays puppets with the tester, and after a while the tester's puppet expresses a desire to play with the prohibited toys. Some children in the study were able to resist temptation, saying in effect, "Didn't you hear my mommy? I better not play with those toys. We better not either" (1988a, p. 36). Emde and his colleagues concluded that these children had an internalized sense of the mother, her rules, and their obligatory role in relation to both. This internal sense of the "other" gave them a sense of control with which they were able to resist temptation.

Compliance with certain demands of the introject is facilitated by reaction formations that incorporate the earliest self-critical functions; the reaction formations of this period reflect phase-appropriate developmental conflicts, especially around issues of body management such as toilet training or the control of hostile aggression. Feelings of disgust at loss of sphincter control (or related expressions of instinctual gratification) are turned on the self, and the painful affect of shame may be experienced along with a loss of self-regard. As one little girl, age two years eight months said, after a wetting accident, "I don't like me." Shame in response to internal criticism (to be differentiated from remorse, embarrassment, and humiliation in response to external criticism) indicates that attempts are being made to comply with the demands of the introject. Defensive reaction formations accordingly guard against instinctual gratification at the same time that they ensure a modicum of self-esteem regulation by warding off the painful affect of shame, an aspect of superego development emphasized by Jacobson (1964).

Compliance with the introject contributes to and later safeguards object and self-constancy. It follows efforts to resolve painful ambivalent feelings toward the object, and it ensures the object's pleasurable responses, reinforcing the loving internal image of mother (Mahler et al., 1975) and the "lovable" self-image (R. L. Tyson, 1983). The child's difficulties in complying with the introject, however, should not be underestimated. In early childhood, ego functioning is relatively weak in comparison to the strength of the impulses. Consequently, even though children as young as two and a half or three may feel remorse, shame, and eventually guilt when their behavior does not comply with the demands of the introject, these painful affects do not function to prevent future transgressions. Whereas a guilty conscience may indicate that parental standards have been internalized, the effective use of guilt as a signal ("moral anxiety"—Freud, 1926) to prevent unacceptable behavior begins only later, a gap in superego functioning discussed by Anna Freud (1936, pp. 116–119).

## INTRASYSTEMIC CONFLICT: CONFLICTING IDEALS AND INTROJECTS

The developmental advance toward the infantile genital phase brings about an increased range of interpersonal and eventually intrapsychic conflict, and a variety of mutually exclusive internalized demands and ideals begins to form. The stage is now set for intrasystemic conflict—that is, conflict within the superego system.

During the infantile genital phase, when pressing gender-identity issues are dealt with (described in part VII), a wide variety of wished-for self-representations in identification with idealized same- and opposite-sex objects emerges. Indeed we believe that a crucial, although insufficiently emphasized, factor in superego formation is the wish for the love of the same-sex idealized parent. Although this idea is implicit in Freud's suggestion of the centrality of castration anxiety for male superego formation, we wish to stress not only the motivation provided by threatened punishment but the motivation provided by the wish to repeat pleasurable interactions with the idealized object. In addition to providing pleasure and a sense of safety, these interactions are a vehicle through which the child makes crucial identifications that enhance a competent and stable sense of masculinity or femininity. Ambivalence felt toward that idealized object can result in a painful sense of alienation; therefore the child complies with and identifies with the directives of that idealized object in efforts to avoid, tolerate, or resolve painful ambivalence. These identifications play a crucial part in superego formation. But the timing of this influence differs in girls and boys. Elsewhere we described how ego ideal formation, based on identification with the same-sex parent as ideal, begins earlier for the girl than for the boy (Tyson and Tyson, 1984). In its core, the girl's ego ideal harbors the fantasized and idealized state of intimate oneness with the mother of infancy.

Identifications with the same-sex parent made during the infantile genital phase stimulate oedipal fantasies, which include hatred toward and love for both parents. These fantasies and ambivalent feelings promote further identifications with them. The child is soon caught in an impossible bind with conflicting gender-related identifications and conflicting hating-and-loving feelings toward each parent. Because the expectations of the parents usually differ, the child senses that being the "ideal child" for one parent risks displeasing the other.

In addition, ideals and wished-for gratifications from earlier developmental stages conflict with infantile genital and emergent oedipal ideals. Attempts to serve one internal demand invariably lead to infraction of another. A little girl's fantasied ideal of oneness with her mother, for example, stands in contrast to an oedipal wish for father. She can hardly be mother to father's baby at the same time that she wishes to be mother's baby.

Such intrasystemic superego conflicts lead to inconsistency in superego functioning and provide a further source of narcissistic vulnerability. Reaching the ideal is impossible as the various parental expectations become embodied in introjects, and phase-appropriate and parent-specific ideals find representation within the ego ideal. Intrasystemic conflict typically begins in early childhood, but the ultimate reconciliation of conflicting standards and ideals, resulting in a more stable narcissistic equilibrium, is an achievement not reached until late adolescence; even then, certain intrasystemic conflicts tend to persist indefinitely.

## IDENTIFICATION WITH INTROJECTS AND IDEALS—GUILT

The Oedipus complex provides a central nidus in the process of superego formation. Preoedipal determinants make important contributions, as we have described, but the Oedipus complex serves to reorganize earlier introjects and ideals so that the superego becomes a more coherently functioning system. As Waelder (1936) long ago pointed out, there is a significant difference between the guilt (we would say remorse) experienced in the presence of a dreaded external object and the guilt experienced in response to an inner institution, the superego.

Having reached the infantile genital phase of psychosexual progression, and having successfully identified with the same-sex parent as a role model (a process we describe in part VII), the child usually engages in the wishful fantasies of the Oedipus complex with its characteristic extremes of love and hate, sadism and masochistic self-sacrifice. Earlier fears of object loss and loss of love take on new dimensions with triadic object relations as both parents become embroiled in the child's oedipal fantasy. Narcissistic vulnerability is also heightened since unfulfilled oedipal wishes are frequently experienced as humiliating rejection.

In addition, fears of retaliatory hostility from the oedipal rival make a contribution to the superego. Fears of retribution are often imagined in the form of bodily injury at this stage of development. Because sexual excitement is now genitally located, boys in particular imagine that genital damage will be the punishment for oedipal wishes, a fear based on the primitive concept of "talion law" (that is, retaliatory, eye-for-an-eye justice; Freud, 1913) prevalent in children at this age and stage of cognitive development. The boy therefore imagines that since his penis is the locus of his sexual excitement, and his narcissistic investment in his penis is central to his ideal image of masculinity, then punishment for oedipal wishes will be castration.

Although the girl may fear genital damage as a result of her masturbatory activity, in a more generalized way she fears any kind of bodily harm as magically representing her mother's retaliatory efforts to attack her beauty and reduce her desirability as a sexual object for her father. One six-year-old, for example, became hysterically upset after being stung by a bee, which she imagined a witch had magically sent. On being questioned, she said, "I have such long eyelashes that people say I'm pretty, and so the witch is jealous!"

These fears are exaggerated because of the narcissistic investment in the body, the nature of the child's fantasy, and the influence of primary process thinking; they are nevertheless based on multiple early childhood experiences of getting hurt and experiencing pain. Helplessness and vulnerability in the face of overpowering adult strength, as in tickling games, physical punishment, sexual or physical abuse, or medical interventions add to these fears.

Fears of body damage further the process of superego structuralization. The child wishes to avoid not only bodily harm but also the loss of the idealized relationship with a parent who is also idealized. Thus the child is motivated to give up incestuous wishes and adhere to parental and internal standards by the triple threat of bodily harm, narcissistic injury, and loss of love, just as earlier reaction formations and fear of loss of the object's love helped in coping with conflicts over anal impulses. Oedipal conflicts accordingly serve as a powerful though not the exclusive motivating force for superego formation, as Freud (1924a) described.

The Oedipus complex also holds the potential for a further step in superego formation—identification with the introjects and ideals. Increasingly the child becomes aware that the parents not only enforce behavioral standards but themselves live by a set of moral and ethical codes. The child's idealization of the parent comes to include idealization of those codes (Hartmann et al., 1946), and he constructs his own internal morality in identification with the rather concretely idealized parental moral standards.

With increasing internalization of conflict, the child begins to fear loss of love from his superego more than from his parents; superego punishment is experienced simultaneously, in differing proportions, as loss of self-esteem and as the painful affect of guilt, the "hallmark" of the superego (Beres, 1958). This sense of guilt may be conscious, or it may be manifested in conscious derivatives of an active, unconscious defensive process (Pulver, 1974)—for example, in the form of self-punishment or additional feelings of inferiority or loss of self-esteem. As the superego becomes a functioning inner source of punishment, fears of inner disapproval for failure to maintain internalized standards are as powerful a motivator to adhere to behavioral standards as were earlier fears of object loss, loss of love, humiliation, castration, or other body damage.

To avoid this sense of guilt, the child normally makes further internal compromises. Then, in seeking expiation, love, and approval from his superego, he strives to identify with the demands and ideals it embodies. In so doing, he becomes less dependent on external sources to ensure his compliance to behavioral standards and obtain adequate self-esteem.

Oedipal resolution is facilitated by the child's eventual (although never total) identification with his own internal moral codes. Although evidence of identification with certain ideals and introjects is apparent before oedipal progression (in the reaction formations of the three-year-old, for example), the child takes a further developmental step when these identifications become more consistent. Conflicts lessen as the identification process proceeds, since introject demands and the standards of the ideal become the wishes and characteristics of the self-representation. By identifying with the ideal, the child feels an increase in self-esteem that in some ways compensates for the relinquished drive wishes. This identification also helps the child feel protected from the dangers of drive expression and the consequent narcissistic mortifications that the Oedipus complex threatens. Furthermore, as guilt comes to serve a signal function, the child becomes more sensitive to avoiding those situations that may arouse intense guilt. In the absence of regression or significant intrasystemic conflict, behavior increasingly becomes automatic or "second nature" in accordance with internalized moral codes and the demands of the introjects.

These crucial identifications mean that the emergent superego, although unstable and subject to externalization, can be considered a coherent functional mental unit. The infantile neurosis is now in place, as the origins of conflict, punishment, and the sources of self-esteem are all internal.

Barring insurmountable conflict or external interference, the child gradually relinquishes his oedipal incestuous wishes, and the related conflicts find some resolution because of the now internal punishing agent, the strict policies of which are in proportion to the intensity of sexual and aggressive impulses. Self-esteem is vulnerable to the extent that punitive, self-judging functions are quick to punish infringement of introject demands or failure to achieve ideal standards, although inner controls remain weak in comparison with drive impulses. To some extent this inconsistency in functioning remains characteristic of the superego, for its functioning is never uniform nor totally reliable. Parental love or some form of external narcissistic supply will therefore be needed to balance inner criticism. Gradually, however, the self-approval gained from adherence to inner ideals and morals begins to outweigh the presumed value of the wished-for pleasure and gratification from external sources, as the infantile neurosis is in place and the voice of conscience is experienced as part of a distinctly separate inner institution.

## OEDIPAL RESOLUTION AND SUPEREGO COHERENCE

On the basis of child analytic experience and child observations, Holder (1982) contends that the contribution of oedipal resolution to superego formation may be overemphasized. He points out that some latency-age children, while still in the midst of oedipal struggles with undiminished rivalry and death wishes toward the opposite-sex parent and strong wishes to take his or her place in the affections of the same-sex parent, nevertheless may have internalized and structured super-egos that function autonomously. Such children do not always demonstrate those kinds of parental identifications that earmark oedipal resolution; they nevertheless seem to be subject to strong feelings of guilt not only as a consequence of actions but also because of certain of their wishes.

Holder's argument reflects what Loewald (1979) calls the "waning of the Oedipus complex" in psychoanalysis. That is, the current predominance of interest in preoedipal development seems to us to have led to a diminished appreciation of the influence that oedipal engagement and resolution, or their absence or insufficiency, has on later development. As we see it, more is required to reach superego autonomy than identification with parental punishing introjects.

We have already pointed out that introjects and ideals are formed early, so that introjection of parental authority and the need for punishment to atone for "crimes" (in fact or fantasy) may exist before oedipal engagement. In spite of early feelings of guilt (or at least remorse), the child may persist in seeking forbidden pleasures with the onset of oedipal impulses, whether in the form of acting on incestuous wishes toward objects or other forms of drive expression.

We maintain, therefore, that it is the internalization of parental values and moral codes and the identification with these internal codes that transform oedipal interpersonal conflicts to intrapsychic conflicts. This implies internal modifications through defense and compromise rather than through continued environmental manipulation. It is only by identifying with his own internalized moral codes that the child takes increasing responsibility for his own actions. It follows that a failure to internalize parental values or to identify with the internalized standards represents a failure in superego structuralization, in which case the child may feel narcissistically entitled to oedipal fulfillment and cheated when his wishes are not gratified. Such a failure is suggested by rapid shifts in self-esteem, by varying values and behaviors in different situations with different people as the child tries to manipulate the environment to obtain instinctual gratification, and by continued reliance on external objects as a means of controlling instinctual impulsive behavior and maintaining self-esteem. An example of this can be seen in one seven-year-old. Caught in sexual play with another girl, she felt no obvious remorse, but rather became furious with her parents—what right did they have to come into her room?

One can then ask whether it is oedipal resolution that consolidates superego functioning leading to autonomy or more consistent superego functioning that facilitates oedipal resolution. Having raised the question, we answer that it must be both. Oedipal wishes ordinarily lead to guilt feelings (especially since the superego does not distinguish between intentions and deeds [Freud, 1930]), and a significant impetus for oedipal renunciation and identification with internalized parental values comes from all the painful affects associated with superego functioning. But in this case the infantile neurosis is in place and psychic structuring advances accordingly. We agree with Jones that "the concept of the superego is a nodal point where we may expect all the obscure problems of Oedipus complex and narcissism on the one hand, and hate and sadism on the other, to meet" (1926, p. 304).

## LATENCY AND THE SUPEREGO AS INNER AUTHORITY

Adequate developmental progression requires that the latency child become accustomed to the superego as an inner voice of authority, and that the superego become more tolerant of drive expression, modifying some of the archaic stringent features of the early introjects. Early in latency, superego functioning tends to be harsh, primitive, rigid, inconsistent, and easily externalized. These gaps and exaggerations in early latency superego functioning result from the fact that the superego is not an exact inner replica of functions previously available from others in the outer world but a distorted and, especially to begin with, an unstable version of them. Consequently, the child may appear at one moment to be a budding delinquent with no internalized moral standards; at the next moment he may be excessively moral and, like a police officer, supervise and report on the transgressions of others and at the same time blame others for his own wrongdoings. At yet another time, he may behave in such a way as to incur repeated punishments to assuage his unconscious guilt, much to everyone's puzzlement (Freud, 1917).

Because the child's capacity for restraint is relatively weak in relation to strong drive pressures, he is frequently unsuccessful in upholding the uncompromising superego standards and ideals. This makes for a period of vulnerable self-esteem in early latency. Character traits appear more marked now than before. Many such traits are based on reaction formations, but they become lasting ethical principles (Freud, 1926). The latency child shows concern with rules and fairness, and especially insists that others obey the rules and be fair.

The superego's detection and control of drive impulses is particularly important to the latency child. Strict restraints are necessary because of the need to repress associated oedipal incestuous wishes. When inhibitions against masturbation are severe, a wide variety of symptoms, such as compulsive rituals, obsessional thinking, pervasive daydreaming, inattentiveness or lack of concentration at school, or even antisocial behavior may appear. If these are unsuccessful, the child may engage in compulsive masturbation, particularly the latency boy. A vicious cycle can be established because of excessive guilt, rigid internal standards, and fears of castration. Bornstein notes that the less displaced and distorted the child's occasional masturbatory activities, the less paralyzing will be the ensuing feelings of guilt (1953, p. 70).

The latency child's expanding social world brings new temptations at the same time that the parents' support of standards diminishes as they expect their child to function more autonomously in this regard. Coping with sexual and aggressive drives with lessening parental support challenges the immature ego and superego, exposing vulnerabilities in superego functioning. Behavior problems in school may result

(A. Freud, 1949) as well as occasional episodes of sexual play among peers, followed by pangs of guilt.

Conflicts and guilt around masturbatory impulses tend to diminish toward the second half of latency. The child has a better integrated defensive structure to ward off intrusive sexual impulses; the superego is less primitive—a bit less harsh and demanding—and masturbation and related fantasies, by now better disguised and displaced from the original oedipal wishes and objects, seem less dangerous. Hence, occasional undistorted genital masturbation accompanied by overt sexual fantasies occurs in the psychologically healthy older latency child.

In its earlier stages, the superego is easily externalized. The boy who trembles all day at the thought of what father will say about his soiling himself, only to hear father say, "Accidents will happen," demonstrates this. The child's future development, however, requires that he begin in latency to take responsibility for his actions and to experience the superego as an internal voice of authority.

In part, the continuing identificatory process with parental morals and values stabilizes superego functioning and affords it progressive independence from the pressures exerted by the first or primitive introjects and the drives (Hartmann and Loewenstein, 1962; E. Jacobson, 1964). As identification with internal rules and standards proceeds, self-criticism and punishment as well as self-reward with a more consistent feeling of well-being become increasingly independent of external authority. As this stability and independence emerges, one can begin to speak of an *autonomous superego.*

As an intermediate step in this process, the child exercises moral standards with peers different from those that must remain effective in the presence of adults. Then, as Anna Freud noted, "True morality begins when the internalized criticism, now embodied in the standard exacted by the superego, coincides with the ego's perception of its own fault" (1936, p. 119).

A dual latency task, therefore, which requires the integration of developing ego, cognitive, and superego functions, is to relax severe superego punishment policies while shoring up, revising, and consolidating moral codes. Piaget (1964), Kohlberg (1981), and Gilligan (1982) have studied morality and the way moral codes change over developmental time. These changes are facilitated by advances in the capacity for abstract thinking, enabling the child to make moral discriminations independent of external support in a more consistent and adaptive manner.

Internalization and consolidation of parental attitudes, authority, and values continue throughout latency; along the way, the child finds other admired figures whose demands and standards may differ from his parents'. These differences allow the child to reevaluate the parents' standards and to modify or add to his concepts of morality in a process of superego depersonification. Freud commented, "In the course of development the super-ego also takes on the influences of those who have stepped into the place of parents—educators, teachers, people chosen as ideal models. Normally it departs more and more from the original parental figures; it becomes, so to say, more impersonal" (1933, p. 64).

Sometimes a child fails to take sufficient responsibility for his own actions, indicating that superego directives have been poorly internalized or are easily externalized, so that he continues to experience authority as lodged in the external world. Lacking superego autonomy, the child remains dependent on others and yet resists the pressure and structure they provide. He continues to operate on the pleasure principle, does not conform to behavioral expectations, and is unable to make identifications with authority figures. He feels misunderstood, mistreated, and abused by the environment. Such a child usually has grave difficulties in adolescence, when morals, standards, and their regulations are ordinarily reexternalized and reevaluated. If he has never achieved internal regulation and superego autonomy, the adolescent tends to continue to expect the environment to conform to his wishes; he predictably feels narcissistically wounded when his conviction that the world owes him something is repeatedly disappointed.

## THE SUPEREGO IN ADOLESCENCE

The biological changes of puberty set in motion what Erikson (1956) called the "normative crisis" of adolescence, for which latency achievements have prepared the ground. Superego functioning plays a crucial role in determining whether the individual realizes his potentials in this period, for new shifts must take place in attitudes toward the drives, objects, and ideals. In addition, if the adolescent is to become fully autonomous he must take significantly increased responsibility for himself and his actions. This implies that the superego must become fully internalized and parental authority relinquished. Finally, ego functioning must predominate over superego functioning.

Freud commented that "one of the most significant, but also one of the most painful, psychical achievements of the pubertal period is . . . detachment from parental authority, a process that alone makes possible the opposition . . . between the new generation and the old" (1905b, p. 227). Jacobson (1961) observed that the definite and final abandonment of practical and mental dependency on the parents is often accompanied by intense grief, which has no parallel in childhood. This is because, as Loewald points out, taking over authority from the parents is in psychic reality tantamount to murdering the parents; not only is their authority destroyed, but they are destroyed as libidinal objects (1979, p. 390). Although the process of assuming responsibility for oneself begins earlier, its completion is a task for adolescence, a time when early ideals and introjects are reevaluated and modified and the superego reconsolidated so that it can function as a stable and durable system in tune with adult realities. At this time, too, optimal development in the adolescent is accompanied by a parallel process in the parents, who must gradually relinquish their power and authority over the young person.

Regressive personification of the superego—that is, externalization of internal authority—is the first step in the adolescent's process of superego reorganization. Rather than feeling the conflict to be an internal one, he now feels himself to be in a constant battle with his parents. Even as he relies upon them to maintain standards and provide stability, he may fight the imposition of those standards bitterly.

On the other hand, varieties of inconsistent superego functioning result when the adolescent's parents differ in their expectations or when a parent is inconsistent. At times a parent may be demanding in one area and yet permissive in another, or demanding of a certain behavior and yet providing a model of the opposite, as a mother's refusing to allow her daughter to date while being promiscuous herself (see Blum, 1985, for a clinical example). Although we discussed the possible detrimental effects of parents' inconsistency in regard to early childhood, their inconsistency during adolescence can have an equally damaging effect because of the instability of the adolescent's superego at this time and the need for external authority.

Relinquishing parents (or their internalized representations) as libidinal objects and as objects of authority may lead the adolescent to feel lonely, unhappy, and isolated, a state of mind Anna Freud (1958) referred to as "inner object loss." To cope with these feelings, he displaces emotional ties as well as superego functions onto the group and replaces identifications with parents by identifications with a strong, idealized group leader.

Freud observed:

The intense emotional ties which we observe in groups are quite sufficient to explain one of their characteristics—the lack of independence
and initiative in their members, the similarity in the reactions of all of
them, their reduction, so to speak, to the level of group individuals. But
if we look at it as a whole, a group shows us more than this. Some of its
features—the weakness of intellectual ability, the lack of emotional restraint, the incapacity for moderation and delay, the inclination to exceed
every limit in the expression of emotion and to work it off completely in
the form of action—these and similar features . . . show an unmistakable
picture of a regression of mental activity to an earlier stage." (1921,
p. 117)

Freud's description of group behavior is particularly relevant to the
understanding of adolescent groups. It is as if the adolescent suffers no
guilt for failing to adhere strictly to his internal standards as long as his
emotional ties and authority are displaced onto the group. The group
functions as a means through which regressive drive impulses and
object-related conflicts can be reworked at the same time that early
introjects and ideals are reexamined. Indeed, the group offers alternative identifications, standards, and emotional support during the chaos
of superego regression and reorganization.

Success in finally breaking away from oedipal ties, establishing new
object relations, and reorganizing psychic structures is achieved only as
long as these changes do not deplete the libidinal investments in, or
eradicate the identifications of, the past (Jacobson, 1964, p. 173). If
group standards differ too greatly from already internalized moral
codes, the adolescent may be thrown into tremendous turmoil and
infantile conflicts will merely be repeated in a new context. The remaining ties to the past are such that, for optimal progress, the adolescent must ultimately negotiate a rapprochement with his parents to
consciously and unconsciously accept and identify with certain of their
adult standards and moral codes while rejecting others. The adolescent's selectively identifying with parental moral standards and integrating them with the moral codes built up from early childhood and
with those derived from peer relationships further his psychic structure elaboration. The superego becomes a more coherent and stable
organization that enables him to be his own authority and to accept
responsibility for himself at the same time that he is becoming increasingly independent of his parents.

We must be careful, however, not to underestimate how long this
process takes. One nineteen-year-old's car was rammed. He was not at

fault, but imagined his father would have to go to court with him. Since he could not imagine himself to be in a position of authority, he could not imagine anyone believing him.

In addition to modifying introjected parental standards, superego reorganization entails modification of early ideals. The idealized parents of infancy are very different from the parents of adolescence, and the goals represented by the infantile ideal may bear little resemblance to reality and the individual's potential capacities. For the adolescent to make such changes requires the revival of infantile bisexual wishes preserved in the ego ideal. Displacing these wishes to the peer group and an admired group leader serves to diminish the anxiety they arouse, although fears of homosexual attachment sometimes work in the other direction. Other displacements are evident as the adolescent looks to teachers, sports heroes, singers, band groups, movie stars— figures that the group or society at large deems to be special—as the adolescent remodels his ego ideal, which normally departs more and more from the original parental figures.

Blos speaks of achieving "secondary object constancy" as a process in which the old idealized omnipotent parental images lodged in the superego become "humanized" (1967, p. 181). The older adolescent reevaluates idealized views of the past parents in the light of a more realistic image of the parents of the present; in so doing, he further modifies ideal object and self-representations to conform to external reality. The optimal outcome is an internalization of ideal goals that are valued and are still within the realistic potential of the individual. This makes it possible for the adult self-representation and ego ideal to become more alike; consequently self-esteem can be more consistently maintained.

As part of this outcome, the superego contains more realistic ideals and moral standards, and it functions more compassionately in its guiding, judging, criticizing, and punishing dimensions. As the voice of authority is again securely lodged within the mind, the superego structure optimally gains individuality, flexibility, and stability, and it becomes a mature, autonomous, coherent, and consistently functioning psychic system.

To some extent this is an idealized picture, for the superego always retains the capacity to revive early primitive introjects, moral directives, and ideals along with the accompanying harsh and retaliatory judgments. Inasmuch as this primitive core remains, the potential for hostile self-recrimination and punishment remains. The superego also remains vulnerable to externalization throughout life, as when we experience revived infantile neurotic conflicts as interpersonal in nature. This occurs in psychoanalytic treatment, for example, where the analyst is often felt to be judging and persecuting. Such an experience illustrates that in spite of later modifications and revisions, preoedipal and oedipal conflicts consolidated in the infantile neurosis remain at the center of the superego.

## SUMMARY

The history of superego development extends from its beginnings in the reciprocal interaction of mother and child to the nodal preoedipal and oedipal conflicts consolidated in the infantile neurosis through latency internalization and adolescent reorganization to some variable point in adult life. Major waves of revision occur with oedipal resolution and in adolescence, but our ideals, values, and morals may be subject to further revision throughout life as we are influenced by new people, new ideas, and new values. The individual's conscience, although continuing to represent "right" and "wrong" categorically, may be flexible in the enforcement of its "laws," depending upon circumstances. Similarly, although our most primitive wished-for ideals persist, we can also reevaluate them in the light of a realistic assessment of potential.

In addition to its modifiability, the superego retains its vulnerability to externalization throughout life. In mastering the Oedipus complex in both the infantile and the adolescent versions, and in making the necessary accompanying changes in superego structure and functioning, we become, however, responsible for ourselves.

We have described the major steps in superego development as follows:
1. Earliest beginnings
2. Formation of primitive introjects and ideals
3. Developmental conflict, compliance with the object, and conflict internalization
4. Internalized conflict and compliance with the introject
5. Intrasystemic conflict: conflicting ideals and introjects
6. The Oedipus complex, identification with introjects and ideals, and guilt
7. Oedipal resolution and superego coherence
8. Latency, the inner voice of authority, and superego autonomy
9. Externalization, modification, and reinternalization in adolescence
10. Ego supremacy

# CHAPTER 14

## GENDER DIFFERENCES IN

## SUPEREGO DEVELOPMENT

Having stressed the common elements in superego functioning and development in females and males, we now turn our focus to gender differences in the ways children experience and cope with their sexuality, their aggression, and their experiences with their parents as these affect superego development. After a survey of explanations offered in rebuttal of Freud's view of superego development and functioning in women, we describe separately the features unique to superego development in the female and in the male.* Our discussion will be limited to early childhood as our focus is on the formation of the superego rather than on later revisions.

### THEORIES OF SUPEREGO DEVELOPMENT IN THE FEMALE

Freud assumed that the voice of conscience is a male one, derived from identifications with the father. To him, a woman's superego organization is inferior to that of a man, the difference resulting from the different relationship in boys and girls between the castration complex and the Oedipus complex. Whereas the castration complex impels the boy to give up his oedipal wishes and leads him to identify with the father, the girl's acceptance of castration leads her to oedipal progression. Only rarely does a girl identify with her father in the same way and to the same extent as does a boy. These considerations led Freud to a tentative conclusion:

> For women the level of what is ethically normal is different from what it is in men. Their super-ego is never so inexorable, so impersonal, so inde-

*It may be less awkward to refer to male or female superego development rather than to superego development in the male or female, but we will avoid this usage because it suggests that the superego has a gender.

pendent of its emotional origins as we require it to be in men. . . . they show less sense of justice than men. . . . they are less ready to submit to the great exigencies of life. . . . they are more often influenced in their judgements by feelings of affection or hostility—all these would be amply accounted for by the modification in the formation of their super-ego. (1925b, pp. 257–258)

Jones disagreed with Freud's speculations about inadequate super-ego functioning in women; his own clinical experience led him to think women suffer guilt as much as men. He suggested that to see castration anxiety as the prime motivator for superego formation was limiting; it ran the risk of confusing female psychology with that of the male and precluded understanding the fundamental conflicts of a woman that would lead her to form a superego.

In Jones's view, a woman's primary fears are of separation and rejection and she develops a superego to cope with these fears. Correcting what he felt to be Freud's overemphasis on the Oedipus complex, he pointed to the importance of a girl's preoedipal tie to her mother. He believed that the girl's fears of being rejected by and separated from the mother are transferred to the father in the oedipal phase. Then, in her efforts to win father's approval and avoid rejection and abandonment, the girl identifies with father's moral ideals. Jones further suggested that penis envy may be prominent because women often develop the idea that men (that is, father) are strongly opposed to feminine wishes and disapprove of femininity (1927, p. 449). Thus the girl's identification with the father in attempts to ward off separation and rejection often comes to include male ideals along with a disparagement of feminine ones.

Jones's ideas notwithstanding, the concept of castration continued to be and to some extent still is the Achilles' heel of theories about superego formation in the female. To support the conviction that a woman develops superego functioning to a degree at least equivalent to that of a man, analysts have tried to find a motivator in the female that is equivalent to male castration anxiety.

Horney (1926), for example, while protesting the comparison of female development to that of the male, nevertheless tied female superego development to fears of genital damage. She thought that when penis envy operates as a dynamic factor in adult women, it indicates a regressive resolution to the Oedipus complex. In her analyses of adult women, Horney found ubiquitous fantasies about an excessively large penis effecting forcible penetration, producing pain, hemorrhage, and destruction. She assumed such fantasies originate in early childhood: a little girl observing the disproportionate size between father and herself will fear vaginal injury as she entertains fantasies of intercourse. According to Horney, this fear forces the girl to give up oedipal wishes and a feminine position; she makes male identifications and wishes for a penis. A woman's wish to be a man then sustains repression of oedipal fears and oedipal guilt; and since castration is taken as evidence of guilt, the possession of a penis would prove the girl to be guiltless.

Melanie Klein also emphasized bodily damage as the motivator for superego formation, although she dissented from Freud's view of superego formation in the female in two ways (1928, 1929, 1930, 1933). First, she postulated that the superego functions much earlier in life than Freud had proposed, and that this archaic superego is characterized by extremes of goodness and severity because of very early identifications. Second, it is an attacking mother, not an attacking father, that the girl fears. Klein believed that the infant girl thinks that her father's penis, feces, and more children are hidden inside her mother's body. The infant girl's envy leads her to an oral-sadistic desire to devour the mother's breast, rob mother's body contents, and destroy the mother. The projection of this fantasy results in the girl's fear that the contents of her own body are vulnerable to seizure, destruction, or mutilation. These fears arise at the time of weaning and represent the little girl's earliest danger situation. Klein thought that fears of being alone, of loss of love, and of loss of the love object are later modifications of this early anxiety.

Müller-Braunschweig (1926) assumed the superego of a woman to be on a par with that of a man. He thought a girl's feminine nature is expressed very early and includes pronounced masochism and passivity, betraying an unconscious knowledge of the passive role played by the vagina. And because a fundamental wish of the female is to be overpowered by the male, incestuous impulses threaten the girl with danger of violation by father, loss of mother's love, and also loss of father's love to the extent that the father represents a judge. Since being overpowered also endangers the ego, penis envy emerges as a reaction formation against the primary, passive, masochistic wish to be violated. This penis-ideal then serves as the foundation for the superego in the female, representing the superego's control over the urge to submit to the demands of the id. According to Müller-Braunschweig, the "deprivation anxiety" connected with the possible loss of the fantasized penis is at least as intense for women as is castration anxiety for men, if not more so.

Sachs also disagreed with the inferiority idea and proposed that a woman's independent superego functioning is based on the ideal of renunciation. That is, the girl has to give up oedipal strivings and tolerate the accompanying frustration. Frustration begins early, for in accepting castration, the little girl finds clitoral masturbation frustrating and unsatisfactory, which propels her toward incestuous oedipal desires. She is then frustrated in her genital desires for father or his baby. In a final effort to cling to the Oedipus complex—that is, to her fixation to her father—she transfers to him "with passionate intensity" oral wishes originally associated with oral frustration and the mother. The fate of these oral wishes, whose object is now father, is an important determinant to the final form of the superego in the female. If the wishes cannot be relinquished, the girl remains fixated to the father and in a dependent manner simply identifies with his (or his substitute's) ego ideal. If the frustration can be tolerated, however, the father is introjected and the girl detaches and functions independently, "accepting deprivation as a life-long ideal" (1929, p. 50).

Jacobson observed women's tendency to devalue their femininity and to defer to the opinions of men (1937) and thought this confirmed Freud's view that a woman's superego is weak and unstable. She was puzzled, though, that these same women also suffer from mercilessly cruel superego demands. Later (1964) she disagreed with Freud's idea that women lack incentive for superego formation; she suggested that superego functioning in the female evolves along a pathway different from that of the male. She thought the girl's discovery that she has no penis is experienced as a narcissistic injury for which she holds her mother responsible. Some restitutive efforts may be attempted; these usually give way to feelings of depression, sometimes with a premature relinquishment of genital activities, and with anal devaluation of her own and the mother's genitals, with which she copes by establishing an ideal of being neat, clean, and obedient. Renouncing sexual activities, she shifts attention from the genitals to the whole body. In an angry turning away from the now devalued mother, the girl makes an intensely ambivalent approach to her father. The narcissism previously invested in her own genitals is displaced to him; fear of penis loss is replaced by fear of loss of his love, and loss of father's love represents loss of the penis, repeating the earlier narcissistic injury.

To guard against loss of father's love, the girl becomes subservient to his ideas and values; thus the female anxiety of conscience becomes a secondary "social anxiety" as the opinions and judgments of the phallic love object become decisive. The basis for the girl's valuing her femininity, Jacobson believed, is the nature of the attitudes of both parents toward her femininity: "The eventual constitution of a self-reliant ego, and of a mature ego ideal and autonomous superego in women is all the more successful the better the little girl learns to accent her femininity and thus can find her way back to maternal ego and superego identifications" (1964, pp. 114–115).

Reich (1953) did not question Freud's view of the superego as an outcome of oedipal resolution, but she thought the ego ideal forms earlier and that disturbances in the ego ideal interfere with superego internalization. In her study of narcissistic pathology, she observed that certain women consistently make narcissistic object choices and use these pathological object relations to master injury to self-esteem and to overcome their feelings of castration. In so doing, they frequently become too dependent on the opinions of others. She thought these narcissistic disturbances are derived from preoedipal pathology in the mother-daughter relationship. The pathology interferes with superego development so that oedipal resolution and full superego internalization do not take place.

Greenacre (1952a) suggested that the girl's superego is influenced by her reactions to her physical body. The girl must accept not having a penis, but she nevertheless assumes its absence to be a punishment for past masturbation since it is often a situation of masturbatory arousal that brings a girl's attention to her "plight." The hypothetical sin for which she has already been punished appears to provide a fund of guilt, which contributes to the enormous enhancement of later guilt feelings in situations of conflict. Greenacre suggested that this fund of guilt contributes to some of the marked but rather diffuse or aimless conscientiousness and worrying tendencies often seen in girls.

Chasseguet-Smirgel (1970) considers the problem of female guilt from a very different angle. She thinks that children of both sexes see the mother as powerful and omnipotent and feel helpless and incomplete in comparison. The boy feels narcissistically satisfied at the thought he has something his mother does not, but the girl must turn to the father to free herself from the mother. Yet the oedipal position means that she must identify with the mother she sees to be castrating. She wants the penis not for its own sake but as a revolt against the person who has caused the narcissistic wound—the omnipotent mother. The woman takes on the moral beliefs of her sexual partner because of her unconscious guilt linked to the powerful admonition from the omnipotent mother—"you must not have your own law." A woman's guilt thus derives from the wish both to incorporate the paternal penis orally or vaginally and to depose the omnipotent mother. To defend against rivalry with the mother, against fears of identifying with the castrating mother, and out of fear of castrating the father, the girl may choose to remain the father's dependent caretaker. In this way she is neither taking mother's place beside father nor identifying with the castrating mother; rather, she remains a subservient child instead of becoming a woman.

Muslin (1972) maintains that the superego of a woman compares equally with that of a man with regard to structure and function, but that the contents of ideals and prohibitions differ from those of a man. He observed that a woman's wish for love and need for approval from parental and other objects continues throughout life. Consequently, fears of loss of love or threats to self-esteem are as important in regulating psychic functioning as are fears of superego punishment in the form of guilt.

Schafer asserts that Freud's traditional values led him to underestimate both the girl's relationship to her mother and the role of pregenital experience when he was constructing his theory of superego development. Schafer suggests that what Freud saw as male rigid moral stability has more to do with isolation of affect and obsessional psychopathology than with morals and values. Schafer also points to the need to better distinguish between superego and morality. To the extent that "a girl does not develop the implacable superego that a boy does . . . she might be better suited than a boy to develop a moral code that is enlightened, realistic, and consistently committed to some conventional form of civilized interaction among people" (1974, p. 466).

Blum (1976) challenges Freud's view that masochism is moral, erotogenic, and feminine, and therefore an important part of the female superego. He points out that masochism is a residue of unresolved infantile conflict and is neither essentially feminine nor a valuable component of female character. An intense masochistic ego ideal is usually associated with impaired object relations and reflects preoedipal and oedipal pathology. Blum further notes that maternal devotion should not be confused with masochistic enslavement or with a preservation of the object from aggression.

Bernstein (1983) criticizes Freud's concept of superego development and functioning on the basis of his assumed timing and assumed motivation, and because he took male characteristics as universal standards for judging adequate superego functioning. She contends that, as measured by drive control, the superego in women is no less effective than that in men, but that the contents of a woman's superego directives differ from those of a man, and the constraints imposed by a woman's superego are derived from sources other than castration anxiety. These sources are fears of the grandiose narcissistic mother of infancy; the spread of anal prohibitions to genital impulses because of confusion and diffusion between genital and anal body zones; and fantasies of having been castrated which give increased validity to fears of bodily harm such as from sexual penetration or childbirth.

## DISCUSSION

The primary idea these various views have in common is that Freud erred in concluding that superego development and functioning in women is inferior to that in men. The reports of psychoanalytic experience presented over the years clearly attest to the intensity of guilt found in women, their tendency toward self-criticism, their sense of insecurity, their tendency to defer to the opinions of others, and the importance of the girl's preoedipal relationship with her mother. All this can be understood as the consequence of an insufficiently internalized superego, or rather more likely, as behavior attesting to the complicated pathway of superego development in the female, intertwining as it does with character development.

It should come as no surprise that we believe that any understanding of superego development in the female must take account of many factors: sexuality, aggression, the mother-child and father-child relationships, the formation of gender identity (which we discuss in part VII), the regulation of narcissistic equilibrium, the varieties of ideals and goals held, and the contributions from experiences and conflicts of preoedipal as well as oedipal and postoedipal developmental stages.

Among these many factors, the consideration of the content of ideals and introjects is of particular importance in considering superego development in the girl. Muslin (1972) points out that, whereas specific ideals, prohibitions, and moral codes vary from culture to culture, in his experience, common elements can be found in the superego contents of women in Western cultures. These include prohibitions against aggressive activity, censorship of sexual activity, restriction of other forms of instinctual expression, ideals of being "sweet, kind, shy" or "unaggressive, clean, neat," and often, the expectation that she should mother her own mother.

Among other contemporary commentators, Schafer (1974) and Bernstein (1983) emphasize that differences in male and female values lead to differences in apparent superego functioning rather than superego weakness. The concept of a "firm" versus a "flexible" structure will illustrate the issue. In our reading of Freud's writings on the superego, we understand him to imply that a firm structure, unaffected by emotions of the past or present, is the more desirable. In contrast, we would say there are times when a more flexible structure, able to access and respond appropriately to present circumstances, is the more moral. From the psychologist's standpoint, Gilligan (1982) demonstrated significant differences in male and female responses to the need to resolve moral dilemmas; she concluded that men more often respond on the basis of adhering to an abstract law, whereas women more often respond on the basis of what is best for a relationship.

In our view, the mistaken conclusion that the superego in the female is weaker reflects the impact of intrasystemic conflict. Such a conflict may begin when, following an early superego directive of obedience to authority, a woman defers to the opinion of another in order to maintain the relationship. Then a superego directive of later origin may encourage her to be assertive and to make an independent decision. But the more archaic introjects are still a powerful influence and contradict the later ones. Given this dilemma, even the most assertive and independent of women may at times suffer indecision, vacillation, and guilt.

The issue of motivation and timing is also important to a discussion of gender differences in superego development. We interpret the developmental evidence to indicate that, in general, girls begin superego formation earlier than boys. To some extent this is facilitated by the well-known fact that girls' cognitive abilities are more advanced than those of same-age boys in the early years.

But we propose that the wish for the love of the idealized, same-sex love object and the fear of loss of that love are of particular importance to superego development. Issues of gender identity, narcissism, and self-esteem are bound closely with this wish. Therefore the need to resolve conflicting feelings of love and hate held toward the idealized same-sex love object is central to superego formation. For the girl, this conflict must be resolved before oedipal progression can take place. For the boy, this conflict is central to oedipal resolution.

We therefore maintain that central to the girl's motivation for superego formation is her wish for the love of the idealized mother. Often this entails a wish for a fantasized, idealized sense of intimacy or oneness that the girl imagines must have been a part of her earliest relationship with the mother of infancy. With genital primacy, this often takes the form of the wish for closeness with an idealized fairy godmother–type figure. Rapprochement conflict, however, with struggles over willfulness and control in attempts to establish a separate identity and a sense of autonomy lead the girl to fear the loss of the love of the ideal. The girl's early steps in superego formation then represent her efforts to resolve this conflict. Often this implies idealization of the mother and formation of harsh introjects that are turned against the self when she expresses sexual or aggressive impulses.

To elaborate: rapprochement conflict and anger at the mother interfere with feeling loved by mother. Loss of the sense of intimacy leads to painful feelings of lonely ambivalence beyond that resulting from the frustration of other wishes. Projections now distort the real mother, but the early identifications made with the demands of this distorted maternal representation in attempts to resolve the intensified and painful ambivalence and to restore the sense of intimacy form the basis of her superego.

Consider the example of three-and-a-half-year-old Beth, referred for treatment by her preschool because of her impulsive behavior; she had alienated all the children by pinching, hair pulling, and biting. Whenever she was frustrated she would strike out; when reprimanded, she would tearfully hide under a table and sob, claiming that no one liked her. She longed for, yet feared, any kind of intimacy in relationships, having an excessive dependence on others for maintenance of her self-esteem. Her mother, fearing a lack of control over Beth, would respond to any misbehavior with abrupt, intense, and frightening expressions of anger and assertions of control, accusing her of never thinking of the other person and often comparing her unfavorably to her two-years-younger sister, until she was completely demoralized and heartbroken. Beth attempted to comply with the directive to think of others (which she understood as either-or, herself or another, since her cognitive development did not yet allow her to truly decenter) by becoming subservient, but still she felt only disapproval to which she responded with anger. The father, attempting to modify the mother's influence, found himself responding in an equally negative fashion to Beth's behavior.

In treatment, a major transference wish emerged that Beth and her analyst be twins. She liked to draw, but felt that if her analyst's drawing was better, hers would seem no good at all; if hers were better, she feared the analyst's jealous anger, which would leave her feeling devastated. Thus she concluded it would be better if she and the analyst were the same—or twins. They spent long hours making "twin drawings," in which the analyst had to do exactly as Beth did. In this way, she re-created in the transference not only her regressive wish for a sense of oneness and attachment but also her search for the approval of an idealized mother.

Although Beth's pathology cannot be taken as an example of normal development, it only exaggerates a picture found commonly in early female development where issues of control and competition (not oedipally based but based on narcissistic comparisons of feminine beauty and competence) are uppermost. These then spoil the chances for the wished-for intimacy with mother. One consequence of these dynamics is that the girl may quickly give up independent strivings in favor of passive compliance and maintain regressive fantasies of being a baby. Because primitive self-critical elements of the introjects and ideals have a lasting influence that is less subject to change than are later, more reality-oriented elements, authority figures continue to be viewed as hostile and harsh, which reinforces the passive compliance. Although the boy's rapprochement ambivalence also leads to inter-nalized conflict, in his case the differences in sex impel him away from a sense of intimacy with the mother and toward a sense of separateness and differentness and toward making identifications with the idealized father rather than so quickly complying with mother's demands.

Because Freud considered superego formation only in relation to the Oedipus complex and chiefly in relation to males, it is not surpris-ing that he concluded that castration anxiety was paramount. Develop-mentally, however, the motivation for superego formation is much less clear-cut, and it changes over developmental time, as we described in the previous chapter. There we pointed out that pleasure in identify-ing with the ideal and the wish to gain the approval of the idealized mother are both potent motivators for superego formation, as the mother's love begins to have conditions.

Indeed, one of the most important aspects of female development is the nature of the powerful tie to the mother and the problem for the girl of moving beyond it. A successful oedipal progression involves more than a simple change of object; in our discussion of gender identity in the next chapter, we detail the difficulties a little girl has in giving up her maternal attachment while at the same time identifying and competing with her. Often she achieves oedipal progression only at the expense of persistent, intense hatred of the mother. Even if she deals with these feelings through reaction formation, they may never-theless contribute to a pervasively harsh, critical, and punitive super-ego. Often the girl is never fully able to give up her mother and remains attached to her throughout life. Balint (1973) describes women who displace this attachment to other women, but they remain preoccupied with how to satisfy and care for them.

Although such struggles are a matter of frequent observation, surprisingly little mention has been made of the role of aggression in women's superego formation. It is true that hostile impulses and related conflicts are implicit in many formulations, but the emphasis is on sexuality—guilt over masturbation, over oedipal wishes, over wishes to take father's penis, and so on. Except for Melanie Klein, conceptualizations of the early relationship with the mother stress disappointment in and anger at her for not providing the girl with a penis.

Recent developmental studies show that the girl's hostile impulses arise from many sources, not simply as reactions to disappointment and narcissistic injury from not owning a penis, as important as these sexual sources are. Mahler, for example, draws attention to the toddler's distancing and disengagement alternating with appeal and approach behavior, to which she gives the name *ambitendency* (Mahler et al., 1975). These phenomena commonly accompany the toddler's building of her own individual identity and capacity for autonomous functioning as her awareness of separation intensifies. At such times, the regressive pull to mother-infant union threatens the girl's autonomy and identity.

Aggression serves to advance the processes of separation and individuation, but intense hatred and anger toward the mother can prematurely disrupt the girl's view of her mother as ideal. The results include a premature and passive compliant character formation or a delay in compliance with the mother, and an interference with resolving developmental conflicts and a delay in tolerating ambivalence. Loss of the idealized view of the mother also interferes with the internalization of guiding, protecting, and comforting introjects. Instead the girl forms a denigrated view of the object and internalizes hostile, uncompromising introjects. Identifications made with the denigrated object then put her at risk for forming a denigrated self-image, and the end result is a person with a harshly self-critical superego and vulnerable self-esteem. Nadelson and her colleagues (1982) point out that mothers often critically disapprove of their daughter's hostile impulses. The little girl then fears her mother's retaliatory withdrawal of love as punishment for her anger; in addition, the girl's own anger is felt to sever the tie, as it interferes with her enjoyment of feeling loved by her mother, with her ability to love her mother, and with the idealization of her. This serves to amplify the hostility of the introjects and so to exaggerate the harshness of the self-criticizing functions of the super-ego.

As fantasies of loss of love intensify, so does the girl's anxiety; her felt loss of the early nurturing maternal ego ideal because of her expressed anger leads to still more anxiety, to self-devaluation with narcissistic hurt, and to further anger at and devaluation of the mother. Out of defensive reparative efforts to resolve ambivalence, the girl tries to be good, clean, and neat in order to regain her mother's love. In so doing, she often evolves a compliant and masochistic attitude toward external authority (and eventually toward her superego) in order to maintain the object tie and avoid loss of love, the fear of which is compounded by projection of her hostile introjects (Blum, 1976).

Although Kernberg's (1976) formulations are not specific to women, they are relevant in regard to the hazards of this early phase of superego formation for the female. He describes how the pathogenic effect of an early preponderance of aggression results in distortion of parental images. This interferes with internalization of later, more realistic oedipal parental images so that the harsh, hostile (Kernberg prefers "sadistic"), unintegrated, and easily projected quality of the superego remains. This in turn interferes with higher levels of super-ego integration and with the development of internalized value systems. Such a failure may take the form of a pathological integration of hostile and idealized self- and object representations; the ideal is then dominated by aggressive features, and it acquires characteristics of hostile demands for perfection, bringing about an excessive repression of instinctual expression.

A similar dynamic picture may emerge because of the mother's psychopathology (Lax, 1977). The birth of a daughter may be upsetting for a mother because of a variety of unconscious meanings the event may have for her. Perhaps she unconsciously longed for a penis and so would have preferred a boy. For this or some other reason, the mother is unable to develop a genuine "maternal preoccupation" (Winnicott, 1956) because the infant does not represent her "fantasy child." The girl's emerging self-representation then incorporates the mother's devaluing attitudes, so that the girl experiences herself as unlovable, worthless, and inadequate. Conflicts of the anal and infantile genital phases add to the sense of denigration; the mother herself is not viewed as ideal but is depreciated, interfering with any pleasure in identifying with her. Internalization of the rejecting, depreciating mother leads to a masochistic, self-defeating attitude and a primitive, harsh, and hostile superego.

A girl's discovery of anatomical differences may compound rapprochement struggles if the idealization of the mother is significantly interfered with in any of the ways described. Rather than feeling pride in being female like mother, the girl then feels further narcissistic injury and experiences more anger and disappointment with her in conjunction with the discovery (Jacobson, 1954, 1964). Penis envy may evolve, as Roiphe and Galenson (1981) observe, but this is secondary to the girl's inability to resolve her ambivalence to the mother (Grossman and Stewart, 1976). Under such circumstances, penis envy is often accompanied by the devaluation of femininity and by an identification with the father and with his ideals, as Jones (1927) described.

Although these circumstances make the girl's oedipal attachment to the father difficult or delay her oedipal involvement with him, oedipal progression may nevertheless take place. Then all love and narcissistic expectation is directed to the father and the unintegrated, excessive preoedipal anger and hostility is attached to the representation of the mother-rival. To the extent that the mother is the recipient of these negative feelings, so also will the introjects, based on early experiences of the mother, take on hostile attitudes that are directed inward, stimulating an even greater need for the father and his love. Consequently, the girl's anxieties over her continuing angry feelings will focus on the narcissistic threat of an unresponsive father, as well as on the fear of mother's retaliatory envy, hostility, and withdrawal of love. Fears of punishment for oedipal wishes then center around frightening images, which may include some form of bodily harm, building on earlier feelings of helplessness and powerlessness. The girl may manifest such fears in various ways. One six-year-old girl, after describing her enjoyment at being tickled by her father, had a dream of being chased by a vampire.

Unresolved conflicts around aggression toward the mother may leave the girl vulnerable to experience the developmentally inevitable oedipal disappointment as an intensely painful rejection. Her feelings of being not pretty enough, not lovable enough, and not good enough are amplified, and earlier disillusionments in the mother are reexperienced with a corresponding resurgence of self-devaluation.

The girl's ultimate consolidation of a superego relatively autonomous from the drives and from hostile introjects and external objects may depend on the extent to which the father can extricate her from rapprochement struggles. The father can help the girl modulate aggression (Herzog, 1982), assistance that is helpful to the girl in modulating her hostility to the mother and also to herself owing to her hostile introjects. This extrication may require that the father provide his daughter with an additional voice of authority and an alternate source of well-being and that he appropriately encourage her oedipal development and be empathetic to her oedipal disappointments. The girl is further helped if the father's relationship with her is such that she feels encouraged to identify with her feminine and maternal ego ideal, as well as with appropriate aspects of her father and his ideals and moral principles.

## SUPEREGO DEVELOPMENT IN THE MALE

Because the mother sets standards and demands in early phases of superego development, the origin of the masculine voice of authority in the superego of the male requires explanation. In our view, the answer lies not only in the way in which preoedipal conflicts are reorganized by the Oedipus complex but also in the nature of the preoedipal and oedipal conflicts themselves. Although the boy has to deal with his ambivalence to his mother in the rapprochement phase, in contrast to the girl he does not have to deal with as much disillusionment and anger at the loss of the idealized sense of oneness with his mother because such oneness threatens his sense of male self. The difference in sex, therefore, provides an impetus to his strivings for autonomy. The boy's narcissistically satisfying thought that he has something mother does not possibly serves to defend against feelings of anger and helplessness evoked by the powerfully and omnipotently viewed mother (Chasseguet-Smirgel, 1970). Furthermore, although his earliest introjects or voices of authority and the accompanying system of values are based on prohibitions and standards set by the mother, with his increasing sense of maleness he looks more and more to his father as an authority. Indeed, the boy may defend against early castration anxiety by idealizing the father. This idealization may lessen his motivation for complying with and identifying with mother's standards. If he experiences mother's demands as excessively intrusive, he may stubbornly refuse to comply in efforts to maintain his sense of autonomy and maleness, a phenomenon often apparent in boys' difficulties in toilet training.

As the boy progresses to the infantile genital phase and establishes genital primacy, his father becomes increasingly prominent in his mind as an ideal, and approaching this ideal affords him narcissistic gratification in his enhanced sense of masculinity. When the boy takes his father as a masculine ideal and strives to identify with him, this paves the way to the positive Oedipus complex (Freud, 1921). Now the father's availability to the boy is of utmost importance not only for ultimate oedipal progression and resolution but for internalizing a secure sense of masculinity (a process elaborated in the following chapters).

When, because of conflicting incestuous wishes, the boy's ambivalence to the father arises, the paternal representation assumes an increasingly authoritative position in his mind. At the same time, the father introject becomes the spokesman, so to speak, of all previous superego injunctions, and preoedipal hostile feelings about mother's demands become reorganized, transformed, and directed toward the father. The boy is then free to turn to mother as the less ambivalently loved libidinal object. Viewing mother in this way mitigates otherwise excessively hostile preoedipal maternal introjects.

While increasing involvement in the Oedipus complex brings pleasurable fantasies of oedipal success, competition with and hatred of the father accompany these fantasies. Because the boy also loves his ideally viewed father, these oedipal fantasies arouse painful feelings of ambivalence in addition to fears of father's retaliation. Both the fear of castration *and* ambivalence toward the father may interfere with the boy's pleasurable sense of masculinity. Ambivalence toward the father may lead to devaluing him and hence to a devaluing of himself as male. Resolving ambivalence ensures his maintaining the pleasurable phallic-narcissistic relationship of shared masculine activities that enhances the competent sense of masculinity as the boy identifies with his father-ideal. A pleasurable sense of masculinity, therefore, depends on the boy's successfully resolving his ambivalence to his father, an achievement reached by giving up incestuous wishes and adhering to the rules of the father and through further idealization of him. The narcissistic gratification gained by thus identifying with the father-ideal and with his moral standards helps balance the narcissistic hurt of oedipal failure.

Just as for the girl, we think that the boy's need to resolve ambivalence toward the idealized same-sex love object provides a powerful motivation for superego formation. The boy's loving and hating feelings toward his father may evoke a variety of fantasies of retaliatory punishment, the avoidance of which provides further motivation to identify with father's rules. As we mentioned earlier, however, the boy also gains an increasing awareness both that the father has rules for him and that the father himself lives by a set of moral standards and rules, and the boy idealizes and identifies with these rules as a part of oedipal resolution.

We have pointed out that the girl begins superego formation at a younger age than boys, that among the consequences one finds primitive elements in her superego that appear less subject to change than are later, more reality-oriented elements. This implies that the boy's representations of authority may not have quite the primitive features as do the early introjects of the girl's superego.

The man's superego at times, however, conveys a quality of rigid and dogmatic adherence to rules that is perhaps, as Schafer (1974) suggests, mostly related to obsessional psychopathology. But an important etiological factor in obsessional psychopathology is the need to adhere to superego directives because of intense castration anxiety. Here we want to emphasize a relatively neglected aspect of the father's early role in helping the young boy to modulate aggression. For a variety of reasons, boys often have more difficulty than girls in controlling their libidinal and aggressive impulses. Because of their greater impulsiveness they are also vulnerable to harsh introjects, and castration anxiety may be a continuing threat. One little boy even expressed this fear as an active wish. He wished he could be a girl, because "girls don't have so much trouble being good!" Just as for the girl, it is essential that the father help the boy learn to modulate, control, or otherwise manage his sexuality and aggression and to identify with the parental injunctions. He does this partly through rough play with the boy. This first excites him, and then the father helps him by calming him to a quieter state. When the father does not perform this function, exaggerated aggressivity with lessened control of it increases the likelihood of harsh introjects, or of real experiences of punishment, both of which increase castration anxiety, so that it continues to exert an overriding influence. Later, rational reasoning may be disrupted and the male may urgently insist that only by following the strictest letter of the law (or the rather rigid directives of his harsh superego) can disaster, or castration, be avoided.

Consider the example of six-and-a-half-year-old Jimmy. Jimmy's parents were divorced when he was three, and both have remarried and share custody. Jimmy admires and adores both his natural and his stepfather, but the two men hold very different values and present contrasting models for identification. His natural father plays in an intimidating, aggressive manner and offers a rough, tough, macho view of masculinity. His stepfather is quiet, soft-spoken, affectionate, but firmly in control. As Jimmy struggles with these two views of masculinity, superego integration and effective functioning suffer. He is small in stature and is quick to anger when teased about his size. He attempts to show off his masculinity by being physically aggressive and attacking, like his father. But he then becomes depressed and views himself as a bad boy, a reaction that reflects harsh introjects and ideals based on the values of his stepfather.

Interestingly, precisely opposite manifest behavior may also indicate intense and persisting castration anxiety. Noncompliance to external or internalized prohibitions and moral standards results in disruptive behavior that brings a boy into conflict with external authority; this behavior is often motivated by the boy's need to exhibit and thereby prove his masculinity. Although attention from authority may be painful as it brings certain shame, it may also confirm to a boy his virility and effectiveness, and so to some extent the negative attention is reinforcing. In this case, however, further superego internalization is delayed with other pathological consequences.

## CONCLUSION

Although we have perhaps not done full justice to the complete range of varieties of gender differences in superego development, and have limited our discussion to early childhood, we hope we have nevertheless refuted Freud's idea that superego functioning in women is inferior to that of men.

Our basic thesis is that the need to resolve ambivalence to the idealized object of the same sex in the service of gender-identity formation is of particular importance to superego development. For the girl this task arises early, at a time when cognitive skills are immature. Therefore, the likelihood is great that the internalization of harsh, severe, and unrelenting introjects results from these efforts. This jeopardizes a pleasurable, narcissistic investment in a sense of femininity and the formation of a loving, comforting superego. It also potentially interferes with the ultimate internalization of an autonomous, independently functioning superego.

For the boy, this task evolves later, when some capacity for reality testing is available because of somewhat more advanced cognitive skills. Furthermore, the boy does not have to deal with disillusionment and anger at the loss of the idealized sense of oneness with the mother because the difference in sex usually provides an additional impetus for his strivings for autonomy. Resolution of ambivalence toward the father is of utmost importance for the boy's superego development. Resolution of ambivalence ensures a competent sense of masculinity as the boy identifies with his father-ideal, and it also ensures identifying with father's rules and moral standards. In this way he postpones fantasies of heterosexual conquest until later in life. In the interim he gains increasing pleasure in being like his idealized father and in sharing activities with him as well as in complying with and identifying with his father's moral code. The voice of authority then gradually becomes a relatively autonomously functioning, reliable, internal presence.

# PART SEVEN

## GENDER

# CHAPTER 15

## GENDER DEVELOPMENT: A

## THEORETICAL OVERVIEW

Freud's theory of psychosexual development lacks the concept of gender identity. Although references to masculinity and femininity are found throughout his writings, his formulations of these concepts are based on infantile sexuality and do not include the correlating contributions of the development of object relations, the sense of self, the superego, and the ego. The concept of gender identity, which takes all of these into consideration, is of relatively recent origin; it emerged with a greater awareness of the range of factors that influence development.

In tracing gender development, we follow Stoller in his preference for the less ambiguous term *gender identity* rather than *sexual identity*. This is because the term *sex* refers to a biological designation, male or female; gender identity is a broader concept. It refers to a psychological configuration that combines and integrates personal identity and biological sex, and to which object relations, superego ideals, and cultural influences make significant contributions. Furthermore, the term *sex* is often used to refer to erotic fantasies or behavior, and so it is more related to psychosexuality than to identity.

A wide variety of feelings, thoughts, fantasies, beliefs, and actions related to patterns of courtship, mating, and child-rearing practices is associated in one way or another with gender (Meyer, 1980). Because of the variety of contributing elements, and also because of the many forms of psychopathology related to one or another of these elements, we find it useful to distinguish among *gender identity, gender-role identity,* and *sexual-partner orientation*. Although all are related in a global sense to gender development, different elements and different developmental configurations contribute to each. By more precisely distinguishing the clinical features of each, we can be more specific about the contributions of developmental factors as well as about the psychopathological elements involved in any given clinical picture.

One further note by way of introduction: psychoanalytic authors have often tended to make generalizations about the development of femininity based on an understanding of male development. In what follows, after a theoretical overview defining the relevant concepts, we discuss the development of a sense of gender for female and male separately in order to clarify their different pathways as best we can with our present knowledge. If making such a separation runs the risk of overlaps, it counteracts the tendency to understand one gender by contrasting it to the other.

## GENDER IDENTITY

*Gender identity* is a broad concept that includes all those characteristics that compose each individual's combination of masculinity and femininity, determined by a wide array of biological, psychological, social, and cultural factors (Stoller, 1968a, 1976). Stoller emphasizes that over the course of development, identifications made with same-sex and opposite-sex objects contribute, so that one's ultimate gender identity—that is, personal identity in combination with biological sex—contains a mix of masculinity and femininity. Even the definition of masculinity or femininity, Stoller says, is a personal one; although cultural influences may contribute, each individual forms a complex system of beliefs about himself, which includes a sense of oneself as masculine or feminine (1976, 1985).

Gender identity is built on the foundation of what Stoller refers to as core gender identity (1968a, 1968b). This is the most primitive, conscious and unconscious, sense of belonging to one sex and not the other. Stoller defines it as the basic "sense we have of our sex—of maleness in males and of femaleness in females. . . . It is part of, but not identical with" the broad sense of gender identity (1976, p. 61). Among the many factors that contribute to the formation of core gender identity are physiological and biological forces, psychological factors, object relations, ego functions, and cognitive capacities, variously discussed by Greenacre (1950, 1958), Kohlberg (1966, 1981), Stoller (1968a, 1976), Money and Ehrhardt (1972), and Roiphe and Galenson (1981), among others.

Stoller (1976) suggests that core gender identity starts as a biological force in the fetus; the sex hormones to which the fetus is exposed make a significant contribution to it. Core gender identity is abetted by the anatomy and physiology of the external genitalia, which under normal circumstances provide the basis upon which sexual assignment is made.

In addition to these biological and anatomical considerations, social and psychological influences make a contribution. Sexual assignment at birth leads the parents to handle the infant in a particular way. They give to the infant a variety of verbal and nonverbal messages that convey the meaning of feminine or masculine as defined by that family; the attitudes of parents and siblings toward a child of that sex as well as a variety of conscious and unconscious fantasies will also be reflected in these cues. Indeed, once the parents know the anatomical sex of the infant (before or after birth), their attitudes toward it take on a distinct tinge, depending on whether it is male or female.

The mother's fantasies and expectations during pregnancy are thought to influence her initial responses to her infant (Kestenberg, 1976; Broussard, 1984). The sensations and moods accompanying the bodily changes of pregnancy tend to invite regression, giving the pregnant woman opportunities to resolve earlier and current conflicts between herself and her mother, as well as to integrate earlier fantasies into a formed fantasy of her infant. Pregnancy represents the culmination of wishes that began in her early childhood, but now, early and later childhood wishes and fantasies along with adolescent modifications and elaborations become integrated with current realities. In addition, pregnancy verifies an identification with the mother, and the ambivalence and conflicts around that identification from all developmental stages reemerge. When the woman's relationship with her own mother has been fraught with conflict, the idea of having a girl or boy may arouse particularly strong emotions.

The degree to which the woman is able to resolve earlier conflicts and integrate earlier wishes and fantasies has a profound effect on her earliest response to and handling of her baby. If the infant is a girl, for example, the woman may fear repeating a conflictual relationship with her daughter. In a worst scenario, the mother may identify her daughter with the denigrated part of her self-representation. Projective mechanisms may then lead her to interpret the baby's behavior accordingly; as one mother said, "The first time I held her she gave me a cold, icy stare, and she turned away!" Neglect or abuse may follow (see Steele, 1970, 1983; Steele and Pollock, 1968). Alternatively, a woman may view having a girl as an opportunity to rework old mother-daughter conflicts and to regain or re-create the fantasized, idealized, lost symbiotic state of early infancy; less happily, she may tend toward total engulfment of the child and discourage independence and autonomy, making it difficult for the little girl to break away from her grasp. If the infant is a boy, fantasies associated with gaining a longed-for penis, or fantasies associated with father or a brother, or even disappointment at not being able to re-create the feeling of unity she believes she could have with a girl, influence a woman's reactions to and her handling of her infant.

Because of a variety of unresolved conflicts and pathological fantasies, women sometimes view motherhood and masochism as synonymous, regardless of the biological sex of the infant (Blum, 1976). In such instances the woman may see the arrival of a baby as a loss of her autonomy and independence, a configuration that sets the stage for a variety of sadomasochistic interactions.

The father's role may affect, directly or indirectly, the mother's response to her newborn. Some evidence suggests that a woman's successful adaptation to pregnancy is facilitated by her husband's support (Shereshefsky and Yarrow, 1973). Also, the relationship with the husband may provide a buffer against a mother's tendency for extreme regression.

The father's influence on the infant's gender identity must also be considered. His prenatal fantasies influence his later handling of the infant, just as with the mother. If the baby is a boy, the father may hope that the boy will share his interests, or he may fantasize repeating with his son meaningful experiences he shared with his own father, or he may hope that he will have experiences with his son that he missed with his father. If the baby is a girl, the father may fantasize about her physical appearance. He may hope that she will be pretty, attract many suitors, and most important, respond to his loving overtures (see Burlingham, 1973). Sometimes a man may worry about how to interact with a girl and not be able to imagine reexperiencing with a daughter his own early interactions with his father. These anxieties are often expressed, albeit unconsciously, through the choice of an ambiguous name, one that while feminine has a masculine diminutive, so that, for example, Veronica comes to be called Ronnie, or Andrea becomes Andy.

From the time the infant is born, fathers interact with their infants differently from the way mothers do. Fathers tend to be more active with both sons and daughters, more stimulating and exciting; Herzog

(1982) suggests this ultimately plays an important role in the child's ability to modulate aggressive impulses. We would add sexuality as well, particularly if father can not only excite but also help the child shift from the excited state to a more quiescent one. As the less "contaminated" object, father can optimally facilitate the eventual resolution of rapprochement conflict by helping to break the exclusive mother-infant tie, thus rendering anal-rapprochement conflict a less noxious influence on gender development. Fathers also convey a view of masculinity that their sons tend to see as ideal. This influences the infant boy's view of masculinity; the degree to which he can match this ideal may influence his confidence in his masculinity. Whereas a mother may have some ambivalence about her daughter's growing femininity, fathers are more ready to express pride (Ticho, 1976) and encourage the girl's feminine identifications with her mother. Where a mother may convey disgust and shaming criticism toward her infant daughter's genital exploration, fathers tend to be less judgmental (Herzog, 1984).

There is some evidence to suggest that a "critical period" may exist in the development of a father's attraction toward and interest in his child. Fathers who have no contact with their infants during the first few months may have difficulty showing affection for the child later on (Greenberg and Morris, 1974). In contrast, when a father becomes the primary nurturing parent, the normal attachments and conflicts usually felt toward the mother are directed toward him (see Pruett, 1983, 1984, 1987).

Core gender identity, or primary femininity and primary masculinity, also accrues from the sense the infant makes about his or her own body. The infant builds a body image through the integration of various oral, anal, urethral, and genital sensations that arise from feeding, diapering, bathing, play, and other intimate, affective interchanges with the mother or primary caregiver. Perceptual, motor, and cognitive functioning, more mature at birth than previously thought, aids the infant in distinguishing body parts, including genitals, and in integrating various body experiences and sensations into a "body self"; this early sense of self based on an emerging body image makes important contributions to core gender identity.

As the sense of self comes to be mentally represented, observations indicate that the infant has some awareness of oral, urethral, anal, and genital bodily zones (Mahler et al., 1975; Roiphe and Galenson, 1981). This seems so evident that we conclude that a basic or core sense of being male or female is an integral part of the self-representation from the beginning. Although Fast (1978, 1979) proposes an undifferentiated gender matrix during the earliest period of life,* the prevailing view has it that by fifteen to eighteen months when there is evidence for an emerging sense of self, there are also indications of an awareness of being male or female with male or female genitals (Kleeman, 1965, 1966, 1971; Stoller, 1976; Roiphe and Galenson, 1981). Between age two and three more clear-cut signs of gender awareness can be observed, as boys take on masculine characteristics and girls assume feminine ones. By this time, core gender identity is so well established that it is generally considered to be unalterable (Money et al., 1955a, 1955b; Stoller, 1985).

Although core gender identity is established in the first few years of life, the broader sense of gender identity continues to become more and more elaborate over the course of development. At various developmental stages contributions are made from selective identifications with each parent. In addition, certain attempts at disidentification have a developmental impact. Early identifications are also elaborated by identifications made at later stages. The final outcome, therefore, is a gender identity that represents a blending of many elements from many developmental stages.

## GENDER-ROLE IDENTITY

Superimposed on but different from core gender identity is gender-role identity, a gender-based patterning of conscious and unconscious interactions with other people. This aspect of the self-representation is built on subtle interactions between parents and child from birth. These interactions are influenced by parental attitudes toward the child's biological sex, as well as by each parent's sense of himself or

*Fast maintains that early experience is undifferentiated and that the child's sense of sex and gender potential is not limited by its actual sex. She concedes that gender-related experiences, which differ for boys and girls to some extent from the beginning, are influenced by biological factors and the differences in handling, but she asserts that the earliest self-representations are indiscriminate as to gender. By the second half of the second year, the child can identify self and others as to maleness and femaleness, but even then the awareness of the limitations of the characteristics of each sex is a more advanced achievement. Her idea has merits, but it also illustrates the difficulties in assigning meaning to observed behavior and the difficulties in discerning which are most important among the many factors influencing the child's defining his own unique sense of masculinity or femininity.

herself as male or female and by the style with which each interacts with others. Along with the infant's earliest representations of self and objects, he creates representations of the interactions, the relationships, and the dialogues with objects (Sandler and Sandler, 1978, p. 239). These "role relationship" representations coalesce with other aspects of gender awareness, so that eventually the self-representation contains elements of one's gender identity together with the role or habitual mode of interaction used in relation to other people vis-à-vis one's masculinity or femininity.

Gender-role identity, as we use it here, should not be confused with socially determined learned roles; rather, it refers to an intrapsychic, interactional representation. As the child matures, his identifications with same-sex objects and his intrapsychic representations of role relationships are indeed affected by cultural and social influences; gender-role identity, therefore, eventually includes significant contributions from culturally determined learned behavior. In this regard, cognitive capacities play an important part. The child's perception of physical and behavioral differences and similarities between same- and different-sex siblings, peers, or parents leads to self-categorization. Categorizing oneself as male or female serves as an organizer for gender experience, and self-labeling guides the child in seeking "self-like objects" as role models with whom to identify (Kohlberg, 1966, 1981, p. 439).

## SEXUAL-PARTNER ORIENTATION

Green (1975) distinguished sexual-partner orientation from other aspects of gender-related experience. Sexual-partner orientation expresses one's preference regarding the sex of the chosen love object. This orientation has origins early in life with preoedipal and oedipal object relations, although the choice may be neither firmly established nor a source of conflict until adolescence, when sexual maturity is reached and early object relations are reworked as a part of the adolescent process.

It is in relation to sexual-partner orientation that the issue of bisexuality and bisexual conflict normally arises. Freud (1905b) saw bisexuality as a normal part of human psychological makeup, becoming manifest particularly in relation to the positive and negative Oedipus complex. Because the term *bisexual* is used in reference to sexual aims directed toward both sexes as well as to identifications made with each parent during the course of development (Moore and Fine, 1968), it blurs gender identity (in its broad sense) with sexual-partner orientation. It therefore suffers from being imprecise. We think it more helpful to distinguish between issues related to object choice and issues related to identifications contributing to gender identity.

## DISCUSSION

The recommended distinctions between gender identity, gender-role identity, and sexual-partner orientation give more precision to our understanding of developmental configurations. By distinguishing the different contributions of each to the developmental process, it is possible to be more explicit about potential hazards; furthermore, the many feelings and behaviors related to gender become more meaningful rather than being viewed in global terms. In addition, differences in male and female development become more obvious.

It has been said, for example, that a girl's psychosexual development is much more complex than a boy's because of her need to change love objects to enter the Oedipus complex. The issue here is sexual-partner orientation. Although various wishes, fantasies, and object-related experiences may undermine a girl's narcissistic investment in her sense of femininity, the establishment of a secure core sense of being female is generally a smooth process. In contrast, the more difficult issue for the male is to establish a secure sense of gender identity. That is, the boy's identifications with his primary love object may undermine his sense of masculinity, so he must disidentify (Greenson, 1954, 1968) with the mother to form a secure masculine sense of self. To contrast the boy to the girl, we could say that although oedipal progression may be smooth for the boy, his identity formation is more complex because of the need to change objects. Gender-role identity also relies on this process taking place. Entering the Oedipus complex for the boy, then, involves not a change of object but a change in role in relation to the object. Such a change in role may be possible only to the extent that the boy's sense of being male is secure.

Distinguishing gender identity, gender-role identity, and sexual-partner orientation is also useful clinically. Consider an adult man who complains of not finding a suitable love object and of sexual inadequacy. Analytic investigation may suggest that his gender identity is secure and his sexual-partner orientation is heterosexual. But if he has not been able to identify with father and a male gender role, his continuing to feel like a "little boy in a grown-up world" would contribute to feeling inadequate in sexual relations with women. The pathology, therefore, is primarily in the area of gender-role identification. Directing interventions accordingly can prove to be clinically beneficial. A different scenario would ensue if the pathology were in the area of insecurity in the sense of masculinity, which might lead the man to fear any woman as intrusive and castrating. Although the presenting symptoms might be the same, different interventions would be called for. Consider, for example, a man who fancied himself as endowed with phallic omnipotence and power. The macho ideal of this sort has been described by Person (1986, p. 3) as a man with a large, powerful, untiring phallus able to make women crazy with desire. Even though he saw himself thus, he complained of premature ejaculation. On closer investigation, it appeared that he obtained his primary pleasure from masturbation because, in contrast to his fantasies of conquering countless women, an unconscious castration anxiety led him to fear loss of his penis through intercourse. His idealization of phallic omnipotence was thus a defense against an insecure sense of masculinity, castration anxiety having undermined his establishing a secure sense of his masculine self.

## SUMMARY

The conceptual distinctions we have drawn among gender identity, gender-role identity, and sexual-partner orientation provide a framework for understanding the developmental evolution of gender. In the next chapter, we describe the ways in which these three strands of gender development interact with, influence, and are influenced by the child's other simultaneously developing psychic systems.

# CHAPTER 16

## GENDER DEVELOPMENT:

## GIRLS

We now examine the girl's establishment of core gender identity or primary femininity and then consider how object relations and superego formation in the second and third years contribute to broader aspects of gender identity. Following this, we study the girl's emerging gender-role identity. Then we discuss the ways in which both gender identity and gender-role identity contribute to oedipal configurations, forming the foundations for later sexual-partner orientation. We then trace further developments during latency and adolescence.

### CORE GENDER IDENTITY

The girl's sense of femininity depends on the coalescence of her core gender identity. Stoller remarked that, once established, primary femininity is "a piece of identity so firm that almost no vicissitudes of living can destroy it" (1968b, p. 48).

In addition to the influences we described previously, such as hormones and parental handling, early identifications with the mother contribute importantly to the infant girl's primary sense of being female. Fantasies of mother-daughter oneness are common in mothers (Chodorow, 1978), particularly as many mothers can so easily identify with the body of their infant girl (Bernstein, 1983). Sometimes the mother's fantasies are accompanied by a tendency to engulf her infant girl and be possessive of her. Although these fantasies and tendencies are potentially noxious, they provide a powerful affective "surround" (Spitz, 1965), which fosters the infant girl's primitive identifications with her mother. As a sense of body-self and then a sense of self-as-mentally-represented emerge, these identifications contribute to a primitive sense of being female.

The building of a body image is an important contributor to a primary sense of femininity. Historically, there has been debate about the girl's vaginal awareness and hence about the extent to which the girl can mentally represent and integrate a sense of her genitals into her body image (see Greenacre, 1950, 1958; Kestenberg, 1956b, 1961, 1968; Barnett, 1966; Moore, 1976; Silverman, 1981). Freud believed that the girl remains unaware of her vagina until puberty, and some contemporary writers such as Plaut and Hutchinson (1986) concur. More than vaginal awareness, however, is involved in genital awareness and representation. The female genitals have several externally observable and touchable parts that give rise to pleasurable sensation—the mons, the labia, the parting between the labia, and the introitus. Girls have no difficulty locating these, and indeed, infant girls regularly finger and explore their genitals during diapering, which suggests they have some genital awareness and experience genital sensations. The mental representation of these external genital parts, Mayer suggests, may constitute early precursors to conceptualization of the vagina insofar as they lead the little girl to experience her genitals as "having an opening and potential inside space" (1985, p. 334). A further step in eventually acquiring a mental representation of the vagina, Mayer thinks, pointing to Barnett's (1966) suggestion, is the awareness of the introitus which prepares the way for vaginal awareness because it suggests a space existing beyond a recognized opening; that is, the girl's associating her genitals with an opening with potential space inside prepares the way for a vaginal representation.

We might conclude that since the girl's genitals and their associated sensations are such an integral and protected part of her body and of her body experience from the beginning, her developing body image will include a sense of genital awareness, however diffuse or vague. Even if early self-awareness may be disconnected and fragmentary, as the infant girl's self-representation emerges it includes some primitive sense of being female, with female genitals. (Silverman, 1981, and Person, 1983, hold similar views.)

It is entirely possible that forming a genitally intact, confident sense of the body self may even be easier for the girl than for the boy because the girl's genitals are not an appendage seemingly vulnerable to loss. Anxieties around genital injury may emerge later because of masturbation guilt, but although the associated conflicts may lead her to sexual fantasies of being beaten, penetrated, or otherwise injured, her anxiety about genital injury does not usually disrupt her integrated sense of body self. (Fantasies of being beaten are not unusual in the course of the girl's development, but much more rare in boys. For the relationship of beating fantasies to the development of masochism, see Glenn, 1984; Galenson, 1988; J. Novick and K. K. Novick, 1972, 1990; K. K. Novick and J. Novick, 1987.)

## NARCISSISM AND GENDER IDENTITY

The woman's pride or shame about her body and herself as feminine—that is, her ultimate narcissistic investment associated with a broad sense of gender identity—has its beginnings in early childhood. In the second and third years, the confluence of separation-individuation conflicts, early superego formation, penis envy, and the father's role is an important influence on the little girl's narcissistic investment in being female.

Caught in the dilemma of struggling for autonomy while still in a state of dependence, the little girl often feels hostile and angry toward her mother. When these feelings are intense, they may interfere with the view of mother as ideal and with the girl's pleasure in identifying with her. The resulting strongly ambivalent mother-daughter relationship may impede the girl's pleasure and pride in her femininity. When aggressive manifestations are not overwhelming, however, they may adaptively enable the girl to separate from and selectively identify with her mother. In this way she can establish a sense of individuality (Mahler, 1981) and also her own unique sense of pleasurable femininity (P. Tyson, 1986a).

Somewhere between fifteen and twenty-four months, girls show a definite awareness of the anatomical differences (Burlingham and A. Freud, 1944; Greenacre, 1953b; Mahler et al., 1975; Kleeman, 1976; Roiphe and Galenson, 1981). Dorothy Burlingham and Anna Freud reported how two little girls each gave obvious signs of distress upon noticing a boy's genitals. They commented that children often react to these first observations negatively: instead of remarking on the difference in the genitals they have noticed, children stress the similarity of some other parts of their bodies—for example, showing a special interest in each other's navel and breasts (1944, pp. 626–627).

Observations of little girls' reactions to the discovery of anatomical differences have often been interpreted as indicating a sense of castration or of penis envy (Mahler et al., 1975; Roiphe and Galenson, 1981). These reactions undoubtedly occur, but we question whether they are the bedrock of normal female development, as Freud (1940) asserted. To understand the meaning of a girl's reaction we must take account of her relationship to her parents, including the father's emotional (rather than sexual) availability, as well as the mother's sense of her own femininity. When the mother-child relationship has been "good enough" and the mother is comfortable with her own femininity, the little girl may show surprise on discovering anatomical differences; she may even demonstrate a transitory fascination with or awe of the penis (Greenacre, 1953b), be excited by and seek every opportunity to see a penis, and express wishes to have one. But at the same time she also has a sense of pride in being female. When father is libidinally available, this fascination may lead to some early identifications with him. Frequently penis fascination may be directed toward urinary functions, as when a little girl experiments with urinating standing up. This may express penis envy, or it may be an expression of envy of a boy's urinary prowess and a wish for similar bodily control. As Kestenberg noted, the little girl "wants a penis as a tool for control rather than an organ for pleasure" (1975, p. 223; see also Horney, 1924).

If the early separation-individuation phases are troubled, however, the girl may react to the discovery of anatomical differences with intense penis envy. Galenson and Roiphe (1976) report mood changes in some girls of this age, which they attribute to the discovery of sexual differences. Mahler and her colleagues (1975) observe similar mood changes but attribute them to the rapprochement crisis, during which the depressive mood expresses a sense of loss of the idealized feeling of oneness. The wish for a penis may here express an attempt to defend against the anxiety about object loss that is part of the separation-individuation process.

In its various forms, penis envy may undermine the girl's self-confidence and further strain the mother-child relationship, compounding anal-phase and rapprochement difficulties. For example, if the girl believes the acquisition of a penis would make her more acceptable to mother and open the possibility of reestablishing the early mother-child closeness, penis envy may become a vehicle for expressing rapprochement conflicts. Grossman and Stewart (1976) suggest that in such instances penis envy could be understood as a developmental metaphor that comes to represent a general sense of worthlessness, narcissistic vulnerability, inadequacy, deprivation, and a sense of damage; that is, it expresses all the conflicts of the rapprochement phase, including the underlying fantasy that mother would have preferred a boy.

In order to make sense of the infant girl's reaction to the discovery of anatomical differences, we need to consider her progression along a

variety of developmental lines. For example, conflicts in object relations and early steps in the emerging superego as well as drive impulses
make significant contributions to what may otherwise appear to be
simply a manifestation of penis envy.

It is also timely that we reconsider, in addition to penis envy, whether
or not castration anxiety is a central feature of female development.
The female sense of inferiority has frequently been interpreted adulto-
morphically as related to the idea that the little girl reacts to awareness
of genital differences with a sense that she has been castrated. It is not
hard to trace the origin of this idea. In a 1920 footnote to his "Three
Essays on the Theory of Sexuality," Freud categorically stated, "We are
justified in speaking of a castration complex in women as well. Both
male and female children form a theory that women . . . lost it by
castration" (1905b, p. 195). At about the same time Abraham (1920)
described psychopathology resulting from the female castration complex.

The present state of our knowledge would lead us to hesitate to
make so categorical a statement. Early trauma and the experiencing or
witnessing of physical injury are known to arouse confusion capable of
undermining the stability of the body image (Greenacre, 1953a). Furthermore, wishes, fantasies, conflicts, and fears in relation to experiences with the mother or father during the separation-individuation
process can easily lead a girl to experience anxiety about loss of the
object. Freud observed that early separation anxieties were easily generalizable to anxieties about body integrity (1926, pp. 136–139). Settlage (1971) reported a case in which a clear link existed among a
disruption of the early object relationship, intense separation anxiety,
and the girl's preoccupation with her body and her fear of bodily
injury. Similarly, we know of a two-year-old girl who underwent surgery to repair a bilateral hernia shortly after her mother had returned
to full-time employment, so that the toddler had to spend long hours in
day care. The combination of the confusing bodily injury, separation
from mother, and the conviction that her mother preferred her older
brother led the little girl to fantasize that the surgery had removed her
penis. She was emphatic that it would grow back, and in the meantime
she withheld her feces so as not to lose any other valued part of her
body.

Mayer (1985) distinguishes such fantasies from uniquely female
fears of genital damage or loss, which Horney (1924) described as
female genital anxiety. Mayer points out that not only do some women
fear genital damage as a result of masturbation or penetration, but

some women seem to fear loss of access to their genitals, as if they might be closed up and no longer open and receptive.

These uniquely female genital concerns, which evolve and change over the course of development, suggest a developmental line for female genital anxiety. This might begin with the girl's early curiosity about her inner and outer genitals (Kestenberg, 1976) and then progress to her fears of damage through masturbation, to later fears of inner damage derived from confusion about childbirth, to adolescent fears of damage from penetration, and to the pregnant woman's anxiety about inner damage from her expected baby.* We would emphasize that such genital concerns follow rather than precede the establishment of primary femininity and do not themselves lead to a sense of inferiority.

The father's role in the girl's development is an important influence on her growing sense of femininity. His importance as a protector against the threat of maternal engulfment has often been emphasized. Girls in the second year commonly turn to father in a new and apparently erotic way, seeking mother only during periods of stress. This development is not seen when the early mother-child relationship has been of poor quality; in the latter cases the girl's hostile dependence on the mother is often enormously aggravated by the discovery of sexual differences, and the father may then be viewed as an intruder. This turn to the father may be misunderstood as a precocious oedipal involvement (for example, Ogden, 1987), but because it is not accompanied by other indications of triadic object relations, we believe that it is probably a defensive move against the regressive pull toward the mother from whom the small girl is trying to separate (see Mahler et al., 1975; Parens et al., 1976; Roiphe and Galenson, 1981). Nonethe-

---

*As we noted earlier, the automatic assumption that an adult woman's fear of penetration derives from an early childhood fantasy of intercourse is more than likely a genetic fallacy in which later fantasies are assigned an earlier origin. Unless the girl has experienced sexual molestation or primal scene exposure (which usually leads more to confusion of sexuality and aggression than to an understanding of intercourse), little girls rarely fully understand sexual intercourse and its function in procreation. One six-year-old, for example, after being read a book on the subject, gleefully described how the sperm spurts from the penis to the egg. She imagined little sperm with great wings, flying around until they found the egg, much like a mother bird. She had totally failed to grasp the intercourse aspect of the information. Much later the girl may nevertheless experience neurotic suffering when she understands the incestuous sexual implications of her infantile wishes for father's baby.

less, the father's role is crucial in reinforcing the little girl's sense of femininity and may help her cope with feelings of inferiority in reaction to the discovery of anatomical distinctions.

## INFANTILE GENITAL PHASE AND THE BROADENING SENSE OF FEMININITY

Beginning about the third year, the girl displays a variety of new behaviors. Increased exhibitionism, an anatomical preoccupation or a fascination with the bodies and genitals of both sexes, scopophilia, and increased genital masturbation suggest that infantile genital phase dominance has been established.

As noted in our discussion of psychosexuality, optimal development requires that the little girl accomplish two major tasks during the early or preoedipal part of the infantile genital phase. She must assume a feminine gender role (see below) and also consolidate a narcissistically valued body image. The latter includes building on core gender identity as an overall sense of gender identity expands. In the process, exhibitionism becomes prominent. Many little girls appear to enjoy the kinesthetic pleasures in such activities as running, jumping, dancing, and tumbling, and enjoy showing off their bodies in every way. They seek and enjoy the praise received from both parents, praise that enhances the little girl's narcissistic pleasure in being female.* These activities ordinarily facilitate the girl's formation of a feminine, narcissistically valued gender identity. At the same time, girls typically show continuing and more elaborate interest in being like mother, often expressing wishes to adorn themselves with particular accoutrements in imitation of her and as concrete expressions that to them define femininity.

A girl's interest in, curiosity about, and concern for her genitals also become apparent when genital masturbation, possibly involving both vaginal and clitoral stimulation, becomes a primary focus of sexual excitement. Insofar as the only known function of the clitoris is to serve as an erotic focus for sexual stimulation (Masters and Johnson, 1966;

---

*In his book on dreams, Freud (1900) introduced the idea that people sometimes use their bodies in a way that suggests the body symbolically represents a phallus. Lewin (1933) subsequently broadened the body-phallus symbolic equation to other areas. Even though material from the analyses of some adult patients of both genders suggests that unconscious body-phallus fantasies may have been present from childhood, we know of no evidence that such fantasies are ubiquitous or a usual part of female development.

Clower, 1976), it is not surprising that masturbation in girls is primarily clitoral, although occasionally the girl fingers or introduces objects into her vagina. A girl may also use indirect and disguised forms of masturbation such as squeezing her thighs or rocking on her foot or her father's knee.

Penis envy seems to be ubiquitous in the infantile genital phase. Although it may begin much earlier, at this stage it tends to express phase-specific rivalry with boys and to be part of the continuing process of defining a narcissistically valued female body image. When it is exaggerated and accompanied by a sense of inferiority and low self-esteem, it can usually be traced to earlier problems in object relations that led to narcissistic vulnerability (Grossman and Stewart, 1976). In such instances, the development of a secure, pleasurable sense of femininity may be compromised and positive oedipal development delayed. If a girl is to negotiate this phase successfully, she must find a way of coping with penis envy and of finding a narcissistically valued view of her own female body.

In addition to penis envy, girls have a fascination with and envy of the mother's breasts. This reflects idealization of mother's mature body and envy of and competition with her, which may become more obvious in oedipal elaboration and may lead, Greenacre (1950) suggests, to an illusory expectation of superiority after puberty. This aspect of female development has been insufficiently appreciated, except for Melanie Klein who attributed to the very young infant fantasies and conflicts related to breast envy (1952b, 1957). Analytic experience with prelatency girls has shown convincing evidence of the influence of breast envy (or indeed an envy of anything they don't possess, a universal characteristic of children). Breast envy may equal or be greater than penis envy (P. Tyson, 1989b).

## GENDER-ROLE IDENTITY

As we have already noted, gender-role identity refers to conscious and, especially, unconscious ways of interacting with other people that reflect one's gender identity. What we can classify as feminine role identifications begin at a remarkably early age. Mannerisms, gestures, and interactions that are unquestionably feminine can be seen even before the little girl walks, Stoller (1976) observes. These not only demonstrate the early establishment of a primary sense of femininity but also indicate the early beginnings of feminine gender-role identifications.

Another important manifestation of gender-role identity is the wish to nurture a baby (P. Tyson, 1982a). Evidence for such a wish has been observed, manifested particularly in doll play, as early as twelve to eighteen months. Freud viewed the little girl's wish for a baby as a substitute for a penis and thought it was a typical way of coping with penis envy during the infantile genital phase, although he also mentioned fantasies of having a baby in connection with anal-phase struggles (1916–1917, pp. 318–319). Although wishes and conflicts of anal and infantile genital phase origin may come to be represented in the girl's wish for a baby, current analytic opinion considers the girl's wish for a baby a basic expression of femininity. Indeed, Kestenberg (1956a) suggests the existence of a maternal "instinct." Parens and his colleagues (1976) think the girl's wish for a baby is an inborn gender characteristic. McDevitt (1975) explains it as an identification with mother, part of coping with the awareness of separation and the conflicts of the rapprochement phase.

We think that the wish for a baby is also a manifestation of gender-role identification, an idea that in no way invalidates the suggestions just mentioned. As an expression of gender-role identity, it is among the first and emerges long before the infantile genital phase and oedipal triadic object relations. Indeed, as a sense of primary femininity emerges and the infant girl is increasingly aware of being female, she begins to identify with her mother's (often unconscious) style of interacting with others and with her mother's nurturing and caretaking interactions with her. Wishful fantasies of being a mother with a baby in a dyadic relationship then form the core of her female gender role as well as her ego ideal. At this stage a little girl's expressed wish for a baby as well as her turning to the father in an erotic fashion (Abelin, 1971; see also below) may therefore be a manifestation of gender-role identification at a dyadic preoedipal level rather than reflecting triadic oedipal dynamics.

Once the girl enters the infantile genital phase, consolidating a female gender role is a requirement for oedipal progression. That is, in order to have wishes and fantasies of taking mother's place in relation to father, she must both take pride in being feminine like mother and identify with mother's role in interaction with father. Instead of being the baby or daddy's little girl, she wishes to be "mistress of the house," daddy's chosen love object. Bride fantasies frequently appear now. Again, these should not automatically be assumed to reflect oedipal wishes; when they first emerge they more often indicate an enjoyment of sharing in female activities with an idealized mother figure and an elaboration of the female gender role. The wish to be the object of father's exclusive love evolves from these fantasies. As a female gender role becomes firmer through these fantasies, the little girl struggles to interact with her father in a more mature feminine manner, simultaneously extending the depth and breadth of her identifications with her mother.

The wish for a baby and playing at nurturing and caretaking continue as expressions of a female gender role. During the infantile genital phase these fantasies often become more elaborate not only because of the extension of identifications made with the mother (as well as an increased capacity for fantasy) but also because of the change in role in relation to father; now she wants father's baby. As one little girl, age four years five months, said after her mother had given birth to a baby sister, "But I dreamed that daddy gave me five baby dolls."

## THE OEDIPUS COMPLEX AND THE FOUNDATION OF SEXUAL-PARTNER ORIENTATION

Oedipal progression for the girl implies that more and more she takes her father as her love object and constructs elaborate fantasies around the "glamorous figure of her phallic father" (Jacobson, 1964, p. 114). In so doing, the little girl takes the first major step toward an eventual heterosexual orientation.

According to Freud, the girl's oedipal progression is based on her acknowledgment of her inferior castrated state, turning away from her mother in anger and disappointment and then taking her father as her love object; thereafter her mother is seen as a sexual rival. Our broader understanding of the female Oedipus complex is in the context of gender-identity development. Rather than stress the girl's total rejection of mother (which happens only in pathological situations and which may predispose the girl to give up and not fully pursue an oedipal attachment to her father), we believe it is important to understand how her attachment to the mother shifts and changes.

These changes are based on the developmental tasks of the preoedipal infantile genital phase, from which a narcissistically valued (instead of inferior) sense of femininity and a female gender role evolve. These are built upon the girl's preoedipal attachment to her mother. When she has significantly resolved her preoedipal ambivalence toward her mother and achieved a useful degree of libidinal object constancy, she feels herself to possess a lovingly available internal mother. Now, under the guiding influence of her female ego ideal and wishing to expand her female gender role, she can become preoccupied with fantasies about being chosen by her father, unhampered by fears of abandonment by her mother but rather confident of her continuing love. As the girl acquires the capacity for triadic object relations, she loosens her exclusive attachment to her mother. She does not reject her; she wishes for a relationship with her father that is different from the kind she has with her mother. Anxiety now centers on the fear of loss of father's as well as mother's love.

Although in fantasy the little girl displaces her mother by imagining herself the object of her father's love, she continues to count on the support of the idealized fairy godmother maternal image. Indeed, her fantasies are elaborated in connection with that image, and she feels anxious if she believes that libidinal wishes for her father jeopardize her anaclitic attachment to her mother. One little girl, age three years eight months, illustrated this in her announcement that she wanted to be a "baby-married"—that is, she did not want to wait until she grew up. She did not appear to anticipate her mother's criticism although she was at times competitive, but rather she looked for her mother's support in various elaborations of her fantasy. Some relinquishment and resolution began to be apparent when she asked to see her mother's wedding dress and requested that her mother promise to let her wear it when she eventually did marry.

The girl's positive oedipal progression is not always as smooth as this description may imply. It depends partly on the nature and extent of father's responsiveness to her, now that she has achieved the capacity for a triadic relationship. His admiration of her bolsters her pride and self-esteem, encourages her identifications with her feminine ego ideal, and fosters oedipal consolidation. If father is more seductive than admiring, however, the little girl may become overexcited yet flooded with loyalty conflicts and guilt and may then regressively reattach herself to her mother. Other possible difficulties in the father-daughter relationship (see Leonard, 1966) include the girl's tendency either to idealize her father (or men in general) or to see him as overly sadistic or punitive when he is relatively absent, unresponsive, or critical.

Another obstacle to the girl's oedipal progression is her feelings about her mother. Difficulties in resolving rapprochement conflicts may delay oedipal progression. Once forward movement begins, excessive preexisting conflict may facilitate ease of regression. Then, instead of the girl's engaging in oedipal pursuits, her envy of her mother or her conscious guilt over oedipal wishes leads her to fear the loss of her mother's love. In addition, because superego formation begins early for the girl, in response to efforts to resolve rapprochement conflicts, idealization of the mother and self-criticism from harsh introjects may compromise her confidence in her femininity. The confluence of these factors may lead her to withdraw from oedipal competition and regress to her early attachment to her mother, remaining frozen in a state of childlike dependency. Submissive, compliant, and masochistic character traits then predominate. Freud's exquisite case of a homosexual woman illustrates some of these issues. (See P. Tyson, 1989b, for elaboration.)

It has been an integral part of psychoanalytic formulations to postulate a negative Oedipus complex prior to the positive Oedipus. The girl identifies with her father, assumes an active phallic role in relationship to the mother, and competes with father for mother's love in triadic object relations (see Lampl-de Groot, 1927; Deutsch, 1930, 1932, 1944, 1945; Freud, 1931; Brunswick, 1940; Nagera, 1975). Freud noted that the girl's attachment to her father is preceded "by a period before it that is governed by the negative complex"—that is, "by a phase of exclusive attachment to her mother which had been equally intense and passionate. Except for the change of her love-object, the second phase had scarcely added any new feature to her erotic life" (1931, pp. 225–226).

Although oscillations and conflicts in relation to object choice are a part of the idea of bisexuality, the little girl's dyadic preoedipal ambivalent tie to her mother accompanied by her view of the father as a troublesome intruder should be distinguished from a triadic so-called negative oedipal attachment. Although the preoedipal mother-daughter relationship may be "intense and passionate," Edgcumbe and her colleagues (1976) report analytic investigations that find that the intensity and passion are pregenital and focused on control struggles, not triangular competition for an object. They therefore conclude that a negative oedipal position is not an obligatory phase of female development. We agree, but would add a proviso. We find that if a negative oedipal attachment to the mother does take place, it follows rather than precedes the positive Oedipus and suggests disturbed object relations (see P. Tyson, 1986a, for elaboration).

Freud (1925b) noted that oedipal resolution for a girl does not have the urgency it has for a boy; oedipal wishes may be only slowly abandoned or dealt with by repression or they may persist for an indeterminate length of time. We agree that since girls have many conflicts to resolve before moving into a positive oedipal position, once achieved, a triadic heterosexual configuration may continue. The fear of narcissistic mortification, or of the loss of mother's love, and increasing pressure of guilt from the superego, however, motivates the girl to repress oedipal libidinal wishes for her father. In that way she preserves affectionate relationships with both parents. It is not uncommon, however, for a girl to continue to seek attention and affection from her father. This not only helps reinforce her pleasure in her femininity, but it also facilitates her making selective identifications with her father that broaden her gender identity. As long as mother's envy does not arouse undue guilt, and as long as the affection is in appropriate proportions and the unconscious incestuous wishes do not become conscious, the girl can retain a positive oedipal configuration until adolescence; then the upsurge of sexual impulses may cause her to employ reaction formations against her father's affection and look for extrafamilial objects.

We should not, however, confuse a girl's proclivity to remain in a positive oedipal heterosexual position with a failure in superego formation, as Freud did when he failed to differentiate the early development of the male and female. As we detailed in our discussion of the superego, the girl's pathway to superego formation is different from the boy's. It begins early, and the need to resolve ambivalence to the mother to *enter* the Oedipus complex makes fundamental contributions. Later modification depends on the girl's successful progression to and resolution of the Oedipus complex, during the course of which she makes selective identifications with her father.

## LATENCY

During latency the girl reworks earlier issues and consolidates and elaborates on all aspects of her gender development. Gender identity broadens and becomes firmer as latency progresses. Expanding social relations bring the girl into contact with a wider peer group and greater opportunities for finding new objects for idealization and identification. Because peer relations may become competitive and reawaken earlier insecurities, the girl, in order to bolster her confidence in her sense of femininity, may embrace and exaggerate stereotypic and somewhat superficial aspects of femininity. In contrast, tomboyish behavior is common among some latency girls and may represent an elaboration of masculine identifications. It may also provide a means of compensation for girls whose sense of femininity is for some reason insecure or undervalued.

Freud (1933) believed that the attainment of adult femininity requires the girl to relinquish infantile wishes for a penis and repress awareness of genital pleasure—that is, she has to give up masturbation. This idea resulted from his erroneous belief that clitoral stimulation exacerbates penis envy—he equated the clitoris with a "little penis." Clinical experience, however, has clearly shown that neither masturbation nor the capacity for genital sensation disappears in the healthy latency girl (see Bornstein, 1953; Fraiberg, 1972; Clower, 1976). Because of strong superego prohibitions, direct stimulation of the genitals may be less frequent, but there are manifold disguises that involve indirect genital stimulation—for example, rhythmic activities or tactile stimulation from riding bicycles or horses, sliding down banisters, or urinating frequently. Unconscious masturbation guilt and fears of genital damage may also be displaced, sometimes accounting for the hypochondriacal concerns about bodily damage shown by some latency girls. Girls may separate conscious and unconscious masturbation fantasies from the masturbatory act, thereby providing an important means for the elaboration and consolidation of a sense of femininity as preoedipal and oedipal conflicts and wishes, and gender-related themes are worked out in disguised ways.

Gender-role identity becomes more elaborate during latency, a time for practicing gender roles. During these years girls pretend to be mothers, caretakers, housekeepers, hostesses, teachers, businesswomen, dancers, lovers, and so forth, with varying levels of awareness, as their gender-role identification begins to take on aspects of socially learned behavior, and they identify with women other than their mother. A unisex ideal or attitude—which nowadays parents often espouse—may be a source more of anxiety than of comfort for the latency girl because her own personal and gender identity is not yet too secure.

Sexual-partner orientation is not a strong issue during latency, and peer relationships tend to have a bisexual orientation. A girl may have a crush on a particular boy, but she pays close attention to female peer relationships, reflecting aspects of preoedipal and negative oedipal object relations. Girls form small cliques or best-friend couples; if the dyad is interrupted by a competitor, much unhappiness and pain can follow. Attempts to form threesomes often fail.

## ADOLESCENCE

A woman's ultimate mix of masculinity and femininity, her gender role, and her sexual-partner orientation consolidate as a result of her resolution of the expectable adolescent developmental conflicts. The final blending of all these strands is usually established by the end of adolescence.

A woman's eventual ability to find a satisfying and narcissistically valued sense of femininity and to experience sexual pleasure is largely influenced by her response to the developmental tasks heralded by menarche. Indeed, Ritvo (1976) suggests that menarche has all the characteristics of a normal developmental crisis and that it can provide a stimulus or be an obstacle to development. It serves as an organizer for a more mature sense of femininity and a nidus around which a revised body image is built, an image that must integrate acceptance of and pleasure in the body as feminine, as sexually active, and as potentially childbearing. (Many have written about this, but see especially Kestenberg, 1961; Blos, 1967; Hart and Sarnoff, 1971.)

Important revisions in her body image accompany the girl's menarche. From the little girl of latency, the adolescent acquires a mature body with breasts almost overnight, it may seem. The young girl must adjust her view of herself and her body to accommodate these physical changes. In a relatively brief time, these bodily changes bring into focus the increasingly obvious differences between female and male, child and adult. Unresolved conflicts in any of these areas soon become apparent, often through a bodily preoccupation as the girl tries to cope with disappointing discrepancies between her own and an "ideal" body.

Acquiring an adult body is a powerful reminder to the young girl that she is like, yet separate from, her mother. Whether consciously or preconsciously, this reminder revives unresolved mother-child wishes and conflicts from all developmental levels. The difficulties in resolving these conflicts are apparent in, among other indications, the prevalence of eating disorders among adolescent girls as they try to alter the shape of their adult body.

Menarche may be a rite of passage, but many attitudes of secrecy, inferiority, shame, and insecurity can exist alongside feelings of pride, confidence, self-assurance, and adequacy about the new development. Menstruation typically stimulates unresolved conflicts around anality. In contrast to urine and feces, menstrual flow cannot be controlled by voluntary sphincter action; the possibility of uncontrollable soiling brings feelings of helplessness, passivity, and shame, and fears of humiliation. Reaction formations contribute additional stress. A little girl may have developed feelings of disgust in relation to her menstruating mother, to her breasts, or simply to mother's or her own body products and odors. If she is to accept and cope with her mature body functioning, however, she must modify these reaction formations.

Fears of bodily damage may also arise with menarche. Coping with menstrual flow or irregularities arouses anxiety, perhaps because of pregnancy implications, but more often because of uncertainty about mysterious internal processes. Considerable anxiety is often manifested if the girl uses tampons (Shopper, 1979), for then she must experience her vagina directly. This anxiety may be related to earlier fears of genital damage, or the fears may arise anew owing to the complexities of tampon use.

Because of the intense anxiety about the body in puberty, Plaut and Hutchinson (1986) maintain that the events of puberty are even more important than the oedipal phase for the girl's psychosexual development. In their view, the feminine body image before puberty lacks the coherent organization that is provided to the male by the penis. The lack of visibility of the vagina creates a sense of mystery, incompleteness, anxiety, and inferiority. With the onset of menarche comes a greater vaginal awareness. Vaginal sensations become more conscious and more clearly localizable and so can be integrated into the feminine body image. This view may accurately reflect the developmental experience of some but not all young girls, for some are better able to discriminate early vaginal sensations and so are able to establish a feminine body representation prior to menarche. Most girls, however, do appear to benefit from the greater vaginal awareness and the further coherence of body image integration that come with menstrual functioning.

As a concrete confirmation of being female, menarche sometimes revives penis envy as well as feelings of deprivation, narcissistic vulnerability, and uncertainties about an acceptable body image. Although potentially noxious, these feelings may be counteracted by the adolescent girl's newfound pleasure and pride in finally developing at least an approximation of an ideal female body, as preoccupation with the size of her breasts in comparison with those of her mother or some other admired woman replaces preoccupation with penis envy. The girl may then rapidly swing away from the tomboyish behavior she previously enjoyed, as if the experience of menstruation and breast development fortifies her pride in the feelings of feminine identity (Jacobson, 1964).

Biological changes also revive and intensify the girl's sexual urges. Increased masturbation as well as some sexual activities with others are not uncommon, although these activities typically bring anxiety, shame, and guilt before the restructuring of the superego. In addition, curiosity and fantasies about intercourse frequently lead to anxiety, for fantasies of pain and damage on penetration are ubiquitous.

Gender-role identity is also revised and finalized during adolescence. Mature sexuality exerts a pressure toward finding new ways of interacting with others, especially with potential lovers. Often in reaching puberty a girl finds a new sense of self-confidence; she may move from cautiousness and shyness to a haughty flirtatiousness, sometimes bordering on the castrating and sadistic in her interactions with the opposite sex—not only with her male peers but also with her father. In its early stages the girl's style of interacting with boys and men may resemble a caricature of a feminine role, betraying underlying anxiety; but the ultimate role the woman assumes in interacting with love objects begins to take its final form in early adolescence.

The wish for a baby also reemerges in the adolescent girl—a wish that reflects both revived oedipal incestuous wishes and modifications and additions to earlier gender-role identifications. Indeed, consciously unwanted but unconsciously hoped-for pregnancy in the young adolescent girl is not uncommon, and the wish finally to assume a female gender role by nurturing her own baby is evident in the many girls who keep and try to mother their babies. But teenage pregnancy is a more complicated matter than the girl's simply consolidating her gender-role identity. The boyfriend often represents a substitute mother, and the sexual relationship may be primarily an expression of early dependency longings. Frequently the boyfriend disappears once the baby is born, if not before, and the girl returns to her own mother. For some this provides a means of satisfying an unconscious wish to have a baby both as a way of returning to her own mother while resisting the regressive pull (now they are equals), and as an unconscious regressive attempt to regain or create for the first time the fantasized, idealized, wished-for mother-daughter oneness through close attachment to the baby.

A variety of socially learned roles and educationally inspired possibilities may also be added to earlier gender-role identifications if the adolescent girl has contact with an increasingly wide social world. Identification with a broader range of male and female figures is apparent as the adolescent girl considers career possibilities. Since nowadays a woman can enter many occupations that were once male preserves, and she can do so in her own feminine way and relate to others as a female, judgments about a woman's gender role on the basis of occupational choice should be made with caution. Socially learned or inspired roles nonetheless make a contribution, and we conclude that a woman's final gender-role identity represents a synthesis of early childhood and adolescent identifications and aspirations.

Sexual-partner orientation is primarily an adolescent issue. Conflicts over object choice begin with the Oedipus complex, although in early childhood conflicting object-related wishes can exist side by side without being particularly painful or "noisy." But in adolescence, the girl's sense of identity comes to be linked to her sexual preference, so that the resolution of conflicts over the choice of love object becomes a major task.

Explicit interest in romance often appears in early adolescence as girls develop crushes on boys. Such an infatuation may indicate the girl's strivings for the fulfillment of feminine interests and her wish to make a heterosexual object choice. These relationships can be elaborated and become a source of pleasure and love to the extent that incestuous urges remain repressed. Should heterosexual activity arouse unconscious fantasies of oedipal fulfillment, a sense of guilt may lead the girl to quickly abandon it. Premature heterosexual activity may also represent a defense against the regressive pull of the preoedipal mother. Although the intimacy of a best-friend relationship provides a displacement for this regressive pull, and this relationship may initially provide an opportunity for both girls to elaborate fantasies about heterosexual escapades, the dyadic oneness may lead to homosexual longings and experimentation. If so, this relationship may become so intense and gratifying that movement to a heterosexual position is delayed or thwarted altogether (Blos, 1979).

The adolescent girl's pathway for resolving her conflicts over object choice is through the ego ideal. Infantile images of self and of object must be revised and de-idealized. The girl's image of the all-good nurturing mother with whom she fantasizes having had total symbiotic oneness (or the split image of a depriving, abusive mother and a longed-for, all-good fairy godmother) is more myth than reality—as are the pleasures involved in such a fantasy. Dispelling these myths makes it possible for the girl to integrate a mature ego ideal based on identifications with a revised view of mother combined with identifications with other admired female figures. Narcissistic gratification then comes through identifications with the ego ideal as a sense of femininity becomes consolidated. The girl is now free to make a heterosexual object choice.

## SUMMARY

Establishing a comfortable sense of femininity, or a female gender identity, begins with primary femininity (core gender identity). A broader sense of gender identity, incorporating some masculine as well as feminine characteristics, has a long developmental pathway. Indeed, additions and revisions can be made throughout life. Experiences of courtship, marriage, pregnancy, childbirth, and motherhood, as well as other major life events, all make further significant contributions.

Gender-role identity has its own separate developmental course. The wish for a baby is often an early manifestation, reflecting identifications made with mother in her nurturing and caretaking interactions with others. Yet other, more subtle role-relationship identifications are also part of a woman's gender-role identity. These influence, consciously or unconsciously, the form of a woman's interpersonal interactions. Pregnancy, childbirth, and motherhood also represent stereotyped gender roles that our society holds to be consistent with femininity. Although socially learned roles do ultimately become an important part of gender-role identification, it is well to be cautious in making judgments about a woman's sense of femininity on the basis of culturally determined, learned gender roles.

Sexual-partner orientation, while related to gender identity and to gender-role identity, is a separate issue, and its final outcome has its own developmental course. Conflicts over object choice begin in early childhood during the Oedipus complex and the establishing of triadic object relations. Adolescence brings pressure to resolve infantile and adolescent conflicts over object choice. The final orientation depends on the process of conflict resolution during adolescence. Although conflicts over object choice may never be fully resolved and some individuals may change their orientation even fairly late in life, the sex of a woman's chosen love object is usually firmly established by late adolescence or early adulthood.

# CHAPTER 17

## GENDER DEVELOPMENT:

## BOYS

The boy's gender identity and a se-
cure sense of masculinity are established by a process similar to that in
girls. In this chapter we describe the issues and conflicts that are
different.

### CORE GENDER IDENTITY

Sex assignment at birth, parental fantasies, and parental sex hormones contribute to the initial phase in the establishment of male core
gender identity. Next, the boy must define his body self, which includes
his discovering his penis. In most reported cases—for example, in Loewenstein (1950), Kleeman (1965), and Roiphe and Galenson (1981)—
this discovery occurs in the second six months of life along with early
phases of separation and individuation and with Piaget's Stage IV of
sensorimotor development, when the infant begins to have usable
object permanence (that is, when the infant assumes an object still
exists even though it is hidden and not directly visible). As part of this
process, pleasurable tactile, kinesthetic, and visual experiences gained
through general body exploration, genital sensations, and genital manipulation become integrated into the emerging self-representation.

Loewenstein (1950) gives us a memorable description of a mother's
observation of her ten-month-old son discovering his penis. The little
boy, lying naked in his crib and playing with his arms and legs, sat up
while kicking his feet back and forth. His heel touched his penis several
times. He peered down, evidently to see what caused the sensation. His
protruding abdomen prevented him from seeing his penis, and he
started playing with his navel, pushing it in. Then he did the same with
his stomach and suddenly saw his penis. He slowly brought his finger

into contact with it and, beaming, looked up at his mother. Over the next several minutes he repeated the maneuver several times, crawling away, sitting, pushing in his stomach, and touching his penis with some uncertainty. It took the baby a few minutes to realize that his penis was indeed a part of his body, that it belonged to him.

Because the discovery of the penis is usually followed by intentional reaching and self-stimulation together with affectionate glances at the mother (Kleeman, 1965; Roiphe and Galenson, 1981), several analysts stress the importance of mother-infant reciprocity as a necessary ingredient in the process of defining body boundaries and establishing genital awareness (Greenacre, 1953a, 1958; Spitz, 1962; Kleeman, 1965; Francis and Marcus, 1975).

In the second year the practicing toddler begins to experience greater control and pride in every aspect of his bodily functioning, particularly pride in urinary functioning as sphincter control becomes possible. The little boy's pleasure in urination is a part of the pleasurable interchange with his mother, but now a greater interest in his father and his urinary stream becomes increasingly apparent (see Loewenstein, 1950; Kleeman, 1966; Roiphe and Galenson, 1981).

It is in connection with the urinary interest and closely associated genital arousal (the combination of which Ferenczi [1924] labeled urethral eroticism) of the second year that a boy usually discovers the difference between the sexes (Fenichel, 1945). Whether or not he discovers this in relation to siblings, peers, or parents, he gradually becomes aware, at least at times, that his genital body image differs from that of his mother. Because at this early stage the boy's own body image is still somewhat unstable, fears of castration frequently accompany the discovery of anatomical differences. The boy, egocentric in his thinking at this age, typically assumes that everybody has a penis and so mistakenly understands the female genital to be the result of its loss. One little boy, age eighteen months, for example, observed in a daycare setting a little girl being diapered. Although he had routinely witnessed such procedures, on one particular day his reaction was different. When the teacher said it was his turn, he ran, screaming "No! No!" and clutching his diapers. As his diapers were being changed, he continued to clutch his penis, crying "No! No!" Although the teacher explained anatomical differences to him, he remained obviously anxious when being diapered for several days.

Projected aggression typical of the anal-rapprochement phase adds credence to the boy's castration theory. As expectations and prohibitions are levied, he may fear castration as punishment and may imagine that his mother, who has issued these prohibitions, is therefore to be feared.

Toilet-training efforts may also engender early castration reactions. In addition to the anxiety aroused by the developmental conflict between mother's and toddler's wishes, anxiety may be aroused by successful use of the potty for defecation, as the child sees his narcissistically invested product discarded and lost (Heimann, 1962). Kleeman (1965) describes a boy who, during a period of heightened genital awareness and interest in father's urination, began tugging at his own penis, saying "Off!" or "Broken!" which coincided with his successes at using the potty (see also Roiphe and Galenson, 1981).

Greenacre (1953a, 1958) emphasized the importance of the first eighteen months for the stability of the boy's ultimate gender identity. Observing that the genitals are a source of interest, pleasure, and anxiety long before the phallic phase, she thought that trauma, continual exposure to female genitals, or a significant disturbance in the mother-child relationship can lead to body-image confusion and uncertainty, predisposing the boy to severe castration reactions. It should be noted, however, that the appearance of early castration anxiety gives evidence that a step has been taken toward core gender identity in that the boy is aware that he is a male.

An example is provided by a two-and-a-half-year-old who stubbornly refused to use the potty; when undressed, he would spread his scrotal sac and run about flapping it like wings, saying "Butterfly! Butterfly!" Although in most areas the mother-child relationship seemed a good one, the mother found herself struggling with the boy over toilet training. Further investigation revealed that not only was the boy repeatedly exposed to parental nudity, but he had recently witnessed the ceremonial circumcision of his baby brother. The boy described a favorite story about a caterpillar who went to sleep and woke up as a butterfly and flew away. Analysis revealed that the exposure to female genitals, witnessing the circumcision, and the anal struggles with his mother had become organized around castration anxiety. His cognitive immaturity led him to fear that his penis, like the butterfly, would fly away as a punishment for his angry struggles with his mother. Defecation, to him, offered proof of the potential for loss of a body part.

Optimally the father helps to minimize the boy's early castration anxiety and to stabilize core gender identity. He can reduce the influence of a mother's engulfing tendency as well as facilitate resolution of rapprochement conflict, thereby rendering the castration threat implicit in these conflicts less noxious. As a male figure for identification, the father becomes still more important to the boy who is increasingly aware of being male and who looks for males with whom to identify; identifying with his father, it is easier for the boy to disidentify (Greenson, 1954) with his mother. Identification with the father fosters a sense of masculinity and confidence in intact genitals, and the boy's body image becomes more stable.

The central role of the father for the boy's establishing a secure sense of masculinity should not be minimized. Freud declared that "anatomy is destiny," implying that a sense of maleness is guaranteed by possession of a penis (1912, p. 189; 1924a, p. 178). Stoller (1985), however, concludes that a secure sense of masculinity is an achievement. Because the sense of self accrues partly through identifications with the mother, the boy has a built-in vulnerability. To establish a confident sense of maleness, he must have a sense of being different from the mother, a sense that is enhanced when he has a male with whom to identify. When father is not readily accessible, identification with him may be delayed or not possible, and the boy's establishing a secure sense of primary masculinity is compromised.

The difficulty in counteracting identifications with the mother when no father figure is available was exemplified when one three-year-old was psychologically evaluated. On successfully pointing to all body parts on a picture of a small boy, his single mother reached under his shirt and insisted he point to his "boobies." She explained that the flowery jacket he was wearing was a hand-me-down from a friend's little girl and wasn't he lucky—it fit! About his long curls, she admitted they made him look like a girl, but they were so pretty she hated to cut them.

One particularly important manifestation of a male identity is upright urination, which the boy typically learns in imitation of his father, whether by seeing it or by being told by mother or father, "Boys do it standing up, like daddy." Pride in the urinary stream that he can produce helps the boy come to terms with toilet-training struggles. When father is absent or uninvolved, interest in urinary functioning has been seen to be delayed (Roiphe and Galenson, 1981), so upright urination may also be delayed. This often suggests an insecurity in the sense of masculinity (see P. Tyson, 1982b).

## PHALLIC NARCISSISM AND GENDER IDENTITY

Maturational forces lead eventually to the stage of genital primacy when genital interests and pleasures dominate and genital masturbation becomes the leading autoerotic activity. As we said earlier, certain phase-specific tasks must be accomplished in the early part of the infantile genital phase, which Edgcumbe and Burgner (1975) called the phallic-narcissistic phase. First, the boy must find a narcissistically valued view of his intact male body and his sense of masculinity; second, he must assume a male gender role.

In the course of the boy's finding a narcissistically valued sense of masculinity—a narcissistic investment that significantly contributes to consolidating his core gender identity (Stoller, 1968a)—a primacy and, indeed, an idealization of the phallus becomes manifest, expressed by one four-year-old who said, "I know, Superman's power comes from his penis." Possession of a large and potent penis becomes a wished-for aspect of the male ego ideal and attempts to reach the ideal are evident as phallic sexuality comes into full bloom. Now great displays of phallic exhibitionism, whether in the form of direct genital display or derivatives, become common. The boy shows great interest in his own genitals, in those of his peers, and in those of adult males—especially his father's. Many boys become envious of those with a larger penis.

In addition to penis envy and penis preoccupation, the boy is typically fascinated with the anatomy of both sexes and expresses envy of the woman's breasts, of her womb, and of her ability to have a baby (Kestenberg, 1965a; Van Leeuwen, 1966; Ross 1975). He may even express a wish to be a girl. Although he may occasionally voice such a wish, however, the boy also values his own genitals. Great concern about their being damaged or lost appears in a resurgence of castration anxiety at this time. Although earlier a boy may have denied anatomical distinctions because of his cognitive immaturity, continued denial or confusion extending into this phase indicates a defensive process against mounting castration anxiety.

The boy's self-esteem is often vulnerable during the infantile genital phase. This is related partly to a waning sense of omnipotence and resurgent castration anxiety, and partly to a sense of genital inferiority engendered by exhibitionism, penis envy, and the awareness that his genitals are small in comparison to the ideal. An optimal narcissistic investment in his penis, his male body image, and his sense of masculinity is notably enhanced when both parents show visible pride in his prowess. The child then internalizes the parents' pride, and his self-confidence in his masculinity is reinforced.

The role of the father is especially important at this juncture. As we have stressed elsewhere, the father helps the boy modulate aggressive behavior (Herzog, 1982). Its importance derives from the fact that boys often use aggression in attempts to defend against castration anxiety and feelings of phallic inferiority. If the father, instead of helping modulate the boy's aggression, becomes a stern disciplinarian, he may intensify the boy's castration anxiety, stimulate his son's hostile competition with him, and interfere with the boy's idealization of him. Not infrequently such a father becomes hostile and competitive in response to the boy's hostile competition and, setting himself up as an invincible, phallic, macho ideal, belittles and teases his son in order to make him "tough." Such behavior only heightens the boy's defensive hostility. In any event, whether because of a father's passivity or unavailability or because of his stimulating hostile competition, a boy's persistent, exaggerated displays of phallic power (in identification with the aggressor) usually suggest his insecurity rather than confidence in his masculinity, betraying an underlying lingering fear of castration.

Transsexual wishes may be primarily related to a failure to accomplish the tasks of the phallic narcissistic phase. Failure to find narcissistic value in the male body image and in the sense of masculinity, as well as failure to assume a male gender role (see below), leads to the descriptive state of feeling "trapped in the wrong body." Such a transsexual state may be due either to developmental psychopathology and partially arrested development or to defensive regression (Socarides, 1978) to the point where ideals and identifications are opposite to that of core gender identity.

## GENDER-ROLE IDENTITY

During the first two years the boy's major relationship is usually with his mother or female caregivers who provide him with his first role model. Identifications with mother and the female role are therefore ubiquitous in early childhood. The boy imitates his mother in her daily household tasks and often gives evidence of a specific wish to bear and nurse babies as the mother does, especially during the anal phase when anal-genital sensations may become associated with fantasies of having a baby (Ross, 1975). Freud noted in the case of Little Hans that "in phantasy he was a mother and wanted children with whom he could repeat the endearments that he had himself experienced" (1909a, p. 93, note).

The boy may use his identification with his mother and her gender role in several ways. It may help him cope with the feelings of object loss engendered by increasing separation awareness or resolve feelings of ambivalence toward her by becoming like her. Although childbearing fantasies and attitudes in very small boys can be considered phase-appropriate, the boy, in order to establish a male gender role, must switch his identification from mother to father. It is the boy's successful disidentification with his mother that is crucial to his finding a firm sense of masculinity (Greenson, 1968). Attempts at disidentification and the accompanying role confusion are demonstrated by the little boy who dons a flowery wide-brimmed hat and caresses a baby doll and then tosses doll and hat in the air and puts on his cowboy hat.

The father is so important in encouraging masculine attitudes (Stoller, 1979) that his availability as a role model is crucial. With the foundations of his primary masculinity in place and his sensorimotor intelligence supplemented by beginning representational intelligence, the boy now has the cognitive skills to enable him to differentiate male and female. He can begin at this point to seek "self-like objects" (Kohlberg, 1966) as role models with whom to identify.

As he approaches the phallic phase, the boy looks increasingly to his father as an adored ideal. He wishes to be with his idealized father and to be gratified by him, and builds a wished-for view of himself on the model of this paragon of perfection he has created in his mind. Freud viewed this idealization and identification with the father as a prerequisite for entry into the oedipal phase (1921, p. 105). As the boy identifies with his father's way of interacting with others, he begins to wish to interact with his mother in a different way.

The father's easy availability to his son in a variety of activities clearly is important if the boy is to identify with a male gender role; when father is not available or is overly aggressive or competitive, a variety of potentially maladaptive consequences may follow (see Tyson, 1982b, 1986b). The boy's increasing awareness of his father's part in procreation also helps him identify with his father's instead of his mother's way of relating to him. This helps him cope with the disappointment of not being able to have a baby and thus further disidentify with mother (see Ross, 1982a, 1982b; P. Tyson, 1980; 1982b), and it also furthers his male identifications. He can then look forward to being a father just like his father. Although disidentification with the mother may never be complete and the wish for a baby never completely disappear, a basically male gender role is consolidated with idealization of the father and identification with that ideal. Remnants of maternal identifications may then be evident primarily in nurturing and supportive attributes that may exist alongside masculine traits.

The quality of the relationship between the parents is important both for the boy's narcissistic investment in his masculinity and for his acquisition of a male role. If their relationship is fraught with ambivalence, being undermined by the unavailability and unreliability of the father, or with the mother devaluing the father, the boy may fear that as a male he too will be devalued. He may then fail to make the shift adequately from identification with mother to identification with father and the male gender role.

## THE OEDIPUS COMPLEX AND GENDER IDENTITY

Having established genital primacy, a confident and narcissistically valued sense of masculinity, and a male gender role, successfully disidentifying with mother, the boy moves toward the positive oedipal phase. Now he begins to seek a different type of relationship with his mother. He wants to appear more masculine in relation to her; instead of being her baby in anaclitic dependency, the boy wants to take his father's place with the mother and have an exclusive relationship with her (Freud, 1921).

The fantasy play of a five-year-old boy illustrates such wishes and also the related dangers. Using a female doll, a male doll, and a smaller boy doll, he pretends one day that the woman is confronted by a lion. The boy rescues her, kills the lion, and takes her behind the horse stable where they hug and kiss. Then the woman's husband appears, chastises the boy, and takes her home, where they go to bed, naked. The child giggles excitedly. On another day he pretends a princess is captured and put into the dungeon. The king plans to kill her. But he pretends to be a jester and tries to save the woman by tricking the king. Just as he is stealing away with the woman, the real jester appears and exposes him as an impostor—only a child. "Well," he explains to his captors, "I was just trying to keep everyone happy and entertained." The impostor is then killed.

Movement to the oedipal phase for the boy implies no outward change of love object but rather a change in fantasies about the object and a change of role in relation to the love object. Increased intensity of the genital impulses accompanies genital ascendancy—expressed by one boy who, while playing with horses, wondered "What will tame the horses?" He thought perhaps a rider would help (he had not yet read Freud!). These impulses intensify the boy's libidinal longings for his mother. Genital masturbation, the only phase-appropriate sexual outlet available to him, often increases along with associated fantasies. Unlike preoedipal dyadic competition in which the father is simply a rival for mother's attention with the boy merely wanting to retain or regain center stage, the oedipal triadic wish is to replace the rival with himself. Now the boy wants to possess his father's large penis as the outward symbol of masculinity and to eliminate the father to assure himself of an exclusive relationship with the mother for whom he then plays the role of husband-lover. In other words, he identifies with as well as wants to replace the rival.

The boy comes to feel very guilty because of his heightened sexual excitement about his mother and his "inadmissible impulses" (Freud, 1924a).* Castration anxiety again emerges, but now it is father, not mother, whom he fears.

Immature cognitive functions serve to heighten castration anxiety. The boy fears that his powerful father magically knows his thoughts and fantasies and will retaliate. He fears damage to or loss of his penis. Puzzling penile erections and detumescence may intensify this fear. The boy may not yet associate spontaneous erections with genital excitement, and not being in control, he may feel anxious. With detumescence the boy may fear that as the penis gets smaller and smaller it will disappear altogether (Solnit, 1979). In fact, he may associate detumescence with his father's feared magical punishment. Fears of castration may, in this way, lead to a cycle of maladaptive compulsive masturbation that only increases castration anxiety and tension.

In view of the many possible factors at various developmental phases that may undermine the sense of masculinity, castration anxiety, rather than simply coming into florescence and completion in the phallic phase as Freud suggested, may be better thought of as a developmental metaphor like penis envy (Grossman and Stewart, 1976), which takes on a variety of meanings and vicissitudes at various developmental stages (P. Tyson, 1989b). According to such a formulation, we can describe three phases in which castration anxiety arises.

In infancy, body integrity, identification, and the need to disidentify with the mother are crucial developmental issues. Castration anxiety deriving from this early period betrays a basic disturbance in the mother-child relationship, manifested in an insecurity in separateness

---

*Although the boy has fantasies related to his sexual impulses and about being his mother's lover, as we said earlier, these early childhood fantasies do not include a realistic or accurate depiction of intercourse. A child's sexual theories are confused and confusing for him. Because the child's feelings are so intense, efforts to "educate" him beyond his cognitive and emotional capacity to take in and comprehend the details often contribute to the distortion, a fact discovered in the early years of child analysis.

and in differentness, an insecurity in a sense of body integrity, and an insecurity in an intact male sense of self.

In the early infantile genital (or phallic-narcissistic) phase, the consolidation of a narcissistically valued and intact body image and a delineation of a male gender role are the crucial issues. Castration anxiety deriving from this period, which may be manifested in phallic exhibitionism, voyeurism, demeaning attitudes toward women, and idealized exaggerations of macho sexuality, indicates inadequate narcissistic investment in and continuing insecurity about the male body as well as some disturbance in object relations.

Castration anxiety deriving primarily from the oedipal phase is manifested in defensive competition with father or other males and fears of loss of love, of humiliation, or of punishment from the father. As the child matures, derivatives of oedipal phase castration anxiety may be manifested in fears of superego punishment.

Viewed as a developmental metaphor, castration anxiety can be considered not only as an anxiety about loss of the penis; with development and efforts to become like the ego ideal, it becomes related also to the fear of one's masculinity being undermined, as fears of actual genital damage or loss generalize to concerns about one's effectiveness or one's potency, and about measuring up to the ideal. Clinically, the problem then is to distinguish among castration anxiety representing unresolved oedipal conflict with continuing superego threat, castration anxiety representing vulnerability of phallic narcissism and failure to assume a male gender role, and castration anxiety representing a severe disturbance in early object relations, with a basic insecurity in an intact male sense of self.

## SEXUAL-PARTNER ORIENTATION

The little boy comes to form a close attachment to his father in the course of idealizing and identifying with him. Because of this, negative oedipal wishes—that is, wishes for the father as the primary love object with libidinal longings directed toward him—may emerge and conflict with positive oedipal wishes and libidinal longings for the mother. This is the foundation for conflicts over sexual-partner orientation.

Usually the little boy gives evidence of experiencing libidinal longing toward both parents (positive and negative oedipal strivings), and he may picture himself in a male or female role in relation to either of his parents. The boy's negative oedipal position in which he pictures himself consciously as feminine is usually shorter in duration than the positive position. This is commonly understood to result from his castration anxiety; if he were to persist in attempting to take mother's place and in identifying with her gender role—thus in fantasy becoming female—it would entail the loss of his precious penis. This would imply failure to reach the phallic-narcissistic goal of his ego ideal. Furthermore, since the close relationship with father was established on the basis of idealization of maleness and identification with father, female identifications might cause him to lose rather than gain father's admiration and love.

Negative oedipal aspirations not only risk loss of father's love and failure to reach the ideal, but taking mother's place would also jeopardize his preoedipal anaclitic attachment to her; this is an additional threat because the boy at this age continues to be dependent on mother for physical needs, feelings of well-being, and positive self-regard. The boy therefore turns his attention ardently to his phallus, denies any feminine wishes, repudiates anything about himself that may be feminine, and attempts to reach the ideal, endeavors that lead him to make further identifications with his father. This is only a temporary solution to conflicts over object choice, however; the ultimate resolution is deferred until adolescence (Blos, 1979).

The positive oedipal position is also ultimately and inevitably a disappointment to the boy; the mother falls short of fully satisfying his positive oedipal libidinal wishes for which he finds gratification ordinarily only in fantasy. In fact, he finds that neither parent responds sufficiently to his libidinal overtures and may not even take his longing seriously; rather, they may think he is "cute." Parental ridicule or unresponsiveness signifies to the boy he is inadequate and has not lived up to his ego ideal, which may inhibit the full flowering of his Oedipus complex.

Even when the validity of his libidinal longings is acknowledged, the boy can experience oedipal disappointments as a blow to his self-esteem at a time of great narcissistic vulnerability. Furthermore, the castration threat persists as long as the libidinal wishes persist. At this time the castration threat involves feared loss of the penis, the loss of father's love, and increasingly, superego punishment. In order to preserve his sense of self-worth and narcissistic balance, and for his optimal development, the boy must come to terms with the reality that oedipal gratification comes only in fantasy. In order to escape castration fears and to preserve his narcissistic integrity and balance, he gradually sets aside his oedipal wishes.

Giving up oedipal wishes is aided by an increasing repertoire of defenses available by superego development and the implied elaboration of an ego ideal and internalization of parental directives, and by increasing access to the widening social world where libidinal wishes can be displaced. Eventually, oedipal wishes become repressed, modified, or sublimated, making it possible for the boy to maintain an affectionate relationship with both his parents.

## IDENTIFICATION WITH THE FATHER

In Freud's discussion of the male Oedipus complex, he described the part played by identification with the father both as a step toward the Oedipus complex and as a means of its resolution. The first step is often underemphasized and the process misconstrued to imply that identification with the father is a defensive stance to protect the boy against projected hostile oedipal wishes, and that it is the vehicle to resolution of oedipal conflicts. But several authors have noted, and close observations of young children demonstrate, that nondefensive identification with father begins very early (see, for example, Loewald, 1951; Abelin, 1971, 1975; Edgcumbe and Burgner, 1975; Stoller, 1979; P. Tyson, 1982a, 1986b). Freud viewed identification as "the earliest expression of an emotional tie with another person" (1921, p. 105). Identification is therefore not per se defensive; furthermore, identification with the father is a prerequisite for beginning the Oedipus complex. It is by identification with father in his male gender role that the boy can himself acquire a male gender-role identity and in fantasy make the switch from being mother's baby to becoming her lover. As Abelin (1971) points out, oedipal rivalry presupposes an empathic identification with the father rival. It is only later when the boy notices that his father stands in the way of his positive oedipal fantasies, that "his identification with his father then takes on a hostile colouring and becomes identical with the wish to replace his father in regard to his mother" (Freud, 1921, p. 105).

Identification with the father continues throughout the infantile genital phase. Freud described how oedipal resolution comes about through taking father as an ego ideal and identifying with that ideal in the course of superego development (1921, 1924a). We have already described ego ideal formation in which the father plays such an important part. Now cognitive advances enable the boy more often to take the other person and his wishes into consideration—to think less egocentrically. He is thereby increasingly able to empathize with his father's wishes and to recognize that his father has rules not only for him but for himself. Increasingly father's rules and moral standards become idealized and internalized as the superego becomes more elaborate and complex, and narcissistic gratification comes with identification with the ideal. Fears of castration and of guilt provide powerful motivations for the boy to give up libidinal wishes toward his mother and to identify with the parental introject. In so doing, he preserves the affectionate relationship with both parents and suspends any further resolution of the Oedipus complex until a later date.

## LATENCY

When the boy reaches latency, the basic psychic structures should be in place. He now, ideally, enters a period of psychic integration and consolidation, including gender identity. A firm sense of masculinity is based on the identifications he has made with his father. Remaining insecurities and castration fears are evident, however, as exemplified in the way phallic narcissism reigns supreme, as latency boys tend to competitively show off their masculine prowess and to tease and yet avoid girls. The wider social opportunities of this period help the boy further integrate a sense of masculinity by giving him opportunities to experience a variety of relationships with peers, with older boys, and with other men. Idealizations of these figures become incorporated into the ego ideal and persist; narcissistic satisfaction is found when the boy successfully identifies with these idealizations. In this way, the wider social contacts give the boy an opportunity to extend his sense of gender identity.

Latency social relationships essentially reflect a phallic-narcissistic, idealized father-son attachment, which at this time is nonconflictual and helps maintain repression of lingering oedipal wishes, defends against feminine wishes and identifications, and wards off further threats of castration. The latency period is also a time during which the boy can practice many forms of male roles. In this way the intrapsychic role relationships established earlier are elaborated by social and cultural influences, and a broader sense of gender role results.

## ADOLESCENCE

The biological changes of preadolescence and adolescence challenge the boy's sense of his masculinity, his sense of his gender-role identity, and his previous position regarding choice of love object. As drive pressures increase, conflicts from all previous developmental levels may be

revived. Preoedipal passive longings conflict with active male identifications, feminine identifications conflict with male idealizations, incestuous conflicts threaten castration and superego integrity, and conflicts over object choice threaten the sense of masculinity. These
conflicting currents intensify inner disharmony, so much so that the
border between normality and pathology often becomes blurred. The
boy may tolerate revived positive oedipal affectionate feelings as long as
his incestuous wishes remain repressed (see Shengold, 1980), but the
reappearance of negative oedipal wishes arouses simultaneously his
longings for male companionship and his dread of homosexuality. Occasional homosexual contact—for example, in the form of mutual
masturbation—is apt to bring up a wide variety of questions, anxieties,
and problems of sexual identity. The adolescent may fear that attachments to or sexual activities with other boys indicate a fixed homosexual
position. In anxiety, he may regress to preoedipal attachments.

Such regression, however, further complicates the bisexual conflict.
Revival of early feminine identifications may undermine a precarious
sense of masculinity, while revival of anal-rapprochement conflicts re-
arouses castration anxiety—in particular, fears of the castrating mother. A representation of the mother as phallic and castrating may be
generalized to all women, causing the boy to turn away completely
from contact with women. Because some girls at this age tend to have a
rather harsh assertiveness—characteristically they "chase" boys—they
can appear to susceptible boys as threatening and reinforce fear of
women and admiration of men.

In some boys the admiration of men arouses such anxiety about
their basic sense of masculinity that to prove their sense of their masculine self, they may turn prematurely to heterosexual activity. Because of the defensive nature of these relationships, based as they are
on phallic-narcissistic pursuits, they are likely to be superficial and of
short duration (or what is sometimes called the Don Juan type). Rather
than confirming a sense of masculinity and helping resolve conflict
over object choice, these relationships function primarily as a defense
against homosexuality. Once established, such a pattern of relating
interferes with the eventual attainment of mature, reciprocal heterosexual relationships.

When conflicts over object choice lead to some kind of homosexual
activity, such an episode may be experienced as a trauma and result in a
"secondary adolescent fixation" (Blos, 1979; p. 478). In this case the
boy remains in what is felt to be a nonelective but nevertheless fixed

homosexual position. Many factors are involved in a homosexual orientation, many of which have earlier roots than their manifestation in adolescence, and we are only beginning to recognize the range of these factors (see Green, 1980; Isay, 1989; Friedman, 1988). But the coming to terms with the homosexual component of pubertal sexuality is an implicit development task for all adolescents. The ultimate sexual-partner orientation will be determined largely by the resolution made at this time.

The successful reorganization of the ego ideal is central to the resolution of the anxieties and conflicts relative to the adolescent boy's gender identity. Pressure arising in adolescence against attachments to infantile objects forces him to find displacements for the expression of his love for his father. So he seeks boys or men who have some of the characteristics of his paternal ego ideal. Consequently, resolution of conflicts over object choice comes about in a manner similar to the resolutions in early childhood—that is, admired characteristics of the object become a part of the maturing ego ideal. Spruiell notes that "just as the prohibiting superego was born in the embers of the Oedipus complex, the basically adult ego ideal is born in the embers of early adolescence" (1979, p. 327). In this way, the infantile masculine ego ideal undergoes revision and a more mature masculine ego ideal is consolidated. The boy then strives to become like the ideal, enhancing his sense of masculinity while leaving him free to make a heterosexual object choice.

As the boy achieves significant resolution of conflicts over object choice and further integrates a more mature ego ideal, questions of gender role appear again. These issues become more clearly defined with a certain amount of sexual experimentation during middle and late adolescence and with expansion of extrafamilial heterosexual relationships. If the boy is not overly burdened by a need to demonstrate phallic prowess, these relationships can serve as proving grounds and provide a foundation for the building of mature heterosexual reciprocal relationships with increasing consolidation of the young man's gender-role identity.

By the time he reaches adulthood, the young man usually has a fairly stable sense of his overall gender identity. Optimally, he has integrated a certain mix of masculinity and femininity; his position regarding sexual preference is stabilized, for he has a clear idea of the sex of the desired love object; and his gender-role identity vis-à-vis that love object is more or less consolidated.

## SUMMARY

Establishing a secure sense of masculinity is a long process for a boy, beginning in infancy when core gender identity is established. A secure sense of masculinity depends on, among other things, the boy's dis-identification with his mother and his identification with his father. It also depends on his successfully coping with castration anxiety. We have suggested that since castration anxiety is such a prevalent de-velopmental issue, emerging at several developmental way stations, it might be considered a developmental metaphor. The dynamic under-lying conflicts as well as the descriptive manifestations in any particular instance give clues as to the time of its developmental origin.

In addition to gender identity, male gender-role identity must be considered in any complete discussion of gender development. We have pointed out that although identification with the mother and her role is ubiquitous in early male development, it is crucial for the boy's ultimate sense of masculinity as well as for oedipal involvement that a boy disidentify with his mother and assume a male gender-role identity. It is this that paves the way for the boy's oedipal involvement with his mother. Therefore, oedipal movement for the boy includes not a change of object but a change in role in relation to the object.

We have pointed out that sexual-partner orientation is a separate is-sue with its own developmental trajectory. Conflicts over object choice begin in early childhood when, during the course of idealizing and identifying with the father of the phallic narcissistic phase, the boy forms a close relationship with him. In elaborating oedipal wishes, this idealization may be a foundation for wishes for father to be the primary libidinal object. Although many other factors may be involved in object choice, some of which are poorly understood, the final orientation, whether it is homosexual, heterosexual, or bisexual, depends on how the adolescent conflicts are resolved. Although the conflicts may never be fully resolved, a man's sexual-partner orientation is usually fixed by late adolescence.

Finally, we have discussed gender identity, gender-role identity, and sexual-partner orientation separately, but we have also emphasized that they are intertwining strands of gender development. The syn-thesizing and integrating functions of the ego work to establish an adaptive dynamic equilibrium among them during all stages of de-velopment, so that together they contribute to an overall complete sense of gender identity.

# PART EIGHT

## THE EGO

# CHAPTER 18

## THE DEVELOPMENT OF

## THE EGO

Our central premise is that the many diverse aspects of the personality we have been describing grow and develop simultaneously. Any relationship among functions or any integration within the apparent randomness of these many functions occurs because of ego functioning. Ego functioning provides a structure, a kind of order among psychic elements, thereby giving coherence to our minds.

As we have said before, in his early work Freud used the term *das Ich* (translated as "ego") to refer to an experiential sense of one's self. When he proposed his structural hypothesis, he added that the ego could also be thought of as "a coherent organization of mental processes" consisting of all those functions that regulate the drives and adapt to reality (1923a, p. 17). In other words, two levels of abstraction are implied, an experiential, which leads to the formation of self- and object representations, and a nonexperiential, which functions as an organizer, synthesizer, and regulator of the personality. We have already described the experiential; we now turn to the nonexperiential, and after a discussion of some conceptual issues, we propose a formulation for the development of the ego as an organizing structure.

Ego functioning is our first consideration. Freud ascribed to the ego those functions that have the task of adapting to the outer world of reality at the same time as they are concerned with the inner world and with maintaining psychic equilibrium. These inner- and outer-oriented functions are in constant interaction, and with development, the ego acquires a variety of ways of dealing with the inner and outer worlds. Defense mechanisms evolve and aid in the control or delay of instinctual gratification or other peremptory urges. Affects, as we have seen, come to serve in a signal capacity to anticipate danger, whether it be related to drive impulses or to external reality. Through processes of internalization and identification, the superego forms and then supports the ego in the task of adapting to the demands of inner and outer reality.

The tendency to organize and unify the personality is one of the most important functions of the ego; Freud noted that this capacity to synthesize grows stronger as the strength of the ego increases (1926, p. 98; see also Nunberg, 1931, for further emphasis). Hartmann (1956) commented that, in recognizing the synthesizing function together with the functions of adaptation and control (which Hartmann referred to as the ego's powerful triad of functions), Freud depicted the ego not only as an organization but also as an *organizer* and *harmonizer* of the three systems of the personality. We would add that it is this synergistic functioning of the ego that accounts for the coherence and durability of a sense of self. (Neubauer [1980, p. 33] described the differences between the organizing, synthesizing, and integrative functions of the ego, valuable distinctions but ones we do not maintain here for purposes of clarity.)

When we consider the ego as an organizer of the personality, the question rises as to how we should view its development. If the ego is understood to be simply a group of similar functions, recognizing that Freud arranged mental processes according to their functions in conflict and in adaptation, then tracing the evolution of its various functions would be one way of evaluating ego development. We take another approach, however. We follow Loewald's emphasis on the internal organization of the ego and conceptualize the stages of ego development on the basis of the linking of various ego functions (1978, p. 210). In other words, rather than stressing the evolution of various individual functions, we focus on the evolution of integration, as the ego develops toward becoming a coherently organized system.

Some have interpreted Hartmann's concept of the "conflict-free sphere" as being at odds with this integrative view. Although he usefully drew attention to ego functions that do not emerge as a result of conflict—cognition, for instance—some have thought that his idea that certain functions have "primary autonomy" means that they operate somehow in isolation and independently of any other part of the personality.

If the various ego functions are as interrelated as we believe, then cognitive functions do not operate in isolation and so are not autonomous or free of dependent connections in any simple way. Although cognitive capacities develop independently of conflict, the optimal emergence of these capacities depends on adequate mothering (which includes adequate and appropriate sensory stimulation) and adequate drive development, and, of course, they can be disturbed by later conflict. Growing cognitive skills provide pleasure, but they are also employed in progressively more sophisticated ways to achieve gratification of drives and other peremptory urges. Affect, likewise, does not emerge from conflict, but affects later on assume the function of signaling danger in relation to conflict. Emphasis on the interrelatedness of functions leads away from the debate over which functions arise from conflict and which are conflict-free. Instead, the focus is on the ways in which drives, ego functions, and environmental factors interact and influence each other throughout the course of development.

It was to such questions of integration and organization among ego functions that Spitz (1959) turned his attention. As we described earlier, he thought that as discrete processes come to be linked and formed into a coherent unit, a pattern emerges that reflects increased integration and structuralization of the ego. Then, with each successive step in structuralization, the response to experiences will be not in terms of unrelated, discrete component processes but in terms of the integrated functioning of the unit as a whole.

We find Spitz's suggestion that newly emergent affects and behaviors indicate organizational shifts and progressive organizational coherence a helpful one in understanding the sequential steps in ego development. Accordingly, we use his scheme to provide the basis for the organization of this chapter. Although Spitz concerned himself with only the first two years of life, developmental shifts are recognizable through adolescence. Because of this, one of us (P. Tyson, 1988) has suggested that Spitz's scheme of psychic organizers could usefully be extended at least through the Oedipus complex, and we are now extending his scheme through latency and adolescence.

We use the emergence of new affective expressions and new behaviors as indicators of progressive shifts in ego organization, complexity, and coherence. The indicators we discuss are the social smile, stranger distress, negativism in gesture and speech, anxiety and shame resulting from internalization of conflict, libidinal object constancy with self-comforting responses and the use of affects as signals, the infantile neurosis and guilt, pleasure in industry with latency integration, affective lability signaling the intrapsychic shifts of adolescence, and mood stability reflecting ego supremacy over instinctual impulses and archaic superego directives as adolescence comes to a close.

At this point a cautionary note is in order. The ego is a hypothetical, nonexperiential concept, to be sure, but the temptation to anthropomorphize is ever present. If we occasionally refer to the id, ego, and superego as battling, negotiating, striking bargains, warding off content, and the like, we hope the reader will understand that, as Anna Freud once commented, we are "just pretending." "To personify the idea of the ego for the moment, it seems to me that the ego doesn't mind. . . . What the ego minds is the content becoming conscious" (Sandler and Freud, 1985, p. 33).

## THE UNDIFFERENTIATED PHASE

The beginning of life was labeled the "undifferentiated" phase (Hartmann, Kris, and Loewenstein, 1946) or the stage of "nondifferentiation" (Spitz, 1959) because of an absence of observations warranting an inference that id and ego are operative as psychic systems, or that a differentiation between pleasure and unpleasure exists. Hartmann (1939) recognized that the infant's state of "preadaptiveness" to the environment is not governed by an intrapsychic organization but is influenced primarily by physiological needs and by affective and sensorial feedback from the environment.

Recent multidisciplinary research findings have brought about changes in our views of the human infant and expanded our knowledge of the preadaptiveness of which the infant is capable. Far from being a tabula rasa, or a "bed of buzzing confusion" (W. James, 1890) in a prolonged state of primary narcissism (Freud, 1914) or "normal autism" (Mahler et al., 1975), the neonate is active, stimulus-seeking, cognitively competent, and socially interactive. He has a complicated organization of endogenously determined behaviors that function to regulate the system and maintain physiological homeostasis.

Although the newborn moves steadily toward psychological functioning, we cannot yet speak of an ego as a psychologically operating system that regulates behavior. The neonate's inherent repertoire of highly organized behaviors is related to the synchronization of his internal state (Emde, 1980c; Sander, 1983). As Spitz and his colleagues stress, "The physiological way the innate copes with its environment is not the way the psyche does it" (Spitz, Emde, and Metcalf, 1970, p. 433).* This early integrative synchronization is facilitated by the

*Because of the complexity of these endogenously determined functions that are operative at birth, Stern (1985) argues against the idea of an un-

affective ambience of mother-infant reciprocity, which in turn is made possible by a mother with appropriate "attunement" (Stern, 1984) and an intact infant. This synchrony provides a physiological basis for the emerging synthesizing ego. Should this integrating, regulating, synchronizing function be overwhelmed—for example, by organismic distress or intense tension states (whether owing to a physiological disturbance, disrupted mother-infant synchrony, or repeated delays or insufficiencies in need satisfaction)—a variety of defective ego functions, or deficiencies, precocities, or unbalances in ego organization and synthesizing capacities may result (Spitz, 1959; Sander, 1962, 1969; Spitz and Cobliner, 1965; Sander et al., 1970; Weil, 1970, 1978).

An example of premature but unbalanced ego development is offered by James (1960) who described the development of an infant chronically underfed for the first three months of her life. Care was given primarily by a nurse, who fed the infant on a fixed schedule and tied her hands in a napkin before feeding. The infant was observed to be hyperalert, tense, and jumpy, and in her chronically hungry and restless state, mouthed the napkin-tied hands. James tracked the child's development for several years and observed precocities and imbalances in several areas, which he attributed to the undermining influence of this early experience. At three months the baby's facial expression in a quiet state was described as something between bewilderment, discouragement, and depression. This alternated with a state of hypersensitivity to stimulation. By eight months she had developed a quality of appealingness, which James thought suggested object hunger. From the time of first walking, the infant showed a subtle disorder of motility but an unusual mental plasticity. At two she strove to read and write, teaching herself the alphabet, in imitation of an older sibling going to school, but she tended toward delays in motor activities. At the age of

---

differentiated phase. He maintains that since the neonate is capable of making perceptual distinctions between inside and outside, self and other, there must be some form of a core self at birth. Mandler points out, however, that the capacity to make perceptual distinctions does not require a conceptual form of representation (1988, pp. 117–118). There is a vast difference between a percept or something seen, and a concept or something thought. The latter is required for even a primitive concept of, or sense of, self. In addition, since we view the ego as a *psychic* system that regulates behavior, we understand it as something that evolves out of and cannot be equated with physiological state regulation. Therefore, although perhaps less undifferentiated than Hartmann thought, the concept of an undifferentiated phase we think remains useful.

five she had developed a charming "public personality," taking on the mannerisms, postures, and interests of others with whom she came into contact, yet this was devoid of affect. At eight years the child had a wool fetish, wrapping her hands in and picking at a wool comforter while sucking her thumbs, tickling her nose and upper lip with the wool she picked, reminiscent of the way she had sucked at her tied, napkin-wrapped hands as an infant. James concluded that the early traumatic feeding situation and substitute mothering interfered with the establishing of competent object relations; her personality integration was in this way undermined and a severe narcissistic disorder was the result.

## THE SOCIAL SMILE

According to Spitz (1959), the first discernible shift in psychic organization occurs between two and three months of age, evidenced by the emergence of the social smile. (Earlier "endogenous" smiling has different characteristics and is unrelated to social interaction, as we noted in our discussion of affects.) The social smile denotes progress beyond inborn capacities and indicates responsiveness to external stimuli. The mother is stimulated by the smile to stimulate the infant; she quickly becomes the best elicitor of this smile, after which the smiling response becomes part of an exchange of signals in the emerging dialogue that provides the basis for later communication. The smiling response also indicates an emerging capacity for anticipation, and as such it comes to play an important part in mother-infant interactions.

Many early mother-infant interactions occur in the context of feeding experiences, along with nonnutritional pleasure sucking and play. The infant's urge to repeat the pleasurable experiences inherent in these activities leads to id-ego differentiation as his oral pleasures come to acquire psychological meaning and form part of a primitive motivational system, eventually part of the id (Loewald, 1978).

In addition, the infant's experiences of playful interactions apart from feeding gain increasing importance for structuralization of self-regulatory ego functions. For the most part, the mother regulates interaction at the beginning. An optimal balance between gratification and frustration in these interactions fosters the infant's internalization of and identification with maternal regulative functions. As mentioned earlier, however, studies show that the smile indicates a readiness for interaction; the infant seems to anticipate and to a limited extent is able to regulate interactional exchanges (Brazelton et al., 1974; Stern,

1974b, 1977; Beebe and Stern, 1977; Tronick et al., 1977; Beebe, 1986). So we see mother-infant interactions contributing importantly to ego development.

Mahler's use of the word *symbiotic* emphasizes the optimal affective relationship at this time: mother and infant "in tune." Should this synchrony fail, or should the infant suffer overwhelming distress, such as sudden separation from the mother, extreme delay in the satisfaction of hunger or sucking needs, or physical maltreatment as in episodes of abuse, psychic trauma results. That is, these situations provide the essence of a traumatic situation—an experience of helplessness on the part of the (emergent) ego in the face of the accumulation of excitation or intensifying stimuli. Should the distress be persistent— such as being exposed to a depriving, anxious, or unstable and unpredictable environment, chronic frustration and delays in hunger or sucking satisfaction, or frustration of motor and kinesthetic expression (as in the case of infants treated for congenital orthopedic problems, discussed by Roiphe and Galenson, 1981)—the progress of ego organization, drive differentiation, and object attachment may be disrupted or distorted owing to the effects of "strain trauma" (Kris, 1956, p. 224) or "cumulative trauma" (Khan, 1963). As a result, the infant may develop a predisposition to experiencing excessive anxiety and/or excessive rage (Greenacre, 1941; Weil, 1970, 1978). Also, primitive self-regulatory functions may be undermined, and varieties of premature, delayed, or unbalanced ego development may occur (Bergman and Escalona, 1949; A. Freud, 1967; Call, 1983).

Joey, born prematurely, remained hospitalized for four weeks. At four months he was again hospitalized with failure-to-thrive syndrome. Multiple illnesses, neglect, and abuse characterized his infancy. At three years, eight months, Joey could not yet combine words into sentences, and he was functioning with a mental age of 2.9 (Stanford-Binet I.Q. 64). In addition, he was aggressive and unruly and his mother controlled him with a leash and carried a whip. Although many genetic and socioeconomic factors must be considered, Joey seems to have been one of those children where a combination of a vulnerable physiological state and mother's inability to attune to his special needs interfered with the baby's attachment to her. The failure in reciprocity undermined the push to explore and compromised emerging cognitive and synthesizing functions resulting in a profound developmental interference.

From three to six months the infant shows signs of developing rudimentary yet durable concepts about himself, as we described in discussing the emerging sense of self. Soon a "primitive self-feeling" can be surmised (Mahler and Furer, 1968). Combining various kinesthetic, tactile, visual, and olfactory sensations with motor activity and recognition memory to form this body image is an early example of synthesizing, integrative ego functioning (Hoffer, 1949, 1950b; Greenacre, 1969). Indeed, Freud suggested as much, although his comment that "the ego is first and foremost a bodily ego" (1923a, p. 26) has been a source of confusion, especially if we read ego to mean a psychic system. This seems to be one of those instances in which an experiential sense of self, not an organizing system, is implied. If we retranslate the phrase to read "the sense of self is first and foremost a bodily self," the meaning would be that the sense of the self first emerges as a sense of the body comes together.

## STRANGER DISTRESS

A second major developmental shift in ego organization takes place somewhere between seven and nine months. Fear and distress in reaction to the unfamiliar suddenly appear in the course of the gradual integration of perception, memory, thought processes (means-ends connections), locomotion, and judgment. In distinguishing the known from the unknown, the infant now has the capacity to express distress when confronted with a stranger, apparently in anticipation of something feared. He also now has the capacity to be reassured or warned by the mother.

Spitz (1959) viewed the emergent distress as the affective indicator that the mother has become the "libidinal object proper"—the person who is preferred over all others. The establishment of the mother as the libidinal object is important for ego development because at this time mother comes to serve as a social referent. The infant now responds to her affective expressions as a signal of safety or danger (described in our discussion of affects); in this way she guides and influences the infant's adaptive response to novel stimuli. Her reassuring affective signal supports the infant's self-regulatory functions and encourages adaptive exploration, which is essential for the expansion of intellectual horizons. Further, appropriate maternal intervention in danger situations protects against disorganizing panic and at the same time optimizes the infant's progressive development of defenses and use of the signal function. Eventually the synthesizing, organizing, regulating functions of the ego will be supported by its own activities as in using affects as signals and instituting defenses to avoid danger.

## NEGATIVISM IN GESTURE AND SPEECH

The affective indicator of the next developmental shift, which appears between fifteen and eighteen months, is the emergence of negativism, expressed by the "no" in gesture and word. The developmental reorganization at this level includes the linking of speech and the accompanying capacity for representational thinking and symbol manipulation with a mentally represented, gender-differentiated sense of self and sense of the other. These linkages bring an emergent capacity for self-reflection and reflection on the other, and the beginnings of the capacity for defense.

To elaborate, Spitz (1957) thought that the gesture and the spoken "no" that follow shortly indicate the beginnings of useful language, that this is the earliest example of the infant's replacing action by communication. Once available, language fosters independent functioning; not only does speech make communication possible, but it organizes thought processes and mental operations. Language becomes a tool for thinking, organization, reflection, and mastery. Accordingly, an awareness of the self as male or female, as separate from mother, and as small and dependent rather than omnipotent begins to emerge. Furthermore, as we suggested in discussing cognition, the spoken word makes it possible to infer beginning differentiation between the inner world of psychic reality and the outer world of objective reality. And so, the toddler begins to formulate wishes and simple fantasies and to distinguish these from the demands of external reality. Awareness of these distinctions ushers in the period of stubbornness, negativism, ambivalence, and the ensuing conflicts and complexities of object relations development.

Spitz also believed that the infant's "no," in gesture and in speech, was an identification with the aggressor and, as such, a defense mechanism.* A notable advance in ego development is evident in the use of defense mechanisms. In the earlier stages of development the internal structures necessary for accurate perception of, reflection upon, and integration of an event to trigger defense mechanisms have not as yet evolved. Although responses suggesting denial, flight, and avoidance are evident, these are based on the use of mother as a social referent—the infant's responses are based on the affective cue received from the

*Defense mechanisms are a necessary part of normal development and are not in themselves pathological. Some prefer to use "coping mechanisms" to differentiate nonpathological from pathological means of defense.

mother indicating her evaluation of the situation, not on his internal evaluation of the situation. (Stolorow and Lachmann, 1978, Fraiberg, 1982, and Wallerstein, 1983, all discuss this subject.) With the mental capacities that come with representational intelligence, the toddler can now reflect on events and mobilize defense mechanisms in response to his inner evaluations. Among the possible ones any particular child might use are identification with the aggressor, repetition, and turning passive into active, now possible with the beginnings of a fantasy life and symbolic play. Denial, flight, and avoidance are also common early defenses.

Developmental consolidation following the emergence of speech accordingly includes further differentiation between self and object, male and female, love and hate, conscious and unconscious, and primary and secondary processes. Greater integration and organization within the ego can be surmised with representational intelligence and the functioning of defense mechanisms. These advances provide the foundations for the next step in ego formation—the internalization of conflict as a beginning of superego functioning.

## INTERNALIZATION OF CONFLICT: SUPEREGO FORMATION

The appearance of anxiety and shame at about twenty-four to thirty months indicates the internalization of conflict and the beginnings of superego formation. The eventual consolidation of a functioning superego makes stable interpersonal and intrapsychic harmony possible. As we described earlier, once the capacity for representational thinking is available, early steps in superego formation follow, apparent with the formation of mental representations of parental rules and admonitions. Then the voice of authority becomes an internal presence as well as an external one, and conflict becomes increasingly internal—that is, between internal directives and internal wishes. Anxiety appears in relation to conflictual wishes, and one can often see shame following drive expression. Superego formation thus makes further demands on the integrating, organizing, and regulating functions of the ego, and so beginning superego formation implies advances in ego functioning.

Accordingly, we propose that internalization of conflict, reflecting early stages of superego structuralization, indicates that another level of ego organization has been achieved. Anxiety (distinguished from stranger distress, as described in the discussion of affects) and shame in response to internal criticism (differentiated from remorse, embarrassment, and humiliation in response to external criticism) are the affective expressions that indicate this new level in psychic organization and integration.

Some elaboration may be helpful. Symbolic thinking makes it possible for feelings to be linked with ideas. Affects then come to represent multifaceted psychological experiences—that is, as complex structures with interconnected motivational, somatic, expressive, communicative, emotional, and ideational components, as we described in discussing affects. Symbolization also makes self-reflection possible, and as the toddler recognizes mother as the source of his well-being, he also recognizes that mother's love has conditions. Now interpersonal conflicts combine with fantasies of feared consequences. The danger situations outlined by Freud (1926) may all be imagined and feared. Emotional storms resulting from the awareness of conflict between internal wishes and external demands threaten to undermine the as yet relatively weak synthesizing and regulating functions of the ego; the modulation and management of aggression are clearly central developmental issues of the second year, challenging both the object and the toddler's immature ego (Mahler, 1972b). Phase-specific conflicts thus provide the setting for what has been characterized as the confrontation between the immature ego of early psychic development and the as yet untamed aggression of the id (Loewald, 1974; Ritvo, 1974; Settlage, 1975, 1980). A wider range of defenses, including reaction formation, undoing, externalization, condensation, displacement, projection, reversal of affect, and turning aggression against the self, can be detected as efforts are made to resolve conflict. When these defenses are unsuccessful, hostile aggression is often mixed with anal eroticism, and sadomasochistic interactions and character traits emerge and may persist (see Galenson, 1986, for examples).

Developmental conflict between mother and toddler poses a dilemma; the toddler wants to retain his mother's love and he also wants instinctual gratifications that threaten the loss of that love. The toddler becomes intolerant of the simultaneous presence of incompatible feelings (McDevitt and Mahler, 1980; Settlage, 1980), and compliance with and then internalization of mother's rules offer a way to ensure her love. If this happens, the developmental conflict between the toddler's wishes and the mother's wishes becomes an intrapsychic conflict.

Toilet training is an arena in which these events are clearly played out, although no area of life is exempt. Toilet training begins with a clash between the mother's and the toddler's wishes. Shared pride and a sense of accomplishment follow successful conformity; anger and unhappiness follow refusal and altercation. Optimally, conformity leads to introject formation and later to identification with the introject, as mother's standards around toileting become the toddler's own. The early superego then takes on, in part, the threatening and punishing functions of the mother, and the toddler feels shame when "accidents" occur; he may become anxious if facilities are not immediately available or anxious around anything smelly or dirty as reaction formations take hold. These new affects of anxiety or shame are independent of the signaling or punishing reactions of the object and are indications of this advance in psychic structuralization.

Optimally, identification with mother includes identification with her consistent organizing, regulating, and harmonizing functions. These identifications facilitate the capacity of the young child's ego to deal adaptively with conflict and painful feelings. Identification with parental attitudes about instinctual pleasures thus brings the possibility for a new degree of self-regulation and self-control. The child's successful mastery of anal-stage tasks is then accompanied by pride, a pleasurable feeling of mastery, and a more self-regulated sense of self-esteem.

The formation of introjects and ideals creates a greater potential for intrapsychic conflict, but it also provides a tool for the restoration of interpersonal harmony and fosters new potentials for self-regulation. The regulative, integrative efforts of the ego now come to be reinforced by superego functions, and new defenses help the young child cope with strong libidinal and aggressive impulses. The affective expressions of anxiety and shame signal this developmental advance.

## LIBIDINAL OBJECT CONSTANCY AND AFFECTS AS SIGNALS

Beginning at about thirty to thirty-six months, if all goes well, the young child achieves a useful degree of libidinal object constancy—he internalizes enough of the mother's caretaking functions that he can rely on his mental representation of her for comfort, sustenance, and love during the short periods when she is absent. We suggest that regarding and using his own affects as signals and responding with self-comforting, organizing, and protective measures are the affective and behavioral indicators of this developmental advance (P. Tyson, 1988).

Therefore, it would appear that the mother makes a crucial contribution to the child's ego functioning by facilitating his use of affects as signals. As we discussed in relation to object relations and affects, this begins with the mother's consistent comforting, harmonizing, regulating, and organizing responses to the infant's emotive displays. Identification with mother then includes identification with her response to emotional expression.

Understood in this way, the young child's acquiring some measure of libidinal object constancy suggests that he has taken a significant step in ego development, for it implies that the mother's functions in responding to an affective signal are now internalized ego functions. If this is so, the child is better able to perceive and evaluate affect and limit it to manageable proportions by the employment of the appropriate defenses. Self-regulation is thereby enhanced and self-control is more often possible.

The result is that anxiety or other feelings accompanying conflict are more easily managed, and so internal compromise in response to conflict, interpersonal or intrapsychic, whereby both sides give up something (Loewald, 1974) is more often possible. Compromise can then be accompanied by pleasurable feelings of mastery, and it usually elicits reinforcement from the object.

Consider another example from the case of Johnny, referred to in chapter 8. One day, after bursting out in anger at his analyst, he drew a picture of an unhappy-looking man who had been put in jail by a robber. A policeman then captured the robber, put him in jail, and released the now happy man. Clinical material is always open to various interpretations: Johnny's difficulty controlling angry outbursts could reflect a structural deficit; his fantasy of the policeman and robber might be evidence of lack of integration of good and bad maternal or paternal representations; his sadness could reflect a narcissistic injury consequent on his analyst's failure, in the transference, to provide sufficient empathic nurturing. While these interpretations are all possible, it seemed also that Johnny was describing conflict aroused in him because of his aggressive urges as well as his experience of himself. Because he was not regulating his instinctual urges, which he came to call his "robber feelings," and was not getting sufficient help from his "policeman feelings," he was suffering a painful lowering of self-regard as well as jeopardizing his relations with important persons in his life, including his analyst. His picture also included his attempts to evolve effective inner restraints to guard over and police his instinctual urges in order to preserve inner as well as interpersonal harmony. He responded to an interpretation of these issues by making a paper airplane and pretending to throw it at the analyst; but instead he laughed, and said, "My policeman stopped me!"

Internalizing the mother's regulating, comforting, and organizing responses to the child's anxiety states fosters increasing ego strength and stability. These are reflected in the child's increasing ability to tolerate conflict and its accompanying affect. Whether resolution, regression, or deviation results when oedipal conflicts are confronted depends on how well the child's ego is able to utilize the related affects as signals for defense and compromise.

Consider another example from the case of Susie (compared with Johnny in the earlier discussion). One day Susie pretended to be Cinderella and imagined her fairy godmother gave her a wonderful dress and helped her go to the ball and marry the prince. A sparkle in her eye and coquettish gestures accompanied the fantasy. Suddenly, projecting her guilty self-criticism, she imagined her analyst to be the wicked stepmother who then killed Cinderella so that she could marry the prince instead. Susie's propensity to be overwhelmed with anxiety had delayed internalization and internal compromise in response to conflict, so that she broke into a temper tantrum whenever a wish was frustrated, attempting to manipulate her mother. But in the face of oedipal wishes, regression and deviation were her only alternatives, seen in her version of the Rapunzel story. Imagining herself to be Rapunzel, Susie taunted the witch about what a bad mother she was, telling the witch that her prince gave her candy, which she liked much better than the bones and mice the witch gave her to eat. As in the traditional story, hearing of a rival, the furious witch cut Rapunzel's hair, banished her to the desert, and blinded the prince. But in Susie's version, when Rapunzel found the prince wandering blindly in the desert and restored his sight with her tears, Susie-Rapunzel abandoned the prince to search for her real mother, the lost, fantasized, all-giving, nurturing mother of infancy.

Children like Susie, who fail to internalize the signal function and to respond with self-regulatory responses, are left vulnerable to being repeatedly overwhelmed by disorganizing affect. The resulting structural deficit can be found in a number of pathological outcomes, including narcissistic and borderline syndromes.

Our comments here and these clinical examples are relevant to Hartmann's (1952) cautionary note against the tendency to oversimplify the mother's role in the child's ego development. He pointed to instances in which a child was repeatedly overwhelmed by affective storms, unable to use anxiety as a signal, and remained dependent on the mother as an auxiliary ego despite what appeared to be a good mother-child relationship. He suggested that any judgment of the adequacy of the relationship should include an assessment of the child's ego functioning.

## THE OEDIPUS COMPLEX AND THE INFANTILE NEUROSIS: GUILT

The preoccupations of the infantile genital phase of psychosexual development pose further challenges for the young ego. Gender-identity tasks and narcissistic concerns lead the child to make new identifications with the idealized same-sex parent; these identifications pave the way for the Oedipus complex that typically arouses conflict with accompanying fantasies, fears, and oscillations in self-esteem.

There are many possible variations of oedipal conflict as the child strives to satisfy libidinal, aggressive, and other peremptory urges, to gain a measure of impulse control (Lustman, 1966), to meet the standards of his emergent superego, to consolidate a narcissistically valued gender identity, and to maintain self-esteem in the face of ungratified wishful fantasies. The resources available to the ego to respond to and deal with oedipal conflict have important consequences for the child's subsequent development.

The Oedipus complex forms the core conflict of what Freud called the *infantile neurosis* (1909a, 1918). The term refers to that particular structure and organization of the mind characterized by internalized conflict and a functioning superego. As we described in our discussion of superego development, the first steps in superego formation begin with the formation of introjects and ideals and the internalization of conflict, but these early fragments do not as yet operate as a well-organized, coherent, and durable system exerting effective controls as well as administering punishments. But the child's making identifications with the moral codes and ethical standards of his parents in efforts at oedipal resolution and his attempting to adhere to these now internal standards entail his making further internal compromises, and the superego becomes a more coherent, integrated, and functional system. Accordingly, the origins of conflict, the origins of punishment in the painful affect of guilt, and the sources of self-esteem are all now internal, and they come to be largely removed from and inaccessible to external influence and modification.

The infantile neurosis, therefore, implies a new kind of integrated psychic organization. As such, it represents an attempt to organize previous (preoedipal) and current developmental (oedipal), inner (active-passive, masculine-feminine), and neurotic conflicts into a single, more reality-adapted, socially acceptable organization. It represents the highest level of psychic organization the young child can reach.

For this, the child pays a price. Freud's case of Little Hans illustrates the possible range of suffering (1909a). Freud commented that although the infantile neurosis represents the outcome of a struggle between the interests of self-preservation and the demands of the libido, a struggle in which the ego is victorious, the price is severe suffering and renunciation: "The price we pay for our advance in civilization is a loss of happiness through the heightening of the sense of guilt" (1930, p. 134).

An example of the intensity and pain that can accompany the infantile neurosis is illustrated by the case of Colin. Colin's oedipal competition with his father had become displaced to his siblings who seemed always to stand between him and his mother. His guilty feelings then led him to displace death wishes toward his siblings on to other children, and on one particular day he verbalized a wish to "kill all the children in the world except those at home." He chewed a plastic doll, accidentally using his brother's name, but then denied hostility toward his siblings. He ran to the window and shouted profanities and murderous threats to some children playing outside. His analyst interpreted the displacement, and he responded, "Then I'd have my mummy all to myself, then I'd kill her too!" Immediately he became overwhelmed with anxiety, displaced the death wish onto his analyst, and tried to attack her. Being restrained from doing so, he expressed a self-destructive fantasy of falling out the window. His analyst interpreted his use of aggression as a defensive maneuver and suggested that what he was looking for was a loving response from others. He solemnly replied, "I'm so bad inside, no one could ever love me," and he pleaded, "Please take away my horrible worries!"

Anna Freud said that even though the infantile neurosis can be severe and crippling and may be accompanied by painful symptoms, the conflicts underlying it are normal ones. She thought, therefore, rather like her father, that the infantile neurosis was "the price which has to be paid for higher human development" (1970a, p. 202).

Because of its central position in early childhood, and because it represents a marked advance in ego functioning and organization, we designate the infantile neurosis as the sixth psychic organizer; guilt is the associated affect signaling this advance in ego organization. Since the conflicts, the sources of approval or disapproval, and the means for resolution are all now chiefly internal (although assistance from the outside world is occasionally needed for reinforcement), the infantile neurosis implies that the ego increasingly functions autonomously— more independently of external support.

## LATENCY AND PLEASURE IN INDUSTRY

At age six or seven, another major developmental shift occurs in association with the stage of latency. It is marked by the affect of "pleasure in industry" which indicates the eventual mastery of the child's inner and outer worlds, an achievement significantly supported by the capacity to sublimate.

Freud (1905b) originally described latency in terms of a diminution of outward manifestations of infantile sexuality and the capacity to sublimate drive impulses. Nowadays we would also include the child's more or less successful oedipal conflict resolution, and a reorganization of the ego's defensive structure influenced by superego development. These psychic achievements should be distinguished from chronological age: the child between the ages of seven and eleven is often referred to as "a latency-age child" without considering whether the underlying psychic changes have occurred.

Because latency is far from uniform, because several different psychic tasks are uppermost at different times, and because the period spans several years, theorists have tried to subdivide this phase of development (see Alpert, 1941; Bornstein, 1951; Williams, 1972; Sarnoff, 1976). We prefer Bornstein's division, describing latency in terms of an early and a late phase, as she based her criteria on changes in ego and superego functioning reflected in the child's behavior.

As we described in our discussion of cognition, Shapiro and Perry (1976) found that significant changes coincide at about the age of seven in areas of cognitive, neurological, maturational, moral, and social functioning. Concrete operational thinking begins, and the secondary process becomes dominant; now a more definite separation between rational thinking and fantasy life is apparent as the primary process is increasingly unconscious and confined to private life. As a consequence, attitudes and thinking are less influenced by the demands of the inner world and become more reality- and logic-oriented. The child is better able to view things from another's perspective (decentering) and able to evaluate others more objectively. This facilitates greater social and personal awareness, which provides a motivation for decreasing impulsive behavior.

As the child approaches age seven, his outer world expands. School activities offer possibilities for mastery, for creativity, and for meeting the new challenges of the widening vista of motor, social, and intellectual involvements. The larger peer group, with its focus on organized games, also affords socially acceptable avenues for both channeling aggression and stabilizing superego directives; the group usually places heavy emphasis on the rules, and children of the same age or older can serve as models for behavioral standards in addition to the family. Peers and teachers also broaden the scope of the latency child's defensive repertoire by representing him with more possibilities for displacement of oedipal wishes and fantasies (A. Freud, 1979).

Drive pressures do not disappear in latency. Although many children continue to masturbate to some extent, the act of masturbation and the associated fantasies frequently become separated. Then the fantasies themselves become an important pathway for drive gratification, with forbidden wishes expressed in symbolic form and increasingly displaced from oedipal themes or objects, as seen in family romance fantasies or fears of monsters.

An additional task for the ego in latency is to accommodate and become accustomed to the superego as an internal watchman, judge, and critic. Because of the strength of drive impulses and other peremptory urges in comparison to the ego-controlling functions, the newly consolidated superego tends to be painfully harsh and strict in early latency. To avoid the pain of self-accusation, the child projects and sees others as watching and judging him. Therefore, he tends to blame others for his own wrongdoings.

In early latency the organizing skills of the ego are still weak in comparison to the tasks at hand, so that some psychic disharmony is typical. As latency progresses, more sophisticated coping mechanisms and defenses emerge. Fantasy content shifts from imagined idealized figures to real objects. Superego contents are gradually modified from primitive, somewhat distorted parental introjects to more realistically based standards. Now a more harmonious relationship is possible among the three mental structures.

Greater narcissistic gratification is gained from sublimation and both facilitates and indicates this increased harmony. Although they can be observed at earlier periods (Harries, 1952), the capacity to develop sublimations with their associated gratifications, rather than simply to defend against any form of instinctual satisfaction (Gross and Rubin, 1972), is a crucial ingredient of optimal latency development. Successful sublimation is demonstrated by the latency child's many new interests and achievements. The child's increasing competence becomes a self-generated source of subjective and social approval, gradually allowing the child to diminish his dependence on his parents for maintaining self-esteem and at the same time establish a more harmonious relationship with them.

Greater harmony in the internal world is accompanied by an integration of defenses and a greater stability of mood and affect. Ego functioning becomes less vulnerable to regression, leading to increased independence from drives and parental objects. As Buxbaum pointed out, the consolidation of ego functions may aid the inhibition and control of drives, whereas the biologically diminished drive may facilitate the consolidation of ego functions: "It is not a question of priority, but a question of mutual influences" (1980, p. 123).

Erikson (1959) speaks of a "sense of industry" to describe the latency child's need to proceed beyond fantasy and to be useful—to make things. Insofar as we observe a diminution of self-esteem as well as behavioral difficulties in children of this age who fail to master basic age-appropriate skills, we would take Erikson's term a step further and emphasize *pleasure* in industry, which becomes available with the capacity to sublimate. Using the emergence of a new affect as an indication that a higher level of organization has been achieved, we suggest that "pleasure in industry" indicates the child's successful mastery of his inner and outer worlds in the latency phase.

## ADOLESCENCE: AFFECTIVE LABILITY AND PSYCHIC RESTRUCTURING

Biological maturity at puberty, with the accompanying increase in drive pressure and rapid physical, cognitive, and social changes, challenges the adolescent ego's defensive and integrating functions. The relative calm and harmony among the psychic systems of late latency is replaced in adolescence by inevitable shifts, tensions, and imbalance. The ego's major task now is to restore the psychic balance so that a unique, individuated, and autonomous identity emerges with an integrated, stabilized character structure.

During the course of this imbalancing and restructuring process, unpredictable and uncontrollable mood swings are typical. The adolescent swings from elation to depression; from narcissistic overexpansion, or "narcissistic boom," as Jacobson (1961) calls it, to self-hatred and despair; from love to hate, often enough directed toward the same object; from passionate crushes and commitment to boyfriend and girlfriend to cool indifference. The degree of anxiety associated with the affective fluctuations is related to the strength of the ego in relation to the pressures from the drives, the superego, and the external world. Mood shifts, behavioral changes, and transient symptoms often blur the boundary between normality and pathology and reflect significant conflicts between and within the various psychic structures, as well as attempts at conflict resolution through compromise formation.

Because affective fluctuations are an outward sign of biological and psychological imbalancing and restructuring processes, G. Stanley Hall (1904) dubbed adolescence as the time of Sturm und Drang. Indeed, early psychoanalytic writers tended to overemphasize the possible range and intensity of pathology in adolescence (see Aichhorn, 1925; Bernfeld, 1938; Deutsch, 1944; Katan, 1951; Fraiberg, 1955). Offer (1969), in response, claimed that turbulence does not necessarily accompany the development of adolescents. We believe that this claim is equally invalid. The maturational and developmental tasks to be accomplished during adolescence produce major changes among the psychic systems, and these changes do not occur without inner turmoil and stress. Although inner turbulence need not be "noisy" and therefore apparent to the external observer, it nevertheless is a necessary part of the adolescent process. Both Geleerd (1957) and A. Freud (1958) pointed out that a degree of turmoil is an indication that the psychic restructuring process is under way; its absence may be a sign of pathology. Because turmoil is so characteristic of adolescence, we propose, in keeping with our earlier hypothesis that the emergence of a new affect signals a developmental shift, that this *affective lability* be designated as the eighth psychic organizer. Its appearance indicates the psychic disequilibrium that characterizes the adolescent process.

The way in which the individual copes with the impact of increased hormone secretion, increased drive pressure, and the disturbed balance among psychic structures is significantly determined by the degree to which the ego has become integrated, stabilized, and autonomous (the degree to which its functioning is not disrupted by conflict and not dependent on adult reinforcement) during latency. To the extent that this has taken place, the conflicts and issues specific to adolescence will emerge unburdened by earlier problems, and the individual's resources will be undiminished by prior claims. To the extent that the individual's development falls short of this ideal, then the tasks of adolescence must also include, take into account, and try to find acceptable solutions for the unintegrated residues of prior periods (Blos, 1958; Harley, 1961).

Before the young person reaches adolescence proper, we speak of preadolescence—that phase of psychological adjustment leading up to and accompanying the emergence of secondary sexual characteristics and the earliest pubertal changes. Preadolescence is a transitional period characterized by diffuse unrest, regression, and instability of mood and temperament during which affects and behavior become more fluid and unpredictable. Progressive and regressive forces and new biological and psychological demands produce intrapsychic disequilibrium. Accordingly, Erikson suggested that preadolescence marks the onset of a *normative crisis*—that is, a normal phase of increased conflict characterized by a seeming fluctuation in ego strength, and yet one with a high growth potential (1956, p. 116). This normative crisis becomes more manifest as adolescence proceeds.

The developmental tasks of preadolescence focus around psychological mastery of physiological changes within the body, changes in the self-representation, and mastery of changing family and peer relationships. A noticeable increase in affective lability and mood swings and a degree of sullenness and defensiveness are practically universal during this phase, marking the psychic stress of this process. Neither a new love object nor a new instinctual aim can be discerned in preadolescence; conflicts are focused mainly around regressive drive impulses, regressive urges toward parents, and defenses against these regressions.

The ego in preadolescence is under great stress. Sexual and aggressive impulses increase in strength with biological maturity, so that previous defenses and adaptive measures may be inadequate. Rapid and continually shifting body changes require constant revision of the body image and self-representation. Narcissistic strivings are bound up with bodily changes as ideal-self images may not match the perceived bodily changes. Consequently, affective reactions to the body range from pride and exhilaration to shame and a sense of inferiority.

Biological changes and physical maturation are accompanied by an intensification of existing object-related conflicts. Physical maturation is an outward indication that the child is coming to resemble the same-sex parent. Gender-identity tasks emerge as old identifications and idealizations are revived, but reinforcement of identifications with the parent may be invaded by conflict and threaten a resurgence of dependency. There may also be marked efforts toward disidentification in attempts to resist the regressive pull.

Pubertal maturation marks the end of preadolescence and the beginnings of early adolescence. Blos (1979) subdivides adolescence into three periods—early, middle, and late—which we think is useful for organizing the ego tasks we are discussing. Once biological maturation has been reached (girls often being two or more years ahead of boys), both boys and girls tend to give up pregenital regressive urges and eventually establish genital primacy. Pregenital impulses henceforth usually find expression within the context of genital activity.

In many respects, early adolescence continues the processes begun in preadolescence. Because of social and intrapsychic pressures, however, the ego is under additional stress to master regressive urges. With physical maturation and an adult, sexually mature, and sexually functioning body, this may be an enormous task in the face of increasing sexual hormone secretion, given that little outlet is available other than self-stimulation.

At the same time, intense anxiety and shame may accompany an adolescent's masturbation, as we described in the discussion of psychosexual development, and a host of fantasies, conflicts, and anxieties about the body and its functioning may surface. Harley (1961) notes that alongside the mobilization of genital forces there may be an overlibidinization of intellectual or other ego activities, expressed in an overcharged and overlabile investment in ever-shifting interests and hobbies.

Because of the relative strength of instinctual urges and the relative weakness of the ego in the face of them, early adolescence is often a time of drug, alcohol, and sexual experimentation, which may arouse enormous conflicts about loyalty to parents and adherence to superego standards. Frequently superego standards are repersonified, and peers assume the role previously taken by the superego.

Probably the most important task for the young adolescent is to complete certain gender-identity tasks. This includes revising the body-self image, coming to terms with identifications or disidentifications with the same-sex parent, and revising the ego ideal. This facilitates the adolescent's finding a new sense of identity as he finds new love objects and approaches middle adolescence.

Indeed, by middle adolescence, a degree of sexual experimentation has usually begun. Unresolved bisexual conflicts—conflicts over masculine and feminine identifications and conflicts over object choice— arouse anxiety. The adolescent's resolving these conflicts facilitates the adaptive move toward his finding new love objects outside the family.

Now the second individuation process (Blos, 1967) begins. During the course of disengaging from the parents, both as love objects and as objects of authority, bringing about a reorganization within the superego, the adolescent faces a further task: achieving a new balance between the ego and the superego. These several tasks bring added pressure to the ego's organizational, self-regulatory, and adaptive capabilities. Accordingly, a variety of phase-specific defenses against objects as well as defenses against impulses emerges (see A. Freud, 1958).

Blos (1967) points out that the regressive revival and externalization of early object-related conflicts at this time make it possible for the residues of infantile trauma, conflict, and fixation to be modified because of the now-extended resources of the adolescent ego. For example, the more mature ego can reevaluate the fear of abandonment and loss of love and decide that even failure to comply with the object's (or the introject's) wishes will not render the adolescent helpless and without resources. Early introjects and ideals, including early ideal parental representations are, accordingly, reexamined, in the course of which they (ideally) lose some of their compelling power.

In addition to these major revisions in object relations and within the superego, the adolescent individuation process includes a shift in the relationship between the ego and superego. At the beginning of latency when the superego consolidates, ego capacities in controlling drives are weak. Therefore superego directives tend to be restrictive, and punishments harsh. Adaptive adolescent functioning, however, necessitates that the adolescent accept ownership of his body and its sexuality, and accept responsibility for himself and his actions. This involves not only deidealization of infantile ideals but also ego supremacy over early introjects and ideals so that the adolescent can make new identifications with sexually active parents who will grant the adolescent indulgence in sexual activities (Jacobson, 1961), while being responsible for these activities. The adolescent exercises greater freedom of choice while taking present reality into consideration rather than automatically complying with the demands of the superego. Gradually the adolescent's ego comes to be less directed by the superego and more in charge of it. As a result, the adolescent gains a sense of instinctual freedom, freedom of object choice, and freedom of thought, feelings, and action; he is more autonomous, more independent of external influences and archaic id and superego pressures. To the extent that the ego gains autonomy and strength to maintain a stable and durable control system in accord with adult reality, these freedoms can be guaranteed.

The process of adolescent individuation is a long one, and it may not culminate until very late in adolescence or in early adulthood. The process is aided, however, by the maturation of cognitive capacities that support an orientation toward reality and away from the domination of guilt, shame, and the authority of early introjects and ideals. This new way of thinking helps the adolescent to be self-conscious: instead of being self-centered, he is able to be self-aware and to take himself clearly as an object of thought. This allows him to come to a new sense of personal identity, as detailed by Erikson (1956).

The establishment of identity neither begins nor ends with adolescence, for various aspects of the self-representation are added and discarded throughout life. What distinguishes the adolescent identity process is that it takes place for the first time in the context of a mature physical body and a mature capacity for logical thinking. The integration of this sense of maturity with past representations, identifications, and ideals and with representations of future goals and possibilities implies another step in psychic structuralization toward the consolidated adult personality.

## LATE ADOLESCENCE: EGO SUPREMACY AND MOOD STABILITY

Blos (1968, 1976) has studied how and when adolescence ends. He concludes that in order for a definitive, integrated, and autonomous adult personality structure to emerge, the individual must complete four tasks. The first, part of the second individuation process, is for him finally to assume authority from the parents and from the superego. Now the adolescent comes to take more responsibility for "what he does and what he is" (Blos, 1967, p. 148). The second involves his coming to terms with and giving up grudges about irredeemable childhood events or traumas, such as the consequences of object loss or the effects of special sensitivities or of physical disabilities. The adolescent's third task is to establish a sense of historical continuity with the past. Allowing oneself to know who one is and where one came from makes disengaging from the adult caretaking environment possible without disorganizing disruption. The fourth task involves the final resolution of bisexual conflicts so as to consolidate gender identity and sexual preference. Then the individual is free to find an appropriate adult love object.

The successful completion of the adolescent tasks in the various psychic systems we have described optimally brings a new level of ego integration, consolidation, and dominance over other psychic systems. Ego functioning becomes relatively free from early archaic superego influences, dominates the peremptoriness of the instinctual drives, and is relatively free from but not indifferent to environmental forces. As this level of ego supremacy is reached, affects and their expression fluctuate more within a tolerable range (Zetzel, 1965; Blos, 1968) and are better contained and better modulated. A new harmony between the inner and the outer worlds and within the inner world is achieved and becomes more secure. The pattern of the ego's self-regulating, adaptational, organizing, and synthesizing responses becomes more predictable and assumes a definitive character or style, as reaction patterns become more automatic, and self-esteem regulation assumes a more definite pattern (Reich, 1958). As stability of identity is achieved (Erikson, 1956), an integrated adult personality emerges. This greater harmony is reflected in a greater stability of mood. Accordingly, we suggest that the appearance of *mood stability* is a signal that a new level of psychic stability has been reached and that the adolescent process has been completed.

## SUMMARY

Following Spitz, we have utilized the appearance of a new affect or a new quality of affect to indicate a new level of coordination and integration among ego functions, implying a new level of ego organization and development. Although the appearance of a new affect early in life is dramatic and easy to observe, as development proceeds each event becomes more subtle, but is still identifiable.

Accordingly, we have proposed that new levels of organization and synthesis are signaled by the emergence of the social smile (two to three months), signaling progress beyond inborn capacities and the beginnings of psychological functioning; stranger distress (seven to nine months), denoting the establishment of the libidinal object; negativism (fifteen to eighteen months), signaling the capacity for self-reflection and the emergence of speech; anxiety and shame (twenty-four to thirty months), signaling internalized conflict and indicating the beginning formation of the superego; the use of affects to signal danger and conflict accompanying libidinal object constancy (beginning about thirty to thirty-six months); guilt (three to five years), indicating superego integration and the infantile neurosis; a pleasure in industry (latency), indicating greater autonomy in ego and superego functioning; labile moods (adolescence), indicating the psychic reorganization process of adolescence; and mood stability (late adolescence), indicating a supremacy of the ego over drive and other peremptory impulses and over superego directives, and therefore a completion of the adolescent process.

# EPILOGUE

In presenting an integration of the psychoanalytic theories of development, we have followed the central premise that the many systems of the personality grow and develop simultaneously and interdependently. Each system is defined in relation to all other systems, and in their entirety they compose a single complex system—which is why our mind, surprisingly enough, continues to function coherently throughout life.

In order to describe the developmental process, we have discussed many subjects, some in detail, some in more condensed form. We recognize the danger of oversimplification in the latter, particularly as we could not take into account all the subtle nuances of each subject in an integrative overview like this one. We hope, however, that in our overview, the complexities of the developmental process have become evident as well as the many possible meanings underlying any piece of manifest behavior; to the extent we have been successful, the tendency to reduce any explanation either to external events or to intrapsychic forces will be avoided.

Several topics have been omitted from this overview. The child's relations within the family system other than in relation to his parents, the development of social interactions, and the implications of our theory for psychopathology are examples. These subjects are indeed important, but our focus has been on the intrapsychic aspects of normal development to the extent that we can describe it.

We also realize that at times we have presented something of an ideal picture in that we talk of the roles of the mother and the father, as if the theory were relevant only to a child growing up in an intact family. Although to clinicians there may appear to be fewer functioning intact families every year, we think that an understanding of the developmental role served by both parents is helpful in detailing and conceptualizing optimal development, and in order to access the kinds of vulnerabilities a child might face growing up in alternative situations.

In the course of the book, we may have at one time or another created the impression of certainty, of closure, as if some hypothesis has come to be so generally accepted it has achieved the status of established fact. If we have created such an impression, we would like to correct it now. Psychoanalytic theory is still marked by many unanswered questions and areas of controversy, and the theory, like the model of development we have discussed, is an open, evolving one, always subject to change and evolution as new data appear.

Nevertheless, we hope that the perspective of the developmental process we have presented will prove coherent enough to maintain its integrity and at the same time elastic enough to accommodate new knowledge. We also hope we have presented our ideas in a manner that not only conveys the complexity of the developmental process but also provides a useful way of thinking about the human mind.

# A CASUAL GLOSSARY

Many terms that have come into common usage in psychoanalysis have gradually accumulated a variety of meanings. This casual glossary is intended to clarify the way we use a particular term in this book; it is not meant as an authoritative and comprehensive guide to psychoanalytic terminology. Rather, it is meant primarily to provide those unfamiliar with these terms with an explanation sufficient to permit them to continue reading without having to consult an external source. Four such sources are recommended for those who wish to pursue further any of the terms: L. E. Hinsie and R. J. Campbell, *Psychiatric Dictionary,* 4th ed. (New York: Oxford University Press, 1970); J. LaPlanche and J.-B. Pontalis, *The Language of Psycho-Analysis* (London: Hogarth Press, 1973); B. E. Moore and B. D. Fine, eds. *Psychoanalytic Terms and Concepts* (New Haven and London: Amer. Psychoanal. Assn. and Yale Univ. Press, 1990); and C. Rycroft, *A Critical Dictionary of Psychoanalysis* (Middlesex: Penguin, 1972).

**ACCOMMODATION**   A Piagetian concept referring to a way of relating to the environment in terms of already available information, or what Piaget refers to as "internal schemes." An example would be a child who sees a monkey for the first time and views it as a cat because it is about the same size and he knows about cats. A Piagetian concept similar to alloplastic adaptation.

**ADAPTATION**   The capacity to cope with external or internal reality. This often requires fitting one's inner needs to the environment, but it may also require using a certain defense mechanism, for example, to cope with inner psychic reality.

**AFFECT**   A multifaceted psychological phenomenon having motivational, somatic, emotional (or feeling), expressive, and communicative components, with an associated idea or cognitive component. Should be distinguished from emotion, feeling.

**AFFECT-TRAUMA**   The name often given to Freud's first model of the mind. (See also *Drive-discharge model.*)

**ALLOPLASTIC**   A type of adaptation characterized by the individual's capacity to elicit responses from the environment to meet internal needs or wishes, and to relate to the environment primarily in terms of these needs and wishes. This capacity is crucial to earliest infancy, when the infant must be capable of eliciting a response from the environment in order to survive. But to continue to manipulate the environment as the sole or major means of meeting one's inner needs or of resolving conflict is considered inappropriate and may indicate pathology.

**AMBIVALENCE**  The simultaneous existence of strong opposing feelings, such as love and hate, felt for the same person.

**ANACLITIC**  A dependent type of relationship in which one person relies on another either for the fulfillment of basic needs or for the gratification of physical or psychological needs. The infant's relationship with the mother is always anaclitic.

**ANAL PHASE**  The stage of libidinal development when most pleasurable attention is focused on the functioning of the anal zone. This refers mainly to pleasure in defecation or in retaining feces.

**ANXIETY**  An affective state consisting of an unpleasant, distressing, or painful feeling that is subjectively experienced as worry or panic similar to the fear of real danger. This is accompanied by an anticipation of being overwhelmed by an internal or external force, and the emotion is linked with one or more fantasies or ideas.

**ASSIMILATION**  Creating new internal schemes in response to new information from the environment; a Piagetian concept similar to autoplastic adaptation (see below). An example would be a child who sees a monkey, knows it is not a cat, and creates a new category: animals can be cats or they can be monkeys.

**AUTISM**  A severe developmental disorder of organic origin that results in an impairment in reciprocal social interactions, usually accompanied by a qualitative impairment in verbal and nonverbal communication. Mahler borrowed the term from pathology to refer to the first few weeks of life when the infant, in contrast to later phases, appears less interactive with caregiving objects.

**AUTOEROTISM**  Sexual stimulation and gratification generated without an external stimulus. Masturbation in any of its forms is an example.

**AUTONOMY**  The quality of functioning independently. Regarding psychic systems, the superego, for example, is said to be operating autonomously when its functioning is not disrupted by conflict and is not dependent on adult reinforcement. Hartmann (1958) introduced the term into psychoanalytic theory in relation to ego functions. (See also *Primary autonomy; Secondary autonomy.*)

**AUTOPLASTIC**  The ability to make inner or psychic modifications in response to perceptions of the environment. This ability requires reality testing and in most cases implies internal compromise and the capacity to delay gratification.

**AUXILIARY EGO**  When the mother or other caregiver provides care, protection, and comfort, or shields the infant or child from excessive internal or external stimulation, she is said to be acting in the capacity of an auxiliary ego. The term assumes that some ego functions are already present, but that external assistance is needed of a kind that eventually the child will be able to provide for himself.

**BISEXUALITY**  A mixture of the character traits and sexual wishes that belong to a person's own and the opposite sex, as, for example, the person who sees himself as possessing male and female characteristics and wishes sexual relations with both sexes. Developmentally, its source is the early tendency to identify with various characteristics of each parent and to maintain libidinal feelings toward each parent. It may become the basis for psychic conflict.

**BODY EGO**  The sense of self that first emerges as a sense of the body comes together. Freud used the term to refer to the earliest evidence of ego functioning.

**BODY IMAGE**  The mental representation of the body that evolves gradually and is modified through growth, maturation, and development. It does not necessarily correspond to the objective body.

**CASTRATION ANXIETY**  A term referring to the male's fear, in early childhood, of actual genital injury; the term is used broadly to refer in later life to an exaggerated fear of injury to any part of the body or to a fear of a loss of potency. The term has been generalized and applied to both sexes, referring broadly to fears of genital injury or any bodily injury, although we suggest restricting its use to male psychology.

**CATHEXIS**  A quantity of hypothetical psychic energy that is attached to or invested in something, such as in an external object or the self, or the mental representations of an external object or the self.

**CLOACAL THEORY**  A childhood sexual belief that assumes the anus and vagina to be the same, so that the anus is assumed to be the site of defecation, intercourse, and birth.

**COMPONENT INSTINCT**  A phenomenon in which particular impulses are joined to form a unified drive expression. It refers mainly to pregenital impulses and activities being joined together during the course of normal development to become subordinated to the primacy of the genital zone. A variety of oral, anal, and urethral functions may join together and be expressed through a particular activity, such as looking (as in scopophilia). Often the drives joined together are at variance with each other, as in sadism and masochism, wherein aggression and sexuality are combined in behavioral manifestations.

**CONFLICT-FREE EGO SPHERE**  An area of ego functioning that begins, remains outside of, and does not ordinarily become involved in intrapsychic conflict. Examples would be motility, cognition, or speech. The concept was introduced by Hartmann and is related to his concepts of primary and secondary autonomy (which see).

**CONFLICT, INTRAPSYCHIC** Conflict between opposing systems within the mind, in contrast to opposing forces between the individual and the outside world.

**CONFLICT, INTRASYSTEMIC** Conflict between opposing aspects of one system—that is, within a system, as in conflicting ideals within the superego.

**CONSCIOUSNESS** An awareness of perceptions coming from the outside world or from within the body and mind.

**CORE GENDER IDENTITY** The most primitive, nonconflictual, and basic sense of belonging to one sex and not the other.

**CUMULATIVE TRAUMA** Any condition that is unfavorable, noxious, or injurious over time to the development of the young child.

**DEFENSE MECHANISMS** Various attempts on the part of the ego to protect itself against danger. The danger usually refers to an intrapsychic conflict and arises because a repressed wish threatens to erupt into consciousness, and the gratification of this wish has become associated with a real or imagined punishment. The threat of the wish erupting is signaled by painful feelings of anxiety or guilt, and these feelings motivate the ego to ward off the wish or drive. Defenses operate unconsciously, so that the person is unaware of their employment. They are a normal part of development and of psychic functioning.

**DENIAL** A defense mechanism characterized by the ego's avoidance of becoming aware of some painful aspect of reality, as in a little boy's apparent unawareness of anatomical distinctions.

**DEVELOPMENT** A process whereby the personality forms from the interaction among maturational and environmental influences and personal experiences.

**DISPLACEMENT** A defense mechanism whereby a person exchanges the original object for another or uses one part of his body instead of another. An example is a boy who, instead of feeling angry with his father, feels angry and hostile toward other male authority figures instead.

**DRIVE** The term *Trieb*, translated "instinct," is found throughout the *Standard Edition* of Freud's writings. However, contrary to the stereotyped, automatic behavior implied by instinct as found in lower animals, in psychoanalytic usage the term refers to a psychological phenomenon. It is viewed as the mental representative of a biological force that has a motivational impact—that is, it impels the mind to activity. Unlike the motor activity that follows excitation in animals, in humans the behavior that follows the drive impulse is mediated by the ego. This makes it possible for the response to the drive to be plastic or varied and modified by experience and reflection, instead of being predetermined. Therefore the term *instinct* is more often referred to as *instinctual drive*, or simply *drive*.

**DRIVE DERIVATIVE** Because drives themselves are not conscious, the consequences of their motivational impact become conscious only because of their effects on psychic functioning; a drive derivative may therefore become manifest in thought, impulse, wish, or behavior.

**DRIVE-DISCHARGE MODEL** Freud's first model of the mind. Working on the basis of a hydraulic model and a metaphorical psychic energy. Freud thought the mental apparatus tends to keep the energies within it as low as possible and constant. If the quantity becomes excessive, it must be discharged. Distressing emotions, such as those aroused by early overwhelming childhood experiences with the environment, sexual seductions in particular, were assumed to cause an increase in mental or psychic energy, which results in a disequilibrium in the mental apparatus. This creates a "pressure toward discharge," a "demand" for the restoration of the constant state. Repression of this affect causes the associated energy to be "dammed up," which interferes with the smooth functioning of the mental apparatus. The greater the amount of energy repressed, the more psychic functioning is interrupted and so the more traumatic is the effect. Psychic energy is thus regarded as being augmented or diminished by stimulation or discharge (of emotion), which is why treatment at that time was based on catharsis. Freud thought that this model could provide a neurological basis for psychopathology.

**EGO** A term employed by Freud—*das Ich* in the German—to refer to both an experiencing sense of self and a hypothetical psychic system that functions to organize and synthesize the personality. In Freud's first two models of the mind the term referred primarily to the sense of self as experienced, but since his formulation of the structural model, it is often used to refer mainly to the hypothetical system.

**EGO-DYSTONIC** Wishes, impulses, or thoughts that are experienced as disagreeable, not compatible, or not in harmony with one's desired standards, as, for example, an aberrant sexual thought or a compulsive ritual.

**EGO IDEAL** An ideal image of oneself to which the individual aspires both consciously and unconsciously, and against which he measures himself. It is based on identification, mainly with parents, but it is revised in adolescence when other figures are taken for identification. The ego ideal makes up a part of the superego.

**EGO-SYNTONIC** Behavior experienced as compatible with one's standards, as, for example, a character trait that, although it might be unpleasant for others, causes no discomfort to the individual.

**ENERGY, PSYCHIC** A hypothetical metaphorical force in mental functioning introduced to account for a seeming quantitative aspect of certain elements of psychic life. It was always considered analogous but not equivalent to the concept of energy used in physical science.

**EPIGENESIS** A developmental principle borrowed from embryology. It was first applied to psychoanalytic theory by Erikson (1959) and suggests that personality growth obeys certain laws common to anything that grows. Each kind of organism has a ground plan according to which each part has its time of special ascendancy until all parts form a functioning whole. Accordingly, developmental events that unfold as personality grows appear at a particular rate and in a particular sequence.

**EROGENOUS ZONES**   Areas of the body the stimulation of which results in feelings of sexual pleasure or excitement. In addition to the genitals, other areas of the body can so serve. There is a developmental series that begins in the oral zone and progresses to the anal and then the genital zones; this is the basis for the theory of libidinal and psychosexual development.

**EXHIBITIONISM**   An exposure or display of oneself in order to obtain instinctual gratification through the awareness of being looked at and through the responses of the onlooker.

**EXTERNALIZATION**   A defense mechanism that is characterized by the tendency to put outside of oneself one's own instinctual wishes, conflicts, moods, and ways of thinking, so that these are perceived as originating from someone else. To be distinguished from projection.

**FANTASY**   A more or less connected series of mental images that may be conscious or unconscious and in which images, ideas, or modified external perceptions are often arranged or rearranged to create a gratification of an unfulfilled wish or desire. A fantasy presupposes the capacity to form connected ideas.

**FIXATION POINT**   In libido theory, fixation results from the damming up of libidinal energy at a particular stage of infantile development. It may occur because of trauma, conflict, frustration, or a significant amount of gratification at the time. The place or time at which this occurs is the fixation point, and its occurrence may make further development more difficult. When later obstacles are encountered, regression takes place to the point of fixation. Nowadays, instead of being understood as a spot along a continuum where energy is deposited and to which the psyche must return to gather up its deposited energy, a fixation point is viewed as a thought, a wish, or a behavior associated with pleasure or with pain that continues to be emotionally significant for the individual, and whose continuing influence may be seen especially at times of stress. Viewed in this manner, the occurrence of fixation points is a regular part of normal development, although the term becomes increasingly less useful.

**GENDER IDENTITY**   A psychological configuration that combines personal identity, biological sex, interpersonal experiences, intrapsychic consequences (such as identifications), and social and cultural influences into an individual's overall sense of femininity or masculinity.

**GENDER-ROLE IDENTITY**   The gender-based role one characteristically assumes consciously or unconsciously in interactions with other people.

**GENITAL PHASE**   The final stage of psychosexual development. It begins in puberty and signifies the biological capacity for orgasm. Once the person has reached the genital phase, the component sexual drives from earlier stages of psychosexual development usually become organized in the service of ultimate genital satisfaction, although they may be used for sexual excitation in foreplay.

**ID**   The hypothetical psychic system encompassing the instinctual drives—that is, the motivational forces that have a peremptory quality and function to impel the mind to activity in search of gratification. It is one of the three divisions of the psyche in the structural theory, the other two being the ego and the superego.

**IDENTIFICATION**   Changing the shape of one's self-representation to become more like the perception of an admired person or of some aspect of an admired person. The term is used to refer both to the process of making such changes and to the changes themselves. Identification with a parent emerges early and is a necessary component of normal development. Although identification can sometimes take on defensive aspects, it should not be viewed primarily as a defense. To be distinguished from internalization, incorporation, and introjection (which see).

**IMITATION**   Developmentally, the act of copying an admired or hated object, as in identification, but imitation is usually temporary and most often conscious.

**INCORPORATION**   The primitive fantasy of taking something into one's body through one or another orifice—mouth, anus, ears, nose—in order to appropriate aspects or qualities of the object. The term is also sometimes used with the connotation either of destroying the object or of one's obtaining pleasure by making an object penetrate oneself. To be distinguished from identification, internalization, and introjection (which see).

**INDIVIDUATION**   The developmental processes occurring through the first three years of life whereby the infant attempts to forge a distinct and unique sense of identity, with his own individual characteristics, as differentiated from the representation of the object—usually the mother.

**INFANTILE GENITAL PHASE**   The period of psychosexual development, following the anal stage, when most of the child's sexual attention is focused on the genitals, and oral and anal pleasures recede to the background. (See also *Phallic phase.*)

**INFANTILE NEUROSIS**   An intrapsychic organization characterized by internalized conflict that arouses anxiety and by an ego structure capable of responding to the anxiety signal with appropriate defense and compromise—that is, with internal modification (instead of environmental manipulation). The infantile neurosis begins with internalized conflict and implies a functioning superego. With an internalized set of standards and an internalized source of punishment and reward, drive wishes arouse internal disapproval and punishment (guilt).

Accordingly, the infantile neurosis implies that inner turmoil and compromise solutions are removed from external influence, and the ego and superego function relatively independently of external reinforcement.

**INSTINCT** See *Drive.*

**INSTINCTUAL DRIVE** Experienced as an idea, wish, or impulse that has a peremptory quality that "drives" or impels the mind to activity, the instinctual drive is a mental representative of a hypothetical motivational force of supposedly somatic origins. Originally Freud thought of the drive as having a particular bodily source, but nowadays we emphasize that many factors coalesce to form an instinctual drive, so that in addition to a somatic component, affective experiences and environmental influences also contribute. It is also characterized as having an aim, object, and intensity, but the resulting behavior is mediated by the ego; hence the emphasis is on psychological phenomena. This allows for the response to be plastic and varied, and to be modified by experience and reflection instead of being predetermined and stereotypic, as it is with lower animals.

**INTERNALIZATION** A general term that includes all those processes such as incorporation, introjection, and identification, by means of which internal or psychic representations, functions, structures, regulations, and characteristics are formed from interactions with real or imagined objects.

**INTERNALIZED CONFLICT** A conflict that begins interpersonally, but becomes a conflict between psychic structures, such as a conflict between an instinctual wish and a superego prohibition. Sometimes referred to as a neurotic conflict.

**INTERSYSTEMIC** The id, ego, and superego are the systems of the mind in the tripartite model. When conflict exists between wishes and impulses of different systems, it is referred to as intersystemic conflict. A typical intersystemic conflict is one between an impulse for drive gratification originating in the id and a wish to delay on the basis of reality considerations originating in the ego. (See also *Intrasystemic.*)

**INTRASYSTEMIC** In the tripartite model of the mind, the id, ego, and superego are referred to as systems. When conflict exists between impulses or wishes within one system, it is called intrasystemic conflict. A conflict of ideals is a typical intrasystemic conflict within the superego. (See also *Intersystemic.*)

**INTROJECT** The mental representation that accrues from the process of introjection (which see). We use the term specifically to refer to mental representations that accrue authority in the process of superego formation—the shoulds and should nots. Once formed, they are felt to have all the authority and power, fantasied or real, of the actual original objects. To be distinguished from identification, incorporation, and internalization (which see).

**INTROJECTION** Originally introduced by Ferenczi (1909) to refer to the antithesis of projection—that is, a pleasurable taking-in of aspects of the external world.

Since then it has been used in addition as a synonym for identification, and to refer to a primitive form of internalization, to a primitive form of identification sometimes associated with "psychotic identifications" when the boundaries between self- and object representations are indistinct, and to a defense. It can also refer to a child's taking in the object's demands and making them a part of his mind, so that he reacts in the same way whether or not the object is present. This is the specific way in which we employ the term.

**LATENCY**  The stage in development characterized by a relative diminution of outward manifestations of infantile sexuality, which implies repression of or successful resolution of oedipal conflict, and a reorganization of the ego's defensive structure influenced by superego development.

**LIBIDO**  The metaphorical, hypothetical psychic energy thought to be responsible for the force behind the sexual drive.

**LIBIDO THEORY**  The theory that sexual urges provide a motivation for psychic functioning from earliest infancy, and that the focus of sexual attention shifts from one erogenous zone to another during the course of development—from the oral to the anal to the genital. The theory assumes that the sources of the sexual instinct are derived from somatic processes, and that these are connected with certain aims or wishes that arouse sensual pleasure associated with fantasies about an object.

**MASOCHISM**  The need for physical or mental suffering or pain in order to achieve, unconsciously or consciously, sexual arousal or gratification.

**MASTURBATION**  Self-stimulation of an erogenous zone that produces sexual pleasure.

**MATURATION**  Developmental changes that are genetically predetermined. The sequential progression through the psychosexual stages or the timing of the emergence of certain functions such as upright locomotion and speech, for example, are determined by innate, biologically predetermined factors.

**MENTAL APPARATUS**  The hypothetical division of the mind into various systems or groups of functions. According to the structural model, these groupings are the id, ego, and superego.

**MENTAL REPRESENTATION**  A more or less stable and enduring image formed in the mind of an object or thing existing in the external world. A mental representation combines and is built from a variety of multidetermined perceptions and impressions about the object or thing. A child's mental representation of his mother, for example, is built from a wide range of images and impressions about the mother, as well as from images of the child himself in interaction with the mother.

**METAPSYCHOLOGY**  A term introduced by Freud (1901) to refer to a psychology beyond consciousness to distinguish psychoanalysis from a psychology based on conscious mental activities such as intelligence and perception. Freud referred to a "metapsychological presentation" as the most complete description of any clinical phenomenon that psychoanalysis had to offer (1915, p. 181). Later the term came to refer generally to the theoretical underpinnings of psychoanalytic knowledge. Although during the height of the ego psychology theorizing of the 1950s, metapsychology tended to be abstracted away from clinical experience, this is less the case today. We accordingly view metapsychology as the conceptual tools with which we can understand the functioning of the human mind. Although fundamental, because these conceptual tools are derived from clinical observations, they must also be periodically revised with advances in understanding, so that metapsychology is continually evolving.

**NARCISSISM**  In Freud's original concept, narcissism was the libidinal investment of the ego (self) taken as the object of the libidinal drive. It has come to acquire a variety of meanings—to refer to a sexual perversion, a stage in development, a type of object choice, a way of relating to the environment, and aspects of self-esteem.

**NEGATIVE OEDIPUS COMPLEX**  So called in analogy to a photographic print, this refers to the child's identifying with the opposite-sex parent and having a libidinal interest in the same-sex parent.

**NEUROTIC**  A type of conflict between one or more psychic systems. (See also *Internalized conflict; Infantile neurosis.*)

**NEUTRALIZATION**  A hypothetical psychic process linked to the concept of psychic energy (which see). It supposes that the sexual or aggressive aspects of the motivating drive force become lessened or deactivated—hence desexualization or disaggressivization.

**NONEXPERIENTIAL**  Hypothetical aspects of psychic functions, such as defense mechanisms, or psychic systems, such as the id, ego, and superego. Concepts about psychic functioning are central to the theory of psychoanalysis and are useful clinically in understanding mechanisms underlying behavior, but they are not a part of our experience. They are like the supporting framework to a stage; we can observe the play, but not the underlying supportive structures or scaffolding.

**OBJECT**  In psychoanalytic usage *object* refers to *person*. This unfortunate designation came into common usage with Freud's reference to the object of the libidinal drive—the person through whom pleasure is sought.

**OBJECT CHOICE**  The person chosen to be the most important love object. In the libido theory, this is the person chosen as the object of the libidinal drive. The choice is usually influenced by unconscious determinants and by the stage of development.

**OBJECT CONSTANCY**  A concept introduced by Hartmann (1952) to refer to a stage in object relations wherein the relationship was not destroyed or disrupted by sexual or aggressive impulses. The concept has become confusing because of its similarity to a Piagetian concept and because Spitz, Anna Freud, and Mahler, operating with very different definitions and criteria, used almost identical terminology. Spitz spoke of the *constant libidinal object* at the time (six to eight months) when the infant makes it clear that the mother is preferred over all others. Anna Freud used the term *object constancy* to refer to the point at which the mother continues to be the most important person for the child regardless of whether she gratifies or frustrates his needs (also about six to eight months). *Cognitive object permanence,* or *"thing" constancy,* does not have connotations of interpersonal relationships and of their internalization; rather, it refers to the persistence of a mental representation past the point of its being perceived. Cognitive object constancy, wherein an integrated representation endures in memory and can be evoked at will, becomes stable around eighteen months. Mahler used the term *libidinal object constancy,* which she saw to be attained through a gradual process that requires a firm attachment to the mother to begin with, requires building up an evocable cognitive maternal representation, and finally requires some resolution of loving and hating feelings so that the mother can be viewed as basically loving. Then the mental representation of her can be a loving one that functions to provide comfort and support in her absence, enabling the child to function separately and to progress to more advanced ways of relating.

**OBJECT LIBIDO**   Denotes libidinal energy or psychological attention directed toward external love objects. Object libido is in contrast to narcissistic libido in which the attention is focused on the self.

**OBJECT LOSS**   Either the actual loss of a loved person through separation or the feelings of loss owing to some intrapsychic process.

**OBJECT RELATIONS**   Unconscious mental representations of objects and the sense of self in interaction with them that are built up as development progresses from interpersonal interactions. Representations of the important relationships and experiences of childhood can be found in them, and they profoundly affect the person's interpersonal interactions and object choices. To emphasize the intrapsychic location, the term *internalized object relations* is sometimes used.

**OBJECT REPRESENTATION**   The mental representation of an external object that becomes built up and lodged in the inner world. The representation may correspond to the actual object, but is often altered by unconscious processes, such as loving or angry feelings about the object, or by various fantasies or idealizations.

**OEDIPUS COMPLEX**   The configuration of a child's relationship to his parents based on a fantasy that usually evolves during the height of the infantile genital phase. Specifically, it refers to the child's identifying with the same-sex parent and having a libidinal interest in the opposite-sex parent. This fantasy of replacing one parent so as to live that parent's role in relation to the other parent is usually accompanied by a variety of conflicts because of loyalty to and admiration of the same-sex parent, and because of fears of retribution by the parent who is replaced.

**OPERATIONS** A term used by Piaget to refer to the cognitive ability to think about actions without having to go through the physical motions. He described a child's thinking developmentally as the stages of:
1. Preoperations: the earliest stage of being able to mentally think about actions. Thinking at this early stage is dominated by egocentric thought and prelogical thinking. Perceptions rather than logic influence a child's judgment.
2. Concrete operations: thinking in terms of concrete, existing objects. In this stage the child is able to think about actions mentally, but is not yet able to form hypotheses mentally or consider possibilities.
3. Formal operations: the cognitive ability to reason on hypotheses alone and to be able to mentally test thoughts.

**ORAL PHASE** The first stage of libidinal development, corresponding approximately to the first year of life, when it is supposed that the infant's chief source of libidinal gratification is through pleasurable oral activities such as sucking and biting.

**PENIS ENVY** An unpleasant feeling, often accompanied by low self-esteem, aroused by a covetous attitude toward the male phallus. Freud thought this to be bedrock to female psychology. This notion has been challenged, and boys have also been observed to suffer penis envy when they discover older males possess a larger organ than they do.

**PHALLIC MOTHER** The fantasy that the mother has a penis. The term *phallic woman* is often employed loosely to describe a woman with allegedly masculine character traits.

**PHALLIC PHASE** The stage of psychosexual development of boys that succeeds the anal phase and in which the main focus of sexual attention is focused on the genitals. It was termed *phallic* because the organ of principal interest and anxiety appeared to be the boy's penis. We prefer Freud's original term, the *infantile genital phase,* because it more easily allows consideration of other equally important aspects of this period of development not only for boys but also for girls.

**POSITIVE OEDIPUS COMPLEX** The child's identifying with the same-sex parent and having a libidinal interest in the opposite-sex parent.

**PRECONSCIOUS** Any mental processes, contents, and memories that are more or less available to consciousness, but that are for the moment outside of awareness. The term was also used to designate a system of the mind in the topographical model.

**PREOEDIPAL PHASE**   Those phases in object relations preceding the formation of the Oedipus complex. It is characterized primarily by attachment to the first love object, the mother.

**PRIMARY AUTONOMY**   Inborn characteristics that mature in the course of development independently of external influence. These capacities may be interfered with by conflict or by regression. Cognition and motor capacities are examples.

**PRIMARY OBJECT**   The first and most important person in the infant's life, usually the mother.

**PRIMARY PROCESS**   The mode of thinking associated with the subjective inner world, or the system Unconscious. It is characterized by associational thinking, concretism, condensation, displacement, imagery, and symbolization. Examples are dreams, fantasies, or slips of the tongue. (See also *Secondary process*.)

**PROJECTION**   A defense mechanism characterized by attributing to an external object unacceptable impulses and feelings that are then felt to be directed back toward the self. (See also *Externalization*.)

**PROJECTIVE IDENTIFICATION**   A term introduced by Melanie Klein referring to mechanisms used by the infant in fantasy to handle aggressive feelings toward himself and his mother. It has become broadened to apply to later stages and to include displacement outside; turning the aggression back to the self in association with feelings of persecution; wishes to control and possess the object; a part of countertransference mechanisms; and actual alteration of the object's internal state and self-representation.

**PSYCHIC APPARATUS**   See *Mental apparatus*.

**PSYCHIC REALITY**   Freud used this term to designate whatever in one's mind takes on the force of external, objective, or material reality. In the strict sense, it refers to an unconscious wish and the fantasy associated with it, but it may be used more broadly to include conscious and unconscious thoughts, feelings, dreams, fantasies, memories, and perceptions without regard to their correspondence to external reality. In terms of psychic reality, a wish or fantasy may be reacted to as if it had actually taken place with resulting guilt and distortions of memory, for example.

**PSYCHOANALYSIS**   The study of human psychological functioning and behavior with a particular focus on unconscious mental activity. It includes three aspects—a method of investigating the mind, a systematized body of knowledge about human behavior, and a method of treating emotional illness.

**PSYCHOSEXUAL DEVELOPMENT**   The personality organization that evolves at successive developmental stages and is based on the progressive maturation of erogenous zones; it occurs together with accompanying fantasies and conflicts related to object relations development, superego development, cognitive development, and ego development.

**RAPPROCHEMENT**  Originally a French term denoting the task of renegotiation to restore harmony in a relationship. Mahler used it to refer to the developmental conflict between the toddler and the mother during the second half of the second year of life. The toddler begins to feel a certain separation from the mother, as well as a lack of the omnipotence that was characteristic of the preceding practicing phase. The relationship with the mother must then be renegotiated. Although the conflict begins in the second year of life, the issues involved arise at each new developmental stage, and the parent-child relationship must be renegotiated at each of these stages.

**REACTION FORMATION**  A defense mechanism whereby an infantile wish is warded off through the formation of a character trait representing the opposite instinct. Fastidiousness replaces messing in the anal phase, for example.

**REGRESSION**  A process of seeking pleasure or utilizing behavior patterns characteristic of an earlier developmental phase. Such behavior is observable at times of stress or anxiety. Earlier in psychoanalytic theory such changes in behavior were thought of in terms of a "going back" to a fixation point along a continuum where energy had been deposited.

**REPRESENTATIONAL WORLD**  A concept suggested by Sandler and Rosenblatt (1962) to refer to a collection of images or representations of the objects of the outside world, which, through processes of internalization, become lodged in the inner world, resulting in a kind of experiential map of the phenomena of objective reality as it exists in each individual's mind.

**REPRESSION**  Originally referring to all defensive activity in Freud's early writings, the term has come to be limited to a specific defense whereby psychological activities or contents of wishes, fantasies, or early childhood events are excluded from conscious awareness by a process of which the individual is not consciously aware.

**SECONDARY AUTONOMY**  The state of ego functions that have their origin in areas of conflict but achieve independent functioning free of it. Cleanliness is an example.

**SECONDARY PROCESS**  Thinking characterized by rationality, order, and logic. It relies heavily on verbal symbolism and functions chiefly in adaptation to reality. It can be conscious or unconscious. (See also *Primary process*.)

**SELF-IMAGE**  The image an individual has of himself at a particular time in a particular situation. It consists of his body image and the representation of his inner state at the time. It is derived from and forms a part of the self-representation.

**SELFOBJECT**  A concept central to the theories of Heinz Kohut and self psychology. A selfobject is a person who is used as a functional part of the self to provide a stabilizing structure against the fragmenting potential of stimulation or affect.

**SELF-REPRESENTATION**  More encompassing than the self-image, the self-represen-tation is a mental representation of the self constructed from a variety of realistic and distorted self-images, experiences, interactions, and associated feelings that the individual has had at various times. It also represents the person as he consciously perceives himself.

**SENSORIMOTOR**  The kind of thinking based on sensory perception and motor activity. It is the only kind of thinking available to the infant from birth to about eighteen months, according to Piaget, which is why he referred to the period as the sensorimotor stage. In this stage the infant acts in relation to objects that are perceptually present, and he shows a wholly practical, perceiving and doing, action-bound kind of intellectual functioning.

**STRUCTURALIZATION**  Psychic structure formation—a process whereby a variety of functions become linked to form a coherent and durable system.

**STRUCTURAL THEORY**  The theory of mental functioning that Freud advanced in 1923, in which he suggested grouping mental processes in three systems, the id, the ego, and the superego, according to their functions in conflict and in adaptation. These systems have come to be referred to as structures because of their relative stability and slow rate of change, the constancy of their objectives, and consistency in their modes of operation.

**STRUCTURE**  A conceptual term to describe a slowly changing and evolving, rela-tively stable system, as, for example, the ego or the superego of structural theory.

**SUBLIMATION**  The unconscious deflection of sexual impulses to aims that are more acceptable to the ego and superego. Instead of masturbating and becom-ing engrossed in its related fantasies, the latency child, for example, creates "nice" stories or enjoys handicrafts.

**SUPEREGO**  A hypothetical psychic system that functions to set up and maintain moral standards and wished-for goals and ideals. When functioning optimally, it supports intrapsychic and interpersonal harmony and facilitates social adap-tation. Its functioning is particularly experienced through elevations in self-esteem or through the painful affect of guilt.

**SYMBIOSIS**  A biological term denoting two separate but mutually dependent organisms. Mahler applied the term to describe the type of object relating characteristic of the infant of two to four or five months; she believed that the infant had as yet no sense of being separate from the mother. Because we now recognize that the infant has many cognitive and perceptual skills to differenti-ate inside and outside, self and other, from birth, and that the infant is born preadapted for social interaction, Mahler's view is better expressed in terms of an optimal affective relationship at the time: mother and infant closely "in tune." In this sense, we think it remains useful as a metaphor to refer to an affective ideal, where there is a kind of affective oneness between mother and infant. A fantasy that infancy is a symbiotic state of total need gratification is not uncommon in children, and a fantasy of symbiotic oneness between infant and mother is often maintained by pregnant women. A person may similarly fantasize having had such an experience with mother earlier in life and seek to relive it with another.

**SYSTEM**  An organization of interrelated elements in dynamic interaction with each other.

**TOPOGRAPHICAL MODEL**  Freud's second model of the mind, which divided the mental apparatus into three systems, the Unconscious, the Preconscious, and the Conscious.

**TRANSITIONAL OBJECT**  A concept introduced by Winnicott to refer to the infant's use of a favorite possession, such as a blanket or toy, that functions as a comfort in mother's absence. The transitional object appears to symbolize a link between the infant and his mother and contains qualities of both mother and infant.

**TRAUMA**  A condition that is experienced as overwhelming to the ego's capacity to organize and regulate and that therefore produces a state of helplessness.

**TRIPARTITE MODEL**  A term often applied to the model of the mind, introduced by Freud in 1923, consisting of the id, ego, and superego as the three major divisions of the mind. Also known as the structural model.

**UNCONSCIOUS**  The mental contents and processes that are outside conscious awareness at any given moment. Two kinds of unconscious are recognized in psychoanalytic theory. The descriptive unconscious refers to any content outside awareness. The dynamic Unconscious (distinguished by the capital U) refers to mental contents and processes of the "system" Unconscious of the topographical model that are inaccessible to consciousness and incapable of achieving consciousness because of the counterforce of repression and other defenses.

# REFERENCES

The following abbreviations are used throughout the references.

| | |
|---|---|
| Amer. J. Orthopsychiat. | American Journal of Orthopsychiatry |
| Amer. J. Psychiat. | American Journal of Psychiatry |
| Am. Pediatrics | American Pediatrics |
| Ann. Psychoanal. | Annual of Psychoanalysis |
| Archs. Sexual Behavior | Archives of Sexual Behavior |
| Brit. J. Med. Psychol. | British Journal of Medical Psychology |
| Bull. Anna Freud Centre | Bulletin of the Anna Freud Centre |
| Bull. Hampstead Clin. | Bulletin of the Hampstead Clinic |
| Bull. Johns Hopkins Hosp. | Bulletin of the Johns Hopkins Hospital |
| Bull. Phila. Assn. | Bulletin of the Philadelphia Association for Psychoanalysis |
| Child Develop. | Child Development |
| Child-Fam. Digest | Child and Family Digest |
| Cogn. Develop. | Cognitive Development |
| DHHS | Department of Health and Human Services |
| Genetic Psychol. Mono. | Genetic and Psychology Monographs |
| Int. J. Psychoanal. | International Journal of Psychoanalysis |
| Int. J. Psychoanal. Psychother. | International Journal of Psychoanalysis and Psychotherapy |
| Int. Rev. Psychoanal. | International Review of Psychoanalysis |
| Int. Univ. Press | International Universities Press |
| J. Amer. Acad. Child Psychiat. | Journal of the American Academy of Child Psychiatry |
| J. Child Psychother. | Journal of Child Psychotherapy |
| J. Amer. Acad. Psychoanal. | Journal of the American Academy of Psychoanalysis |
| J. Amer. Psychoanal. Assn. | Journal of the American Psychoanalytic Association |
| J. Communication | Journal of Communication |
| J. Comp. Neurol. | Journal of Comparative Neurology |
| J. Nerv. Ment. Dis. | Journal of Nervous and Mental Disease |
| J. Personal. Soc. Psychol. | Journal of Personality and Social Psychology |
| J. Phila. Assn. Psychoanal. | Journal of Philadelphia Association for Psychoanalysis |
| J. Psychosom. Res. | Journal of Psychosomatic Research |
| Merrill-Palmer Q. | Merrill-Palmer Quarterly |
| Psychoanal. Contemp. Science | Psychoanalysis and Contemporary Science |
| Psychoanal. Contemp. Thought | Psychoanalysis and Contemporary Thought |

| | |
|---|---|
| Psychoanal. Inq. | Psychoanalytic Inquiry |
| Psychoanal. Psychol. | Psychoanalytic Psychology |
| Psychoanal. Q. | The Psychoanalytic Quarterly |
| Psychoanal. Rev. | Psychoanalytic Review |
| Psychoanal. Study Child | The Psychoanalytic Study of the Child |
| Psychosom. Med. | Psychosomatic Medicine |
| Psychother. Psychosom. | Psychotherapy and Psychosomatics |
| S.E. | The Standard Edition of the Works of Sigmund Freud |
| WHO | World Health Organization |

Abelin, E. L. (1971). The role of the father in the separation-individuation process. In *Separation-individuation: Essays in honor of Margaret S. Mahler,* ed. J. McDevitt and C. Settlage. New York: Int. Univ. Press, pp. 229–252.

Abelin, E. L. (1975). Some further observations and comments on the earliest role of the father. *Int. J. Psychoanal.,* 56:293–302.

Abend, S. M. (1982). Serious illness in the analyst: Countertransference considerations. *J. Amer. Psychoanal. Assn.,* 30:365–379.

Abraham, H. C., and Freud, E. L., eds. (1965). *A psycho-analytic dialogue: The letters of Sigmund Freud and Karl Abraham, 1907–1926.* New York: Basic Books.

Abraham, K. (1916). The first pregenital stage of the libido. In *Selected papers on psycho-analysis.* New York: Basic Books, 1953, pp. 248–279.

Abraham, K. (1920). Manifestations of the female castration complex. In *Selected papers on psycho-analysis.* New York: Basic Books, 1953, pp. 338–369.

Abraham, K. (1924a). The influence of oral erotism on character formation. In *Selected papers on psycho-analysis.* New York: Basic Books, 1953, pp. 393–406.

Abraham, K. (1924b). A short study of the development of the libido, viewed in the light of mental disorders. In *Selected papers on psycho-analysis.* New York: Basic Books, 1953, pp. 418–501.

Abrams, S. (1977). The genetic point of view: Historical antecedents and developmental transformations. *J. Amer. Psychoanal. Assn.,* 25:417–426.

Aichhorn, A. (1925). *Wayward youth.* New York: Viking Press, 1965.

Ainsworth, M. D. (1962). The effects of maternal deprivation: A review of findings and controversy in the context of research strategy. In *Deprivation of maternal care: A reassessment of its effects.* Public Health Papers No. 14. Geneva: WHO, pp. 97–165.

Ainsworth, M. D. (1964). Patterns of attachment behaviour shown by the infant in interaction with his mother. *Merrill-Palmer Q.,* 10:51–58.

Ainsworth, M. D.; Blehar, M.; Waters, E.; and Wall, S. (1978). *Patterns of attachment.* Hillsdale, N.J.: Erlbaum.

Alpert, A. (1941). The latency period: Re-examination in an educational setting. *Amer. J. Orthopsychiat.,* 11:126–132.

Als, H.; Lester, B. M.; and Brazelton, T. B. (1979). Dynamics of the behavioral organization of the premature infant: A theoretical perspective. In *Infants born at risk: Behavior and development,* ed. T. M. Field, A. M. Sostek, S. Goldberg, and H. H. Shuman. New York: Spectrum, pp. 173–192.

Amsterdam, B. K. (1972). Mirror self-image reactions before age 2. *Developmental Psychology,* 5:297–305.

Anders, T. F. (1978). Home-recorded sleep in two- and nine-month-old infants. *J. Amer. Acad. Child Psychiat.,* 17:421–432.

Anders, T. F. (1982). Biological rhythms in development. *Psychosom. Med.,* 44:61–72.

Anders, T. F., and Zeanah, C. H. (1984). Early infant development from a biological point of view. In *Frontiers of infant psychiatry.* Vol. 2, ed. J. Call, E. Galenson, and R. L. Tyson. New York: Basic Books, pp. 55–69.

Anthony, E. J. (1957). Symposium on the contribution of current theories to an understanding of child development, the system makers: Piaget and Freud. *Brit. J. Med. Psychol.,* 30:255–269.

Anthony, E. J. (1982). Normal adolescent development from a cognitive viewpoint. *J. Amer. Acad. Child Psychiat.,* 21:318–327.

Anthony, E. J., and Cohler, B. J., eds. (1987). *The invulnerable child.* New York: Guilford Press.

Arlow, J. A. (1969). Unconscious fantasy and disturbances of conscious experience. *Psychoanal. Q.,* 38:1–27.

Arlow, J. A. (1977). Affects and the psychoanalytic situation. *Int. J. Psychoanal.,* 58:157–170.

Arlow, J. A., and Brenner, C. (1964). *Psychoanalytic concepts and the structural theory.* New York: Int. Univ. Press.

Balint, M. (1959). *Primary love and psycho-analytic technique.* London: Tavistock.

Balint, M. (1968). *The basic fault: Therapeutic aspects of regression.* London: Tavistock.

Balint, E. (1973). Technical problems found in the analysis of women by a woman analyst: A contribution to the question "What does a woman want?" *Int. J. Psychoanal.,* 58:289–300.

Barnett, M. C. (1966). Vaginal awareness in the infancy and childhood of girls. *J. Amer. Psychoanal. Assn.,* 14:129–141.

Basch, M. F. (1976). The concept of affect: A re-examination. *J. Amer. Psychoanal. Assn.,* 24:;759–778.

Basch, M. F. (1977). Development psychology and explanatory theory in psychoanalysis. *Ann. Psychoanal.,* 5:229–263.

Beebe, B. (1986). Mother-infant mutual influence and precursors of self- and object-representations. In *Empirical studies of psychoanalytic theories.* Vol. 2, ed. J. Masling. Hillsdale, N.J.: Erlbaum, pp. 27–48.

Beebe, B., and Stern, D. (1977). Engagement-disengagement and early objective experiences. In *Communicative structures and psychic structures,* ed. N. Freeman and S. Grand. New York: Plenum Press, pp. 35–550.

Bell, A. (1961). Some observations on the role of the scrotal sac and the testicles. *J. Amer. Psychoanal. Assn.*, 9:261–286.

Bell, R. Q. (1974). Contributions of human infants to caregiving and social interaction. In *The effect of the infant on its caregiver*, ed. J. M. Lewis and L. A. Rosenblum. New York: Wiley, pp. 1–19.

Bell, R. Q., and Harper, L. V. (1977). *Child effects on adults*. Hillsdale, N.J.: Erlbaum.

Benedek, T. (1959). Parenthood as a developmental phase: A contribution to the libido theory. *J. Amer. Psychoanal. Assn.*, 7:389–417.

Benjamin, J. D. (1961a). Some developmental observations relating to the theory of anxiety. *J. Amer. Psychoanal. Assn.*, 9:652–668.

Benjamin, J. D. (1961b). The innate and the experiential in child development. In *Lectures on experimental psychiatry*, ed. H. W. Brosin. Pittsburgh: Univ. of Pittsburgh Press, 1961, pp. 19–42.

Benjamin, J. D. (1963). Further comments on some developmental aspects of anxiety. In *Counterpoint*, ed. H. S. Gaskill. New York: Int. Univ. Press, pp. 121–133.

Beres, D. (1958). Vicissitudes of superego functions and superego precursors in childhood. *Psychoanal. Study Child*, 13:324–352.

Beres, D. (1981). Self, identity, and narcissism. *Psychoanal. Q.*, 50:515–534.

Bergman, D., and Escalona, S. K. (1949). Unusual sensitivities in very young children. *Psychoanal. Study Child*, 3/4:333–352.

Bernfeld, S. (1938). Types of adolescence. *Psychoanal. Q.*, 7:243–253.

Bernstein, D. (1983). The female superego: A different perspective. *Int. J. Psychoanal.*, 64:187–201.

Bertalanffy, L. von (1968). *General system theory: Foundations, development, applications*. New York: George Braziller.

Bettelheim, B. (1976). *The uses of enchantment: The meaning and importance of fairy tales*. London: Thames and Hudson.

Bibring, E. (1947). The so-called English School of psychoanalysis. *Psychoanal. Q.*, 16:69–93.

Bibring, G. L.; Dwyer, T. F.; Huntington, D. S.; and Vallenstein, A. F. (1961). A study of the psychological processes in the pregnancy and earliest mother-child relationship. *Psychoanal. Study Child*, 16:9–72.

Blos, P. (1958). Preadolescent drive organization. *J. Amer. Psychoanal. Assn.*, 6:47–56.

Blos, P. (1962). *On adolescence: A psychoanalytic interpretation*. New York: Free Press.

Blos, P. (1967). The second individuation process of adolescence. *Psychoanal. Study Child*, 22:162–186.

Blos, P. (1968). Character formation in adolescence. *Psychoanal. Study Child*, 23:245–263.

Blos, P. (1970). *The young adolescent: Clinical studies*. New York: Free Press.

Blos, P. (1974). The genealogy of the ego ideal. *Psychoanal. Study Child*, 29:43–88.

Blos, P. (1976). How and when does adolescence end? In *Adolescent psychiatry.* Vol. 5, ed. S. C. Feinstein and P. Giovacchini. New York: Aronson, pp. 5–17.

Blos, P. (1979). *The adolescent passage.* New York: Int. Univ. Press.

Blum, H. P. (1976). Masochism, the ego ideal, and the psychology of women. *J. Amer. Psychoanal. Assn.*, 24 (Suppl.):157–191.

Blum, H. P. (1978). Symbolic processes and symbol formation. *Int. J. Psychoanal.*, 59:455–471.

Blum, H. P. (1982). Theories of the self and psychoanalytic concepts: Discussion. *J. Amer. Psychoanal. Assn.*, 30:959–978.

Blum, H. P. (1985). Superego formation, adolescent transformation, and the adult neurosis. *J. Amer. Psychoanal. Assn.*, 33:887–909.

Boesky, D. (1988). The concept of psychic structure. *J. Amer. Psychoanal. Assn.*, 36 (Suppl.):113–135.

Bornstein, B. (1951). On latency. *Psychoanal. Study Child*, 5:279–286.

Bornstein, B. (1953). Fragment of an analysis of an obsessional child: The first six months of analysis. *Psychoanal. Study Child*, 8:313–332.

Bower, T. G. R. (1974). *Development in infancy.* San Francisco: Freeman Press.

Bowlby, J. (1958). The nature of the child's tie to his mother. *Int. J. Psychoanal.*, 39:350–373.

Bowlby, J. (1960a). Grief and mourning in infancy and early childhood. *Psychoanal. Study Child*, 15:9–52.

Bowlby, J. (1960b). Separation anxiety. *Int. J. Psychoanal.*, 41:89–113.

Bowlby, J. (1961). Processes of mourning. *Int. J. Psychoanal.*, 42:317–340.

Bowlby, J. (1969). *Attachment and loss.* Vol. 1, *Attachment.* New York: Basic Books.

Bowlby, J. (1973). *Attachment and loss.* Vol. 2, *Separation, anxiety, and anger.* New York: Basic Books.

Bowlby, J. (1980). *Attachment and loss.* Vol. 3, *Loss, sadness and depression.* New York: Basic Books.

Bowlby, J. (1981). Psychoanalysis as a natural science. *Int. Rev. Psychoanal.*, 8:243–256.

Brazelton, T. B. (1973). *Neonatal behavioral assessment scale.* London: Spastics International Medical Publications.

Brazelton, T. B. (1982). Joint regulation of neonate parent behavior. In *Social interchange in infancy,* ed. E. Z. Tronick. Baltimore: University Park Press, pp. 7–27.

Brazelton, T. B., and Als, H. (1979). Four early stages in the development of mother-infant interaction. *Psychoanal. Study Child*, 34:349–369.

Brazelton, T. B.; Koslowski, B.; and Main, M. (1974). The early mother-infant interaction. In *The effect of the infant on its caregiver,* ed. M. Lewis and L. Rosenblum. New York: Wiley, pp. 49–77.

Brazelton, T. B.; Tronick, E.; Adamson, L.; Als, H.; and Wise, S. (1975). Early mother-infant reciprocity. In *Parent-infant interaction*. Ciba Foundation Symposium 33. Amsterdam: Elsevier, pp. 137–154.

Brenner, C. (1959). The masochistic character: Genesis and treatment. *J. Amer. Psychoanal. Assn.*, 7:197–226.

Brenner, C. (1974). On the nature and development of affects: A unified theory. *Psychoanal. Q.*, 43:532–556.

Brenner, C. (1979). The components of psychic conflict and its consequences in mental life. *Psychoanal. Q.*, 48:547–567.

Brenner, C. (1982). *The mind in conflict*. New York: Int. Univ. Press.

Brenner, C. (1987). Notes on psychoanalysis by a participant observer: A personal chronicle. *J. Amer. Psychoanal. Assn.*, 35:539–556.

Breuer, J., and Freud, S. (1893–1895). *Studies on hysteria. S. E.*, 2.

Brody, M. W., and Mahoney, V. P. (1964). Introjection, identification and incorporation. *Int. J. Psychoanal.*, 45:57–63.

Brody, S. (1980). Transitional objects: Idealization of a phenomenon. *Psychoanal. Q.*, 49:561–605.

Brody, S. (1981). The concepts of attachment and bonding. *J. Amer. Psychoanal. Assn.*, 29:815–829.

Brody, S. (1982). Psychoanalytic theories of infant development and its disturbances: A critical evaluation. *Psychoanal. Q.*, 51:526–597.

Brody, S., and Axelrad, S. (1970). *Anxiety and ego formation in infancy*. New York: Int. Univ. Press.

Brody, S., and Axelrad, S. (1978). *Mothers, fathers, and children: Explorations in the formation of character in the first seven years*. New York: Int. Univ. Press.

Broussard, E. (1984). The Pittsburgh firstborns at age nineteen years. In *Frontiers of infant psychiatry*. Vol. 2, ed. J. Call, E. Galenson, and R. L. Tyson. New York: Basic Books, 1984, pp. 522–530.

Bruner, J. S. (1974). From communication to language: A psychological perspective. *Cognition*, 3:255–287.

Bruner, J. S. (1977). Early social interaction and language acquisition. In *Studies in mother-infant interaction*, ed. H. R. Schaffer. London: Academic Press, pp. 271–289.

Brunswick, R. M. (1940). The preoedipal phase of libido development. In *The psychoanalytic reader*, ed. R. Fliess. New York: Int. Univ. Press, pp. 261–283.

Burgner, M. (1985). Oedipal experience: Effects on development of an absent father. *Int. J. Psychoanal.*, 66:311–320.

Burgner, M., and Edgcumbe, R. (1972). Some problems in the conceptualization of early object relationships: Part II, The concept of object constancy. *Psychoanal. Study Child*, 27:315–333.

Burgner, M., and Kennedy, H. (1980). Different types of sado-masochistic behavior in children. *Dialogue*, 4:49–58.

Burlingham, D. (1952). *Twins: A study of three pairs of identical twins*. London: Imago.

Burlingham, D. (1973). The preoedipal infant-father relationship. *Psychoanal. Study Child*, 28:23–47.

Burlingham, D., and Freud, A. (1944). Infants without families. In *The writings of Anna Freud*. Vol. 3. New York: Int. Univ. Press, 1973, pp. 543–666.

Burns, P.; Sander, L.; Stechler, G.; and Julia, H. (1972). Distress in feeding: Short-term effects of caretaker environment of the first ten days. *J. Amer. Acad. Child Psychiat.*, 11:427–439.

Busch, F. (1974). Dimensions of the first transitional object. *Psychoanal. Study Child*, 29:215–229.

Buxbaum, E. (1945). Transference and group formation in children and adolescents. *Psychoanal. Study Child*, 1:351–366.

Buxbaum, E. (1980). Between the Oedipus complex and adolescence: The "quiet" time. In *The course of life*. Vol. 2, ed. S. I. Greenspan and G. H. Pollock. Publication No. (ADM) 80–999. Washington, D.C.: DHHS, pp. 121–136.

Calef, V., and Weinshel, E. (1979). The new psychoanalysis and psychoanalytic revisionism. *Psychoanal. Q.*, 48:470–491.

Call, J. D. (1964). Newborn approach behavior and early ego development. *Int. J. Psychoanal.*, 45:286–294.

Call, J. D. (1979). Introduction to normal development. In *Basic handbook of child psychiatry*. Vol. 1, ed. J. Noshpitz et al. New York: Basic Books, pp. 3–10.

Call, J. D. (1980). Some prelinguistic aspects of language development. *J. Amer. Psychoanal. Assn.*, 28:259–289.

Call, J. D. (1983). Toward a nosology of psychiatric disorders in infancy. In *Frontiers of infant psychiatry*. New York: Basic Books, pp. 117–128.

Call, J. D. (1984). From early patterns of communication to the grammar of experience and syntax in infancy. In *Frontiers of infant psychiatry*. Vol. 2, ed. J. D. Call, E. Galenson, and R. L. Tyson. New York: Basic Books, pp. 15–29.

Call, J. D., and Marschak, M. (1966). Styles and games in infancy. In *Infant psychiatry*, ed. E. Rexford, L. Sander, and T. Shapiro. New Haven: Yale Univ. Press, 1965, pp. 104–113.

Campos, J. J.; Barrett, K. C.; Lamb, M. E.; Goldsmith, H. H.; and Stenberg, C. (1983). Socioemotional development. In *Handbook of child psychology*. Vol. 2, ed. M. Haith and J. J. Campos. New York: Wiley, pp. 783–916.

Cath, S. H.; Gurwitt, A. R.; and Ross, J. M., eds. (1982). *Father and child: Developmental and clinical perspectives*. Boston: Little, Brown.

Chasseguet-Smirgel, J. (1970). *Female sexuality: New psychoanalytic views*. Ann Arbor: Univ. of Michigan Press.

Chess, S., and Thomas, T. (1986). *Temperament in clinical practice*. New York: Guilford Press.

Chodorow, N. (1978). *Reproduction of mothering: Psychoanalysis and the sociology of gender*. Berkeley: Univ. of California Press.

Clower, V. L. (1976). Theoretical implications in current views of masturbation in latency girls. *J. Amer. Psychoanal. Assn.*, 24:109–126.

Colarusso, C. A., and Nemiroff, R. A. (1981). *Adult development: A new dimension in psychodynamic theory and practice.* New York: Plenum Press.

Compton, A. (1980). A study of the psychoanalytic theory of anxiety: Part III, A preliminary formulation of the anxiety response. *J. Amer. Psychoanal. Assn.,* 28:739–774.

Compton, A. (1981a). On the psychoanalytic theory of instinctual drives: Part III, The complications of libido and narcissism. *Psychoanal. Q.,* 50:345–362.

Compton, A. (1981b). On the psychoanalytic theory of instinctual drives: Part IV, Instinctual drives and the ego-id-superego model. *Psychoanal. Q.,* 50:363–392.

Darwin, C. R. (1872). *The expression of the emotions in man and animals.* Chicago: Univ. of Chicago Press, 1965.

Décarie, T. G. (1965). *Intelligence and affectivity in early childhood.* New York: Int. Univ. Press.

Deese, J. (1973). Cognitive structure and affect in language in communication and affect. In *Language and thought,* ed. P. Piner, L. Krames, and T. Alloway. New York: Academic Press, pp. 91–113.

Demos, E. V. (1982). Facial expressions of infants and toddlers: A descriptive analysis. In *Emotion and early interaction,* ed. T. Field and E. Fogel. Hillsdale, N.J.: Erlbaum, pp. 118–129.

Deutsch, H. (1930). The significance of masochism in the mental life of women. In *The psycho-analytic reader,* ed. R. Fliess. New York: Int. Univ. Press, 1948, pp. 223–236.

Deutsch, H. (1932). On female homosexuality. In *The psycho-analytic reader,* ed. R. Fliess. New York: Int. Univ. Press, 1948, pp. 237–260.

Deutsch, H. (1944). *The psychology of women: A psychoanalytic interpretation.* Vol. 1. New York: Grune and Stratton.

Deutsch, H. (1945). *The psychology of women: A psychoanalytic interpretation.* Vol. 2, *Motherhood.* New York: Grune and Stratton.

Dewald, P. A. (1981). Adult phases of the life cycle. In *The course of life: Psychoanalytic contributions toward understanding personality development.* Vol. 3, ed. S. I. Greenspan and G. H. Pollock. Publication No. (ADM) 81–1000. Washington, D.C.: DHHS, pp. 35–53.

Dowling, S. (1977). Seven infants with esophageal atresia: A developmental study. *Psychoanal. Study Child,* 32:215–256.

Drucker, J. (1981). Cognitive and affective growth: Developmental interaction. In *Development: Concepts of cognition and affect,* ed. T. Shapiro and E. Weber. Hillsdale, N.J.: Erlbaum, pp. 240–261.

Edelson, M. (1975). *Language and interpretation in psychoanalysis.* New Haven: Yale Univ. Press.

Edgcumbe, R. M. (1984). The development of symbolization. *Bull. Hampstead Clin.,* 7:105–126.

Edgcumbe, R. M., and Burgner, M. (1975). The phallic narcissistic phase: A differentiation between preoedipal and oedipal aspects of phallic development. *Psychoanal. Study Child,* 30:161–180.

Edgcumbe, R. M.; Lundberg, S.; Markowitz, R.; and Salo, F. (1976). Some comments on the concept of the negative oedipal phase in girls. *Psychoanal. Study Child,* 31:35–62.

Eisnitz, A. J. (1980). The organization of the self-representation and its influence on pathology. *Psychoanal. Q.,* 49:361–392.

Ekman, P. (1984). Expression and the nature of emotion. In *Approaches to emotion,* ed. K. Scherer and P. Ekman. Hillsdale, N.J.: Erlbaum, pp. 35–55.

Ekman, P., and Friesen, W. V. (1975). *Unmasking the face.* Englewood Cliffs, N.J.: Prentice-Hall.

Emde, R. N. (1980a). Emotional availability: A reciprocal reward system for infants and parents with implications for prevention of psychosocial disorders. In *Parent-infant relationships,* ed. P. M. Taylor. Orlando, Fla.: Grune and Stratton, pp. 87–115.

Emde, R. N. (1980b). Toward a psychoanalytic theory of affect: Part I, The organizational model and its propositions. In *The course of life: Infancy and early childhood.* Vol. 1, ed. S. I. Greenspan and G. H. Pollock. Publication No. (ADM) 80–786. Washington, D.C.: DHHS, pp. 63–83.

Emde, R. N. (1980c). Toward a psychoanalytic theory of affect: Part II, Emerging models of emotional development in infancy. In *The course of life: Infancy and early childhood.* Vol. 1, ed. S. I. Greenspan and G. H. Pollock. Publication No. (ADM) 80–786. Washington, D.C.: DHHS, pp. 85–112.

Emde, R. N. (1981). Changing models of infancy and the nature of early development: Remodeling the foundations. *J. Amer. Psychoanal. Assn.,* 29:179–219.

Emde, R. N. (1983). The prerepresentational self and its affective core. *Psychoanal. Study Child,* 38:165–192.

Emde, R. N. (1984). The affective self: Continuities and transformations from infancy. In *Frontiers of infant psychiatry.* Vol. 2, ed. J. D. Call, E. Galenson, and R. L. Tyson, New York: Basic Books, pp. 38–54.

Emde, R. N. (1985). From adolescence to midlife: Remodeling the structure of adult development. *J. Amer. Psychoanal. Assn.,* 33 (Suppl.):59–112.

Emde, R. N. (1988a). Development terminable and interminable: Part I, Innate and motivational factors from infancy. *Int. J. Psychoanal.,* 69:23–42.

Emde, R. N. (1988b). Development terminable and interminable: Part II, Recent psychoanalytic theory and therapeutic considerations. *Int. J. Psychoanal.,* 69:283–296.

Emde, R. N.; Gaensbauer, T.; and Harmon, R. J. (1976). *Emotional expression in infancy: A biobehavioral study.* Psychological Issues, Monograph 37. New York: Int. Univ. Press.

Emde, R. N., and Harmon, R. J. (1972). Endogenous and exogenous smiling systems in early infants. *J. Amer. Acad. Child Psychiat.,* 11:177–200.

Emde, R. N., and Robinson, J. (1979). The first two months: Recent research in developmental psychobiology and the changing view of the newborn. In *Basic handbook of child psychiatry.* Vol. 1, ed. J. D. Call, J. D. Noshpitz, R. L. Cohen, and I. N. Berlin. New York: Basic Books, pp. 72–105.

Emde, R. N., and Sorce, J. F. (1983). The rewards of infancy: Emotional availability and maternal referencing. In *Frontiers of infant psychiatry,* ed. J. D. Call, E. Galenson, and R. L. Tyson. New York: Basic Books, pp. 17–30.

English, H. B., and English, A. C. (1958). *A comprehensive dictionary of psychological and psychoanalytical terms.* New York: David McKay.

Erikson, E. H. (1946). Ego development and historical change. *Psychoanal. Study Child,* 2:359–396.

Erikson, E. H. (1950). *Childhood and society.* New York: Norton.

Erikson, E. H. (1956). The concept of ego identity. *J. Amer. Psychoanal. Assn.,* 4:56–121.

Erikson, E. H. (1959). *Identity and the life cycle: Selected papers.* Psychological Issues, Monograph 1. New York: Int. Univ. Press.

Erikson, E. H. (1968). *Identity: Youth and crisis.* New York: Norton.

Esman, A. H. (1983). The "stimulus barrier": A review and reconsideration. *Psychoanal. Study Child,* 38:193–208.

Eysenck, H. J.; Arnold, W. J.; and Meili, R., eds. (1972). *Encyclopedia of psychology.* Bungay, Suffolk: Richard Clay, The Chaucer Press.

Fairbairn, W. R. D. (1954). Observations on the nature of hysterical states. *Brit. J. Med. Psychol.,* 29:112–127.

Fairbairn, W. R. D. (1963). Synopsis of an object-relations theory of the personality. *Int. J. Psychoanal.,* 44:224–225.

Fast, I. (1978). Developments in gender identity: The original matrix. *Int. Rev. Psychoanal.,* 5:265–274.

Fast, I. (1979). Developments in gender identity: Gender differentiation in girls. *Int. Rev. Psychoanal.,* 6:441–453.

Fast, I. (1985). *Event theory.* Hillsdale, N.J.: Erlbaum.

Fenichel, O. (1941). The ego and the affects. In *The collected papers of Otto Fenichel.* 2nd ser. New York: Norton, 1954, pp. 215–227.

Fenichel, O. (1945). *The psychoanalytic theory of neurosis.* New York: Norton.

Ferenczi, S. (1912). Symbolism. In *Sex in psychoanalysis.* New York: Basic Books, 1950, pp. 253–281.

Ferenczi, S. (1913). Stages in the development of the sense of reality. In *Sex in psychoanalysis.* New York: Basic Books, 1950, pp. 213–239.

Ferenczi, S. (1924). *Thalassa: A theory of genitality.* Albany: Psychoanalytic Quarterly, 1938.

Ferenczi, S. (1925). Psycho-analysis of sexual habits. In *Further contributions to the theory and technique of psycho-analysis.* New York: Basic Books, 1952, pp. 259–297.

Ferenczi, S. (1930). Notes and fragments, II. In *Final contributions to the problems and methods of psycho-analysis.* New York: Basic Books, 1952, pp. 219–231.

Flavell, J. H. (1977). *Cognitive development*. Englewood Cliffs, N.J.: Prentice-Hall.

Fogel, G. I. (1989). The authentic function of psychoanalytic theory: An overview of the contributions of Hans Loewald. *Psychoanal. Q.*, 58:419–451.

Fraiberg, S. H. (1955). Some considerations in the introduction to therapy in puberty. *Psychoanal. Study Child*, 10:264–286.

Fraiberg, S. (1968). Parallel and divergent patterns in blind and sighted infants. *Psychoanal. Study Child*, 23:264–300.

Fraiberg, S. (1969). Object constancy and mental representation. *Psychoanal. Study Child*, 24:9–47.

Fraiberg, S. (1972). Some characteristics of genital arousal and discharge in latency girls. *Psychoanal. Study Child*, 27:439–475.

Fraiberg, S. (1974). Blind infants and their mothers: An examination of the sign system. In *The effect of the infant on its caregiver*, ed. J. M. Lewis and L. A. Rosenblum. New York: Wiley, pp. 215–232.

Fraiberg, S. (1982). Pathological defenses in infancy. *Psychoanal. Q.*, 51:612–635.

Francis, J., and Marcus, I. (1975). Masturbation: A developmental view. In *Masturbation from infancy to senescence*, ed. J. Francis and I. Marcus. New York: Int. Univ. Press, pp. 9–51.

Freedman, D. G. (1965). Hereditary control of early social behavior. In *Determinants of infant behavior*. Vol. 3, ed. B. M. Foss. New York: Wiley, pp. 149–159.

Freud, A. (1922). Beating fantasies and daydreams. In *The writings of Anna Freud*. Vol. 1. New York: Int. Univ. Press, 1974, pp. 137–157.

Freud, A. (1936). *The ego and the mechanisms of defense*. Vol. 2 of *The writings of Anna Freud*. Rev. ed. New York: Int. Univ. Press, 1966.

Freud, A. (1941–1945). Reports on the Hampstead Nurseries. In *The writings of Anna Freud*. Vol. 3. New York: Int. Univ. Press, 1973, pp. 3–540.

Freud, A. (1949). Aggression in relation to emotional development: Normal and pathological. In *The writings of Anna Freud*. Vol. 4. New York: Int. Univ. Press, 1968, pp. 489–497.

Freud, A. (1951). Observation on child development. In *The writings of Anna Freud*. Vol. 4. New York: Int. Univ. Press, 1968, pp. 143–162.

Freud, A. (1952). The mutual influences in the development of ego and id. In *The writings of Anna Freud*. Vol. 4. New York: Int. Univ. Press, 1968, pp. 230–244.

Freud, A. (1955). The concept of the rejecting mother. In *The writings of Anna Freud*. Vol. 4. New York: Int. Univ. Press, 1968, pp. 586–602.

Freud, A. (1958). Adolescence. In *The writings of Anna Freud*. Vol. 4. New York: Int. Univ. Press, 1968, pp. 136–166.

Freud, A. (1960). Discussion of Dr. John Bowlby's paper (Grief and mourning in infancy and early childhood). In *The writings of Anna Freud*. Vol. 5. New York: Int. Univ. Press, 1969, pp. 167–186.

Freud, A. (1962). Assessment of childhood disturbances. *Psychoanal. Study Child,* 17:149–158.

Freud, A. (1963). The concept of developmental lines. In *The writings of Anna Freud.* Vol. 6. New York: Int. Univ. Press, 1965, pp. 62–87.

Freud, A. (1965). *Normality and pathology in childhood: Assessments of development.* Vol. 6 of *The writings of Anna Freud.* New York: Int. Univ. Press, 1965.

Freud, A. (1967). Comments on psychic trauma. In *The writings of Anna Freud.* Vol. 5. New York: Int. Univ. Press, 1969, pp. 221–241.

Freud, A. (1968). Panel discussion with J. Arlow (Mod.), J. Lampl-de Groot, and D. Beres. *Int. J. Psychoanal.,* 49:506–512.

Freud, A. (1970a). The infantile neurosis. In *The writings of Anna Freud.* Vol. 7. New York: Int. Univ. Press, 1971, pp. 189–203.

Freud, A. (1970b). Child analysis as a subspecialty of psychoanalysis. In *The writings of Anna Freud.* Vol. 7. New York: Int. Univ. Press, 1971, pp. 204–219.

Freud, A. (1976). Changes in psychoanalytic practice and experience. In *The writings of Anna Freud.* Vol. 8. New York: Int. Univ. Press, 1981, pp. 176–185.

Freud, A. (1979). Foreword. *Psychoanal. Study Child,* 34:3–4.

Freud, A. (1983). Problems of pathogenesis: Introduction to the discussion. *Psychoanal. Study Child,* 38:383–388.

Freud, S. (1893). On the psychical mechanism of hysterical phenomena. In *S.E.,* 3:25–39.

Freud, S. (1894). The neuropsychoses of defense. In *S.E.,* 3:43–61.

Freud, S. (1895a). On the grounds for detaching a particular syndrome from neurasthenia under the description "anxiety neurosis." In *S.E.,* 3:87–117.

Freud, S. (1895b). Project for a scientific psychology. In *S.E.,* 1:295–397.

Freud, S. (1896). Draft K. The neuroses of defense. In *S.E.,* 1:220–232.

Freud, S. (1900). *The interpretation of dreams.* Vols. 4 and 5 of *S.E.*

Freud, S. (1905a). Fragment of an analysis of a case of hysteria. In *S.E.,* 7:31–122.

Freud, S. (1905b). Three essays on the theory of sexuality. In *S.E.,* 7:125–243.

Freud, S. (1908). Character and anal erotism. In *S.E.,* 9:169–175.

Freud, S. (1909a). Analysis of a phobia in a five-year-old boy. In *S.E.,* 10:5–149.

Freud, S. (1909b). Family romances. In *S.E.,* 9:237–241.

Freud, S. (1911). Two principles of mental functioning. In *S.E.,* 12:213–226.

Freud, S. (1912). On the universal tendency to debasement in the sphere of love. In *S.E.,* 11:179–190.

Freud, S. (1913). Totem and taboo. In *S.E.,* 13:1–161.

Freud, S. (1914). On narcissism: An introduction. In *S.E.,* 14:67–102.

Freud, S. (1915a). Instincts and their vicissitudes. In *S.E.,* 14:111–140.

Freud, S. (1915b). Repression. In *S.E.,* 14:141–158.

Freud, S. (1915c). The unconscious. In *S.E.,* 14:161–215.

Freud, S. (1916–1917). *Introductory lectures on psycho-analysis.* Vols. 15 and 16 of *S.E.*

Freud, S. (1917). Mourning and melancholia. In *S.E.,* 14:237–259.

Freud, S. (1918). From the history of an infantile neurosis. In *S.E.*, 17:3–122.

Freud, S. (1920). Beyond the pleasure principle. In *S.E.*, 18:7–64.

Freud, S. (1921). Group psychology and the analysis of the ego. In *S.E.*, 18:67–143.

Freud, S. (1923a). The ego and the id. In *S.E.*, 19:3–66.

Freud, S. (1923b). The infantile genital organization. In *S.E.*, 19:141–145.

Freud, S. (1924a). The dissolution of the Oedipus complex. In *S.E.*, 19:172–179.

Freud, S. (1924b). The economic problem of masochism. In *S.E.*, 19:157–170.

Freud, S. (1924c). The loss of reality in neurosis and psychosis. In *S.E.*, 19:183–187.

Freud, S. (1925a). An autobiographical study. In *S.E.*, 20:3–77.

Freud, S. (1925b). Some psychical consequences of the anatomical distinction between the sexes. In *S.E.*, 19:243–258.

Freud, S. (1926). Inhibitions, symptoms and anxiety. In *S.E.*, 20:77–175.

Freud, S. (1927). Dostoevsky and parricide. In *S.E.*, 21:175–196.

Freud, S. (1930). Civilization and its discontents. In *S.E.*, 21:59–145.

Freud, S. (1931). Female sexuality. In *S.E.*, 21:223–246.

Freud, S. (1933). New introductory lectures on psycho-analysis. In *S.E.*, 22:3–184.

Freud, S. (1939). Moses and monotheism. In *S.E.*, 23:3–137.

Freud, S. (1940). An outline of psycho-analysis. In *S.E.*, 23:141–207.

Friedman, L. (1980). The barren prospect of a representational world. *Psychoanal. Q.*, 49:215–233.

Friedman, R. C. (1988). *Male homosexuality: A contemporary psychoanalytic perspective*. New Haven: Yale Univ. Press.

Furer, M. (1967). Some developmental aspects of the superego. *Int. J. Psychoanal.*, 48:277–280.

Furer, M. (1972). The history of the superego concept in psychoanalysis: A review of the literature. In *Moral values and the superego concept in psychoanalysis*, ed. S. C. Post. New York: Int. Univ. Press, pp. 11–62.

Furman, E. (1974). *A child's parent dies: Studies in childhood bereavement*. New Haven: Yale Univ. Press.

Furman, E. (1985). On fusion, integration, and feeling good. *Psychoanal. Study Child*, 40:81–110.

Furman, R. A. (1975). Excerpts from the analysis of a prepuberty boy. In *Masturbation*, ed. I. M. Marcus and J. J. Francis. New York: Int. Univ. Press, pp. 223–229.

Gaensbauer, T. J. (1982). The differentiation of discrete affects: A case report. *Psychoanal. Study Child*, 37:29–66.

Galenson, E. (1964). Panel: Prepuberty and child analysis. *J. Amer. Psychoanal. Assn.*, 12:600–609.

Galenson, E. (1984). Influences on the development of the symbolic function.

In *Frontiers of infant psychiatry.* Vol. 2, ed. J. D. Call, E. Galenson, and R. L. Tyson. New York: Basic Books, pp. 30–37.

Galenson, E. (1986). Some thoughts about infant psychopathology and aggressive development. *Int. Rev. Psychoanal.,* 13:349–354.

Galenson, E. (1988). The precursors of masochism: Protomasochism. In *Masochism: Current psychoanalytic perspectives,* ed. R. A. Glick and D. I. Meyers. Hillsdale, N.J.: Analytic Press, pp. 189–204.

Galenson, E., and Roiphe, H. (1971). The impact of early sexual discovery on mood, defensive organization, and symbolization. *Psychoanal. Study Child,* 6:195–216.

Galenson, E., and Roiphe, H. (1974). The emergence of genital awareness during the second year of life. In *Sex differences in behavior,* ed. R. C. Friedman. New York: Wiley, pp. 223–231.

Galenson, E., and Roiphe, H. (1976). Some suggested revisions concerning early female development. *J. Amer. Psychoanal. Assn.,* 24 (Suppl.):29–57.

Galenson, E., and Roiphe, H. (1980). The preoedipal development of the boy. *J. Amer. Psychoanal. Assn.,* 28:805–828.

Geleerd, E. R. (1957). Some aspects of psychoanalytic technique in adolescence. *Psychoanal. Study Child,* 12:263–283.

Gilligan, C. (1982). *In a different voice: Psychological theory and women's development.* Cambridge: Harvard Univ. Press.

Glenn, J. (1984). A note on loss, pain and masochism in children. *J. Amer. Psychoanal. Assn.,* 32:63–73.

Glover, E. (1945). Examination of the Klein system of child psychology. *Psychoanal. Study Child,* 1:75–118.

Golding, W. (1955). *Lord of the flies.* New York: Capricorn Press.

Goldings, H. I. (1974). Jump-rope rhymes and the rhythm of latency development in girls. *Psychoanal. Study Child,* 29:431–450.

Gould, R. L. (1972). The phases of adult life: A study in developmental psychology. *Amer. J. Psychiat.,* 129:521–531.

Green, A. (1975). The analyst, symbolization and absence in the analytic setting. *Int. J. Psychoanal.,* 56:1–22.

Green, R. (1980). Patterns of sexual identity in childhood: Relationship to subsequent sexual partner preference. In *Homosexual behavior: A modern reappraisal,* ed. J. Marmor. New York: Basic Books, pp. 255–266.

Greenacre, P. (1941). The predisposition to anxiety. In *Trauma, growth and personality.* New York: Norton, 1952, pp. 27–82.

Greenacre, P. (1948). Anatomical structure and superego development. In *Trauma, growth and personality.* New York: Norton, 1952, pp. 149–164.

Greenacre, P. (1950). Special problems of early female sexual development. *Psychoanal. Study Child,* 5:122–138.

Greenacre, P. (1952a). Pregenital patterning. *Int. J. Psychoanal.,* 33:410–415.

Greenacre, P. (1952b). *Trauma, growth, and personality.* New York: Norton.

Greenacre, P. (1953a). Certain relationships between fetishism and the faulty development of the body image. In *Emotional growth*. Vol. 1. New York: Int. Univ. Press, 1971, pp. 9–30.

Greenacre, P. (1953b). Penis awe and its relation to penis envy. In *Emotional growth*. Vol. 1. New York: Int. Univ. Press, 1971, pp. 31–49.

Greenacre, P. (1958). Early physical determinants in the development of the sense of identity. In *Emotional growth*. Vol. 1. New York: Int. Univ. Press, 1971, pp. 113–127.

Greenacre, P. (1960). Considerations regarding the parent-infant relationship. In *Emotional growth*. Vol. 1. New York: Int. Univ. Press, 1971, pp. 199–224.

Greenacre, P. (1967). The influence of infantile traumas on genetic patterns. In *Emotional growth*. Vol. 1. New York: Int. Univ. Press, 1971, pp. 260–299.

Greenberg, J. R., and Mitchell, S. R. (1983). *Object relations in psychoanalytic theory*. Cambridge: Harvard Univ. Press.

Greenberg, M., and Morris, N. (1974). Engrossment: The newborn's impact upon the father. *Amer. J. Orthopsychiat.*, 44:520–531.

Greenson, R. R. (1954). The struggle against identification. *J. Amer. Psychoanal. Assn.*, 2:200–217.

Greenson, R. R. (1968). Dis-identifying from mother: Its special importance for the boy. *Int. J. Psychoanal.*, 49:370–374.

Greenspan, S. I. (1979). *Intelligence and adaptation: An integration of psychoanalytic and Piagetian developmental psychology*. Psychological Issues, Monograph 47/48. New York: Int. Univ. Press.

Greenspan, S. I. (1981). *Psychopathology and adaptation in infancy and early childhood: Principles of clinical diagnosis and preventive intervention*. New York: Int. Univ. Press.

Greenspan, S. I. (1988). The development of the ego: Insights from clinical work with infants and young children. *J. Amer. Psychoanal. Assn.*, 36 (Suppl.): 3–55.

Grolnick, S. A., and Barkin, L., eds. (1978). *Between reality and fantasy: Transitional objects and phenomena*. New York: Aronson.

Gross, G. E., and Rubin, I. A. (1972). Sublimation: The study of an instinctual vicissitude. *Psychoanal. Study Child*, 27:334–359.

Grosskurth, P. (1986). *Melanie Klein*. New York: Knopf.

Grossman, W. I., and Stewart, W. (1976). Penis envy: From childhood wish to the developmental metaphor. *J. Amer. Psychoanal. Assn.*, 24 (Suppl.):193–212.

Gunsberg, L. (1982). A selected critical review of psychological investigations of the father-infant relationship. In *Father and child*, ed. S. H. Cath, A. R. Gurwitt, and J. M. Ross. Boston: Little, Brown, pp. 65–82.

Guntrip, H. (1961). *Personality structure and human interaction*. New York: Int. Univ. Press.

Guntrip, H. (1969). *Schizoid phenomena, object relations and the self*. New York: Int. Univ. Press.

Guntrip, H. (1975). My experience of analysis with Fairbairn and Winnicott. *Int. Rev. Psychoanal.*, 2:145–156.

Guntrip, H. (1978). Psycho-analysis and some scientific and philosophical critics. *Brit. J. Med. Psychol.*, 51:207–224.

Haith, M. M., Bergman, T., and Moore, M. J. (1977). Eye contact and face scanning in early infancy. *Science*, 198:853–855.

Hall, G. S. (1904). *Adolescence: Its psychology and its relations to physiology, anthropology, sociology, sex, crime, religion and education.* New York: Appleton, 1916.

Hanly, C. (1978). Instincts and hostile affects. *Int. J. Psychoanal.*, 59:149–156.

Harley, M. (1961). Genitality and structural development of adolescence. *J. Amer. Psychoanal. Assn.*, 9:434–460.

Harley, M., and Weil, A. P. (1979). Introduction. In *Infantile psychosis and early contributions.* Vol. 1 of *The selected papers of Margaret S. Mahler.* New York: Aronson, pp. ix–xx.

Harlow, H. F. (1960a). Affectional behavior in the infant monkey. In *Central nervous system and behavior,* ed. M. A. B. Brazier. New York: Josiah Macy, Jr., Foundation, pp. 3–21.

Harlow, H. F. (1960b). Primary affectional patterns in primates. *Amer. J. Orthopsychiat.*, 30:676–684.

Harlow, H. F., and Zimmerman, R. R. (1959). Affectional responses in the infant monkey. *Science*, 130:421–432.

Harmon, R. J., and Emde, R. N. (1971). Spontaneous REM behaviors in a microcephalic infant: A clinical anatomical study. *Perceptual Motor Skills*, 34:827–833.

Harmon, R. M.; Wagonfeld, S.; and Emde, R. N. (1982). Anaclitic depression: A follow-up from infancy to puberty. *Psychoanal. Study Child*, 37:67–94.

Harries, M. (1952). Sublimation in a group of four-year-old boys. *Psychoanal. Study Child*, 7:230–240.

Hart, M., and Sarnoff, C. A. (1971). The impact of the menarche. *J. Amer. Acad. Child Psychiat.*, 10:257–271.

Hartmann, H. (1939). *Ego psychology and the problem of adaptation.* New York: Int. Univ. Press, 1958.

Hartmann, H. (1950). Comments on the psychoanalytic theory of the ego. In *Essays on ego psychology.* New York: Int. Univ. Press, 1964, pp. 113–141.

Hartmann, H. (1952). The mutual influences in the development of ego and id. In *Essays on ego psychology.* New York: Int. Univ. Press, 1964, pp. 155–182.

Hartmann, H. (1953). Contribution to the metapsychology of schizophrenia. In *Essays on ego psychology.* New York: Int. Univ. Press, 1964, pp. 182–206.

Hartmann, H. (1955). Notes on the theory of sublimation. In *Essays on ego psychology.* New York: Int. Univ. Press, 1964, pp. 215–240.

Hartmann, H. (1956). Notes on the reality principle. In *Essays on ego psychology.* New York: Int. Univ. Press, 1964, pp. 241–267.

Hartmann, H., and Kris, E. (1945). The genetic approach in psychoanalysis. *Psychoanal. Study Child*, 1:11–30.

Hartmann, H.; Kris, E.; and Loewenstein, R. (1946). Comments on the formation of psychic structure. *Psychoanal. Study Child,* 2:11–38.

Hartmann, H., and Loewenstein, R. (1962). Notes on the superego. *Psychoanal. Study Child,* 17:42–81.

Hayman, A. (1969). What do we mean by "id"? *J. Amer. Psychoanal. Assn.,* 17:353–380.

Hayman, A. (1989). What do we mean by "phantasy"? *Int. J. Psychoanal.,* 70:105–114.

Heimann, P. (1962). Notes on the anal stage. *Int. J. Psychoanal.,* 43:406–414.

Heimann, P. (1966). Comments on Dr. Kernberg's paper (Structural derivatives of object relationships). *Int. J. Psychoanal.,* 47:254–260.

Herzog, E., and Sudia, C. (1973). Children in fatherless families. In *Review of child development research.* Vol. 3, ed. B. M. Caldwell and H. N. Ricciuti. Chicago: Univ. of Chicago Press, pp. 141–232.

Herzog, J. M. (1980). Sleep disturbance and father hunger in 18- to 28-month-old boys: The Erlkonig syndrome. *Psychoanal. Study Child,* 35:219–233.

Herzog, J. M. (1982). On father hunger: The father's role in the modulation of aggressive drive and fantasy. In *Father and child,* ed. S. W. Cath, A. R. Gurwitt, and J. M. Ross. Boston: Little, Brown, pp. 163–174.

Herzog, J. M. (1984). Fathers and young children: Fathering daughters and fathering sons. In *Frontiers of infant psychiatry.* Vol. 2, ed. J. D. Call, E. Galenson, and R. L. Tyson. New York: Basic Books, pp. 335–342.

Hoffer, W. (1949). Mouth, hand and ego integration. *Psychoanal. Study Child,* 3/4:49–56.

Hoffer, W. (1950a). Oral aggressiveness and ego development. *Int. J. Psychoanal.,* 31:156–160.

Hoffer, W. (1950b). The development of the body ego. *Psychoanal. Study Child,* 5:18–24.

Hoffer, W. (1952). The mutual influences in the development of ego and id: Earliest stages. *Psychoanal. Study Child,* 7:31–41.

Holder, A. (1982). Preoedipal contributions to the formation of the superego. *Psychoanal. Study Child,* 37:245–272.

Holt, R. R. (1967). *Motives and thought: Psychoanalytic essays in honor of David Rapaport.* Psychological Issues, Monograph 18/19. New York: Int. Univ. Press.

Horney, K. (1924). On the genesis of the castration complex in women. In *Feminine psychology,* ed. H. Kelman. New York: Norton, 1967, pp. 37–53.

Horney, K. (1926). The flight from womanhood: The masculinity complex in women as viewed by men and women. *Int. J. Psychoanal.,* 7:324–339.

Horney, K. (1933). The denial of the vagina. In *Feminine psychology,* ed. H. Kelman. New York: Norton, 1967, pp. 147–161.

Horney, K. (1967). *Feminine psychology,* ed. H. Kelman. New York: Norton.

Hughes, J. M. (1989). *Reshaping the psychoanalytic domain: The work of Melanie*

*Klein, W. R. D. Fairbairn and D. W. Winnicott.* Berkeley: Univ. of California Press.

Inhelder, B. (1970). *Operational thought and symbolic imagery in cognitive development in children.* Chicago: Univ. of Chicago Press.

Inhelder, B., and Piaget, J. (1958). *The growth of logical thinking: From childhood to adolescence.* New York: Basic Books.

Isay, R. A. (1989). *Being homosexual: Gay men and their development.* New York: Farrar, Straus, and Giroux.

Izard, C. E. (1971). *The face of emotion.* New York: Appleton-Century-Crofts.

Izard, C. E. (1972). *Patterns of emotions.* New York: Academic Press.

Jacobson, E. (1937). Ways of female superego formation and the female castration conflict. *Psychoanal. Q.,* 45:525–538.

Jacobson, E. (1946). The effect of disappointment on ego and superego formation in normal and depressive development. *Psychoanal. Rev.,* 33:129–147.

Jacobson, E. (1953). The affects and their pleasure-unpleasure qualities in relation to the psychic discharge processes. In *Drives, affects, behavior,* ed. R. Loewenstein. New York: Int. Univ. Press, pp. 38–66.

Jacobson, E. (1954). The self and the object world: Vicissitudes of their infantile cathexis and their influences on ideational and affective development. *Psychoanal. Study Child,* 9:75–127.

Jacobson, E. (1961). Adolescent moods and the remodeling of psychic structures in adolescence. *Psychoanal. Study Child,* 16:164–183.

Jacobson, E. (1964). *The self and the object world.* New York: Int. Univ. Press.

Jacobson, J. G. (1983a). The structural theory and the representational world. *Psychoanal. Q.,* 52:514–542.

Jacobson, J. G. (1983b). The structural theory and the representational world: Developmental and biological considerations. *Psychoanal. Q.,* 52:543–563.

Jacobson, S. W. (1979). Matching behavior in the young infant. *Child Develop.,* 50:425–430.

James, M. (1960). Premature ego development. *Int. J. Psychoanal.,* 41:288–294.

James, W. (1890). *The principles of psychology.* New York: Holt, Rinehart and Winston.

Jaques, E. (1981). The midlife crisis. In *Adulthood and the aging process.* Vol. 3 of *The course of life,* ed. S. I. Greenspan and G. H. Pollock. Publication No. (ADM) 81–1000. Washington, D.C.: DHHS, pp. 1–23.

Joffe, W. G. (1969). A critical review of the status of the envy concept. *Int. J. Psychoanal.,* 50:533–545.

Joffe, W. G., and Sandler, J. (1965). Notes on pain, depression and individuation. *Psychoanal. Study Child,* 20:394–424.

Joffe, W. G., and Sandler, J. (1967). Some conceptual problems involved in the consideration of disorders of narcissism. *J. Child Psychother.,* 2:56–66.

Johnson, A. M., and Szurek, S. A. (1952). The genesis of antisocial acting out in children and adults. *Psychoanal. Q.,* 21:323–343.

Jones, E. (1916). The theory of symbolism. In *Papers on psycho-analysis*. Boston: Beacon Press, 1961, pp. 87–144.

Jones, E. (1922). Some problems of adolescence. In *Papers on psycho-analysis*. Boston: Beacon Press, 1961, pp. 389–406.

Jones, E. (1926). The origin and structure of the super-ego. In *Papers on psycho-analysis*. Boston: Beacon Press, 1961, pp. 438–457.

Jones, E. (1927). The early development of female sexuality. In *Papers on psycho-analysis*. Boston: Beacon Press, 1961, pp. 438–457.

Jones, E. (1929). Fear, guilt and hate. *Int. J. Psychoanal.*, 10:383–397.

Jones, E. (1933). The phallic phase. In *Papers on psycho-analysis*. Boston: Beacon Press, 1961, pp. 452–484.

Jones, E. (1935). Early female sexuality. *Int. J. Psychoanal.*, 16:263–273.

Jones, E. (1947). The genesis of the super-ego. In *Papers on psycho-analysis*. Boston: Beacon Press, 1961, pp. 145–152.

Jones, E. (1953). *The life and work of Sigmund Freud*. Vol. 1. New York: Basic Books.

Kagan, J. (1978). *The growth of the child: Reflections on human development*. New York: Norton.

Kaplan, E. B. (1965). Reflections regarding psychomotor activities during the latency period. *Psychoanal. Study Child*, 20:220–238.

Katan, A. (1951). The role of "displacement" in agoraphobia. *Int. J. Psychoanal.*, 32:41–50.

Katan, A. (1961). Some thoughts about the role of verbalization in childhood. *Psychoanal. Study Child*, 16:184–188.

Katan, A. (1972). The infant's first reaction to strangers: Distress or anxiety? *Int. J. Psychoanal.*, 53:501–503.

Keniston, K. (1971). Youth as a stage of life. In *Adolescent psychiatry*. Vol. 1, ed. S. D. Feinstein, P. L. Giovacchini, and A. A. Miller. New York: Aronson, pp. 161–175.

Kernberg, O. F. (1969). A contribution to the ego-psychological critique of the Kleinian school. *Int. J. Psychoanal.*, 50:317–333.

Kernberg, O. F. (1974a). Barriers to falling and remaining in love. *J. Amer. Psychoanal. Assn.*, 22:486–511.

Kernberg, O. F. (1974b). Mature love: Prerequisites and characteristics. *J. Amer. Psychoanal. Assn.*, 22:743–768.

Kernberg, O. F. (1975). *Borderline conditions and pathological narcissism*. New York: Aronson.

Kernberg, O. F. (1976). *Object relations theory and clinical psychoanalysis*. New York: Aronson.

Kernberg, O. F. (1977). Boundaries and structures in love relations. *J. Amer. Psychoanal. Assn.*, 25:81–114.

Kernberg, O. F. (1980a). *Internal world and external reality: Object relations theory applied*. New York: Aronson.

Kernberg, O. F. (1980b). Adolescent sexuality in the light of group processes. *Psychoanal. Q.*, 49:27–47.

Kernberg, O. F. (1980c). Love, the couple, and the group; a psychoanalytic frame. *Psychoanal. Q.*, 49:78–108.

Kernberg, O. F. (1982). Self, ego, affects and drives. *J. Amer. Psychoanal. Assn.*, 30:893–917.

Kernberg, O. F. (1984). *Severe personality disorders: Psychotherapeutic strategies.* New Haven: Yale Univ. Press.

Kernberg, O. F. (1987). An ego psychology-object relations theory approach to the transference. *Psychoanal. Q.*, 51:197–221.

Kestenberg, J. S. (1956a). On the development of maternal feelings in early childhood. *Psychoanal. Study Child*, 11:257–291.

Kestenberg, J. S. (1956b). Vicissitudes of female sexuality. *J. Amer. Psychoanal. Assn.*, 4:453–476.

Kestenberg, J. S. (1961). Menarche. In *Adolescence: Psychoanalytic approach to problems and therapy*, ed. S. Lorand and H. Schneer. New York: Harper, pp. 19–50.

Kestenberg, J. S. (1968). Outside and inside, male and female. *J. Amer. Psychoanal. Assn.*, 16:457–520.

Kestenberg, J. S. (1975). *Children and parents: Psychoanalytic studies in development.* New York: Aronson.

Kestenberg, J. S. (1976). Regression and reintegration in pregnancy. *J. Amer. Psychoanal. Assn.*, 14:213–250.

Khan, M. (1963). The concept of cumulative trauma. *Psychoanal. Study Child*, 18:286–306.

Klaus, M. H., and Kennell, J. H. (1976). *Maternal-infant bonding.* St. Louis: C. V. Mosby.

Kleeman, J. A. (1965). A boy discovers his penis. *Psychoanal. Study Child*, 20:239–266.

Kleeman, J. A. (1966). Genital self-discovery during a boy's second year: A follow-up. *Psychoanal. Study Child*, 21:358–392.

Kleeman, J. A. (1971). The establishment of core gender identity in normal girls. *Archs. Sexual Behavior*, 1:117–129.

Kleeman, J. A. (1976). Freud's views on early female sexuality in the light of direct child observation. *J. Amer. Psychoanal. Assn.*, 24 (Suppl.):3–27.

Klein, G. S. (1976a). Freud's two theories of sexuality. In *Psychology versus metapsychology: Psychoanalytic essays in memory of George S. Klein,* ed. M. M. Gill and P. S. Holzman. Psychological Issues, Monograph 36. New York: Int. Univ. Press, pp. 14–70.

Klein, G. S. (1976b). *Psychoanalytic theory: An exploration of essentials.* New York: Int. Univ. Press.

Klein, M. (1928). Early stages of the Oedipus conflict. In *The writings of Melanie Klein.* Vol. 1. London: Hogarth, 1975, pp. 186–198.

Klein, M. (1929). Infantile anxiety situations reflected in a work of art and in the creative impulse. In *The writings of Melanie Klein*. Vol. 1. London: Hogarth, 1975, pp. 210–218.

Klein, M. (1930). The importance of symbol-formation in the development of the ego. In *The writings of Melanie Klein*. Vol. 1. London: Hogarth, 1975, pp. 219–232.

Klein, M. (1933). The early development of conscience in the child. In *The writings of Melanie Klein*. Vol. 1. London: Hogarth, 1975, pp. 248–257.

Klein, M. (1935). A contribution to the psychogenesis of manic-depressive states. In *The writings of Melanie Klein*. Vol. 1. London: Hogarth, 1975, pp. 262–289.

Klein, M. (1940). Mourning and its relation to manic-depressive states. In *The writings of Melanie Klein*. Vol. 1. London: Hogarth, 1975, pp. 344–369.

Klein, M. (1946). Notes on some schizoid mechanisms. In *The writings of Melanie Klein*. Vol. 1. London: Hogarth, 1975, pp. 1–24.

Klein, M. (1948). A contribution to the theory of anxiety and guilt. In *The writings of Melanie Klein*. Vol. 3. London: Hogarth, 1975, pp. 25–42.

Klein, M. (1952a). On observing the behaviour of young infants. In *The writings of Melanie Klein*. Vol. 3. London: Hogarth, 1975, pp. 94–121.

Klein, M. (1952b). Some theoretical conclusions regarding the emotional life of the infant. In *The writings of Melanie Klein*. Vol. 3. London: Hogarth, 1975, pp. 61–93.

Klein, M. (1957). Envy and gratitude. In *The writings of Melanie Klein*. Vol. 3. London: Hogarth, 1975, pp. 176–235.

Klein, M. (1958). On the development of mental functioning. In *The writings of Melanie Klein*. Vol. 3. London: Hogarth, 1975, pp. 236–246.

Klein, M.; Heimann, P.; Isaacs, S.; and Riviere, J. (1952). *Developments in psychoanalysis*. London: Hogarth.

Klein, Milton (1980). On Mahler's autistic and symbiotic phases: An exposition and evolution. *Psychoanal. Contemp. Thought*, 4:69–105.

Klein, Milton, and Tribich, D. (1981). Kernberg's object-relations theory: A critical evaluation. *Int. J. Psychoanal.*, 62:27–43.

Knapp, P. H. (1981). Core processes in the organization of emotions. *J. Amer. Acad. Psychoanal.*, 9:415–434.

Knapp, P. H. (1987). Some contemporary contributions to the study of emotions. *J. Amer. Psychoanal. Assn.*, 35:205–248.

Kohlberg, L. A. (1963). The development of children's orientations toward a moral order. *Vita Humana*, 6:11–33.

Kohlberg, L. A. (1966). A cognitive-developmental analysis of children's sex role concepts and attitudes. In *The development of sex differences*, ed. E. Maccoby. Stanford: Stanford Univ. Press, pp. 82–175.

Kohlberg, L. A. (1981). *The philosophy of moral development, moral stages, and the ideal of justice: Essays on moral development*. Vol. 1. San Francisco: Harper and Row.

Kohon, G., ed. (1986). *The British school of psychoanalysis: The independent tradition.* New Haven: Yale Univ. Press.

Kohut, H. (1971). *The analysis of the self: A systematic approach to the psychoanalytic treatment of narcissistic personality disorders.* New York: Int. Univ. Press.

Kohut, H. (1977). *Restoration of the self.* New York: Int. Univ. Press.

Kohut, H., and Seitz, P. F. D. (1963). Concepts and theories of psychoanalysis. In *The search for the self.* Vol. 1, ed. P. H. Ornstein. New York: Int. Univ. Press, 1978, pp. 337–374.

Kohut, H., and Wolf, E. S. (1978). The disorders of the self and their treatment: An outline. *Int. J. Psychoanal.*, 59:413–425.

Kramer, P. (1958). Note on one of the preoedipal roots of the superego. *J. Amer. Psychoanal. Assn.*, 6:38–46.

Kramer, S., and Akhtar, S. (1988). The developmental context of internalized preoedipal object relations: Clinical applications of Mahler's theory of symbiosis and separation-individuation. *Psychoanal. Q.*, 57:547–576.

Kris, E. (1952). *Psychoanalytic explorations in art.* New York: Int. Univ. Press.

Kris, E. (1953). The study of variations of early parental attitudes. In *The selected papers of Ernst Kris.* New Haven: Yale Univ. Press, 1975, pp. 114–150.

Kris, E. (1956). The recovery of childhood memories in psychoanalysis. In *The selected papers of Ernst Kris.* New Haven: Yale Univ. Press, 1975, pp. 301–340.

Kubie, L. S. (1966). A reconsideration of thinking, the dream process, and the dream. *Psychoanal. Q.*, 35:191–198.

Lacan, J. (1965). *The language of the self,* trans. A. Wilder. Baltimore: Johns Hopkins Press.

Lamb, M. E., ed. (1981). *The role of the father in child development.* 2nd ed. New York: Wiley.

Lamb, M. E. (1984). Mothers, fathers, and child care in a changing world. In *Frontiers of infant psychiatry.* Vol. 2, ed. J. Call, E. Galenson, and R. L. Tyson. New York: Basic Books, pp. 343–362.

Lampl-de Groot, J. (1927). The evolution of the Oedipus complex in women. In *The psycho-analytic reader,* ed. R. Fliess. New York: Int. Univ. Press, pp. 180–194.

Lampl-de Groot, J. (1962). Ego ideal and superego. *Psychoanal. Study Child,* 17:94–106.

Langer, S. (1942). *Philosophy in a new key.* Cambridge: Harvard Univ. Press.

Langer, S. (1957). *Problems of art.* New York: Scribner.

Laufer, M., and Laufer, M. E. (1984). *Adolescence and developmental breakdown: A psychoanalytic view.* New Haven: Yale Univ. Press.

Lax, R. T. (1977). The role of internalization in the development of certain aspects of female masochism: Ego psychological considerations. *Int. J. Psychoanal.*, 58:289–300.

Lazarus, R. S., Kanner, A. D., and Folkman, S. (1980). Emotions: A cognitive phenomenological analysis. In *Theories of emotion.* Vol. 1 of *Emotion: Theory, research and experience,* ed. R. Plutchik and H. Kellerman. New York: Academic Press, pp. 189–217.

Lecours, A. R. (1975). Myelogenetic correlates of the development of speech and language. In *Foundations of language development: A multidisciplinary approach.* Vol. 1, ed. E. H. Lenneberg and E. Lenneberg. New York: Academic Press, pp. 121–155.

Leonard, M. R. (1966). Fathers and daughters: The significance of "fathering" in the psychosexual development of the girl. *Int. J. Psychoanal.,* 47:325–334.

Lester, E. P. (1983). Separation-individuation and cognition. *J. Amer. Psychoanal. Assn.,* 31:127–156.

Levinson, N. A., and Call, J. D. (1987). New developments in early language acquisition. In *Basic handbook of child psychiatry.* Vol. 5, ed. J. D. Noshpitz et al. New York: Basic Books, pp. 51–61.

Lewin, B. D. (1933). The body as phallus. *Psychoanal. Q.,* 2:24–47.

Lewis, M., and Brooks-Gunn, J. (1979). *Social cognition and the acquisition of self.* New York: Plenum.

Lewis, M., and Rosenblum, L. A., eds. (1974). *The effect of the infant on his caregiver.* New York: Wiley.

Lichtenberg, J. D. (1975). The development of the sense of self. *J. Amer. Psychoanal. Assn.,* 23:453–451.

Lichtenberg, J. D. (1981). Implications for psychoanalytic theory of research on the neonate. *Int. Rev. Psychoanal.,* 8:35–52.

Lichtenberg, J. D. (1987). Infant studies and clinical work with adults. *Psychoanal. Inq.,* 7:311–330.

Lichtenberg, J. D. (1988). A theory of motivational-functional systems as psychic structures. *J. Amer. Psychoanal. Assn.,* 36 (Suppl.):57–72.

Lichtenberg, J. D. (1989). *Psychoanalysis and motivation.* Hillsdale, N.J.: Analytic Press.

Loewald, H. W. (1951). Ego and reality. In *Papers on psychoanalysis.* New Haven: Yale Univ. Press, 1980, pp. 3–20.

Loewald, H. W. (1952). The problem of defense and the neurotic interpretation of reality. In *Papers on psychoanalysis.* New Haven: Yale Univ. Press, 1980, pp. 21–32.

Loewald, H. W. (1960). On the therapeutic action of psychoanalysis. In *Papers on psychoanalysis.* New Haven: Yale Univ. Press, 1980, pp. 221–256.

Loewald, H. W. (1965). Some considerations on repetition and repetition compulsion. In *Papers on psychoanalysis.* New Haven: Yale Univ. Press, 1980, pp. 87–101.

Loewald, H. W. (1971). On motivation and instinct theory. In *Papers on psychoanalysis.* New Haven: Yale Univ. Press, 1980, pp. 102–137.

Loewald, H. W. (1973). The analysis of the self. *Psychoanal. Q.,* 42:441–451.

Loewald, H. W. (1974). Current status of the concept of the infantile neurosis: Discussion. *Psychoanal. Study Child,* 29:183–190.

Loewald, H. W. (1978). Instinct theory, object relations, and psychic structure formation. In *Papers on psychoanalysis*. New Haven: Yale Univ. Press, 1980, pp. 207–218.

Loewald, H. W. (1979). The waning of the Oedipus complex. In *Papers on psychoanalysis*. New Haven: Yale Univ. Press, 1980, pp. 384–404.

Loewald, H. W. (1985). Oedipus complex and development of self. *Psychoanal. Q.*, 54:435–443.

Loewenstein, R. M. (1950). Conflict and autonomous ego development during the phallic phase. *Psychoanal. Study Child*, 5:47–53.

Luria, A. R. (1961). *The role of speech in the regulation of normal and abnormal behaviour*. New York: Pergamon Press.

Lustman, S. L. (1966). Impulse control, structure, and the synthetic function. In *Psychoanalysis: A general psychology*, ed. R. M. Loewenstein, L. M. Newman, M. Schur, and A. J. Solnit. New York: Int. Univ. Press, pp. 190–221.

Maccoby, E. E., and Martin, J. (1983). Socialization in the context of the family: Parent-child interaction. In *Handbook of child psychology, socialization, personality and social development*. Vol. 4, ed. P. H. Mussen and E. M. Hetherington. 4th ed. New York: Wiley, pp. 1–101.

McDevitt, J. B. (1975). Separation-individuation and object constancy. *J. Amer. Psychoanal. Assn.*, 23:713–743.

McDevitt, J. B. (1979). The role of internalization in the development of object relations during the separation-individuation phase. *J. Amer. Psychoanal. Assn.*, 27:327–343.

McDevitt, J. B. (1983). The emergence of hostile aggression and its defensive and adaptive modifications during the separation-individuation process. *J. Amer. Psychoanal. Assn.*, 31:273–300.

McDevitt, J. B., and Mahler, M. S. (1980). Object constancy, individuality, and internalization. In *Infancy and early childhood*. Vol. 1 of *The course of life*, ed. S. I. Greenspan and G. H. Pollock. Publication No. (ADM) 80–786. Washington, D.C.: DHHS, pp. 407–423.

McKhann, G. M.; Coyle, P. K.; and Benjamins, J. A. (1973). Nutrition and brain development. *Assn. Research Nervous Mental Diseases*, 51:10–22.

Mahler, M. S. (1952). On child psychosis and schizophrenia: Autistic and symbiotic infantile psychosis. *Psychoanal. Study Child*, 7:286–305.

Mahler, M. S. (1961). On sadness and grief in infancy and childhood: Loss and restoration of the symbiotic love object. *Psychoanal. Study Child*, 16:332–351.

Mahler, M. S. (1963). Thoughts about development and individuation. *Psychoanal. Study Child*, 18:307–324.

Mahler, M. S. (1971). A study of the separation-individuation process and its possible application to borderline phenomena in the psychoanalytic situation. *Psychoanal. Study Child*, 26:403–424.

Mahler, M. S. (1972a). On the first three subphases of the separation-individuation process. *Int. J. Psychoanal.*, 53:333–338.

Mahler, M. S. (1972b). Rapprochement subphase of the separation-individuation process. *Psychoanal. Q.*, 41:487–506.

Mahler, M. S. (1975a). On human symbiosis and the vicissitudes of individuation. *J. Amer. Psychoanal. Assn.*, 23:740–763.

Mahler, M. S. (1975b). On the current status of the infantile neurosis. *J. Amer. Psychoanal. Assn.*, 23:327–333.

Mahler, M. S. (1981). Aggression in the service of separation-individuation: A case study of a mother-daughter relationship. *Psychoanal. Q.*, 50:625–638.

Mahler, M. S., and Furer, E. (1968). *Infantile psychosis.* Vol. 1 of *On human symbiosis and the vicissitudes of individuation.* New York: Int. Univ. Press.

Mahler, M. S., and Gosliner, B. J. (1955). On symbiotic child psychosis: Genetic, dynamic, and restitutive aspects. *Psychoanal. Study Child,* 10:195–212.

Mahler, M. S., and McDevitt, J. B. (1968). Observations on adaptation and defense in statu nascendi. *Psychoanal. Q.*, 37:1–21.

Mahler, M. S., and McDevitt, J. B. (1980). The separation-individuation process and identity formation. In *Infancy and early childhood.* Vol. 1 of *The course of life,* ed. S. I. Greenspan and G. H. Pollock. Publication No. (ADM) 80–786. Washington, D.C.: DHHS, pp. 395–406.

Mahler, M. S.; Pine, F.; and Bergman, A. (1975). *The psychological birth of the human infant.* New York: Basic Books.

Mandler, G. (1980). The generation of emotion. In *Theories of emotion.* Vol. 1 of *Emotion: Theory, research and experience,* ed. R. Plutchik and H. Kellerman. New York: Academic Press, pp. 219–243.

Mandler, J. M. (1983). Representation. In *Handbook of child psychology.* Vol. 3, ed. P. H. Mussen. 4th ed. New York: Wiley, pp. 420–494.

Mandler, J. M. (1988). How to build a baby: On the development of an accessible representational system. *Cogn. Develop.*, 3:113–136.

Masters, W. H., and Johnson, V. E. (1966). *Human sexual response.* Boston: Little, Brown.

Mayer, E. (1985). "Everybody must be just like me": Observations on female castration anxiety. *Int. J. Psychoanal.*, 66:331–347.

Meissner, W. (1980). A note in projective identification. *J. Amer. Psychoanal. Assn.*, 28:43–68.

Meltzoff, A. N. (1982). Imitation, intermodal coordination and representation in early infancy. In *Infancy and epistomology,* ed. G. Butterworth. Brighton, England: St. Martin's Press, pp. 174–192.

Meltzoff, A. N. (1985). Perception, action, and cognition in early infancy. *Am. Pediatrics,* 32:63–77.

Meltzoff, A. N. (1988). Infant imitation and memory: Nine-month-olds in immediate and deferred tests. *Child Develop.*, 59:217–225.

Metcalf, D. R. (1979). Organizers of the psyche and EEG development: Birth through adolescence. In *Basic handbook of child psychiatry.* Vol. 1, ed. J. D. Noshpitz et al. New York: Basic Books, pp. 63–71.

Metcalf, D. R., and Spitz, R. A. (1978). The transitional object: Critical development period and organizer of the psyche. In *Between reality and fantasy,* ed. S. A. Grolnick and L. Barkin. New York: Aronson, pp. 99–108.

Meyer, J. K. (1980). Body ego, selfness, and gender sense: The development of gender identity. *Psychiatric Clinics of North America,* 3:21–36.

Modell, A. H. (1969). *Object love and reality.* London: Hogarth.

Modell, A. H. (1975). A narcissistic defense against affects and the illusion of self-sufficiency. *Int. J. Psychoanal.,* 56:275–282.

Modell, A. H. (1984). *Psychoanalysis in a new context.* New York: Int. Univ. Press.

Money, J., and Ehrhardt, A. (1972). *Man and woman, boy and girl.* Baltimore: Johns Hopkins Univ. Press.

Money, J.; Hampson, J. G.; and Hampson, J. L. (1955a). An examination of some basic sexual concepts: The evidence of human hermaphroditism. *Bull. Johns Hopkins Hosp.,* 97:301–319.

Money, J.; Hampson, J. G.; and Hampson, J. L. (1955b). Hermaphroditism: Recommendations concerning assignment of sex, change of sex and psychologic management. *Bull. Johns Hopkins Hosp.,* 97:284–300.

Montagner, H. (1983). New data in the ontogeny of communications systems and biological rhythms in young children. In *Frontiers of infant psychiatry,* ed. J. D. Call, E. Galenson, and R. L. Tyson. New York: Basic Books, p. 456.

Moore, B. E. (1976). Freud and female sexuality. *Int. J. Psychoanal.,* 57:287–300.

Moore, B. E., and Fine, B. D., eds. (1990). *Psychoanalytic terms and concepts.* New Haven and London: Amer. Psychoanal. Assn. and Yale Univ. Press.

Moran, G. S. (1987). Some functions of play and playfulness. *Psychoanal. Study Child,* 42:11–29.

Müller-Braunschweig, C. (1926). The genesis of the feminine super-ego. *Int. J. Psychoanal.,* 7:359–362.

Muslin, H. L. (1972). The superego in women. In *Moral values and the superego concept,* ed. S. C. Post. New York: Int. Univ. Press, pp. 101–125.

Myers, W. (1976). Imaginary companions, fantasy twins, mirror dreams, and depersonalization. *Psychoanal. Q.,* 45:503–524.

Myers, W. (1979). Imaginary companions in childhood and adult creativity. *Psychoanal. Q.,* 48:292–307.

Nachman, P. A., and Stern, D. N. (1984). Affect retrieval: A form of recall memory in prelinguistic infants. In *Frontiers of infant psychiatry.* Vol. 2, ed. J. D. Call, E. Galenson, and R. L. Tyson. New York: Basic Books, pp. 95–100.

Nadelson, C. C.; Notman, M. T.; Miller, J. B.; and Zilbach, J. (1982). Aggression in women: Conceptual issues and clinical implications. In *Aggression, adaptations, and psychotherapy.* Vol. 3 of *The woman patient,* ed. M. T. Notman and C. C. Nadelson. New York: Plenum, pp. 17–28.

Nagera, H. (1966). *Early childhood disturbances, the infantile neurosis, and the adulthood disturbances.* New York: Int. Univ. Press.

Nagera, H. (1969). Imaginary companion: Its significance for ego development. *Psychoanal. Study Child,* 24:165–196.

Nagera, H. (1975). *Female sexuality and the Oedipus complex.* New York: Aronson.

Neubauer, P. B. (1960). The one-parent child and his oedipal development. *Psychoanal. Study Child,* 15:286–309.

Neubauer, P. B. (1980). The role of insight in psychoanalysis. In *Psychoanalytic explorations of technique,* ed. H. P. Blum. New York: Int. Univ. Press, pp. 29–40.

Neubauer, P. B. (1984). Anna Freud's concept of developmental lines. *Psychoanal. Study Child,* 39:15–27.

Neugarten, B. (1979). Time, age, and the life cycle. *Amer. J. Psychiat.,* 136:887–894.

Novick, J., and Novick, K. K. (1972). Beating fantasies in children. *Int. J. Psychoanal.,* 53:237–242.

Novick, J., and Novick, K. K. (1990). Some comments on masochism and the delusion of omnipotence from a developmental perspective. *J. Amer. Psychoanal. Assn.,* in press.

Novick, K. K., and Novick, J. (1987). The essence of masochism. *Psychoanal. Study Child,* 42:353–384.

Noy, P. (1969). A revision of the psychoanalytic theory of the primary process. *Int. J. Psychoanal.,* 50:155–178.

Noy, P. (1973). Symbolism and mental representation. *Ann. Psychoanal.,* 1:125–158.

Noy, P. (1978). Insight and creativity. *J. Amer. Psychoanal. Assn.,* 26:717–748.

Noy, P. (1979). The psychoanalytic theory of cognitive development. *Psychoanal. Study Child,* 34:169–216.

Noy, P. (1982). A revision of the psychoanalytic theory of affect. *Ann. Psychoanal.,* 10:139–186.

Nunberg, H. (1931). The synthetic function of the ego. *Int. J. Psychoanal.,* 12:123–140.

Nunberg, H. (1932). *Principles of psychoanalysis: Their application to the neuroses.* New York: Int. Univ. Press, 1955.

Offer, D. (1969). Adolescent turmoil. In *The psychological world of the teen-ager: A study of normal adolescent boys.* New York: Basic Books, pp. 174–192.

Ogden, T. H. (1987). The transitional oedipal relationship in female development. *Int. J. Psychoanal.,* 68:485–498.

Olden, C. (1953). On adult empathy with children. *Psychoanal. Study Child,* 8:111–126.

Oster, H. (1978). Facial expression and affect development. In *The development of affect,* ed. M. Lewis and L. A. Rosenblum. New York: Plenum, pp. 43–75.

Papousek, H., and Papousek, M. (1979). The infant's fundamental adaptive responsive system in social interaction. In *Origins of the infant's social responsiveness,* ed. E. Thoman. Hillsdale, N.J.: Erlbaum, pp. 27–32.

Papousek, H., and Papousek, M. (1981). How human is the human newborn, and what else is to be done? In *Prospective issues in infancy research,* ed. K. Bloom. Hillsdale, N.J.: Erlbaum, pp. 137–155.

Papousek, H., and Papousek, M. (1984). The evolution of parent-infant attachment: New psychobiological perspectives. In *Frontiers of infant psychiatry.* Vol. 2, ed. J. Call, E. Galenson, and R. L. Tyson. New York: Basic Books, pp. 276–283.

Parens, H. (1979). *The development of aggression in early childhood.* New York: Aronson.

Parens, H.; Pollock, L.; Stern, J.; and Kramer, S. (1976). On the girl's entry into the Oedipus complex. *J. Amer. Psychoanal. Assn.,* 24:79–107.

Pedersen, F. A., and Robson, K. S. (1969). Father participation in infancy. *Amer. J. Orthopsychiat.,* 39:466–472.

Peller, L. E. (1954). Libidinal phases, ego development and play. *Psychoanal. Study Child,* 9:178–198.

Peller, L. E. (1956). The school's role in promoting sublimation. *Psychoanal. Study Child,* 11:437–449.

Peller, L. E. (1958). Reading and daydreams in latency: Boy-girl differences. *J. Amer. Psychoanal. Assn.,* 6:57–70.

Person, E. S. (1983). The influence of values in psychoanalysis: The case of female psychology. *Psychiatry Update,* 2:36–50.

Person, E. S. (1986). Male sexuality and power. *Psychoanal. Inq.,* 6:3–25.

Person, E. S. (1988). *Dreams of love and fateful encounters.* New York: Norton.

Peterfreund, E. (1971). *Information, systems, and psychoanalysis: An evolutionary biological approach to psychoanalytic theory.* Psychological Issues, Monograph 25/26. New York: Int. Univ. Press.

Peterfreund, E. (1978). Some critical comments on psychoanalytic conceptions of infancy. *Int. J. Psychoanal.,* 59:427–441.

Petersen, A. C. (1979). Female to pubertal development. In *Female adolescent development,* ed. M. Sugar. New York: Brunner/Mazel, pp. 23–46.

Peto, A. (1967). Terrifying eyes. *Psychoanal. Study Child,* 24:197–212.

Piaget, J. (1932). Moral judgment: Children invent the social contract. In *The essential Piaget: An interpretive reference and guide,* ed. H. E. Gruber and J. Voneche. New York: Basic Books, 1977, pp. 159–193.

Piaget, J. (1936). *The origins of intelligence in children.* New York: Norton, 1963.

Piaget, J. (1937). *The construction of reality in the child.* New York: Basic Books, 1954.

Piaget, J. (1946). *Play, dreams and imitation in childhood.* New York: Norton, 1962.

Piaget, J. (1952). *The child's conception of number.* New York: Humanities.

Piaget, J. (1954). *Intelligence and affectivity: Their relationship during child development.* Palo Alto, Calif.: Annual Reviews, 1981.

Piaget, J. (1958). Equilibration processes in the psychobiological development of the child. In *The essential Piaget,* ed. H. E. Gruber and J. J. Voneche. New York: Basic Books, 1977, pp. 832–841.

Piaget, J. (1964). *Six psychological studies.* New York: Random House, 1967.

Piaget, J. (1967). *Biology and knowledge.* Chicago: Univ. of Chicago Press, 1972.

Piaget, J., and Inhelder, B. (1969). *The psychology of the child*. New York: Basic Books.

Piers, G., and Singer, M. B. (1953). *Shame and guilt*. Springfield, Ill.: Thomas.

Pine, F. (1971). On the separation process: Universal trends and individual differences. In *Separation-individuation: Essays in honor of Margaret S. Mahler*, ed. J. B. McDevitt and C. Settlage. New York: Int. Univ. Press, pp. 113–130.

Pine, F. (1974). Libidinal object constancy: A theoretical note. *Psychoanal. Contemp. Science*, 3:307–313.

Pine, F. (1985). *Developmental theory and clinical process*. New Haven: Yale Univ. Press.

Plaut, E. A. (1979). Play and adaptation. *Psychoanal. Study Child*, 34:217–234.

Plaut, E. A., and Hutchinson, F. (1986). The role of puberty in female psychosexual development. *Int. Rev. Psychoanal.*, 13:417–432.

Pollock, G. H. (1981). Aging and aged: Development on pathology. In *The course of life*. Vol. 3, ed. S. I. Greenspan and G. H. Pollock. Publication No. (ADM) 81–1000. Washington, D.C.: DHHS, pp. 549–581.

Prechtl, H. F. R. (1982). Assessment methods for the newborn infant: A critical evaluation. In *Psychobiology of the human newborn*, ed. P. Stratton. New York: Wiley, pp. 21–52.

Provence, S., and Lipton, R. C. (1962). *Infants in institutions*. New York: Int. Univ. Press.

Pruett, K. D. (1983). Infants of primary nurturing fathers. *Psychoanal. Study Child*, 38:258–280.

Pruett, K. D. (1984). Children of the father-mothers. In *Frontiers of infant psychiatry*. Vol. 2, ed. J. D. Call, E. Galenson, and R. L. Tyson. New York: Basic Books, pp. 375–380.

Pruett, K. D. (1985). Oedipal configurations in young father-raised children. *Psychoanal. Study Child*, 40:435–456.

Pruett, K. D. (1987). *Nurturing father: Journey toward the complete man*. New York: Warner.

Pulver, S. E. (1970). Narcissism: The term and the concept. *J. Amer. Psychoanal. Assn.*, 18:319–341.

Pulver, S. E. (1974). Unconscious versus potential affects. *Psychoanal. Q.*, 43:77–84.

Rakic, P., and Yakovlev, P. I. (1968). Development of the corpus callosum and cavum septi in man. *J. Comp. Neurol.*, 132:45–72.

Rangell, L. (1963). Structural problems in intrapsychic conflict. *Psychoanal. Study Child*, 18:103–138.

Rangell, L. (1968). A further attempt to resolve the "problem of anxiety." *J. Amer. Psychoanal. Assn.*, 16:371–404.

Rangell, L. (1972). Aggression, Oedipus, and historical perspective. *Int. J. Psychoanal.*, 53:3–11.

Rangell, L. (1974). A psychoanalytic perspective leading currently to the syndrome of the compromise of integrity. *Int. J. Psychoanal.*, 55:3–12.

Rangell, L. (1980). *The mind of Watergate: An exploration of the compromise of integrity*. New York: Norton.

Rangell, L. (1982). The self in psychoanalytic theory. *J. Amer. Psychoanal. Assn.,* 30:863–891.

Rapaport, D. (1951). Toward a theory of thinking. In *Organization and pathology of thought*, ed. D. Rapaport. New York: Columbia Univ. Press, pp. 689–730.

Rapaport, D. (1953). On the psycho-analytic theory of affects. In *The collected papers of David Rapaport*, ed. M. M. Gill. New York: Basic Books, 1967, pp. 476–512.

Rapaport, D. (1960). Psychoanalysis as a developmental psychology. In *The collected papers of David Rapaport*, ed. M. M. Gill. New York: Basic Books, 1967, pp. 820–852.

Rapaport, D., and Gill, M. M. (1959). The points of view and assumptions of metapsychology. In *The collected papers of David Rapaport*, ed. M. M. Gill. New York: Basic Books, 1967, pp. 795–811.

Reeves, J. W. (1965). *Thinking about thinking*. New York: George Braziller.

Reich, A. (1953). Narcissistic object choice in women. *J. Amer. Psychoanal. Assn.,* 1:22–44.

Reich, A. (1954). Early identifications as archaic elements in the superego. *J. Amer. Psychoanal. Assn.,* 2:218–238.

Reich, A. (1958). A character formation representing the integration of unusual conflict solutions into the ego structure. *Psychoanal. Study Child,* 13:309–323.

Reich, A. (1960). Pathologic forms of self-esteem regulation. *Psychoanal. Study Child,* 15:215–232.

Renik, O. (1972). Cognitive ego function in the phobic symptom. *Psychoanal. Q.,* 41:537–555.

Rheingold, H. L. (1969). The social and socializing infant. In *Handbook of socialization theory and research*, ed. D. Goslin. Chicago: Rand McNally, pp. 779–790.

Riess, A. (1978). The mother's eye: For better and for worse. *Psychoanal. Study Child,* 33:381–409.

Ritvo, S. (1974). Current status of the concept of infantile neurosis. *Psychoanal. Study Child,* 29:159–188.

Ritvo, S. (1976). Adolescent to woman. *J. Amer. Psychoanal. Assn.,* 24:127–138.

Ritvo, S. (1981). Anxiety, symptom formation and ego autonomy. *Psychoanal. Study Child,* 36:339–364.

Ritvo, S., and Solnit, A. J. (1960). The relationship of early ego identification to superego formation. *Int. J. Psychoanal.,* 41:295–300.

Roiphe, H., and Galenson, E. (1981). *Infantile origins of sexual identity*. New York: Int. Univ. Press.

Rosenblatt, A. D. (1985). The role of affect in cognitive psychology and psychoanalysis. *Psychoanal. Psychol.,* 2:85–97.

Rosenblatt, A. D., and Thickstun, J. T. (1977). *Modern psychoanalytic concepts in a general psychology; Part 2: Motivation.* Psychological Issues, Monograph 42/43. New York: Int. Univ. Press.

Rosner, H. (1972). "Of music, magic, and mystery": Studies in adolescent synthesis. *J. Amer. Psychoanal. Assn.,* 20:395–416.

Ross, J. M. (1975). The development of paternal identity: A critical review of the literature on nurturance and generativity in boys and men. *J. Amer. Psychoanal. Assn.,* 23:783–818.

Ross, J. M. (1982a). From other to father: The boy's search for a generative identity and the oedipal era. In *Father and child: Developmental and clinical perspectives,* ed. S. H. Cath, A. R. Gurwitt, and J. M. Ross. Boston: Little, Brown, pp. 198–203.

Ross, J. M. (1982b). Oedipus revisited: Laius and the "Laius Complex." *Psychoanal. Study Child,* 37:169–200.

Rothstein, A. (1980). *The narcissistic pursuit of perfection.* New York: Int. Univ. Press.

Rothstein, A. (1983). *The structural hypothesis: An evolutionary perspective.* New York: Int. Univ. Press.

Rothstein, A. (1988). The representational world as a substructure of the ego. *J. Amer. Psychoanal. Assn.,* 36:191–208.

Rycroft, C. (1956). Symbolism and its relationship to the primary and secondary process. *Int. J. Psychoanal.,* 37:137–146.

Rycroft, C. (1968). *Imagination and reality: Psycho-analytical essays, 1951–1961.* London: Hogarth.

Sachs, H. (1929). One motive factor in formation of super-ego in women. *Int. J. Psychoanal.,* 10:39–50.

Sander, L. W. (1962). Issues in early mother-child interaction. *J. Amer. Acad. Child Psychiat.,* 1:141–166.

Sander, L. W. (1964). Adaptive relationships in early mother-child interaction. *J. Amer. Acad. Child Psychiat.,* 3:231–164.

Sander, L. W. (1969). Regulation and organization in the early infant-caretaker system. In *Brain and early behavior,* ed. R. Robinson. London: Academic Press, pp. 311–332.

Sander, L. W. (1975). Infant and caretaking environment: Investigation and conceptualization of adaptive behavior in a system of increasing complexity. In *Explorations in child psychiatry,* ed. E. J. Anthony. New York: Plenum, pp. 129–166.

Sander, L. W. (1980). Investigation of the infant and its caretaking environment as a biological system. In *The course of life.* Vol. 1, ed. S. I. Greenspan and G. H. Pollock. Publication No. (ADM) 80–786. Washington, D.C.: DHHS, pp. 177–201.

Sander, L. W. (1983). Polarity, paradox, and the organizing process in development. In *Frontiers of infant psychiatry,* ed. J. D. Call, E. Galenson, and R. L. Tyson. New York: Basic Books, pp. 333–346.

Sander, L. W.; Stechler, G.; Burns, P.; and Julia, H. (1970). Early mother-infant interaction and 24-hour patterns of activity and sleep. *J. Amer. Acad. Child Psychiat.*, 9:103–123.

Sander, L. W.; Stechler, G.; Burns, P.; and Lee, A. (1979). Change in infant and caregiver variables over the first two months of life: Integration of action in early development. In *Origins of the infant's social responsiveness*, ed. E. Thoman. Hillsdale, N.J.: Erlbaum, pp. 21–28.

Sandler, A.-M. (1975). Comments on the significance of Piaget's work for psychoanalysis. *Int. Rev. Psychoanal.*, 2:365–378.

Sandler, A.-M. (1977). Beyond eight-month anxiety. *Int. J. Psychoanal.*, 58:195–208.

Sandler, J. (1960a). On the concept of the superego. *Psychoanal. Study Child*, 15:128–162.

Sandler, J. (1960b). The background of safety. *Int. J. Psychoanal.*, 41:352–356.

Sandler, J. (1974). Psychological conflict and the structural model: Some clinical and theoretical implications. *Int. J. Psychoanal.*, 55:53–72.

Sandler, J. (1981). Character traits and object relationships. *Psychoanal. Q.*, 50:694–708.

Sandler, J. (1983). Reflections on some relations between psychoanalytic concepts and psychoanalytic practice. *Int. J. Psychoanal.*, 64:35–45.

Sandler, J. (1985). Towards a reconsideration of the psychoanalytic theory of motivation. *Bull. Anna Freud Centre*, 8:223–244.

Sandler, J. (1987). The concept of projective identification. In *Projection, identification, projection identification*, ed. J. Sandler. Madison, Conn.: Int. Univ. Press, pp. 13–26.

Sandler, J., and Dare, C. (1970). The psychoanalytic concept of orality. *J. Psychosom. Res.*, 14:211–222.

Sandler, J.; Dare, C.; and Holder, A. (1972). Frames of reference: The historical context and phases in the development of psychoanalysis. *Brit. J. Med. Psychol.*, 45:133–142.

Sandler, J., and Freud, A. (1985). *The analysis of defense: The ego and the mechanisms of defense revisited.* New York: Int. Univ. Press.

Sandler, J.; Holder, A.; and Meers, D. (1963). The ego ideal and the ideal self. *Psychoanal. Study Child*, 18:139–158.

Sandler, J., and Joffe, W. G. (1969). Towards a basic psycho-analytic model. *Int. J. Psychoanal.*, 50:79–90.

Sandler, J., and Rosenblatt, B. (1962). The concept of the representational world. *Psychoanal. Study Child*, 17:128–145.

Sandler, J., and Sandler, A.-M. (1978). On the development of object relationships and affects. *Int. J. Psychoanal.*, 59:285–296.

Sarnoff, C. (1976). *Latency.* New York: Aronson.

Schafer, R. (1960). The loving and beloved superego in Freud's structural theory. *Psychoanal. Study Child*, 15:163–190.

Schafer, R. (1974). Problems in Freud's psychology of women. *J. Amer. Psychoanal. Assn.*, 22:459–485.

Schafer, R. (1976). *A new language for psychoanalysis*. New Haven: Yale Univ. Press.

Scharfman, M. (1988). History of child analysis. Paper presented to workshop on the Significance of Child and Adolescent Analysis for Clinical Work with Adults. American Psychoanalytic Association, New York City, November.

Schulman, A. H., and Kaplowitz, C. (1977). Mirror-image response during the first two years of life. *Developmental Psychology*, 10:133–142.

Schur, M. (1960). Discussion of Dr. John Bowlby's paper. *Psychoanal. Study Child*, 15:63–84.

Schur, M. (1966). *The id and the regulatory principles of mental functioning*. New York: Int. Univ. Press.

Schur, M. (1969). Affects and cognition. *Int. J. Psychoanal.*, 50:647–653.

Schwartz, A. (1987). Drives, affects, behavior—and learning: Approaches to a psychobiology of emotion and to an integration of psychoanalytic and neurobiologic thought. *J. Amer. Psychoanal. Assn.*, 35:467–506.

Schwartz, L. (1978). Book review: *The restoration of the self. Psychoanal. Q.*, 47:436–443.

Segal, H. (1978). On symbolism. *Int. J. Psychoanal.*, 59:315–319.

Segal, H. (1979). *Klein: Theories and techniques of the pioneer of child analysis*. London: Harvester Press.

Settlage, C. F. (1971). On the libidinal aspect of early psychic development and the genesis of infantile neurosis. In *Separation-individuation: Essays in honor of Margaret S. Mahler*, ed. J. B. McDevitt and C. F. Settlage. New York: Int. Univ. Press, pp. 131–154.

Settlage, C. F. (1975). On the aggressive aspects of early psychic development and the genesis of the infantile neurosis. Unpublished paper.

Settlage, C. F. (1980). The psychoanalytic theory and understanding of psychic development during the second and third years of life. In *Infancy and early childhood*. Vol. 1 of *The course of life*, ed. S. I. Greenspan and G. H. Pollock. Publication No. (ADM) 80–786. Washington, D.C.: DHHS, pp. 523–539.

Settlage, C. F.; Curtis, Z.; Lozoff, M.; Silberschatz, G.; and Simburg, E. (1988). Conceptualizing adult development. *J. Amer. Psychoanal. Assn.*, 36:347–370.

Settlage, C. F.; Kramer, S.; Belmont, H. S.; et al. (1977). Child analysis. In *Psychoanalytic education and research: The current situation and future possibilities*, ed. S. Goodman. New York: Int. Univ. Press, pp. 49–102.

Shapiro, T. (1979). *Clinical psycholinguistics*. New York: Plenum.

Shapiro, T., and Perry, R. (1976). Latency revisited. *Psychoanal. Study Child*, 31:79–105.

Shengold, L. (1980). Some reflections on a case of mother-adolescent son incest. *Int. J. Psychoanal.*, 61:461–476.

Shengold, L. (1989). *Soul murder*. New Haven: Yale Univ. Press.

Shereshefsky, P. M., and Yarrow, L. J. (1973). *Psychological aspects of a first pregnancy and early postnatal adaptation*. New York: Raven Press.

Shopper, M. (1979). The (re)discovery of the vagina and the importance of the menstrual tampon. In *Female adolescent development,* ed. M. Sugar. New York: Brunner/Mazel, pp. 214–233.

Sifneos, P. (1974). A reconsideration of psychodynamic mechanisms in psychosomatic symptom formation in view of recent clinical observations. *Psychother. Psychosom.,* 24:151–155.

Silverman, M. A. (1971). The growth of logical thinking: Piaget's contribution to ego psychology. *Psychoanal. Q.,* 40:317–341.

Silverman, M. A. (1981). Cognitive development and female psychology. *J. Amer. Psychoanal. Assn.,* 29:581–605.

Slap, J. (1977). The eroding concept of intrapsychic conflict. *Int. J. Psychoanal. Psychother.,* 6:469–477.

Slap, J. W., and Levine, F. J. (1978). On hybrid concepts in psychoanalysis. *Psychoanal. Q.,* 47:499–523.

Socarides, C. W. (1978). *Homosexuality.* New York: Aronson.

Solnit, A. J. (1979). Psychosexual development: Three to five years. In *Basic handbook of child psychiatry.* Vol. 1, ed. J. D. Noshpitz et al. New York: Basic Books, pp. 178–183.

Solnit, A. J. (1987a). A psychoanalytic view of play. *Psychoanal. Study Child,* 42:205–219.

Solnit, A. J. (1987b). Review of *The interpersonal world of the infant,* by Daniel Stern. *J. Amer. Psychiat. Assn.,* 144:1508–1509.

Solnit, A. J., and Neubauer, P. B. (1986). Object constancy and early triadic relationships. *J. Amer. Acad. Child Psychiat.,* 25:23–29.

Sorce, J. F.; Emde, R. N.; and Klinnert, M. (1981). Maternal emotional signaling: Its effect on the visual-cliff behavior of one-year-olds. Paper presented at the meeting of the Society for Research in Child Development, Boston, Mass.

Spillius, E. B. (1983). Some developments from the work of Melanie Klein. *Int. J. Psychoanal.,* 64:321–332.

Spitz, R. A. (1945). Hospitalism: An inquiry into the genesis of psychiatric conditions in early childhood. *Psychoanal. Study Child,* 1:53–72.

Spitz, R. A. (1946a). Anaclitic depression: An inquiry into the genesis of psychiatric conditions in early childhood. *Psychoanal. Study Child,* 2:313–342.

Spitz, R. A. (1946b). Hospitalism: A follow-up report. *Psychoanal. Study Child,* 2:113–117.

Spitz, R. A. (1947). *Grief, a peril in infancy.* Film, New York Film Library. Cited in Spitz and Cobliner, 1965.

Spitz, R. A. (1950). Anxiety in infancy: A study of its manifestations in the first year of life. *Int. J. Psychoanal.,* 31:138–143.

Spitz, R. A. (1952). Authority and masturbation: Remarks on bibliographical investigation. *Psychoanal. Q.,* 21:490–527.

Spitz, R. A. (1953). Aggression: Its role in the establishment of object relations.

In *Drives, affects, behavior,* ed. R. Loewenstein. New York: Int. Univ. Press, pp. 126–138.

Spitz, R. A. (1957). *No and yes: On the genesis of human communication.* New York: Int. Univ. Press.

Spitz, R. A. (1958). On the genesis of superego components. *Psychoanal. Study Child,* 13:375–404.

Spitz, R. A. (1959). *A genetic field theory of ego formation: Its implications for Pathology.* New York: Int. Univ. Press.

Spitz, R. A. (1960). Discussion of Dr. John Bowlby's paper. *Psychoanal. Study Child,* 15:85–94.

Spitz, R. A. (1962). Auterotism reexamined. *Psychoanal. Study Child,* 17:283–315.

Spitz, R. A. (1963). Life and the dialogue. In *Counterpoint: Libidinal object and subject,* ed. H. S. Gaskill. New York: Int. Univ. Press, pp. 154–176.

Spitz, R. A. (1964). The derailment of dialogue: Stimulus overload, active cycles, and the completion gradient. *J. Amer. Psychoanal. Assn.,* 12:752–775.

Spitz, R. A. (1965). The evolution of dialogue. In *Drives, affects, behavior.* Vol. 2, ed. M. Schur. New York: Int. Univ. Press, pp. 170–190.

Spitz, R. A., and Cobliner, W. G. (1965). *The first year of life.* New York: Int. Univ. Press.

Spitz, R. A.; Emde, R. N.; and Metcalf, D. R. (1970). Further prototypes of ego formation: A working paper from a research project on early development. *Psychoanal. Study Child,* 25:417–460.

Spitz, R. A., and Wolf, K. M. (1946). The smiling response. *Genetic Psychol. Mono.,* 34:57–125.

Spitz, R. A., and Wolf, K. M. (1949). Auterotism: Some empirical findings and hypotheses on three of its manifestations in the first year of life. *Psychoanal. Study Child,* 3/4:85–120.

Spruiell, V. (1975). Three strands of narcissism. *Psychoanal. Q.,* 44:577–595.

Spruiell, V. (1979). Alterations in the ego-ideal in girls in mid-adolescence. In *Female adolescent development,* ed. M. Sugar. New York: Brunner/Mazel, pp. 310–329.

Spruiell, V. (1981). The self and the ego. *Psychoanal. Q.,* 50:319–344.

Stechler, G., and Halton, A. (1987). The emergence of assertion and aggression during infancy: A psychoanalytic systems approach. *J. Amer. Psychoanal. Assn.,* 35:821–838.

Stechler, G., and Kaplan, S. (1980). The development of the self. *Psychoanal. Study Child,* 35:85–105.

Steele, B. F. (1970). Parental abuse of infants and small children. In *Parenthood,* ed. E. J. Anthony and T. Benedek. New York: Little, Brown, pp. 449–477.

Steele, B. F. (1983). The effect of abuse and neglect on psychological development. In *Frontiers of infant psychiatry,* ed. J. D. Call, E. Galenson, and R. L. Tyson. New York: Basic Books, pp. 235–244.

Steele, B. F., and Pollock, C. B. (1968). A psychiatric study of parents who abuse infants and small children. In *The battered child*, ed. R. E. Helfer and C. H. Kempe. Chicago: Univ. of Chicago Press, pp. 103–147.

Stein, M. H. (1979). Book Review: *The restoration of the self* by Heinz Kohut. *J. Amer. Psychoanal. Assn.*, 27:665–680.

Sterba, R. F. (1942). Introduction. *Psychoanalytic theory of the libido*. 3rd ed. New York: Brunner/Mazel, 1968.

Stern, D. N. (1974a). Mother and infant at play: The dyadic interaction involving facial, vocal, and gaze behaviors. In *The effect of the infant on its caregiver*, ed. M. Lewis and L. Rosenblum. New York: Wiley, pp. 187–213.

Stern, D. N. (1974b). The goal and structure of mother-infant play. *J. Amer. Acad. Child Psychiat.*, 13:402–421.

Stern, D. N. (1977). *The first relationship: Mother and infant*. Cambridge: Harvard Univ. Press.

Stern, D. N. (1984). Affect attunement. In *Frontiers of infant psychiatry*. Vol. 2, ed. J. D. Call, E. Galenson, and R. L. Tyson. New York: Basic Books, pp. 74–85.

Stern, D. N. (1985). *The interpersonal world of the infant*. New York: Basic Books.

Stern, D. N.; Barnett, R. K.; and Spieker, S. (1983). Early transmission of affect: Some research issues. In *Frontiers of infant psychiatry*, ed. J. D. Call, E. Galenson, and R. L. Tyson. New York: Basic Books, pp. 74–85.

Stoller, R. J. (1968a). *Sex and gender: On the development of masculinity and femininity*. New York: Science House.

Stoller, R. J. (1968b). The sense of femaleness. *Psychoanal. Q.*, 37:42–55.

Stoller, R. J. (1976). Primary femininity. *J. Amer. Psychoanal. Assn.*, 24 (Suppl.): 59–78.

Stoller, R. J. (1979). Fathers of transsexual children. *J. Amer. Psychoanal. Assn.*, 27:837–866.

Stoller, R. J. (1985). *Presentations of gender*. New Haven: Yale Univ. Press.

Stolorow, R. D., and Lachmann, F. M. (1978). The developmental prestages of defenses: Diagnostic and therapeutic implications. *Psychoanal. Q.*, 47:73–102.

Strachey, J. (1961). Editor's introduction. In *S.E.*, 19:3–11.

Sutherland, J. D. (1980). The British object relations theorists: Balint, Winnicott, Fairbairn, Guntrip. *J. Amer. Psychoanal. Assn.*, 28:829–860.

Tennes, K., and Lampl, E. (1964). Stranger and separation anxiety in infancy. *J. Nerv. Ment. Dis.*, 139:247–254.

Ticho, E. A. (1982). The alternate schools and the self. *J. Amer. Psychoanal. Assn.*, 30:849–862.

Ticho, G. (1976). Female autonomy and young adult women. *J. Amer. Psychoanal. Assn.*, 24:139–156.

Tolpin, M. (1971). On the beginnings of a cohesive self: An application of the concept of transmuting internalization to the study of the transitional object and signal anxiety. *Psychoanal. Study Child*, 26:316–352.

Tolpin, M. (1978). Self-objects and oedipal objects. *Psychoanal. Study Child*, 33:167–184.

Tomkins, S. S. (1962). *The positive affects*. Vol. 1 of *Affect, imagery, consciousness*. New York: Springer.

Tomkins, S. S. (1963). *The negative affects*. Vol. 2 of *Affect, imagery, consciousness*. New York: Springer.

Tomkins, S. S. (1970). Affect as the primary motivational system. In *Feelings and emotions: The Loyola Symposium*, ed. M. B. Arnold. New York: Academic Press, pp. 101–110.

Tomkins, S. S. (1978). Script theory: Differential magnification of affects. In *Nebraska Symposium on Motivation*. Vol. 26, ed. E. H. Howe, Jr., and R. A. Diestbier. Lincoln: Univ. of Nebraska Press, pp. 201–236.

Tomkins, S. S. (1981). The quest for primary motives: Biography and autobiography of an idea. *J. Personal. Soc. Psychol.*, 41:306–329.

Tronick, E.; Als, H.; Adamson, L.; Wise, S.; and Brazelton, T. B. (1978). The infant's response to entrapment between contradictory messages in face-to-face interaction. *J. Amer. Acad. Child Psychiat.*, 17:1–13.

Tronick, E.; Als, H.; and Brazelton, T. B. (1977). The infant's capacity to regulate mutuality in face-to-face interaction. *J. Communication*, 27:74–80.

Tronick, E. Z., and Gianino, A. (1986). Interactive mismatch and repair. *Zero to Three*, 6:1–6.

Tyson, P. (1978). Transference and developmental issues in the analysis of a prelatency child. *Psychoanal. Study Child*, 33:213–236.

Tyson, P. (1980). The gender of the analyst: In relation to transference and countertransference manifestations in prelatency children. *Psychoanal. Study Child*, 35:321–338.

Tyson, P. (1982a). A developmental line of gender identity, gender role and choice of love object. *J. Amer. Psychoanal. Assn.*, 30:59–84.

Tyson, P. (1982b). The role of the father in gender identity, urethral eroticism, and phallic narcissism. In *On fathers: Observations and reflections*, ed. S. Cath, A. Gurwitt, and J. Ross. Boston: Little, Brown, pp. 175–187.

Tyson, P. (1986a). Female psychological development. *Ann. Psychoanal.*, 14:357–373.

Tyson, P. (1986b). Male gender identity: Early developmental roots. *Psychoanal. Rev.*, 73:405–425.

Tyson, P. (1988). Psychic structure formation: The complementary roles of affects, drives, object relations, and conflict. *J. Amer. Psychoanal. Assn.*, 36 (Suppl.):73–98.

Tyson, P. (1989a). Two approaches to infant research: A review and integration. In *The significance of infant observational research for clinical work with children, adolescents and adults*, ed. S. Dowling and A. Rothstein. Madison, Conn.: Int. Univ. Press, pp. 3–21.

Tyson, P. (1989b). Infantile sexuality, gender identity, and obstacles to oedipal progression. *J. Amer. Psychoanal. Assn.*, 37:1051–1069.

Tyson, P. (in press). The adolescent process and adult treatment. *The signifi-*

*cance of child and adolescent analysis for clinical work with adults,* ed. S. Dowling and A. Rothstein. New York: Int. Univ. Press.

Tyson, P., and Tyson, R. L. (1984). Narcissism and superego development. *J. Amer. Psychoanal. Assn.,* 32:75–98.

Tyson, R. L. (1983). Some narcissistic consequences of object loss: A developmental view. *Psychoanal. Q.,* 52:205–224.

Tyson, R. L. (1986). The roots of psychopathology and our theories of development. *J. Amer. Acad. Child Psychiat.,* 25:12–22.

Tyson, R. L. (1989). Psychological conflict in childhood: A developmental view. Paper presented at the Seminar for Clinicians, American Psychoanalytic Association, New York.

Tyson, R. L. (in preparation). *The psychoanalysis of the prelatency child.*

Van Leeuwen, K. (1966). Pregnancy envy in the male. *Int. J. Psychoanal.,* 47:319–324.

Vigotsky, L. S. (1934). *Thought and language.* New York: MIT Press, 1962.

Waelder, R. (1930). The principle of multiple function: Observations on overdetermination. In *Psychoanalysis: Observation, theory, application,* ed. S. A. Guttman. New York: Int. Univ. Press, 1976, pp. 68–83.

Waelder, R. (1932). The psychoanalytic theory of play. In *Psychoanalysis: Observation, theory, application,* ed. S. A. Guttman. New York: Int. Univ. Press, 1976, pp. 84–100.

Waelder, R. (1936). The problems of the genesis of psychic conflict in earlier infancy. In *Psychoanalysis: Observation, theory, application,* ed. S. A. Guttman. New York: Int. Univ. Press, 1976, pp. 121–188.

Wallerstein, J. S., and Kelly, J. B. (1980). *Surviving the breakup.* New York: Basic Books.

Wallerstein, J. S., and Blakeslee, S. (1989). *Second chances.* New York: Ticknor and Fields.

Wallerstein, R. S. (1981). The bipolar self: Discussion of alternate perspectives. *J. Amer. Psychoanal. Assn.,* 29:377–394.

Wallerstein, R. S. (1983). Defenses, defense mechanisms, and the structure of the mind. *J. Amer. Psychoanal. Assn.,* 31:201–225.

Wallerstein, R. S. (1988). One psychoanalysis or many? *Int. J. Psychoanal.,* 69:5–22.

Weil, A. P. (1970). The basic core. *Psychoanal. Study Child,* 25:442–460.

Weil, A. P. (1976). The first year: Metapsychological inferences of infant observation. In *The process of child development,* ed. P. Neubauer. New York: Aronson, pp. 246–265.

Weil, A. P. (1978). Maturational variations and genetic-dynamic issues. *J. Amer. Psychoanal. Assn.,* 26:461–491.

Weinshel, E. M. (1970). Some psychoanalytic considerations on moods. *Int. J. Psychoanal.,* 51:313–320.

Weissman, P. (1954). Ego and superego in obsessional character and neurosis. *Psychoanal. Q.,* 23:529–543.

Werner, H., and Kaplan, B. (1963). *Symbol formation*. New York: Wiley.

Widzer, M. E. (1977). The comic-book superhero: A study of the family romance fantasy. *Psychoanal. Study Child*, 32:565–604.

Williams, M. (1972). Problems of technique during latency. *Psychoanal. Study Child*, 27:598–617.

Winnicott, D. W. (1949). The ordinary devoted mother. In *Boundary and space*, ed. M. Davis and D. Wallbridge. New York: Brunner/Mazel, 1981, pp. 125–130.

Winnicott, D. W. (1952). Anxiety associated with insecurity. In *Collected papers*. New York: Basic Books, 1958, pp. 97–100.

Winnicott, D. W. (1953). Transitional objects and transitional phenomena. In *Playing and reality*. New York: Basic Books, 1971, pp. 1–25.

Winnicott, D. W. (1956). Primary maternal preoccupation. In *Collected papers*. New York: Basic Books, 1958, pp. 300–305.

Winnicott, D. W. (1959). The fate of the transitional object. In *Psychoanalytic explorations*, ed. C. Winnicott, R. Shepherd, and M. Davis. Cambridge: Harvard Univ. Press, 1989, pp. 53–58.

Winnicott, D. W. (1960). Ego distortion in terms of true and false self. In *The maturation processes and the facilitating environment*. New York: Int. Univ. Press, 1965, pp. 140–152.

Winnicott, D. W. (1962a). Ego integration in child development. In *The maturational processes and the facilitating environment*. New York: Int. Univ. Press, 1965, pp. 56–63.

Winnicott, D. W. (1962b). The theory of the parent-infant relationship. In *The maturational processes and the facilitating environment*. New York: Int. Univ. Press, 1965, pp. 37–55.

Winnicott, D. W. (1965). *The maturational processes and the facilitating environment*. New York: Int. Univ. Press.

Winnicott, D. W. (1967). Mirror-role of mother and family in child development. In *Playing and reality*. New York: Basic Books, 1971, pp. 111–118.

Winnicott, D. W. (1971). *Playing and reality*. New York: Basic Books.

Wolf, E. S. (1988). Case discussion and position statement. *Psychoanal. Inq.*, 8:546–551.

Wolff, P. H. (1959). Observations on newborn infants. *Psychosom. Med.*, 21:110–118.

Wolff, P. H. (1960). *The developmental psychologies of Jean Piaget and psychoanalysis*. Psychological Issues, Monograph 5. New York: Int. Univ. Press.

Wolff, P. H. (1966). *The causes, controls, and organization of behavior in the neonate*. Psychological Issues, Monograph 17. New York: Int. Univ. Press.

Wolff, P. H. (1981). Normal variation in human maturation. In *Maturation and development*, ed. K. J. Connolly and H. F. R. Prechtl. London: Heinemann, pp. 1–18.

Yakovlev, P. I., and Lecours, A. P. (1967). The myelogenetic cycles of regional maturation of the brain. In *Regional development of the brain in early life,* ed. A. Minkowski. Oxford: Blackwell, pp. 3–70.

Yasmajian, R. V. (1966). The testes and body-image formation in transvestitism. *J. Amer. Psychoanal. Assn.,* 14:304–312.

Yasmajian, R. V. (1967). The influence of testicular sensory stimuli on the dream. *J. Amer. Psychoanal. Assn.,* 15:83–98.

Yogman, M. W. (1982). Observations on the father-infant relationship. In *Father and child,* ed. S. H. Cath, A. Gurwitt, and J. M. Ross. Boston: Little, Brown, pp. 101–122.

Yorke, C. (1971). Some suggestions for a critique of Kleinian psychology. *Psychoanal. Study Child,* 26:129–155.

Yorke, C., and Wiseberg, S. (1976). A developmental view of anxiety. *Psychoanal. Study Child,* 31:107–135.

Zetzel, E. R. (1965). A developmental model and the theory of therapy. In *The capacity for emotional growth.* New York: Int. Univ. Press, 1970, pp. 246–269.

# INDEX

187–191; and ego formation, 297; and gender development, 252; and superego formation, 203; social, 195, 204; theory of, 15, 16, 17, 18, 20, 38; to reality, 164, 168

Adolescence, 30; affect in, 159; and gender identity, 255, 258, 271–276, 287, 289, 291, 292; and identity stability, 129; and psychosexuality, 61–65; cognitive development in, 187–191; ego formation in, 287, 298, 302, 313–319, 320; object relations in, 89, 98, 100, 113–117, 129; superego in, 202, 205, 206, 216, 223–227

Adultomorphic bias, 13, 54, 88, 262

Affect, 23, 24, 29, 133–140, 323; affective core, 123; affective expression, 17, 18, 53n, 55, 56, 57, 122, 127, 134, 136, 149, 150, 153, 163, 187, 208, 257, 258, 297, 299, 302, 303, 305; affective feedback, 97, 99, 147; affective interaction, 52, 93, 143, 253; affective response, 32, 51; and cognition, 164, 179, 181, 252; and drives, 140–143; and ego development, 143–146, 295, 297, 300, 305–307, 308, 313–319; and facial expression, 24, 100, 124, 134–135, 147, 150, 151, 176, 178, 208, 211, 299; and object relations, 69, 70, 71, 72, 79, 80, 97, 114, 116, 123, 125, 129, 146–148; and psychosexuality, 42–44; differentiation of, 146, 152; fear, 134, 135, 149 (of retaliation, 59)

Aggression, 9, 16, 25; and affect, 140–143; and cognitive development, 163, 186; and ego de-

velopment, 301, 305, 306, 309, 311, 313, 315; and gender development, 252n, 260, 263, 278, 281, 282; and object relations, 87, 88, 105, 108, 114, 121; and psychosexuality, 41, 45, 47, 48, 49, 54, 55, 56, 64; and superego formation, 197, 210, 212, 214, 219, 221, 228, 233, 234, 236, 238, 239, 240, 243, 244

Aim, 44, 105, 141, 275. *See also* Motivation

Alienation, 114, 125

Ambitendency, 238

Ambivalence, 12, 27–29, 324; and ego formation, 303, 304; and gender development, 251, 253, 260, 267, 269, 270, 282, 284; and object relations, 75, 86, 105, 106, 114, 116, 127; and psychosexuality, 47, 48, 56; and superego formation, 209, 210, 213, 214, 215, 236–242, 244

Anal erotism, 305

Anal phase, 8, 44, 55–57, 86, 105, 157, 203, 239, 261, 266, 278, 282, 306, 324

Anal-rapprochement phase. *See* Rapprochement phase

Anal zone, 49, 253

Anatomical difference, 57, 59, 197

Anlage, 207

Anxiety, 324; around genital injury, 229–230, 259, 262–263, 271, 273, 284, 285, 286; as affect, 133, 136–138, 140, 141, 157, 179, 204, 297, 306; in ego formation, 304, 307, 313, 316, 319; in structural theory, 74; moral, 214; object related, 71, 73, 291; persecutory, 71, 73; predisposition to, 100, 146, 301; separation, 76, 155, 156, 229, 262; signal, 139–140, 197, 308;